Penguin E

Psych
visual arts

Penguin Modern Psychology Readings

General Editor
B. M. Foss

Psychology and the visual arts

Selected Readings

Edited by James Hogg

Penguin Books

Penguin Books Ltd, Harmondsworth,
Middlesex, England
Penguin Books Inc., 7110 Ambassador Road,
Baltimore, Maryland 21207, U.S.A.
Penguin Books Australia Ltd, Ringwood,
Victoria, Australia

First published 1969
This selection copyright © James Hogg, 1969
Introduction and notes copyright © James Hogg, 1969

Made and printed in Great Britain by
C. Nicholls & Company Ltd
Set in Monotype Times

Contents

Contents

Introduction

There is a very real ambivalence in our attitude towards the psychological study of art. On the one hand the experience of art is felt to be so personal and private, and so intimately related to our individual personality that no mere psychological theory, let alone one dependent upon 'objective' techniques, could possibly probe and elucidate its significance. On the other hand the very fundamental nature of, and importance we ascribe to, such experiences suggests that for any psychology to account successfully for the relations we form with the world it must also say something about the function art serves.

Whichever of these attitudes we tend towards, it might appear easier to find reasons for thinking psychological theories lacking in their application to art, than reasons that convince us of their relevance. Among the most familiar in the former category are:

1. The 'stimuli', namely works of art, are complex and dependent upon structural relations in time and space, and are not amenable to the reduction of cues that we might feel legitimate in, for example, a study of depth cues or shape discrimination.
2. The 'response' is private and at least in part non-verbal, and any attempt to externalize it has already removed it some way from what is its actual nature. Further, the meaning of a particular work of art is not objective in the sense that we can specify, for example, the brightness of light, and hence the attribute of the work of art to which the person is responding may be indeterminate.

It is hoped that neither of these arguments caricature real arguments, for it is not intended to lay them low, but to indicate that if we are going to admit psychological theory to our study of art it cannot be done by asking of the explanations offered that they in some way reproduce in us the experience of the object itself. In other words explanations offered can only have the status of other explanations within the science, namely hypotheses held with varying degrees of caution.

Regarding the first argument it is certainly true that psychological theory is as ill-equipped at present to account for the processes by which structural relations are perceived and utilized, as it is to account for the fact that complex structural behaviour is generated by human beings. However, given that such problems are amenable to research, then the fact that the experience of art is dependent upon cognition of complex structure does not automatically remove it from the realm of psychological research.

The second argument regarding the private nature of our response is obviously valid and we must decide whether any externalization or indication of the response is acceptable. If the answer we receive is that it is not, then clearly the experience must be left to silent contemplation. However, the majority of people are not only willing to verbalize their experience of art but are anxious to do so, and a sufficient number of individuals earn a living doing this to assume some interest on the part of the rest of humanity (or a section of it). The question then becomes one of developing techniques (whether of sophisticated scaling methods or content analysis) by which to explore verbalizations, or by evolving complementary techniques to investigate the strategy by which a person engages his experience with a work of art. The meaning and significance to him of the latter situation is clearly involved in this question, for though the work of art has an objective physical existence, interpretation is notoriously variable.

A further answer might be given to the latter part of the second argument against a psychology of art. Namely, that given time the objective properties of works of art will become specifiable. I personally doubt this. Increasingly the evidence suggests that such a search is in vain. As Moyles *et al.* (Reading 20) conclude after such an investigation '. . . it seems likely that for most subjects the determinants of preference are item-specific interactions between the unique properties of each design and the subject's idiosyncratic aesthetics.' These doubts must be qualified by the admonition that failure to find 'objective' determinants of a particular type of response can never prove conclusively that such determinants do not exist. However, the failure to find general determinants does not exclude the study of these idiosyncratic aesthetics in as far as they are related to the way in which a person organizes or structures his perceptual and cognitive experience. This is a general problem to which I return in Reading 2, and which recurs in several papers in these readings, notably Readings 7, 12, 13, 18 and 20.

If these arguments, even in part, are acceptable, then clearly the psychological investigation is legitimate and is going to clarify and offer explanations of certain aspects of the experience of art. However, what we mean by 'psychology' is not a homogeneous discipline. While the division into schools has considerably diminished, differences in approach do exist, and are certainly clearly marked in studies of art. In the readings a variety of approaches is illustrated.

Each author is involved in attempting to understand some feature of the psychological response to art and is highly selective in what he chooses to consider relevant. For this reason the psychology of art is not going to be restricted solely to an understanding of the effect of various formal properties of art on judgements or responses, any more than it is going to be restricted solely to a study of the psychological implications of symbols and images.

The view adopted is that all evidence is potentially admissible. The framework in which the selections have been made therefore is based on a simple attitude to the subject matter.

The main questions that have been approached are:

1. What motivates people to look at the visual arts; what function is served by this activity; and can we indicate what characteristics of a picture subserve this function?

2. In such a context, what can be said about the meaning of paintings from the point of view of content, either in terms of interpretation of symbols or the connotative and expressive qualities they are judged as having?

3. How do individuals organize their total experience of a whole area of the arts? That is, how do they see paintings as differing, and what kind of discriminations can they make?

4. Implicit in all the above is the assumption that psychological theories must account for individual differences, and that the reasons people engage in looking at paintings vary across and within individuals and, similarly, the nature of the resolution may vary as well. Assumptions about the ultimate function and

significance of art and the 'true nature of the aesthetic experience' are not useful to the psychologist, and are rejected by many philosophical writers on aesthetics.

In our declaration of intent we have generally referred to paintings although titling the book 'Psychology and the Visual Arts'. The majority of the papers do deal directly with painting and graphics, or second-order material such as two-dimensional stimulus material produced for experimental purposes. Obviously the visual arts extend well beyond this, but sculpture and the movies (admittedly a mixed media) are poorly served by psychological writers. I have avidly pursued such titles as *The Psychology of Cinema* only to find out that the author likes Chaplin and that close-ups isolate some part of the action, and sadly papers specifically on these topics are not included.

Before going on to discuss the selection of papers bearing on the questions above, three points about their scope should be made. Firstly, in general they are concerned with the response to art, not with its creation. Artificially we start with the object and look at how people experience it. Occasionally this rule is infringed – but it would be even more artificial to exclude references when they occur. The same may be said about the limitation to the visual arts. The psychological literature tends to deal with music and the latter together, contrasting them with the literary arts. Therefore authors on occasions illustrate points by musical examples and in general such references have not been excluded. Thirdly, the recent growth in modern painting in exploration of the processing characteristics of the visual system could well receive attention by bringing recent psychological and physiological information together. That is, papers not directly related to the visual arts could have been included. The problems involved, however, would embrace so many aspects of this subject that they would take a book to themselves, while only in fact being a small part of the story.

To some critics the experimental psychological approach to art has appeared most sterile and it is useful before discussing the selections to indicate why this is so, and the nature of the conceptual problems that confront the experimenters.

Certainly experimental studies of the experience of art have in the past disappointed, and psychologists themselves have tended to reject such work. Hearnshaw (1964) in reviewing the progress of early research in the area comments that they felt it had '. . . failed to reach the heart of the aesthetic experience'.

This early failure is attributable to several factors. Firstly, early work was limited by small samples and inadequate statistical techniques. Indeed, re-analysis of some of the earlier data by more sophisticated methods had led to conclusions contrary to those drawn by the original authors. For example, von Allesch (1925) had claimed that colour preference was an individual matter with no general agreement shown between people, a conclusion 'confirmed' by Chandler (1928) and endorsed by Woodworth (1938). Eysenck's (1941a) re-analysis of von Allesch's data, however, showed that a general order of colour preference was statistically demonstrable.

Secondly, there is the problem of the basis on which the psychologist is to select material (colours, shapes, pictures) with which to confront people in order to analyse their judgements and reactions. And, related to this, what kind of responses does he consider relevant to his studies? Both these questions derive from a more general problem. Choice of materials will reflect his own preconceptions about art, for when the psychologist uses such words as 'art' and 'aesthetic response' he becomes involved in extra-psychological issues about the nature of art. It is loose usage of such terms that leads to disagreements with aestheticians, some of whom contend that the psychologist is not 'really' dealing with aesthetic judgements or responses. Yet it is clearly the meaning the terms have for the psychologist (implicitly or otherwise) that will determine his choice of experimental material and what response he will investigate.

In connexion with this problem, the behaviourist attempts to fall back on operationalism. He talks of *aesthetic behaviour*, and postulates a continuum of visual material from single patches of colour in simple geometrical shapes to complex paintings, all of which are designated 'objects' of aesthetic behaviour. This begs the issue, for such a position leaves us with the problem of distinguishing this behaviour and these objects from the study of attentional activity and its objects in general. Such a distinction may rest not on superficial aspects of the situation that are behaviourally obvious but on psychologically important features such as the intention of the perceiver and the types, or categories, of judgement he considers relevant to the two situations.

These problems are raised specially by Berlyne's article (Reading 5). He writes that 'discussions of the psychological aspects of art, whether by psychologists, critics or laymen, depend too often on implicit assumptions that are pre-behaviourist and pre-operationalist.'

However, the concept of 'art' itself is both pre-behaviourist and pre-operationalist, as are some of the terms – for example, 'aesthetically satisfying' and 'aesthetic preference' – that Berlyne himself uses. The assumption that extensive physiological and behavioural measures are relevant to an understanding of re-actions to art requires a considerable amount of pre-operationalist and pre-behaviourist conceptualizing. The assumption that these techniques can usefully supplement verbal reports also involves a pre-experimental judgement about the phenomena with which we are dealing. Berlyne's own findings that the relation between physiological, behavioural and verbal indices is complex or lacking (that is, that verbally expressed preference does not tie in easily with physiological measures) is not in itself proof that there is something to be gained by looking at the latter in this context. Pike (1967), adopting a quite different *a priori* standpoint opposed to Berlyne's behaviouristic attitude, might argue that verbal analysis of conscious awareness and organization of our experience of art *is* the crucial element and anything accompanying this experience that is beyond consciousness is irrelevant.

These arguments are not directed against the approach chosen by Berlyne, but illustrate that psychology cannot confront the problem of studying people's experience of art from one of its particular standpoints (in this case behaviourism) without implicitly evolving a non-objective view of art in the process. The more explicitly this view is stated, the more easily we can talk about the success of the approach in handling what are judged to be problems in the area. Experimental psychologists do not get around the basic two problems mentioned earlier regarding choice of experimental materials and responses by invoking operational and behaviourist techniques.

In view of these difficulties it has seemed useful not to include discrete experimental inquiries of the kind reviewed by Valentine (1962) and mentioned by Munro in Reading 1, but to represent experimental work that potentially relates to general psychological theories.

Berlyne's work, already referred to, represents such an approach and promises to be a major step forward in the application of experimental techniques to the visual arts. This improvement is related specifically to the attempt to integrate reactions to art with a general psychological theory of attention and arousal. Other progress represented in the readings stems from the development of highly sophisticated scaling techniques, as in Skager *et al.* (Reading 18), where the possibility of representing the way in which individuals organize their experience of a particular area of art is shown. The possibility of relating these techniques with the study of cognition and art (dealt with by Child in Reading 7) is mentioned in Reading 2. Such a combination of experimental techniques probably offers the best course for moving away from the aesthetic typologies criticized by Gregson (Reading 14).

However, if we have chosen to start our discussion of these readings from the point of view of experimental psychology, the papers included go well beyond experimental studies. Almost from the beginning psychoanalysts have turned their attention to the arts, and numerous writers have evolved highly individual, even idiosyncratic, psychoanalytic theories of art. Some of these positions not represented here will be more conspicuous than others. In Reading 3 Waelder gives an account of the Freudian position, and this is followed in Reading 4 by Ehrenzweig's theory developed in response to the limitations of the Freudian theory. Whereas, prior to Berlyne's work, experimental studies were defective in explaining why people should choose to look at pictures or listen to music, the functions served by these activities is explicit in psychoanalytic theories, though the function assumed differs between the Waelder and the Ehrenzweig papers. The extent to which one prefers a comprehensive theory of this sort to limited experimental 'revelations' will depend upon one's attitude to psychoanalysis itself, and this problem is explored further in Reading 2.

One of the contrasts between Readings 3 and 4 is the differing emphasis given to form and content as variables in psychological considerations of art. Reverting to our earlier point regarding the connexion between aesthetic theory and psychological approaches, it is worth noting that the desire on the part of psychologists to look for common formal properties in works of art is fairly general. Berlyne does not deny the influence of associational factors and meaning in art, although the level of analysis at which he chooses to operate excludes these aspects. This exclusion may or may not be effective in that even different random shapes have been shown to have different associational values (Vanderplas and Garvin, 1959), to which the subject may be reacting. However, the attempt to demonstrate an aesthetic factor relating to formal properties over and above content has been made through factor-analytic techniques (Eysenck, 1941b). Such a demonstration might seem to indicate that there is a psychologically valid distinction to be made between the form and content in visual material. However, the interpretation of the psychological meaningfulness of factors is far from unanimously accepted (Overall, 1964). For purposes of investigation some such tentative distinction between form and content might be preserved. An over-emphasis on the former would be inappropriate as a comprehensive psychological theory of the visual arts must also understand that the meaning of a painting's content for an individual is crucial. Meaning in this sense is used in a twofold way – meaning in terms of associations, implications, overtones and such-like connotative meaning in fact, and meaning in the sense of identifying natural objects and symbols. Professor Gombrich's paper (Reading 6) deals with this latter aspect of the psychological study of art, and offers an antidote to over-preoccupation with formal properties of paintings.

The general problems of representation in painting and drawing receive attention in Part 4 of this volume. The major work on this topic utilizing much psychological information on perception is, of course, Gombrich's *Art and Illusion*. In Reading 8 Gombrich takes '. . . stock once more and presents some after-thoughts' on the arguments of the book. Green and Courtis (Reading 9) also utilize the concept of schemata in their fascinating consideration of representation and recognition made at the expense of recent attempts to encompass certain of the problems of figure perception by information theory. Two further papers connected with the objective specification of visual form – what has been called the metrics of visual form – are included as Readings 12 and 13.

In discussing meaning, attention has been firstly concentrated on representational factors as such. Meaning as related to expression and connotation are dealt with elsewhere in the readings. Readings 10 and 11 deal with what is the most influential psychological theory of expression – that derived from Gestalt psychology. Some reference to the present status of the theory and of Arnheim's use of it appears in Reading 2. The connotations of paintings (Reading 15) and colours (Readings 16 and 17) have been investigated through the use of the semantic differential.

Finally, three short articles deal with the attempt to evolve objective tests of 'good' aesthetic judgement. It is sometimes claimed that it is in the field of intellectual assessment that psychology has made its greatest contribution. Certainly this conclusion cannot be extended to tests of design judgement which would appear to fail to hold out any real answers to current problems in selection and assessment in art training. The problem of what is determining preference for one well-known test is dealt with in Reading 20 by Moyles *et al.* In Reading 21 Lansdell reports an intriguing finding relating to changes in performance on another design test as a result of neurosurgery. Again the problem of what aspect of the designs relate to the reported changes is obscure.

One notable approach to the study of art has been omitted in these readings – namely the cross-cultural study of the psychological function of art in various societies. This omission cannot entirely be laid at the door of shortage of space. With solid information on the psychological processes involved in the experience of art so limited, the useful information that can be found in simple comparison of preference judgements from two cultures seems slight. Only when the process involved in forming such judgements is understood to some degree can hypotheses be formulated that predict similarity or dissimilarity of judgement on the basis of known characteristics of the cultures concerned. It is in such a context that the study of theories of visual illusions has found a stamping ground and where cross-cultural investigations have proved fruitful.

The implications of this view are naturally applicable to the function served by art in any given society. While much of the writing in these readings suggests that individual needs can be served by art, little can be said about the general social necessity of art. What sections of society and how many of the population experience such needs is a genuine question but one as yet unanswered. The justification for the necessity of art (which results in expenditure by society on such 'amenities') cannot be found in psychological studies at this juncture. Further, in discussion of this problem, the ultimate function of art as a satisfier of individual needs (a view obviously unacceptable to many) is but one function among numerous social motives ranging from the search for prestige to the need to justify the machinery set up to provide for 'The Arts'.

Finally, the omission of any paper before 1943 should not be taken as indicating a simple rejection, on my part, of all earlier work. On the contrary, the mass of writing on taste in the eighteenth century is particularly stimulating and relevant to many of the problems with which psychologists are now concerned. In considering papers for these readings I have been impressed by the fact that explanation by writers such as Alexander Gerard are still being used (with little awareness of their origins) and some writers come perilously close to blunders that he was careful to avoid. The omission of earlier experimental work of the nineteenth and twentieth centuries does reflect a judgement that this is frequently inadequate methodologically, and that the recent studies included clearly supercede it.

References

CHANDLER, A. R. (1928), 'Recent experiments in visual aesthetics', *Psychol. Bull.*, vol. 25, pp. 720–32.

EYSENCK, H. J. (1941a), 'A critical and experimental study of color preferences', *Amer. J. Psychol.*, vol. 54, pp. 385–94.

EYSENCK, H. J. (1941b), 'The general factor in aesthetic judgement', *Brit. J. Psychol.*, vol. 31, pp. 94–102.

HEARNSHAW, L. S. (1964), *A Short History of British Psychology, 1840–1940*, Methuen.

OVERALL, J. E. (1964), 'Notes on the scientific status of factors', *Psychol. Bull.*, vol. 61, pp. 270–76.

PIKE, A. (1967), 'Some notes concerning the aesthetic and the cognitive', *J. Aesth. art Crit.*, vol. 13, pp. 378–94.

VALENTINE, C. W. (1962), *The Experimental Psychology of Beauty*, Methuen.

VANDERPLAS, J. M., and GARVIN, E. Q. (1959), 'The association value of random shapes', *J. exp. Psychol.*, vol. 57, pp. 147–54.

VON ALLESCH, G. J. (1925), 'Die aesthetische Erscheinungsweise der Farben', *Psychol. Forsch.*, vol. 6, pp. 1–91.

WOODWORTH, R. S. (1938), *Experimental Psychology*, Holt.

Part One Approaches and Problems

There is no one psychological approach to the study of the
experience of art, any more than there is one central problem with
which such approaches have to deal. Nor is the attempt to make
such a study new to this century. These readings do not begin with
statements of various historical approaches and schools of
psychology, but with an extensive review by Professor Munro. This
will serve the reader well in providing an introduction to the whole
field. Reading 2 takes up the point that the application of a theory,
or its acceptability when applied, is going to be no greater than the
credence we give to the theory itself. It offers some criticisms of
both the theories and their application which reflect the editor's
attitude to some of the papers included in later sections of these
readings.

1 T. Munro

The Psychology of Art: Past, Present, Future

T. Munro, 'The psychology of art: past, present, future', *Journal of Aesthetics and Art Criticism*, vol. 21 (1963), pp. 264–82.

1. Its Various Approaches and Unorganized Condition

This is a brief sketch of a large and widely scattered subject. It is difficult to summarize, partly because it is not a definitely integrated science or branch of scholarship with consistent methods, accepted aims and boundaries. Important contributions to it have been made in many other fields – in philosophy, general psychology and psychoanalysis, art criticism, anthropology and elsewhere. It is hard to draw a line between these contributions and the psychology of art as a subject in its own right. At present, it is a rather vaguely defined area of discussion and research, highly diversified in method and subject-matter, and broken up into many almost unconnected lines of thought. Yet many of the problems with which it deals are widely recognized as important for the understanding of human nature and civilization. They also have important bearings on educational policy.

The chief present need, as I see it, is to draw some of these threads together as a step toward theoretical integration and co-operative research. I will try to restate some of the main problems and sketch the history of past attempts to deal with them.

Certainly, the psychology of art cannot claim to be a fully-fledged science or branch of science at the present time. It is usually regarded as a branch of psychology, sometimes under the name of 'psychological aesthetics', 'aesthetic psychology', or 'experimental aesthetics'. Some would call it a kind of applied psychology, in the sense of applying general psychological knowledge to a specific type of cultural activity and product. It would then be analogous to the psychology of religion or law. But it is not 'applied science' in the sense of being devoted to practical uses. It is primarily descriptive, a search for knowledge in a certain field of phenomena. Like all pure, descriptive sciences, it can also be applied in practice, for example, in art education and therapy. But the present essay will consider it mainly as a quest for knowledge and understanding.

The psychology of art is also classed as one of several branches of aesthetics. That subject includes aesthetic axiology (value theory) and aesthetic morphology (the study of form in the arts). Morphology, art criticism and art history emphasize works of art, while the psychology of art emphasizes the behavior and experience of the people who make and use them. But all these branches overlap. To understand the work of art one must pay some attention to its human context, and vice versa. In the psychology of art we try to avoid making moral and aesthetic value judgements, but this cannot be done completely.

It is well known that, since the late nineteenth century, psychology has had a revolutionary impact on Western thought in every field. Scholars have come to interpret each set of phenomena, such as law, religion, medicine and art, in terms of how people think about it; how it affects or can affect human experience. The pioneers in this revolution were not professional psychologists, for there was no such profession then. They were men in other fields, such as philosophy and physiology, who helped to change the old 'philosophy of mind' into an empirical science.

From its beginnings as an experimental science in Germany, psychology laid considerable stress on aesthetic problems. This interest lasted on to some extent through the first decades of the twentieth century, then diminished greatly in recent years. Indeed, as a branch of experimental science, with rigorous ideals of exact measurement, statistical and laboratory procedure, the psychology of art is less active and less influential today than half a century ago. At that time, under the influence of Helmholtz, Fechner, Wundt, Külpe, Münsterberg and other German scientists, a number of European and American psychologists began conducting research on aesthetic phenomena. Among them were Bullough, Witmer, Legowski, von Allesch, Angier and

Thorndike. (Their work is summarized by A. R. Chandler and C. W. Valentine.) While psychology as a whole has grown and ramified prodigiously, the percentage of its active workers specializing in art or aesthetics has grown steadily less. During and after the First World War, the psychological interpretation of art and artists received a great stimulus from psychoanalysis, which promised to solve many of its problems. This interest continued as Freud and Jung dealt more explicitly with artistic subjects, but art is hardly a major concern in present psychiatry or psychoanalysis.

On the other hand, the educated public outside scientific psychology has shown a steadily increasing interest in the psychology of art and artists. It is actively discussed, not only by writers on the arts, but in anthropology, education and other social and cultural fields. Much of the discussion is mere amateur psychologizing, none too well informed, often speculative and dogmatic. Some emphasizes the sensational, as in stories and films about Van Gogh and Toulouse-Lautrec. Some is by serious scholars, well aware of what has been done in scientific psychology. The comparative lack of leadership from scientific psychology is unfortunate since laymen, however intelligent and well read in a casual way, tend to drift into unsupported speculation or to misinterpret the ideas of specialists. But even without much professional aid, the psychological approach in general continues to thrive in all branches of humanistic scholarship, including the arts.

After the Second World War, several factors combined to discourage scientific work in the psychology of art. One was the adverse effect of two world wars, which almost eliminated German scholarship in psychology, philosophy and aesthetics. That effect still lasts. The tendency everywhere is to favor engineering and other practical subjects rather than aesthetics and the cultural sciences. This is evident in psychology itself, in the growing emphasis on industrial and clinical tests.

Another unfavorable trend was the growing insistence in American psychology on exact, behavioristic, quantitative methods. Some kinds of human behavior toward art can be easily observed from the outside. Some can be experimentally produced, controlled and measured in a laboratory; other kinds cannot. Some of the most important processes of art and aesthetic experience are subjective; they occur inside an individual and cannot be directly observed by anyone else. Their nature must be inferred from external evidence, which is often misleading. These include the creative imagination and much of the aesthetic response to art: that which happens within us when we listen to music, read poems or look at pictures. An especially large and vital part of experience related to the arts is inaccessible to outside observation.

A large part of human thought and experience in every realm, toward every kind of object, is likewise subjective and concealed from external observation. For this reason any account of general psychology which limits itself to strictly behavioristic methods, avoiding all inference from subjective reports and introspective data, must have enormous gaps in its coverage. There will be vast, important realms of human experience which it leaves undescribed. These gaps, often unacknowledged or concealed in psychological texts, concern especially the more complex, cortical processes of abstract reasoning and the more subtle fantasies, emotions, and desires which do not manifest themselves externally to any great extent. Like the psychology of art, that of religion, philosophy, science, love and friendship cannot be adequately dealt with in purely quantitative or behavioristic terms.

Moreover, experience on the most highly evolved and civilized levels, as in the arts and sciences, cannot be adequately described in terms of general psychology. These terms are too abstract and basic, applying to many types of situation and levels of development. To cover its whole field, the psychology of art must consider the highly civilized, technical manifestations of art and aesthetic experience as well as the more rudimentary, universal ones.

The foundations of a pre-scientific psychology of art were laid centuries before psychology became a science. They were laid by philosophers and literary theorists such as Plato, Aristotle and Longinus. To the strict behaviorist or laboratory psychologist their theorizing seems highly speculative. But, on the other hand, what the laboratory psychologists have been able to achieve by exact methods, from Fechner to the present day, adds up to comparatively little from the standpoint of those who deal directly with the arts. As summarized in general surveys, it deals with the more marginal, superficial aspects of art and aesthetic experience, with statistics on preference, optical illusions, verbal associations, and the like, or with the more obvious aspects of form and technique in the arts. It never reaches those levels which artists and scholars in the arts regard as most central and important to the phenomena concerned. Observations made on behavior in a laboratory toward such highly simplified objects as dots on a page, shapes of rectangles, or isolated bits of music, are not necessarily applicable to the experience of complex works of art under free conditions. Endless statistics on expressed preferences may tell us very little about what happens inwardly when people look at art. Such researches have their value but do not cover the ground. Seeing the lack of progress, many psychologists have lost interest in aesthetic problems and have moved on to more productive areas.

There is another alternative, however. It is that of a broader, more diversified approach to aesthetic problems on several fronts. For those who prefer it, there is still much to be done along quantitative, experimental lines. But this can be supplemented by less exact methods and by more synthesis, more mutual checking and verification of hypotheses from different sources. Workers in the non-scientific fields of art scholarship could profit from more contact with experimental psychology. I believe that such co-operation could do much to revive an interest in the psychology of art. I am not asking that psychologists abandon their ideals of exact, objective knowledge. Let them keep on using measurement as far as it will take them; but not rely on this approach exclusively or ignore the results of other approaches.

The situation calls for more active co-operation between psychologists and other types of scholar in the arts. Art historians, critics and aestheticians should learn more about psychology, and vice versa. It seems obvious that, to do research on the psychology of art, one should know something about art as well as psychology. But to find an American-born, American-trained psychologist who has more than a slight acquaintance with the visual, musical and literary arts is a difficult piece of research in itself. Such persons do exist, but they are hard to find.

The road I have in mind is a broad, well-traveled one in European thought. It includes, in the first place, the cautious but extensive use of *introspective* data, such as reports by individuals on their own artistic and aesthetic experience. These are not to be taken at their face value, of course, for their unreliability is obvious. But systematic efforts can be made to check and interpret them significantly, somewhat as a psychiatrist interprets the introspective reports of his patients. The events of inner experience such as dreams are a kind of phenomena. A broadly empirical psychology will not ignore them.

In the second place, a broad conception of 'behavior' must recognize that *art itself is a kind of behavior*. So is art criticism. The making, performing, using and enjoying of art all have their overt, active phases, in addition to their inner, subjective phases. The former at least can be observed and described from the outside, to yield empirical data for the psychology of art. Everything that is written or said about art and artists is a kind of behavior. Not only what artists do, but also what critics, teachers, patrons and the general public do and say in relation to art, comes under the general heading of behavior. This includes what people read, buy to put in their homes and offices, or pay to see or hear in theaters. It includes the way artists make a living, and the way other persons in their culture treat them.

Much of this can be classed as data for sociology or social psychology, but it is also relevant to the psychology of art. It is being considered to some extent by historians, critics and social scientists; but all of these have their own special interests. They tend to neglect the aspects which are most important from a psychological point of view: the inner motivations, the modes of thought and feeling, the development of creative and aesthetic abilities, which lie behind the external manifestations.

A third requirement is for more attention to the *philosophical* aspects of psychology. This need is greater here [America] than in Europe because of the greater prominence given there to philosophical studies. These tend to encourage a broad, systematic approach in any field. American research is recognized as being, on the whole, too highly particularized and lacking in theoretical synthesis.

Much European psychology has a different weakness, which

disqualifies it from the American point of view. It is too much pervaded by metaphysics, especially of the idealistic or dualistic school. This is obvious to the present day in general texts on aesthetics and in the statement of theories such as empathy (*Einfühlung*). American psychology inclines more toward empiricism and naturalism, but in a rather vague, implicit way, without thinking out its own philosophic position. This tends to make it superficial and sometimes unaware of its intellectual assumptions. One great need is to restate such theories as empathy in a more acceptable way, detached from their old metaphysical associations; but this cannot be done without some philosophical training.

The fourth main requirement, as I see it, is for a more *historically*, *socially* and *culturally* oriented approach. Early psychology emphasized those traits of behavior and experience which were thought to be universal in human nature, characteristic of all normal individuals. Later on, many of the traits which it described were found to be peculiar to our modern, Western culture. In dealing with art, people have acted, felt and thought very differently in other periods and cultures. Recent psychology has become more aware of these differences. But much research and writing on the psychology of art is still based only on present, local data, while its conclusions are stated as if true of people in general. The need for more awareness of cultural change and variation is especially great in studying the phenomena of art and aesthetic taste. Yet the psychologist too often feels that art history, culture history and anthropology are none of his business. This fault is not entirely limited to American psychology. It exists wherever education, science and scholarship have become too rigidly compartmentalized.

2. Its Central Problems: the Creative and Appreciative Processes in Art. Variable Factors Involved

The main connecting link between these different approaches is a common interest in certain perennial problems. The general task is to *describe and explain the phenomena of human behavior and experience in relation to works of art*. These phenomena fall into two main groups, closely interrelated: those of *creation* and *appreciation.* Like the problems of philosophy, they have been discussed for centuries without final solutions. They involve philosophical issues as to the nature of the mind and experience in relation to the outside world, but their psychological aspects can be detached to some extent and investigated on an empirical level. They are too large and difficult to be handled all at once; hence they are divided into many specific problems for research.

The term 'art', in this connexion, is meant in its aesthetic sense as including the visual, musical, literary and theater arts – all the types of skill and product which commonly have as a function the arousal of some kind of satisfactory aesthetic experience. From the standpoint of the artist, they involve the expression and communication of his own emotional experiences. They include the so-called 'fine' arts and the 'useful' arts, such as architecture, which combine aesthetic with utilitarian functions. How to describe more specifically the kinds of experience now vaguely indicated by such terms as 'aesthetic satisfaction', 'the sense of beauty', 'creative inspiration', and the like, is a perennial task of aesthetics and psychology.

By definition, the psychology of art is concerned primarily with art. But in practice, the subject can hardly be so limited. Many of the processes involved can be directed toward objects other than art – toward nature, humans and products of science. All these can be felt as beautiful, ugly, sublime, and the like. To call the subject 'aesthetic psychology' or 'psychological aesthetics' indicates a somewhat larger field; but in any case the arts are its central area.

The two main divisions of the field have been made under various names since ancient times. One deals with the *artist* (as creator, performer or craftsman); the other with the *observer* of art, the looker, listener or reader, the user, appreciator or critic of art. Economists have called them the 'producing' and 'consuming' phases of art.

What functions, abilities and processes are involved in each of these phases? How are they related to the basic functions of human nature, as described in general psychology? Are they distinct in kind, or different only in degrees of acuteness and in application to different types of situation? How do they vary and develop from culture to culture, period to period, and from childhood to maturity in the same individual? What determines individual differences in taste, aptitude and type of art production? To what extent are they innately predisposed, and to what extent culturally influenced? What factors, within the individual and in outside objects such as works of art, combine to cause various types of experience and behavior? How are they related to the various styles of art and to the general cultural climate of an age and people? What is creative imagination? How does it operate and how is it motivated? What distinguishes and causes different degrees and types of creative ability in individuals? Is the difference between mere talent and genius a matter of degree or more fundamental?

The modern approach to these problems is usually more pluralistic and relativistic than the ancient one. It was formerly supposed that there was only one kind of genuine artist, worthy of the name, and one kind of genuine art, obeying the eternal laws of beauty. There was only one right way to create good art, though individual genius might vary the process in detail: hence one might correctly speak of 'the artist' or 'the creative process'. Likewise, there was only one general set of standards for 'good taste', though minor differences among superior persons might again be allowed. The tastes of the lower classes were regarded as hardly worth studying. In the light of this basic uniformity, one might correctly speak of '*the* standard of taste', '*the* aesthetic judgement', or '*the* sense of beauty'. Today, we assume that there are many kinds of each, and that none is necessarily right or best. There are many kinds of artist, many kinds of taste, many ways of creating and responding to art. Each may have its own values and limitations. The task of descriptive science is not to judge these but to observe and generalize on their nature, varieties and interrelations. Consequently, the field of phenomena being investigated is now much larger, since it is not arbitrarily limited to a few varieties.

For more specialized research, the field is further subdivided in various ways: for example,

(a) As to occupation and attitude: the phenomena of artistry; how artists create, perform, and execute; how they think, feel, imagine, get ideas, work them out mentally and in a medium. The

31

phenomena of appreciation: how people perceive, understand, and otherwise respond to works of art; how they use, enjoy and judge them.

(b) As to art and medium: differences in creation and appreciation among the various arts: for example, as emphasizing visual, auditory, or verbal perception, imagination and construction.

(c) As to different social groups, cultures, and periods: how these processes vary in different cultural settings; the role of art and artists in different social and cultural environments and on different socio-economic levels. This leads to developmental studies of the history and evolution of the processes and abilities involved in the arts. How the artist reacts to the styles, techniques, and standards of value which he inherits at a certain place and time.

(d) As to different types of person: how abilities and processes vary in relation to age, sex, personality type, intelligence, special aptitude, general education, and special training in some art. This leads to developmental studies of individuals, as to the growth and differentiation of abilities, tastes, and tendencies in the making, performing and appreciating of art.

(e) As to different temporary moods, interests, attitudes, situations, physical and mental conditions which affect appreciation and production.

An individual's art production or response to art is influenced by many variable factors, internal and external, social and cultural, including his previous experience of art. The effect of a certain piece of music may be very different as experienced in a church, a dance-hall, a military parade or a scientific laboratory. A child's behavior toward art and the preferences he expresses may be very different if he is alone, with other children, or under the eyes of parents or teachers. One cannot isolate an aesthetic phenomenon from its actual or usual context in life without changing its nature and destroying or distorting some of its original characteristics. Psychologists once made the mistake of thinking that, if people respond in a certain way to a certain picture in a laboratory, they will do so always and everywhere. Now we see that aesthetic responses vary greatly, not only in relation to the age and ability of the individual concerned, but in relation to his temporary attitude and the circumstances under which his experience takes place.

This complicates the task of psychological inquiry and necessitates a more relativistic approach. We need to know in great detail *how different kinds of art affect different kinds of person in different kinds of situation.* In ordinary life, each of these factors contains a great many variables. Most of them are constantly changing and producing highly complex, transitory configurations in behavior and experience. Since they are all hard or impossible to measure, the task of discovering their correlations is enormous. Nevertheless, one can simplify it somewhat for the purposes of a special experiment. One can try to hold some of the factors approximately constant within the limits of an experiment, for example, the immediate environment, the particular works of art shown, or the kind of person to whom they are shown.

Knowledge of this type can be applied in evaluation, as in deciding what kinds of effect we want to produce on different kinds of person. But this takes us out of psychology as a descriptive science.

3. Early Theories about the Psychology of Art

There are two main reasons, at least, for briefly reviewing the history of the field. One is for its intrinsic interest as an important set of threads in cultural history. The other is because it takes us back before the field became so highly specialized along different lines; when its main problems were stated more simply and directly by a few discerning philosophers. Their answers to these questions do not satisfy us today, but we can see throughout the past few centuries a gradual accumulation of knowledge and resources for investigation. A summary of this progress may help us to see the underlying unity of the subject and how it could be more effectively reorganized in future.

An interest in the two main types of aesthetic phenomena, which we now call artistic creation and appreciation, was shown in early Greek poetry and philosophy. Why, then, did it take so long to develop a scientific approach to them? The answer lies mainly in the slow achievement of the scientific attitude and method in general, especially in the humanistic fields. The dominant approaches were those of religious mysticism and metaphysical absolutism. Early attempts at an empirical, naturalistic approach, such as that of Lucretius, were beaten down repeatedly. The old, anti-scientific attitudes persisted in aesthetics through the Renaissance and up to the present time. Any talk of scientific method in the study of art still meets determined resistance from influential scholars as well as from artists and the general public.

The origin of psychological theorizing about the arts can be traced to the wide-spread primitive belief in the supernatural power and inspiration of the artist. It was thought that some artists, like shamans, priests and oracles, could be divinely inspired; their artifacts, chants and dances could have magical power for good or ill. The right kind of statue, temple or ritual dance could please the gods, who apparently liked some kinds better than others. Said Hesiod, 'by grace of the Muses and archer Apollo are men minstrels upon the earth and players of the lyre.' Both Homeric epics begin with an invocation to the Muses. Implicit in this religious explanation is a true psychological insight: that artists often feel and act as if their best creative work were directed by some outside power over which they have little control, not consciously willed and planned from within. To explain this is still a scientific problem on which some light has recently been thrown by the psychoanalytic theory of the unconscious. Lucretius, as a naturalistic philosopher, argued that man had originated the arts himself by accident, reason, skill and industry.

The other basic problem, as mentioned above, is that of the effects of different kinds of art on observers. Here again, poetry foreshadowed science in pointing to a psychological fact: the power of music over the emotions. Pindar sang, in one of his odes, of how music can calm the violence of Ares, god of war. Plato showed how musical training in youth affects character. 'Musical training is a more potent instrument than any other, because rhythm and harmony find their way into the inward places of the soul.' Simple old-fashioned music helps to form a self-controlled and spirited youth; soft, Lydian airs and complex rhythms tend to soften and disintegrate character. Plato's theory of artistic creation is religious and mystical. A kind of divine madness, he says, takes hold of the soul of a true artist; mere skill is not enough to make a good poet. However explained, the phenomenon called 'inspiration' is a real one, and psychology still seeks to understand it.

Aristotle described appreciation in a more empirical way by stating that each type of art (for example, tragedy and comedy) can arouse a special type of pleasure. He explained the effect of tragedy as 'arousing pity and fear', wherewith to purge the emotions. That theory is still debated. Much remains to be said on how an event, which would be painful to watch in real life, can arouse a satisfactory emotion in art; perhaps even a pleasant one. Abhinavagupta, tenth-century Indian philosopher, analysed the different kinds of *rasa* (aesthetic quality, mood or flavor) which could be conveyed by the drama and other arts.

Horace, the Roman Epicurean, took an empirical, hedonistic view of art. He tried to formulate rules whereby the artist could delight and instruct his audience. But in Plotinus and Neoplatonism, the empirical and rationalistic approaches were overwhelmed by a mystical religiosity. It influenced St Augustine and medieval Christian thought toward emphasizing the moral and theological aspects of art, especially the danger of temptation from sensuous beauty. Neoplatonism remained a powerful influence on aesthetic theory during the Renaissance and on into the eighteenth century. In Italy, Girolamo Fracastoro and Marsilio Ficino labored to reconcile the growing naturalism and humanism of life and art with the Platonic ideals of supernatural, purely spiritual beauty. Seventeenth-century philosophy began to move away from Platonism and back toward naturalistic empiricism in Bacon, Hobbes and Locke; but these great baroque philosophers had comparatively little interest in art, which they associated with irrational fantasy and uncontrolled emotion. On through the eighteenth century and into the nineteenth, German philosophy approached aesthetics largely from the standpoint of metaphysical idealism. It speculated on the general nature of art and beauty as an expression of the world spirit in sensuous form, and paid comparatively little attention to empirical phenomena.

The empiricism of John Locke undermined the Platonic and Cartesian belief in innate ideas, including 'recollections' of heavenly perfection. It opened the way to revolutionary thinking in the eighteenth century by raising sensation in esteem, not only as the only source of true knowledge, but as the chief source of pleasure and pain, hence of moral and aesthetic value. Le Bossu, in France at the end of the seventeenth century, developed a somewhat technological approach to art as a systematic adaption of means to ends. The ends were specific 'passions' or other mental effects, and the means were specific kinds of form and content in art. Rules for success in art could thus be devised, he believed.

David Hume, eighteenth-century Scottish philosopher, developed an empiricist, hedonist approach in aesthetics. In psychology, empiricism developed the 'associationist' theory, which sought to explain imagination and knowledge by showing how small units of sensation (impressions, images or ideas) rearranged themselves into complex forms in the mind through contiguity, similarity and other 'laws' of association. Associationism also undertook to explain how objects and ideas take on emotional quality, including pleasantness or unpleasantness, by association with more primary pleasures and pains. This had an obvious bearing on the formation of tastes in art, and on the causes of an artist's attitude toward certain subjects, forms and styles. Investigation along this line might well have become more experimental, leading to the kind of research which Pavlov did on the conditioned reflex in the twentieth century; but in method it long remained somewhat literary and impressionistic.

Like some aestheticians in France, notably Du Bos and Voltaire, Hume relied strongly on the concept of 'taste', i.e. good taste, the taste of the innately sensitive and experienced connoisseur. There was considerable disagreement as to the possibility of rules for the connoisseur and artist; also as to whether the ability to make good art could be taught. This implied a psychological issue as to whether the processes of art, both creation and appreciation, were predominantly rational (hence subject to generalized rules) or predominantly sensuous, imaginative and emotional. Opinion moved gradually away from the dogmatic rationalism of the seventeenth century toward a refined, sensuous Epicureanism of cultivated taste; then, with the advent of romanticism at the end of the eighteenth century, toward a still further emphasis on the non-rational elements in art and aesthetic experience.

English, French and some German theories of art criticism, in the eighteenth century, became psychological in tone, moving partly away from metaphysics and theology. In particular, they tried to analyse the creative and appreciative processes. Joseph Addison, early in the century, explained pleasant imagining as due to three sets of qualities in the object: greatness or sublimity, surprise or uncommonness and beauty from the harmonious adaptation of parts to wholes. Edmund Burke went on to distinguish the experience of beauty from that of sublimity. He emphasized passion and the social instinct rather than reason, thus moving toward romanticism. Feelings of sublimity he traced to the instinct of self-preservation in confronting pain or danger. Feelings of sympathy help explain our pleasure in tragedy; ambition or emulation leads us to admire the sublime; the pleasure of imitation makes painting and poetry agreeable. Coleridge distinguished between imagination and fancy in poetry: the one emphasizes and integrates many parts of a subject, the other selects only a few or allows irrelevant discrepancies, as in burlesque.

Blake, Shelley, Wordsworth, Coleridge and Hazlitt, in the early romantic period, all glorified imagination and emotion in contrast with reason as a source of vital richness in the arts. They insisted that great art could not be produced by any sort of rational rules or mere skill in controlling the observer's feelings. Genius makes its own rules, and proceeds mainly by expressing its own spontaneous visions and emotions. But most of the great romantic artists attempted some intellectual analysis of the psychological processes of art. By emphasizing the irrational or non-rational elements in art, romanticism turned the attention of the theorists toward what was later called 'the unconscious'. The main sources and motives of art, it appeared, were not to be found by studying either the rational or sensuous elements. They were found at times in dreams, drug-induced fantasies, sickness and insanity.

Kant, at the end of the eighteenth century, followed the English aestheticians in describing aesthetic pleasure as 'disinterested', i.e. as not mixed with any desire for a practical, ulterior end. His classification of the arts was mainly empirical. But he moved away from psychology and back toward metaphysics in seeking an *a priori* basis and sanction for judgements of aesthetic value: not how men *do* judge art, but how they *should* judge it. A judgement of taste sets itself up as universally valid, said Kant; we demand of all men that they agree with us when we esteem something beautiful. Psychologically, this generalization is questionable if not obviously false. From it Kant proceeded to set up an *a priori* standard of taste: that of design or system. His vast influence on European thought, followed by the more explicit spiritualism of Hegel, helped to turn aesthetic theory away from psychological and sociological studies of art and artists and back to philosophic speculation. The remaining naturalists and empiricists in the field, such as Auguste Comte in France, were not influential enough to keep the psychology of art alive. After a period of inaction, it revived again in the mid-nineteenth century.

4. Some Nineteenth-Century Contributions to the Subject

Like the older theories just mentioned, the more recent ones all have controversial aspects. They are still much discussed and contemporary writers often go to extremes in polemic attacks on them by contrast with their own ideas. Thus one often hears that the theory of evolution in art and culture is 'a discredited Victorian illusion', or that the concept of empathy has been 'abandoned'. Space is lacking in this article to discuss the points at issue, but I believe there is an element of truth in most of the past theories mentioned in this article. They all need correction and amplification to bring them up to date, but all have added important insights to our understanding of aesthetic phenomena. They opened valuable paths for exploration. Their influence did not end with the nineteenth century, and all of them are still vital elements in the twentieth-century investigation of art.

The evolution of art and aesthetic abilities

As the great intellectual achievement of the eighteenth century was the theory of progress, so that of the nineteenth century was the theory of evolution. The two were organized into one continuous system by Herbert Spencer. Organic evolution, as described by Lamarck and Darwin, included the early development of life and the origins of man. The progress of mind and civilization covered only the last few chapters of the story. The history of the arts was shown as an integral part of the progressive evolution of culture, along with technology, social organization, religion, philosophy and science. The nineteenth-century conception of evolution in art and culture was incorrect in many ways and has been subsequently revised. It was oversimplified and too optimistic about inevitable progress. But it did make some lasting contributions.

Art and all the psychological processes involved in its making and use were shown as subject to change and development – not fixed and eternal. The methods of the artists, the styles of art and the standards of value by which it is judged are all products of cultural evolution and subject to change; they have no absolute authority, but express changing culture-patterns of various groups. Even the finest, most civilized products of art are the cultural descendants of primitive, prehistoric art, which came into being along with early magical and utilitarian techniques. Naturalistic evolutionists regarded the origin and development of art as continuous with the physical evolution of man, and as a result of the psychophysical equipment he inherited through natural selection and the struggle for survival.

The naturalistic approach to psychology

The evolutionary account of the natural origins of all man's mental abilities, including those employed in art, strengthened the naturalistic world view. This helped to lay the foundations for psychology as an empirical science. It opposed the metaphysical approach, especially the dualistic and idealistic theories of the mind. Attention turned more to the physiology of the brain and nervous system as the mechanism directly responsible for man's higher mental processes and products including art. Several of the early physiological psychologists were much interested in the processes of art, and regarded their work as filling in the general framework of evolution. Among them were Grant Allen in England, Helmholtz and Wundt in Germany. The James–Lange theory of emotion, stressing its physical basis, was also influential in building a naturalistic framework for the psychology of art. John Dewey carried on this evolutionary approach to psychology in the twentieth century. Like the founders of evolutionary naturalism, he attacked the dualistic conception of art as something in the clouds, esoteric and purely spiritual. He emphasized instead the influence of Darwin on all realms of thought, the biological origins and functions of intelligence in dealing with environment, the continuity of art and aesthetic experience with ordinary experience and the functions of art in a democratic society.

The socio-economic interpretation of art

This approach was led by Karl Marx and his collaborator, Engels. They were interested primarily in the coming social revolution, for which they laid the theoretical basis; but incidentally their ideas had far-reaching implications for the history and psychology of art. The Marxist theory dominates all thinking about art in the communist world today. Non-communist scholars consider it oversimplified in attributing cultural events, including those of art, primarily to socio-economic factors. They insist that other factors, such as the innate predisposition of the individual artist and the inherent tendencies of stylistic change in art, also play major roles.

In general, the idea that socio-economic factors influence art and attitudes toward art is now generally accepted. Most historians of the arts pay some attention to the social background of each period and nation, and to the ways in which styles are related to socio-economic conditions. This bears upon psychology in that the artist is said to acquire and express in his works, often without realizing it, the ideology and economic interests of his social class and the system of which it is a part. It applies also to the phenomena of taste and preference and to aesthetic principles, which are likewise explained as resulting mainly from social conditions. The same is said of the religious and philosophic beliefs of the period. Like the Freudian approach, the Marxist one provides a method of interpreting works of art, as well as the lives and behavior of artists, in terms of motivations which are often hidden and unconscious.

Taine's theory of the psychological environment and other causal factors in art

Much of the credit for introducing the sociological approach to art history and psychology belongs to Hippolyte Taine, French historian and critic, whose major works began in the sixties. He laid less stress on economic factors, but emphasized instead the role of the psychological 'climate' in which art is produced. Three main types of factor, he said, were responsible for the distinctive styles and tastes of each nation and period. One was environment, including the physical as well as the social and psychological; another was hereditary race, on which he laid more stress than present-day scientists would; a third was 'moment', by which he meant the temporary, changing configuration in art and culture in a certain group at a certain time. Taine proposed an objective, empirical, scientific approach to art and aesthetics. He was also a pioneer in what we now call social psychology.

Fechner's psychometric approach to aesthetics

Fechner's *Vorschule der Ästhetik* (1876) had little to do with art directly, or with the social and evolutionary backgrounds of art, but it initiated one line of empirical, experimental research on aesthetic behavior. He gathered statistics on individual preference for various shapes of rectangle and other simple forms, working out the curves of distribution objectively instead of trying to lay down rules for what people ought to like. Along with Francis Galton in England, he pioneered the experimental, quantitative approach to psychology and thus helped to bring in the scientific era in that subject as a whole. Along with Taine, he deserves credit for introducing 'aesthetics from below' (i.e. based on sensory observation) as opposed to the old 'aesthetics from above' (derived from metaphysical assumptions).

Genius, heredity and eugenics

Galton also pioneered along another line of great importance to art and aesthetics: the nature of genius and the question of its transmission through biological inheritance. He assembled statistics on large numbers of eminent persons in various fields including the arts, to indicate the extent to which specific, innate abilities descend in a family lineage. He also speculated on the possibility of producing genius through genetic control. Without the aid of Mendel's laws of inheritance (almost unknown to the world until about 1900) he could not proceed very far along these lines; but the paths he opened still call for continued research.

The Apollonian, Dionysian and Socratic types

Nietzsche distinguished these opposing tendencies in Greek art in his book, *The Birth of Tragedy* (1871). At the same time, he suggested their wider occurrence throughout the history of art. Greek sculpture was Apollonian, he said, and music Dionysian; the two tendencies being combined in Attic tragedy. Apollo personified the calm and clear perfection of the dream-world; Dionysus, the blissful, self-forgetful ecstasy of drunkenness, merging individuality in a sense of mystic oneness. Socratism, stressing knowledge and intelligence, differed from both.

This conception has been fruitful as a starting-point for distinguishing opposite types, not only in the arts, but in the personalities of artists and the attitudes of different culture-epochs. As an artist himself, Nietzsche described other aspects of the creative process, including the 'sudden flash' of inspiration.

Children's art

Modern interest in the child's aesthetic experience and expression goes back at least to Rousseau and Froebel. Spencer and others wrote of the value of art activities in the child's mental development. One of the earliest discussions of children's drawing and modeling from a psychological standpoint was that of Corrado Ricci (*L'Arte dei Bambini*, 1887). He described in some detail the forms characteristic of successive age-levels.

The theory of empathy (*Einfühlung*)

The theory of empathy as a universal tendency or process in aesthetic experience can be traced back to Aristotle; but it was brought to the fore and developed along psychological lines by such German writers as Vischer, Volkelt and Lipps. Vernon Lee and Langfeld further developed it as an aesthetic principle in the early twentieth century.

Briefly, the theory of empathy seeks to explain aesthetic

responses to art and other objects by showing how the observer tends to project his imagination or 'feel himself into' the outside object. It thus helps to explain the processes of art appreciation. In seeing a stage play or reading a story, one tends to imagine oneself as in the represented place and situation, perhaps as watching and taking part in the action through the eyes of an imaginary character. In looking up at the piers and vaulting of a Gothic cathedral, one may imagine oneself as flying upward along it, or thrusting up or down as if identified with certain parts of the building. The form of a complex work of art provides a stimulus and framework for the empathic responses of a qualified observer.

5. Some Twentieth-Century Approaches

Psychoanalysis; depth psychology

Freud's momentous writings, comparable in revolutionary impact to the theories of progress and evolution, appeared from the turn of the century on into the Second World War. They emphasized the evolutionary survival of basic animal and primitive drives in man, with reverberations in his art. They pointed to consequent problems of controlling and sublimating man's aggressive inheritance in civilization, in order that genuine progress may go on.

There is space here only to list a few of the topics most relevant to the psychology of art. Freud's earlier works were clinical and concerned with neurotic personality-types. They portrayed the artist as inclined to neurosis but often able to escape it and compensate for his frustrations through finding a 'way around to reality' and success. This he could do by expressing his fantasies in forms satisfying to others. In his later works Freud assigned a more constructive, normal role to art and the artist, and dealt more extensively with the phenomena of art as related to dreams, folklore, primitive religion and the perennial warfare between destructive and constructive forces in civilization. His writings threw considerable light on the symbolism of all the arts; their imagery and the reasons why certain images come to have emotive power of a positive or negative, pleasant or unpleasant sort. He maintained that certain almost universal, unconscious conflicts arise in man from early infancy, mostly from the conflict between basic sexual impulses and the moral and practical inhibitions imposed by civilization. Some individuals resolve and sublimate them in what we call a normal way, and art is one great means to this; others fail and resort to neurosis, crime, or other courses which society disapproves. He went on to describe the structure of personality as including three main regions: the id or repressed, unconscious area; the superego or severe, repressing area, also unconscious, and the ego or area of more or less conscious adjustment between these warring parts and between the individual and the outside world.

These seminal ideas, all more or less controversial today, were enthusiastically applied by laymen to the problems of art and aesthetics, often in a mistaken or distorted way, so that a reaction against the psychoanalytic approach to art set in. But if used with caution and supplemented by other data, the psychoanalytic interpretation of art and artists can still be deeply revealing.

Jung's version of psychoanalysis emphasized the role of archetypal images in art and of the extrovert–introvert polarity in personality structure. He showed how certain ones, such as the mandala pattern and the figures of the old wise man, the great mother and the eternal child, recur not only in dreams but also in art and religion. Jung wrote more extensively on art than Freud did. The innate archetypes, he said, act as frameworks into which each people and each individual pours its own specific experiences. Jung's belief in a vitalistic metaphysics and in the transmission of acquired psychological characteristics is highly controversial.

The Freudian and Jungian theories, and those of several lesser psychoanalysts such as Adler, Stekel, Abraham, Riklin, Reik, Ferenczi, Kris and Ernest Jones, have been applied to both the creative and appreciative aspects of art. Maud Bodkin and Herbert Read have applied those of Jung to art criticism and education.

Studies of the creative imagination

T. Ribot's *Essay on the Creative Imagination* appeared in French in 1900 and in English in 1906. It dealt especially with the differences between the merely reproductive imagination, as in memory, and the creative or constructive imagination, as in art and science. It also discussed the mystical and other varieties, often expressed in art. Some years later John Livingston Lowes, in a much-discussed book on Coleridge (*The Road to Xanadu*), described three factors which interplay in imaginative creation: first, the storing of the 'well' of remembered experience; next, the creative 'flash' of vision, when details fall suddenly into place; and afterwards the long task of translating the vision into actuality through elaboration, correction and refinement. As Lowes points out, much the same steps occur in original scientific thinking.

Why and how the crucial flash of inspiration occurs in some if not all creative artists remains something of a mystery. The previous phase, the 'storing of the well', is not to be understood as a mere piling up of inert memories. It usually includes the learning of some technique by which one's imaginings can be expressed and communicated through an external medium, and also some tentative, preliminary sketches of the germinal idea. Today, these inquiries are linked with the study of dreams, myths, reveries, hallucinations and other types of fantasy. They also require consideration of the effects of different culture-patterns on the creative process.

Experimentation under standardized conditions with creative imagining is at present next to impossible. Some interesting experiments are being done on related processes, however, such as the effect of certain drugs in stimulating vivid fantasies and unusual states of mind. Some drugs produce experiences similar to those of ecstatic, mystic revelation. Some are much used by jazz musicians. The term 'psychedelics' has been coined to denote the so-called 'mind-revealing' agents, such as lysergic acid and mescaline, which produce quasi-mystical experiences. Other techniques for stimulating creative fantasy, without the harmful effects of most drugs, are being sought. Many artists have used drugs for this purpose in centuries past, usually with disappointing results.

Studies of artistic processes, production and performance

Imagination is only one of the constituent functions in artistic creation. All are partly internal, partly overt. They operate in complex, ever-changing configurations, mostly inaccessible to observation. Many theoretical attempts have been made to describe recurrent general traits of artistic production and performance and also some of the main varieties, especially in relation to different personality types. As data, the reports of artists on how they think out and execute their work differ greatly in value. More significant data are sometimes available in series of preliminary sketches and rough drafts, showing a work at various stages of development. Some recent artists (such as Van Gogh and Henry James) have shown themselves capable of acute, though never quite objective self-analysis in letters, memoirs and answers to questions. Recent historians and ethnologists have described the varied roles and methods of artists in different types of society.

The artistic process varies greatly as to the artist's type of personality (for example, planful or impulsive, introverted or extroverted) and also as to the styles and theories of art which are current at the time. Today, the desire of some contemporary painters to create impulsively and automatically has been encouraged by the teachings of Zen Buddhism, which is not always thoroughly understood.

Comparisons have been made between such art and the work of young children or even of animals. Serious studies have been made (for example, by Desmond Morris) of the behavior of chimpanzees when provided with finger paints and allowed to make pictures. Abstract painters usually resent such comparisons as unflattering, but the resemblance of some (not all) abstract expressionist art to that of the chimpanzees is too obvious to ignore. Also, as Morris points out, much recent art is regressive from an evolutionary standpoint. It tries to avoid all inherited styles and sometimes all rational processes of thought.

Artistic processes also differ considerably from one art or medium to another. In some, such as architecture, more practical, technological thinking is required as well as attention to economic factors and the tastes of the patron. In others, such as painting and poetry, the artist is often more free to express his personal fantasies and impulses. Generalizations must be made in relation to many such variables.

Studies of appreciation, evaluation, and criticism

This large and important area of aesthetic experience has not received much empirical study as a whole in recent years, although many of the approaches mentioned in this list have thrown some light upon it. Perception and preference have received most of the experimental research. But their functioning is not limited to the appreciative side of art, and they are not the only processes involved in appreciation.

Efforts have been made to analyse 'appreciation' (or the 'aesthetic response', the 'sense of beauty', or some related concept) into its main components, configurations and varieties. Both the appreciation and creation of art are now seen as highly diversified, variable processes. The appreciative or aesthetic attitude differs from the artistic in not being actively directed toward making any outside product, any work of art. It tends to emphasize a detailed, sensitive, emotional response to the perceived object, including imagination, empathy and apprehension of meanings. It may or may not involve evaluation and preference for certain types or examples. It differs from free fantasy (without an external object) and from intellectual inquiry.

Under civilized conditions, appreciation often leads to explicit verbal criticism, involving the search for appropriate words as well as rational interpretation and judgement of the work of art or artist. This provides one more type of variable process for psychology to describe.

The writings of I. A. Richards in the 1920s applied psychological ideas to the appreciation and criticism of literature. They have been followed by many others, usually with special reference to a particular art.

The semantic approach

Influential in contemporary philosophy as a whole, the study of words and meanings has important bearings on aesthetics and psychology. Much art is wholly or partly verbal. Criticism, evaluation and other responses to art are commonly expressed in verbal terms. So is all theorizing about the arts. Sometimes the ambiguity of words is valued for aesthetic and emotive reasons. In science and scholarship it can be a hindrance. Man's use of verbal and other symbols for conceptual thought and communication is one of his most distinctive and momentous achievements. Works of art can be analysed in terms of symbols, iconic signs and various types of meanings. The ideas and attitudes expressed in art and in talking about art are deeply affected by the meanings and associations attached to words and also by logical and illogical statements and inferences.

There are many theories about the metaphysical and epistemological status of symbols and meanings; also about how concepts should be formed, defined and used. But to some extent semantics can be treated as a part of psychology; as a descriptive study of verbal and other symbolic thinking and its role in behavior. A number of recent aestheticians have done so with special reference to art and aesthetic experience.

Cultural psychology

All kinds of behavior and experience toward the arts vary considerably from one culture to another and from one period to another in the same culture. We have noticed the importance of recognizing and describing this diversity in the psychology of art. It has been forcefully revealed by anthropological and archeological studies during this century, especially of tribal and oriental cultures remote from our own. To see how the arts develop and function in a total culture-pattern, including its social, political, economic, technological, religious and intellectual components, can be deeply illuminating. To see the pattern as a whole helps us understand how art develops in certain ways within it – the status and function of the artist, the standards used to judge his work. By comparing our own with exotic cultures, we understand our own more clearly and objectively. All styles of art, all creative and appreciative processes, can be integral parts of the culture as a whole. They are influenced by it and influence it in return. The patterns change at varying speeds; many are now becoming more similar because of cultural diffusion.

One important phase of this study is to discover and compare the value systems of different cultures – what people want, enjoy, admire, detest, hate, fear; what they feel guilty or ashamed about, and so on. (See Benedict, Kardiner, Kluckhohn, Linton, Mead and others.) Such evaluative attitudes become loosely integrated into systems. They are expressed to some extent in the arts, in addition to being used in judging art. Some research in this field has combined the anthropological and psychoanalytic approaches. It asks, for example, to what extent the Oedipus complex occurs in a primitive culture such as that of the Marquesas Islands. It also overlaps the study of cultural history and of styles in various arts as related to their cultural settings.

Morphological and stylistic studies of the arts

These are not psychological in a strict sense, because the emphasis is on the work of art rather than the artist or appreciator. It is well to maintain this distinction, but not to exaggerate it into a wall of separation. We can hardly describe artistic creation and appreciation without observing the varieties of product which emerge from the former and which stimulate the latter. We can hardly describe a work of art without reference to the kinds of attitude, belief, and past experience it expresses, and to the kinds of response it arouses in observers.

Much has been done in recent years toward analysing and comparing the forms of art (symphonies, poems, pictures, films) as biology does with plant and animal forms. This has to be largely in psychological terms. Anthropologists such as Franz Boas and art historians such as Riegl and Wölfflin contributed to this approach by analysing types and styles of art in relation to their cultural settings. A style such as the Byzantine was explained as a way of seeing and imagining.

Gestalt psychology

A German import like many other contributions to the subject, this one has its negative and positive sides. Negatively, it is an attack on eighteenth-century associationism as too 'atomistic', as falsifying experience by describing it in terms of unitary ideas, sense-impressions, and the like. Accordingly, it tends to reject the traditional associationist view of how sense-data (in art and elsewhere) take on emotional, 'tertiary' quality through being associated with pleasant and unpleasant experiences. Positively, this school prefers to think in terms of large, complex configurations in art and other experience. Its investigations have emphasized aspects of visual perception, such as the various ways of seeing relations between figure and ground in a picture. The total process of perception is not a simple one of sensing and interpreting. It varies greatly according to the expectations, desires, and emotional attitudes involved.

Gestalt psychologists have raised anew the old question of how visual art and music seem to have emotional qualities. Some hold that the music is, in a true sense, 'really sad'; that sadness is not merely a projection of the observer's feelings into the sound. The Gestalt approach has recently been extended to deal with motivation in social behavior, which again has important bearings on art. Its main contributions to the psychology of art have been on the side of perception and appreciation.

Theories of personality and character; diagnostic tests and interpretations of art

Analysis of personality types and individuals have an obvious bearing on the arts. It is often asked whether 'the artist' is a distinctive personality type, perhaps akin to the neurotic. The consensus today is against that theory. There are many kinds of artists, as there are of other occupational types. Certain personality types such as the normal and neurotic, introvert and extrovert, are said to cut across these occupational divisions. There is considerable interest in classifying and characterizing, not only artists, but also persons in other fields, including the superior and inferior, genius and moron, socially adjusted citizen and criminal.

Every individual in modern civilization develops several 'selves' or 'personae', different configurational aspects of his personality. These he habitually presents in different types of situation or to different types of person, including himself. An artist presents certain aspects of his personality in his art, but not his whole personality. Much depends on the social environment, what it requires of the individual, and how he adjusts his own desires to this environment.

Besides the psychoanalytic approach to personality diagnosis, many others have been tried in recent years with varying success. These include the attempted correlation of physique and glandular secretion with personality (Kretschmer, Berman); the Inkblot test (Rorschach), and the Thematic Apperception test (Murray, Rapaport). Some tests involve the interpretation of ambiguous visual forms to reveal character traits in the interpreter. They assume that one's response to visual forms, somewhat like those of art, can project and reveal one's own traits of personality. There are also tests of general intelligence and probable learning rate, tests of special interests, questionnaires for comparative analysis of an individual by different persons, resultant 'profiles' of personality and moral character. Some procedures and modes of interpretation in this field, such as graphology, are more respected in Europe than in the United States. All are applicable to artistic phenomena.

It is fairly easy to devise a test or a questionnaire on preference, give it to a number of persons, and treat the results statistically. But interpretation is difficult and liable to error, especially when used to diagnose some individuals as 'normal', others as having neurotic or psychotic tendencies. In interpreting the Rorschach, for example, there has been a tendency to regard any unusual, bizarre, emotional, or highly imaginative response as neurotic. Thus a potential artist or other creative mind can be too hastily branded as pathological. This tends to perpetuate the old, mistaken association of genius with insanity, as in the theories of Lombroso.

Much the same uncertainty surrounds the popular practice of psychoanalysing students' or patients' drawing as a clue to possible neurotic or psychotic conditions. For a number of years, Freudian principles were thus applied in a rather mechanical way with misleading results. Freud himself had cautioned against assuming that a symbol in dreams or works of art necessarily had the same meaning always. The interpretation must be made, he said, in relation to other data about the individual. Over-imaginative interpretations by the teacher or psychiatrist have often led to suspecting a pathological tendency where none exists.

Much depends on contemporary styles in art and standards of what is normal and admirable. At the present time, no particular kind of aesthetic taste or of artistic product is necessarily a pathological symptom. Sane artists produce works which, in other

51

days, would have been considered as symptoms of insanity. Some deliberately try to suggest that condition. A really insane artist may, on the other hand, produce an anxiously careful, orderly, conventional picture.

Art and psychotherapy

The supposedly therapeutic effects of art work are still very unsure and very little understood. Any kind of harmless, object-focused activity, such as handicrafts, may have some therapeutic value in releasing internal anxieties. For this, the quality of the product is not the main consideration. The attempt to create a serious work of art in any medium can be a release in some ways and a very tense, anxious, wearisome task in others. It has contributed to many artists' mental breakdown. The same can be said of other kinds of difficult work, and does not imply that art is especially akin to neurosis.

All this is said by way of caution. There is no doubt that art can have great values in psychiatry and orthopsychiatry, for both diagnostic and therapeutic purposes. But it must be used understandingly, along with other methods of diagnosis and treatment. The kind of art material and activity used, and the ways of using them, will have to be varied in relation to the case at hand. In general, art offers a promising means of helping the disturbed patient to become more conscious of his own unconscious conflicts, and thus of being able to adjust them intelligently.

From the standpoint of descriptive psychology, the importance of therapeutic activities in art lies in the opportunity they give to experiment with different kinds of art and different methods of making and using them. Just as Freud's clinical work with neurotic patients led to discoveries about all human nature, so experiments with art for such patients can lead us to more knowledge about the processes of art in general. Common human traits and tendencies often appear in the neurotic or psychotic personality in a magnified, hypertrophied, uncontrolled form. A certain type of art may arouse a mild emotional response in the normal adult and a similar but far more intense one in the neurotic. By studying the latter, we learn about the former, which in itself might pass unnoticed.

Studies in the growth of individual art ability

In the period between the two world wars, important studies were made in Germany, Austria, France and elsewhere in Europe of the artistic development of individual children. Examples were kept of the drawing, painting and clay-modeling of certain ones from infancy to maturity. Successive stages, observable in the drawings of all normal children, were distinguished in such terms as 'scribble', 'schematic' and 'realistic'. An effort was made not to direct or hasten the child's artistic development into adult styles, but to let his powers of visual conception as well as execution mature freely. His artistic development was studied as a part of his general personality development and as contributing to normal maturation. Some of the researchers went on to discuss possible analogies between such individual growth and the development of world art from prehistoric times.

Innate individual differences always appear in the child's work, over and above any such general, typical stages. The influence of the child's artistic environment and school instruction is also evident in spite of all attempts to keep him free from it.

On the technical side of artistic performance, as in learning to sing or play the piano, studies have been made of the learning process. They seek to show how it can be accelerated in pursuit of desired aesthetic qualities.

Skills can also be developed in the perception and appreciation of art, with or without any skill in production or performance. The ability to perceive and understand complex forms in music, painting and literature involves considerable knowledge and technical training. Most civilized persons develop some of this, as in looking at motion pictures. But there are many levels of such ability. Little has been done to investigate the learning process in these fields. The problem is often confused by different theories as to how one *ought* to look at or listen to works of art and to judge their value.

Tests of art ability

Following the success of the Binet–Simon and other tests of individual intelligence, and of the group intelligence tests developed in the First World War, there was a demand for tests of mechanical, artistic and other abilities and aptitudes. They promised to be of use in grading, not only army recruits and business employees, but students and prospective students of all ages in the crowded public schools and colleges. Such tests and standardized rating scales were devised to measure various types of art ability. Most of them undertook to measure good taste and ability to recognize and judge good art, rather than to create it. But it was sometimes inferred that persons who did well in them were potentially good artists. Many tests were based on the assumption (later challenged) that objective art values could be determined within a group of paintings, poems, musical selections, and the like, by securing a consensus rating by professional experts in the field, such as artists, art teachers and heads of academies. The subject's ability to recognize good art was then rated in terms of his conformity with the 'authoritative' rating. Some tests involved 'spoiling' or altering a picture or piece of music by some well-known artist, in the belief that the spoiled version would necessarily be worse. To prefer it would then be a sign of bad aesthetic judgement. Critics pointed out that the 'spoiled' version might be as good or even better in certain ways, for certain aesthetic effects. The result of such tests was to give a high rating to subjects who preferred the conventional examples, and to penalize those of unconventional or avant-garde tastes. A few tests undertook to judge performance in drawing and other artistic skills, by comparison with a scale of examples, supposedly arranged in order of merit. But these too rested on fallacious assumptions, in that conformity to conventional adult standards of realistic representation was usually the implicit criterion. Other tests undertook to estimate, not 'ability', but stage of maturation in drawing, by comparison with the normal series of stages from 'scribble' to 'realistic'.

Confidence in tests of art ability, both creative and appreciative, has declined in recent years. This is partly due to trends in art itself, in that realistic and other conventional types of form have been widely abandoned by contemporary artists. Dissonant types of music are often preferred over consonant ones, and violation of traditional rules is common in all arts. It is harder to assume, then, that production of any particular kind of art, or preference for it, is a sign of superior ability. Even the possibility of checking a test by success in a later artistic career becomes dubious. What is success in art, and who is successful?

However, the potential value of tests and measurements in the arts does not rest entirely on their power to evaluate ability. They can be used in more objective ways, as means of estimating certain traits and tendencies in the subjects tested, without any implication of superiority or inferiority. Thus used, they can be correlated with the results of other diagnostic methods as part of a comprehensive analysis of taste and personality. The range and distribution of such traits, in both the production and appreciation of art, can lead to significant generalizations.

Propaganda and commercial advertising

The role of the 'strategy of terror' in the Second World War and that of communist propaganda in the subsequent cold war, both conducted with the aid of psychological science, called attention to 'thought control' and 'brainwashing' as practical applications. The arts have been extensively used as means of indoctrination and emotional incitement. Propagandist art is, of course, not new, since art has been used for millennia to glorify rulers and to spread religious doctrines. But now, like other methods of warfare, it has the powerful aid of science.

The same is true of art as used for advertising and commercial inducement – not only in obvious, visual layouts, but in films, music and dramatic skits over radio and television, and in the 'hidden persuaders' which try to influence people unawares, perhaps by almost imperceptible words concealed in motion pictures. Subtle appeals are addressed to the motivational mechanisms of different types of person, for example, through disguised erotic symbolism in pictures. Highly paid psychologists confer with advertising directors and sales organizations on how to use science for their purposes. The effects of various kinds of packaging have been tested in this way. The appearance and message of greeting cards are carefully thought out so as to appeal to certain types of personality and social status.

Advertising and other propagandist art is not necessarily bad; it is capable of good or bad, important or trivial, selfish or public-spirited use. But now it is being used for predominantly commercial and partisan ends. Psychology might well try to understand such uses better, if only to guard against their dangers. It is also worthy of note that large sums are being expended for research in the psychology of advertising, much of which is relevant to the psychology of art in general: for example, research on the ways in which different kinds of picture, song, etc., affect different kinds of observer – different age-levels, sexes, personality types, and educational levels. Aestheticians look forward to the day when equivalent funds and brains can be used for developing the psychology of art in general, for the sake of knowledge and of higher cultural values.

Relations between the psychology of art and art education

These can run in both directions. The influence of psychological ideas on education in every field is enormous, as for example in Dewey's emphasis on arousing the interest of the student and helping him to think for himself; to learn by doing. Theories of normal personality growth and of age-level traits therein have been so frequently applied to education in the arts that I do not need to stress them here. It should be said in passing, however, that the psychological approach is often praised in educational theory and ignored in practice.

As in regard to psychotherapy, I would like to emphasize here the role of education as a *potential laboratory for the psychology of art*. The schools, museums, studios and other places where art is taught provide an excellent testing-ground for psychological investigation in that field. At present, they are not much used for that purpose. Many practical difficulties stand in the way or experimentation in the schools, and it can be overdone. But it should be possible to do a little more than we are now doing. The amount of work done is not as important as the way in which it is done; a small amount, with careful control of procedure and interpretation of results, is better than much of the vague, informal kind. Experimentation on a scientific level is not merely 'trying out' this or that special method or device, such as finger-painting with music or quick recognition of pictures briefly exposed. Without careful preparation, the results are always inconclusive, if not meaningless. The aims, the standardized conditions and procedures, the resultant phenomena to be interpreted must all be planned in advance and controlled.

What information, of value to psychology, could be obtained through properly controlled educational experimentation? The answer is further light on all the problems discussed in this article. In general, it might give some verified conclusions, not mere guesswork and wishful thinking, on the results of different ways of teaching both creation and appreciation, or of fostering them without direct teaching. The question is not merely which are best, but what observable effects, if any, result from each method and each different set of materials, including exposure to different kinds of art at different ages. How can various specific, desired abilities be most effectively developed? Having a child under observation and care for year after year, the schools might throw more light on the processes of learning and emotional maturation as manifested in the arts, together with the factors which can encourage it or distort and arrest it.

In this connexion, educators might try to think out, together with psychologists, the ideal goals which both would approve. What kinds of person are we hoping to produce through education? What kinds of artist, of art, and of cultivated layman? Or is it best to leave all these outcomes to chance and free impulse? These questions take us again outside the realm of descriptive science; but more psychological knowledge about the processes involved would be of great value to the educator.

6. Conclusions

These are by no means all the important, present and potential approaches to the psychology of art. But they are enough to illustrate the wide ramification of that field and the need of more integration within it. I have not tried to evaluate their relative importance. Even where the work done to date along a particular line seems unsound or inadequate, the problems remain and the path lies open for better solutions.

In mentioning so many lines of research I do not imply, of course, that any one individual should try to be active in all of them. Any of them can be a life work in itself. But one can specialize and also pay some attention to what is being done along related lines. Thus to see one's own specialty in a larger context can help to give it greater significance and more far-reaching effects. It can suggest needed research along supplementary lines. Meanwhile, individuals with more philosophic interests can specialize on synthesis, with profit to all concerned.

The newly activated and extended subject of aesthetics promises to offer some help in that direction. It is bringing together psychologists of different persuasions, such as the behaviorist, the Freudian, the Gestaltist, the Marxist and the Neo-Thomist, along with scholars from many other fields. It brings the psychologist face to face with artists, historians, critics, and others who deal directly with works of art in the outside world. More collaboration between them all will help to throw light on the darker areas of this field, still largely unexplored by science.

Bibliography

(*Note:* This is an introductory sampling of different approaches to the subject. It is not intended as a list of the most important references in the field, or as an endorsement of all the views expressed. Most of the titles listed below contain additional bibliographies.)

L. E. ABT and L. BELLAK, *Projective Psychology*, New York, 1959.

K. ALLSOP, 'Jazz and narcotics', *Encounter*, vol. 16 (1961), pp. 54–8.

R. H. ALSCHULER and L. W. HATTWICK, *Painting and Personality*, Chicago, 1947.

R. ARNHEIM, 'Agenda for the psychology of art', *J. Aesthet. art Crit.*, vol. 10 (1952), pp. 310–14.

R. ARNHEIM, *Art and Visual Perception*, Berkeley, California, 1954.

R. ARNHEIM, *Picasso's Guernica, the Genesis of a Painting*, Berkeley, California, 1962.

R. ARNHEIM, R. AUDEN, *et al.*, *Poets at Work*, New York, 1948.

F. BOAS, *Primitive Art*, Oslo, 1927.

M. BODKIN, *Archetypal Patterns in Poetry*, Oxford, 1934.

E. BULLOUGH, *Aesthetics: Lectures and Essays*, Stanford, California, 1957.

A. R. CHANDLER, *Beauty and Human Nature*, New York, 1934.

A. R. CHANDLER and E. N. BARNHART, *A Bibliography of Psychological and Experimental Aesthetics*, Berkeley, California, 1938.

J. DEWEY, *Art as Experience*, New York, 1934.

H. ENG, *The Psychology of Children's Drawings*, New York, 1931.

H. ENG, *The Psychology of Child and Youth Drawing*, New York, 1957.

P. R. FARNSWORTH, *Musical Taste: its Measurement and Cultural Nature*, Stanford, California, 1950.

B. GHISELIN, *The Creative Process*, Berkeley, California, 1952.

R. GOLDWATER and M. TREVES, *Artists on Art*, New York, 1945.

E. H. GOMBRICH, *Art and Illusion*, New York, 1960.

W. W. HARMAN, 'The humanities in an age of science', *Main Currents in Modern Thought*, vol. 18 (1962).

A. HUXLEY, *Heaven and Hell*, New York, 1956.

A. KARDINER, *et al.*, *The Psychological Frontiers of Society*, New York, 1945.

C. KLUCKHOHN and H. A. MURRAY (eds.), *Personality in Nature, Society, and Culture*, New York, 1949.

E. KRETSCHMER, *The Psychology of Men of Genius*, New York, 1931.

E. KRIS, *Psychoanalytic Explorations in Art*, New York, 1952.

M. LASKI, *Ecstasy*, Bloomington, Indiana, 1961.

R. LINTON, *Cultural Background of Personality*, New York, 1945.

V. LOWENFELD, *The Nature of Creative Activity*, New York, 1939.

J. L. LOWES, *The Road to Xanadu, a Study in the Ways of the Imagination*, New York. 1927.

D. B. LUCAS and S. H. BRITT, *Advertising Psychology and Research*, New York, 1950.

F. L. LUCAS, *Literature and Psychology*, London, 1951.

R. LYNES, *The Taste-Makers*, New York, 1949.

L. MACHOVER, *Personality Projection in Drawing the Human Figure*, Springfield, Illinois, 1949.

N. C. MEIER, *Art in Human Affairs*, New York, 1942.

B. MEYER, *Emotion and Meaning in Music*, Chicago, 1957.

D. MORRIS, *The Biology of Art*, London, 1962.

T. MUNRO, *Art Education: its Philosophy and Psychology*, New York, 1956.

T. MUNRO, *Toward Science in Aesthetics*, New York, 1956.

H. A. MURRAY, *Exploration in Personality*, New York, 1938.

J. L. MURSELL, *The Psychology of Music*, New York, 1937.

M. NAUMBURG, *Psychoneurotic Art: its Function in Psychotherapy*, New York, 1953.

M. NAUMBURG, *Schizophrenic Art*, New York, 1950.

R. M. OGDEN, *The Psychology of Art*, New York, 1938.

V. PACKARD, *The Hidden Persuaders*, New York, 1957.

R. C. PANDEY, *Comparative Aesthetics, I: Indian – Aesthetics*, Varanasi, 1959.

R. S. PETERS (ed.), *Brett's History of Psychology*, London, 1953.

W. PHILLIPS (ed.), *Art and Psychoanalysis*, New York, 1957.

C. C. PRATT, 'Aesthetics', *Ann. Rev. Psychol.*, vol. 12 (1961), pp. 71–88.

D. RAPAPORT, *Diagnostic Psychological Testing*, Chicago, 1945.

H. READ, *Education through Art*, London, 1942.

I. A. RICHARDS, *Principles of Literary Criticism*, New York, 1926.

C. A. RUCKMICK, *Psychology of Feeling and Emotion*, New York, 1936.

M. SCHOEN, *Art and Beauty*, New York, 1932.

L. L. SCHÜCKING, *The Sociology of Literary Taste*, London, 1944.

M. W. SMITH (ed.), *The Artist in Tribal Society*, London, 1961.

C. W. VALENTINE, *Experimental Psychology of Beauty*, London, 1962.

V. VAN GOGH, *Dear Theo*, Boston, 1937.

2 J. Hogg

Some Psychological Theories and the Visual Arts

An original paper written for this edition.

Introduction

Scott Fitzgerald once wrote disparagingly of ' . . . that most limited of all specialists, the "well-rounded man" ', and denied his assertion was merely epigrammatic since '. . . life is much more successfully looked at from a single window.' Certainly a consistent point of view in looking at psychological problems has advantages. It makes it easier to relate diverse observations within the same framework, and increases the possibility of detecting inconsistencies.

But there is no one theoretical point of view nor any one methodological approach in psychology that has attempted to deal with all the main problems raised in the psychological study of the visual arts. To try to benefit from the advantages of a consistent approach would lead either to a highly restricted view of the subject matter at one extreme, or to all-embracing generalities at the other. Indeed, Munro (1963) argues for a diversity of approaches.

Nevertheless, when discussing the psychology of art, it may be advisable to group material according to problem areas rather than by the various approaches. Organization of this sort reflects an important feature of the psychological study of art; namely, that the different approaches in general do not set out to offer differing explanations of the same phenomena, but tend to gravitate towards particular areas of the subject. Explicit disagreements in explanation are rare (and a few of these will be indicated) though general criticisms of a whole approach – such as Eysenck's criticism of the psychoanalytic theories of art – are more frequent.

60

Having chosen to treat the psychological investigation of the visual arts in terms of problems and processes rather than schools, the limitations of the theories on which we have drawn must not be overlooked. In some cases these theories are sufficiently explicit to enable us to make some preliminary comments on them, while other papers stand outside any formal theory and tend to reflect generalized approaches to psychological problems.

In the former category are the papers based on psychoanalytic theory by Waelder (1965) and Ehrenzweig (1962), and by Berlyne (1965) whose paper rests on his theory of curiosity and arousal, while Child's (1965) study is based on the theory of cognitive controls. Green and Courtis (1966) criticize the application of information theory to visual perception and Arnheim (1943, 1949) applies Gestalt theory to the arts.

Psychoanalytic Approaches to the Arts

The extent to which psychoanalysis offers a general theory of psychological functioning is often not appreciated. While it is clearly seen to be related to motivational aspects of behaviour it is less apparent that it also sets out to handle perceptual and cognitive phenomena. We will see in our subsequent discussion of cognitive controls the extension of psychoanalytic concepts to these latter processes.

In his introduction to the best-known psychoanalytic study of an artist – Freud's biography of Leonardo – Farrell (1963) draws attention to the central problem that confronts the layman interested in studying the application of psychoanalysis to the arts, and though he is dealing specifically with hypotheses proposed by Freud in relation to Leonardo, many of his comments are applicable to the more general consideration of psychoanalysis and visual art that we are making here. Farrell points out (pp. 13–16) that there is a lack of any 'consensus of scientific opinion about psychoanalysis' and the consequent difficulty the layman has in establishing criteria by which he can make a critical assessment. He notes (p. 71) that our credence of a psychoanalytic interpretation of an artist's personality and works is dependent on the weight we are willing to attach to the theory from which it is derived. However, while Farrell is critical of certain aspects of psychoanalytic theory in itself (for example, its dependence on interpretation of clinical data for validation), he points out that at least it is offering a framework in which to approach highly complicated human activity (such as the work of Leonardo) and concludes that Freud's essay in itself tells much about psycho-analytic methods – and their weaknesses.

Farrell also attempts to indicate the attitudes that various individuals might adopt towards Freud's essay, depending on their previous disposition and training (pp. 82–4). However, while there is no short cut to assessing Freudian, or any other, psycho-logical theory, the non-psychological reader should be aware that serious criticisms have been made at all levels of the theory, and before going on to deal with the papers derived from this approach in the readings, some of these are briefly noted.

Theoretical criticisms

Nagel (1959) has produced what must be considered the severest challenge to psychoanalytic theory's scientific status, scientific here being taken to mean its verifiability through observation. He criticizes psychoanalysis not for dealing with theoretical concepts, but for not specifying operationally their nature or the rules of correspondence between them and behaviour. Further, the theory does not lead to clear-cut determinant predictions, partly because the language in which it is couched is 'metaphorical' and 'open-textured'. Like Farrell, he doubts the faith put in clinical inter-pretation as a method of validating psychoanalytical concepts.

It can be, and has been, argued that criteria applicable to the physical sciences are not relevant to the understanding of per-sonality. If such a view is adopted then Nagel's criticisms will be judged irrelevant to the issue and rejected – which takes us back to Farrell's point, that our opinion on psychoanalysis will be determined by our personal choice of criteria.

Anthropological criticisms

It has become commonplace to note that Freud evolved a uni-versal theory of personality by observing a very restricted cultural group, and the universality of the Oedipus complex has become the key issue in anthropological studies of psychoanalytic theory. The apparent failure to demonstrate its existence in several non-

Western-European societies has been cited as evidence against the Freudian position, though this claim has been disputed and the question is still being actively investigated. (A non-technical review of the controversy, 'Freud and anthropology', appeared in the *Times Literary Supplement*, 21 March 1968.)

Clinical criticisms

There is no reason why psychoanalytic theory should not be 'correct' even though methods of treatment based on it are ineffective. Nevertheless, demonstrations of its therapeutic ineffectiveness tend to weaken conviction in the theory, and Eysenck (1961) has drawn attention to numerous studies which tend to show the shortcomings of psychoanalytic therapy. In considering these studies, the most favourable view of such therapy is that its efficacy has not been adequately demonstrated – a conclusion with which some psychoanalysts would agree.

The reader's attitude to the two papers representative of psychoanalysis will therefore be affected by his degree of acceptance of the theory, in the light of the difficulties that present themselves to it.

Ehrenzweig's (1967) position, though derived from Freud's psychoanalytical approach to art and in response to its failings, is in many respects an introspectionist theory. This he acknowledges: '... hypotheses of the kind I am proposing are really only verified by introspection into one's past experiences ...' (p. 86). At the same time he does present a theory relying heavily on psychoanalytic concepts, though he is far from merely attempting to extend Freudian clinical insights to art, arguing that Freud's own attempt to apply his theory to art failed: his success in dealing with the joke did not lead to a 'triumphant entry into the core of aesthetics ...' (p. 266) since the method was inapplicable. Ehrenzweig accepts Freud's account of the unconscious origins of the structure of the joke, but considers that the structure of art differs in an important respect. Both the joke and a work of art involve clear-cut organizations or configurations. However, in the latter there is structure beneath the organized surface. It is this that has to be perceived to make an authentic response to art. The joke remains superficial, but art has an unconscious structure which has to be grasped unconsciously. Ehrenzweig proposes that we are able to do this through what he calls 'undifferentiated' perception. Such perception is dependent upon what he calls 'unconscious scanning', and is likened to Piaget's term 'syncretistic' – the ability to grasp something as a whole. Perception of this kind is essential since Ehrenzweig (pp. 21–2) considers:

The complexity of any work of art, however simple, far outstrips the powers of conscious attention, which, with its pinpoint focus, can attend to only one thing at a time. Only the extreme undifferentiation of unconscious vision can scan these complexities. It can hold them in a single unfocused glance and treat figure and ground with equal impartiality.

In what has been said about Ehrenzweig's theory so far we have discussed the 'grasping' at an unconscious perceptual level of a work of art. But what kind of response to a work of art is he attempting to account for? It is not easy to pin this down as Ehrenzweig is rarely specific about one response – and it is even questionable whether he is dealing with only one type. In describing reactions to works of art he variously mentions 'vividness' (p. 14), 'emotional impact' (p. 30), 'heaving, pulsating pictorial space' (p. 59), 'beauty' (pp. 265 and 266); and it would be tiresome to take exception to these terms and ask if in fact he is talking about qualitively different experiences. He is more specific in dealing with what appears to be the essential experience of art within his theory which is the experience of being 'enveloped' (p. 119) in a work of art – especially with reference to modern art. The experience of being enveloped is characterized by the 'oceanic' feeling that Ehrenzweig suggests accompanies perception of certain works of art.

How then does the operation of unconscious vision relate to the 'oceanic' experience? Ehrenzweig describes the relation in the following way:

Perception ... sets apart from the outset a large part – perhaps even much the larger part – of its function as an unconscious subliminal substructure into which id phantasy can penetrate with the greatest ease. The ease of the id's penetration is, of course, explained by the extreme undifferentiation of unconscious vision. Its wide all-embracing sweep can use almost any object form as an assembly point for an immense cluster of other images that, for conscious analytic vision at least, have nothing in common. Any objects, however different in shape or outline, can become fully equated with each other, on the unconscious syncretistic level. On a new oceanic level outer perception and inner phantasy become indistinguishable (p. 272).

Ehrenzweig's theory, as we have said, is in part introspectionist, and in part psychoanalytical, and in this is open to the general criticisms and difficulties mentioned earlier. Yet he is concerned to draw on evidence that will support his position and this should be commented on. Much of this evidence is intentionally non-scientific. He cites anecdotes (pp. 16–17), artists, comments (p. 22) and qualitative aspects of pictorial space (pp. 80, 82), and such evidence illuminates his position but offers little confirmation to the sceptical reader. Perhaps more convincingly he draws on two sources of evidence of a more rigorous kind, namely from studies of the blind who have had their sight restored, and experimental evidence on perception.

The former evidence is used to attack Gestalt theory, the application of which to art conflicts with Ehrenzweig's position. Thus Arnheim (1943) draws a parallel between the approach of Gestalt psychology and Cézanne, 'The artist may think here of the saying attributed to Cézanne, that nature can be seen as cubes, spheres, cones, etc. . . .' and compares this view with that of the Gestaltist that perception organizes sensory material into good Gestalten. Ehrenzweig (p. 113), however, denies Cézanne the 'precise focal vision' which would be involved in seeing the world as organized into geometrical shapes. He claims Cézanne's pictures represent a 'syncretistic' (p. 117) handling of a 'total (undifferentiated) visual field . . .' (p. 113). However, despite the strength of Ehrenzweig's assertion, his evaluation of Gestalt psychology is inadequate in many respects.

Specifically he refers to the work of von Senden (1960) and Gregory (1966) on cured blind people as a crucial test of the Gestalt position which would predict immediate organization of the visual field. 'None of these predictions came true!' (p. 13), concludes Ehrenzweig. Wertheimer (1951) has analysed the limitations of these observations. He has pointed out the inadequacies of source material with its lack of controlled observation, and also the inhibiting effect of certain post-operative factors – eye muscle fatigue, dazzle, and the accompanying emotional disturbances. He concluded that the work does not constitute a clear-cut rejection of the Gestalt position as Ehrenzweig states. If Gestalt theory is to be attacked at all, it must be on more sophisticated grounds than this (see below). In effect, Ehrenzweig fails to give convincing argument for his 'depth' account of the perception of art over the 'surface' account proposed by the Gestalt theorists.

If Ehrenzweig fails to gain support for his theory from the negative aspects of Gestalt theory, he also fails when drawing attention to the positive relevance of subliminal perception to his case. 'The superior efficiency of unconscious vision in scanning the total field has been confirmed by experiments in subliminal vision. "Subliminal" is only another word for unconscious . . .' (p. 32). In making these claims he seems unaware of the body of experimental work that has followed the earlier, much publicized, demonstrations of so-called 'subliminal advertising'. Any simple assertions about the 'superior efficiency of unconscious vision' must be doubtful in the light of this later work, and further, the sense of the term 'unconscious' in this situation has also been questioned. The conclusion of one review (Forgus, 1966) of this work was that 'it appears that the organism is extracting information continuously from the stimulating situation and, likewise, there is no need to introduce the notion of unconscious. What we call unconscious is merely the condition wherein the subject is extracting very little information from the stimulus' (p. 266).

Farrell's point that our assessment of Freud's study of Leonardo is dependent on our attitude as to what constitutes valid evidence for psychoanalytic propositions is applicable to Ehrenzweig's theory. If we introspectively compare our own experience of art with his then our assessment will depend on how far the two experiences coincide. There are many areas in which we can make the comparison, for he extends his fundamental explanatory concepts to cover creativity (p. 47 ff.), child art (p. 5 ff.), serial music (p. 33 ff.), art training (p. 55 ff.) and conducting (p. 65 ff.), as well as to neolithic art (p. 131) and schizophrenic art (p. 128 ff.). While the strict experimentalist will see the theory as lacking in evidence and full of insubstantial inferences, it is a theory that had made a considerable impact in art circles, offering as it does both an explanation and justification for certain recent trends in painting. More circumscribed psychological theories of art tend to pale besides the all-inclusive explanatory power it claims.

However, a Gestalt-based argument against Ehrenzweig's position has been developed by Pike (1967) from a phenomenological standpoint. While this argument is specifically connected with the application of the view to music, it is extendable to the visual arts. In brief, Pike argues that the phenomenological approach '... is preoccupied with problems of perception, experience and meaning arising directly from these musical events rather than with a concern for referential, extra-musical data, or unconscious symbolism' (p. 398). In other words, the experience of art is essentially a conscious activity dealing with Gestalt-like structures, requiring no hypothetical unconscious perception (a contradiction in terms, according to Pike) to account for it.

We have noted Ehrenzweig is intent on displacing the content of art from the central position which we see it to occupy in Waelder's (1965) lucid exposition of the Freudian position. Equally we feel the inadequacy of explanatory power in the latter's references to 'certain configurations or Gestalten... which may be seen as *patterns of tension and discharge ...*' and which depend for their pleasing effect upon some unspecified function involving '... the increase or diminution in the quantity of excitation *in a given period of time*'. The suggestion that 'formal beauty' provides an 'incentive bonus' in making the unconscious content of art acceptable is an attitude particularly at odds with the Ehrenzweig position for in the latter's view unconsciously perceived structure is something to be grasped *in spite of* the immediate 'Gestalt-like' organization of a work of art that forces itself upon our attention.

Berlyne's Theory of Curiosity, Arousal and Art

If concepts such as 'tension' and 'discharge' are going to be introduced into psychological theories of art with any conviction, we must turn to the far more carefully worked out hypotheses developed in the context of experimental psychology by Berlyne (1965) and his co-workers. In linking psychoanalytic theory with Berlyne's approach we are not suggesting an intimate conceptual similarity. However, both approaches do emphasize the need to experience art and the ensuing resolution of the motivating state when such an experience is engaged in.

Berlyne's first comprehensive statement of the implications of his study of curiosity and exploratory behaviour appear in his book *Conflict, Arousal and Curiosity* (1960). Like Ehrenzweig he criticizes Freudian aesthetics for over-emphasizing content, though not denying 'the importance of associated factors, conscious and unconscious' (p. 231), he is himself most concerned to direct his attention to formal or structural aspects of art.

This attempt to apply his theory of curiosity and arousal to artistic experience has produced the most comprehensive theory of the response to art based on experimental psychology so far developed, and further work by him and his associates has subsequently explored some of its implications.

The position adopted is, in the main, a testing out of possible analogies between curiosity and arousal in the laboratory setting, and artistic experience. Much of the theory goes beyond what has been experimentally demonstrated, and involves a speculative reinterpretation of certain aspects of artistic experience. However, the adequacy of some of the parallels is worth considering.

Berlyne's theory sets out to explain two aspects of the response to art. Firstly, why do people engage in behaviour which will result in them perceiving a work of art, i.e. why are they motivated to seek such situations out? Secondly, granted that pleasurable (rewarding) arousal results from the perception, what formal or structural aspects of the situation (picture or piece of music) lead to this pleasure being optimized (Berlyne, 1960, p. 229)?

It is a useful starting point to note that Berlyne identifies form and structure with properties of his collative variables (p. 229). These are represented by pairs of pictures [See Figure 1, p. 131] differing in some respect (for example, symmetry) to which people attend differentially. This identification is questionable on two grounds. Firstly, it is easy to give a verbal description to a pair of pictures, for instance, heterogeneity of elements, but very much more difficult to express the difference quantitatively, i.e. to actually measure the degree of heterogeneity. This problem of measuring visual form or pattern – the attempt to evolve a metrics of visual form – is discussed later when we consider the application of information theory to the problem. Suffice to say now that the attempt to develop such metrics is beset with difficulties, and Berlyne's collative variables are not adequately quantified. This is not merely an academic point, for unless the figures are quantified in various ways it is difficult to specify which aspect of the picture a person is attending to. For example, is it heterogeneity of elements or degree of asymmetry that attracts attention? One study at least (Hoats, Miller and Spitz, 1963) suggests that the assumed difference between the figures is not really the effective one.

Secondly, what objective validity have categories such as 'form' and 'structure' in art? Berlyne accepts, perhaps only as a convenient working assumption, the traditional assertion of the necessity for structural organization involving 'unity in diversity' or 'uniformity in variety'. Although he is able to point to several aesthetic theories proposing varieties of the view, its adequacy has certainly not gone unchallenged by aestheticians, nor by psychoanalytic theorists, such as Ehrenzweig. Heyl (1943) considers the view that valued works of art have some common property that leads to a judgement of 'aesthetic quality' or 'beauty' and characterizes such a view as 'objectivist'. He indicates that various objects are valued for all sorts of reasons and asks '. . . what can they, or do they, have in common? Such a sensible answer as "unity" in fact helps little, since there are as many sorts of unity as there are types of art objects . . .' (p. 108). After analysing assertions about basic characteristics such as 'unity' and 'structure' of aesthetically valued objects, he concludes that

there is no *a priori* reason to suppose the existance of a common, intrisic and inexplicable *quale* connoted by the terms. Unless, then, one assumes a naïvely objective attitude toward beauty and aesthetic quality, the situation regarding such a *quale* is analogous to a similar situation regarding the causes of death: 'Of all the things which cause death we can say if we like that they are all lethal, but we are no longer tempted to think that we are saying anything more about them than that death did occur in connexion with them.'

Berlyne's acceptance of an essentially traditional view in this respect is interesting in the light of his obvious dissatisfaction with aesthetic theory in general, and with the many *a priori* assumptions involved in it which he leans towards rejecting.

Given, then, Berlyne's doubly doubtful linking of the 'ideal' structural organization of a work of art and his collative variables, the following assertion must be treated cautiously:

The principle of diversity can readily be identified with the conditions which drive arousal up to high levels. It is associated with variety and multiplicity, in which we recognize two factors that make for complexity, namely heterogeneity and numerosity of elements. It can evidently also embrace novelty, ambiguity and surprise. The opposing principle of order or organization seems, on the other hand, to represent the conditions that make for clear-cut cortical responses that allow arousal to be moderated (Berlyne, 1960, p. 232).

In the statement, however, there is the additional problem of the relation between organization of a stimulus and level of arousal. While this is no place to attempt to appraise the status of the arousal concept, the relation between various indices of arousal and behaviour is extremely complex – as Berlyne's subsequent work has shown. Nevertheless, these criticisms should not conceal the fact that the above statement is an early formulation essentially hypothetical in nature, and fulfills Berlyne's objective of moving aesthetic experience (he would prefer 'aesthetic behaviour') into the ambit of contemporary experimental psychology.

The claimed dependence, at least in part, of artistic experience on the manipulation of arousal by structural properties of the work of art is one way of conceptualizing the relation. However, Berlyne does tend to impose it upon the artist's intentions and art history in a curious fashion. It seems as if he sees the artist as intentionally setting out to manipulate the course of arousal in a spectator, and seeing this as the object of the creation of a work of art. Thus, 'We can take a look at some of the devices that are available to the musician for operating on arousal' (Berlyne, 1960, p. 248) or again, 'The scheme of progress toward mounting arousal followed by progress toward relief has thus to work through content rather than form in literature and cognate arts, and the means that are applied to its realization are well known'

(p. 253). His comments on the movement from early Renaissance to Baroque art, suggesting that the movement involves varying manipulations of arousal value, might be considered a less useful way of considering stylistic change than that of art historians. This application of the theory, then, tends towards a curious example of the intentionalist fallacy. However, it could be argued that Berlyne is not really claiming that artists *do* set out to manipulate arousal (intuitively or otherwise). Therefore when a critic writes, 'like all Haydn's mature quartets, they are a passionately civilized expression of the ideals of the Enlightenment, seeking unity from egalitarian diversity', he is not necessarily asserting that this was Haydn's intention any more than Berlyne would be asserting Haydn's intention was the organization of diversity in unity to manipulate arousal. (At least, one hopes he is not.)

It is with problems of this sort that the psychologist dealing with art inevitably finds himself confronted. He is pushed towards adopting or evolving an aesthetic or critical theory himself. It is questionable that a purely psychological theory of art *can* be developed, because so many conceptualizations about the nature of art intervene. If for example in defending Berlyne's view of the arousal effects of art we maintain that the intentions of the artist are irrelevant, then we are immediately aligning our position with a general (and perfectly respectable) critical attitude that thinks likewise, but which is not accepted by all.

Berlyne's (1965) paper is exceptionally useful in that it gives the essential features of his approach and a considerable amount of experimental work bearing upon it. Improvement in the objective characteristics of his collative stimuli, in the concept of arousal and in physiological indices of arousal will enable this work to bear more closely upon the nature of the response to art. At present there seems to be a gap between Berlyne's laboratory-induced reactions and the latter, deriving largely from the conceptual shortcomings dealt with above. It is also clear that the gap is being closed in a more effective way than has been achieved in earlier psychological studies of art.

Cognitive Controls and the Experience of Art

In discussing psychoanalysis we mentioned that Freud had dealt with the relation between cognition and perception, and motivation. This was further developed by writers such as Hartmann, in the context of psychoanalytic ego-psychology, and has been explored further experimentally through the investigation of what have been called 'cognitive controls'.

Child (1962, 1965) has studied the relation between numerous personality variables and aesthetic judgements, including several cognitive control variables. While this is undoubtedly the most useful and stimulating research on picture preference and personality variables yet carried out, there are several basic problems that present themselves. Although the study of cognitive controls forms only a part of Child's work, some of the difficulties it raises have general relevance to the psychological study of personality and the visual arts. The following consideration then, is limited mainly to Child's research on cognitive controls.

Gardner, Holzman, Klein, Linton and Spence (1959) have produced the basic reference on cognitive controls, though much research has been done since 1959. The nature of these controls and their place in psychoanalytic theory can best be characterized by quoting the following paragraph:

Freud recognized the adaptive characteristics of behaviour by postulating an arrangement of structures concerned with such matters as (a) the gratification of drives, (b) the modulation and delay of drive consummations, (c) appraisal of reality and reconciliation of environmental forces and internal tensions. He conceived cognitive development as following a course intimately linked to, and partly determined by, development changes in drives themselves. He considered perceiving, remembering and thinking to involve a matrix of structures which limit and mediate motivational influences. In our view, a cognitive control describes an organizational tendency that relates the functioning of these structures to each other within the person. It is an intervening structural condition accounting in part for the *particular* impact of a need or cognition (Gardner *et al.*, 1959, p. 4).

While the cognitive control may be compared with a psychoanalytic defence mechanism, the former does not necessarily serve a defensive end. The various types of cognitive control operate across a range of situations and change slowly within any individual, though a given control may or may not operate in a particular situation.

In connexion with the latter point, it may not be individual cognitive controls that influence a person's response, but the particular combination of typical cognitive control performances. A person performing high on Control A and low on Control B may adopt quite a different strategy to cope with a situation than a person high on A and high on B, the two strategies not being predictable in any simple additive fashion from performance on the two tests. The particular combination of controls a person displays constitute his *cognitive style*. Thus 'Style ... may allow more effective prediction to molar aspects of behaviour within and outside the laboratory, some of which may not be evoked by specific adaptive requirements' (Gardner *et al.*, 1959, p. 116). This is a much more specific sense of 'cognitive style' than that which Child uses in his papers.

Finally, cognitive controls do not all relate to the same type of cognitive activity. One may relate to memory, another to the deployment of attention. This is obviously important if we are concerned to make predictions about the influence of cognitive controls on the experience of art, since the part they play in the over-all experience will differ.

In case we have been too abstract, let us note the main types of control that have been studied by Child. These are either derived directly from the work of Gardner and his colleagues, or suggested by it: Tolerance of Ambiguity, Ambivalence and Unrealistic Experiences; Scanning; Sharpening; Narrowness of Equivalence Range; Flexibility; and Field Independence. The nature of these controls are described in Child's (1965) paper.

Difficulties inherent in Child's approach

The rationale linking cognitive controls to the response to art. On what grounds can we assume a cognitive control is likely to have a bearing on the reaction made?

(a) It has been argued that cognitive activity is not involved in the response to art, and such an argument is highly dependent upon certain *a priori* assumptions about the nature of art.

Employing a more restricted view of cognition than that used by psychologists, Aiken (1955) argues admirably that this is not the case. Most psychologists would accept his view, and reject the notion that a 'pure' response to art uncontaminated by cognition is likely. We may grant, then, that in general terms the study of the part played by cognition in the response to art is quite valid.

Certainly those who have developed the work on cognitive controls have pointed this way. Cognitive control principles may 'in . . . some ways become "motives" in themselves. The exercise of mediating structures may in itself entail gratification, as when one seeks out particular kinds of tasks, or pursues a particular hobby that allows free expression to his particular organization of adaptive propensities' (Gardner, Jackson and Messick, 1960).

(b) Granted this, what aspects of cognitive activity are we going to consider? Child's approach here is typical of the logic involved in many correlational studies, in that numerous measures of individual variation in cognitive activity are related to aesthetic judgement on the basis of tenuous verbal analogies and suppositions. Thus, Child (1962) in dealing with the cognitive control of scanning writes:

The variable of scanning seems likely to be related to an understanding of art, and hence to judgement, on two separate grounds. One is that understanding of a complex work of art involves the ability to attend simultaneously to various aspects of its stimulus value. The second is that interest in art (and hence an understanding of it) seems most likely to develop in scanners, since objects of art are constantly present as a part of one's environment from early childhood but may be reacted to solely for their practical significance except by the scanner (p. 56).

Firstly this view of the effect of a high level of scanning on aesthetic judgement goes far beyond what experimental work has demonstrated about the nature of scanning. Secondly, the fact of the correlation found between scanning and aesthetic judgement throws no further light on an explanation as to *why* the two variables *should* be linked. For other personality variables Child proposes equally 'reasonable' hypotheses linking them to aesthetic judgement and the outcome is not significant or even tends in the opposite direction to the prediction. Thirdly, it is probably the case that almost any personality variable could be linked to aesthetic judgement by some vague hypothesis of this sort.

This loose approach may be contrasted with Gardner *et al.*'s (1959) stricture that, 'formulating hypotheses from a control principle to a new situation in which the control principle may be relevant must be preceded by careful consideration of the problems confronting the subject in the new test situation' (p. 141). And again, 'more effective generality studies are rooted in careful analysis of the functional implications of the control principles' (p. 141).

(c) It might be argued that if, despite the above criticisms, positive relations do emerge between some cognitive controls and 'good' aesthetic judgement, then this is sufficient as it points the way to further research. This is only partly the case. Firstly, because the hypotheses are loose, almost any personality test can be made to appear relevant and no initial constraint is put on the selection of variables. This means that the variables arbitrarily chosen may not be those of most interest and we are left dealing with fringe contributions. Secondly, this approach has ignored the contribution of cognitive style, in the sense of a person's placement (high or low) on several cognitive control measures. We have noted Gardner *et al.*'s (1959) comment on the fact that a consideration of cognitive style will allow more adequate prediction to molar behaviour than the individual controls. Negative findings on the latter may lead to them being ignored when in terms of their contribution to style they are highly relevant. Thirdly, the gap between the formulation of a hypothesis and the interpretation of a positive relation is such that Child's conclusion to his paper (1965, p. 510), while being highly attractive and reasonable, goes beyond the actual findings.

Many of the above difficulties relate not to Child's study as such, but to the necessity for further research on cognitive controls. There are two aspects of this that could enable us to develop hypotheses about their relation to the reaction to art.

Firstly, although cognitive controls are conceived of as being motivated, the function and development of the postulated motivation is in general unknown. We cannot, therefore, suggest with any exactness what relation between the motivated control and the need served by the experience of art is – given even that we can say anything about the latter.

Secondly, the concept of cognitive style itself is poorly worked out, and broad categories of cognitive style have not been defined. Their introduction into a study of responses to art would therefore require much original work on them involving an extremely large sample of respondents.

What response to art? If we are going to link measures of cognitive controls to response to art then we must be clear as to what we are interested in in connexion with the latter. Psychologists concerned with studies of the response to art have often leant heavily upon whether or not subjects do or do not agree with expert opinion. It must be said, however, that because an experimenter commits himself to use of expert opinion in an experiment, as Child does, he is not necessarily endorsing an objectivist approach to art, though elsewhere this would appear to be his position (Child 1966). While the implicit approval towards 'good aesthetic judgement' is apparent in Child's (1965) conclusion, it is never explicitly objectivist in this paper. This is as it should be, for as Heyl (1943) has indicated in discussing the diversity of evaluations about art:

... first, it presents cogent empirical evidence against the notion of uniformity in expert value judgements; second, it actually *explains* the fact that certain works of art are highly praised by very different persons and by very different cultures . . . ; and third, it points to a basic variety in the attitudes or points of view which determine critical appraisals (p. 103).

This lack of 'uniformity in expert value judgements' begins to show itself in the complex relations between tests setting out to measure 'good' aesthetic judgement all validated on expert samples.

The question of 'good' aesthetic judgement is a genuine problem. It does, however, appear to beg the issue in some psychological studies. What is really involved is not whether a person agrees with the experts, but what are the characteristics (training, personality, philosophical outlook, etc.) of the experts with whom he agrees. If we wish to see what the characteristics are of a person showing so-called 'good' judgements, why not take the experts who made the original 'good' judgements and compare them with a group who significantly differ in their judgements? Obviously this is not what is needed if an 'objective' test is being evolved *as* a test. But if the test is being evolved to assess, for example, the personality characteristics of a people making a certain type of judgement, why not study those people directly? Equally as interesting to the psychologist should be the characteristics of *any* group who make relatively uniform assessments of art. So-called 'good' taste is of no more psychological interest than so-called 'bad' taste.

Granted, then, that research has been over-concerned with conformity to expert opinion, it might also be noted that it is over-preoccupied with verbally expressed preference. This is a point made by Berlyne (1965) who has cast doubt on the relation between such expressions of preference and actual behaviour. However, Child explicitly distinguishes between aesthetic judgement and aesthetic preference, and in his (1965) paper is concerned with the former. Granted this, are we necessarily choosing the most interesting aspect of the response to art – namely evaluation of some sort? In so far as the outcome of confronting a work of art is frequently a value judgement, the answer is that this is probably the case. However, of considerable importance as well is the strategy by which a person engages in this confrontation with a work of art. It is at this level of strategy that the study of cognitive controls and cognitive style appears so relevant, and yet it is this level that is by-passed in the leap to compare evaluation with expert opinion.

Recent work on multidimensional scaling is particularly relevant here. We may take a set of pictures that we have classified as varying in a number of different ways, i.e. on a number of different dimensions. These may be degree of complexity, amount of colour variation, and so on. However, people will be likely to differ in whether they notice certain dimensions at all. Further they are likely to organize the pictures on dimensions of their own. Clearly their evaluations are going to be affected, for in some sense they are 'seeing' the pictures differently. It will involve a more or less explicit 'schemata' about art that will be more or less sophisticated. It is in such a case that Gombrich's analyses of the significance of iconographic aspects of art and the nature of style are so important and necessary. Indeed, as Child (1965) effectively points out, such an approach is almost demanded by his extraordinary finding of a positive relation between 'good' aesthetic judgement and preference for Baroque over High Renaissance art.

The foregoing suggests that at the bottom of our understanding of the effect of individual differences on the response to visual arts, there is a twofold conceptual short-coming. We are not clear in even an elementary way about the responses we are trying to explain, nor are we able to specify the anticipated effect of individual psychological differences on the responses. Obviously the two go hand in hand. What is demanded is more conceptual analysis of the situation in which a person confronts a painting, and perhaps more *observation*, as distinct from experiment, of the situation.

While Child's study is so easy to criticize in these terms, it is done with such a high degree of technical skill that its findings are to be taken seriously and it forms, and will form, a starting point for further investigation in this area.

Gestalt Theory and Art

Gestalt theory was not just a psychological theory but a total approach to systems and organizations whether biological or physical. Also, though its predominant application in psychology was in the field of perception where it was most convincing, few psychological functions have not been considered in Gestalt terms. The application of Gestalt theory to art – especially the visual arts and music – was as 'natural' (for quite different reasons) as the application of psychoanalytic theory. These points are brought out in Arnheim's (1943) paper, and at the end of that paper and in more detail in his later paper (1949), Arnheim elaborates on the specific application of a Gestalt derived approach to *expression*.

However, the importance of Gestalt theory in relation to perceptual processes (in the widest sense) in contemporary psychology is considerably diminished. Certainly few would be willing to describe its position as '... the academic theory of perception...' as Ehrenzweig (1967, p. 263) does in referring to its earlier status. There are many reasons for this. An obvious one is that physiological studies of perception are throwing light on shape perception and do not require the invocation of hypothetical neuro-electrical fields of the sort the Gestalt psychologists postulated. J. Z. Young has written: 'millions of words have been written about the problem of "Gestalt". In essence it becomes simply the problem of how the mechanism sets up a response appropriate to the stimulation of a particular array of points on the receptor surface' (1964, p. 139).

Furthermore there are logical difficulties in the Gestalt theory which were pointed out relatively early in its development (Petermann, 1932) and which have received further attention in the light of evolving views on the philosophical bases of science by Nagel (1952). One of the key criticisms offered by Petermann relates to the Gestaltist's effort to characterize the nature of a true Gestalt by pointing to the criterion that the effect of the latter was unpredictable from a knowledge of its parts and their relations. Thus Koffka (1915) quoted by Petermann (1932) notes 'The endeavour to derive the whole from its parts or to erect it above its parts has often failed. The whole does not arise from a compounding of parts . . . Hence nothing can be known as to how the experience will eventuate merely from information about the stimulus.' Köhler (1924) attempts to define the criterion by which we judge the existence of a Gestalt as being '. . . that the characteristic properties and effects cannot be put together out of the properties and effects of a like sort of its so-called parts.' However, Petermann points out, it is this very independence of the whole from its parts that the Gestalt psychologist is initially setting out to explain. As he puts it (1932, p. 49) the formulation of the concept of Gestalt '. . . *ceases to be in any way considered as a problem. Rather it has become the explanatory principle* from which, as a primary given fact, the phenomena may be deduced'.

Nagel effectively takes up this criterion of Köhler's and comments that unpredictability of this sort cannot be established '. . . as a matter of inherent logical necessity' (1952 [1963 edn, p. 140]). In other words, because at a particular point in time we cannot predict the effects of a complex system from its parts, this does not mean that the appropriate relations *cannot* be found. No number of failures to find the relations will 'prove' they do not exist.

Petermann's and Nagel's criticisms become anything but academic when we look at experimental attempts to test the Gestalt hypothesis. This has been done with reference to the prediction of judgements of colour combinations from judgements of single colours by Eysenck (1941), Granger (1955) and Hogg (1969). How do we test, in a limited way, the Gestalt position is this situation? If we find that responses *are* predictable then the Gestaltist can argue that we have not refuted his position because the combinations of colours are not true Gestalt – and Gestaltists do admit the existence of complex wholes that are not true Gestalt. If, however, we fail in our prediction, we have only demonstrated the inadequacy of the particular predictive technique we have used, and have not cast any doubt on the Gestalt position. Further, that colours as well as other visual stimuli interact is not in dispute, but interaction itself is not necessarily 'Gestalt-like' for it may be quite lawful.

Both in its physiological assumptions and in its logical structure, then, the Gestalt position is in question. What of Arnheim's (1956, 1967) applications of the theory to art? The first point to be made is that the links between Gestalt theory and Arnheim's analyses of various paintings and perceptual situations are nowhere near as intimate as those between psychoanalytic theory and Ehrenzweig's similar application. Ehrenzweig is dealing with a highly specific sequence of postulated psychological events resulting in various characteristic experiences when confronted with works of art. Arnheim is not always as explicit. He attempts to illuminate such experiences by working within an analytic framework that assumes certain types of experience to be inherent in the perceiver–perceived situation, though experience and training can modify the basic perception. This assumption derived from the Gestaltists varies in its obtrusiveness in different papers. On occasions more specific Gestalt concepts, such as that of isomorphism, are dealt with; in others, explicit Gestalt theory is below the surface. In Arnheim's (1949) paper on expression, the key concept of isomorphism is one which cannot be dealt with through observation but has the status of a hypothetical construct occurring throughout the explanatory sequence he proposes.

The crucial psychological extremes of this sequence are unobservable. To appeal for direct evidence in order to evaluate Arnheim's work would be to miss the point that he has set out to establish a way of looking at the psychological experience of art, rather than of producing a body of experimental detail or specific points. His writings have given rise to surprisingly little experimental work by others, partly due to the unfashionable nature of the psychological research on art, and partly due to the lack of testability of many of his views.

Earlier we noted that Ehrenzweig contrasted the unconscious structure of a work of art with the Gestalt 'surface' view. There is no obvious way of resolving this disagreement, though to anyone not wedded to either approach the necessity of coming out on one side rather than the other will appear doubtful.

Information Theory and the Visual Arts

The fact that human beings gain information from events they perceive made the suggestion that information was measurable highly attractive to psychologists. Nevertheless, the meaning of 'information', as developed in the theory of communication known as information theory, is such that the application of concepts and measurement from the theory to psychological problems has often been merely by analogy. Pierce (1962) has drily commented: 'I have read a good deal more about information theory and psychology than I can or care to remember. Much of it was a mere association of new terms with old and vague ideas. Presumably the hope was that a stirring in of new terms would clarify the old ideas by a sort of sympathetic magic' (p. 229). And more specifically Staniland (1966) comments:

Attneave began a recent book (1959a) with the remark, 'The idea that information is something measurable in precise terms was not widely appreciated until 1948. . . .' This is not an inaccurate statement, but it is of the kind that can encourage confusion as to the significance of measurement. The distinction between finding measures that can be applied to things and talking about 'measuring things' as though this were equivalent to giving a complete description is not a difficult one to make when the field is a familiar one. But it can easily be overlooked when the object of measurement is as evasive and non-material as information (p. 33).

However reasonable it seems then that paintings or sculptures convey some form of aesthetic information, the danger is often of identifying, in too facile a way, such information with information in the technical sense.

Attneave (1959b) has put forward the claim for the relevance of information measures to aesthetic experience:

Perhaps the most fundamental concept of information theory is that of a continuum extending from extreme lawfulness, or redundancy, or regularity on one hand, to extreme disorder, or unpredictability, or uncertainty on the other. One end of this continuum is homogeneity, the other chaos. It seems fairly evident, on the face of things, that those objects which are most pleasing to an observer lie somewhere between these two extremes. One does not stare for long at a blank canvas, because it is too simple, nor at the detail of a gravel road, because it is too complex.

There are many paths, qualitatively different from one another, leading from the homogeneous to the chaotic. Some of these almost certainly have greater aesthetic merit than others; still for any particular path aesthetic merit may be highly dependent upon complexity or uncertainty. Information measures of one sort or another may be used to quantify this variable. It should be admitted at once that in the cases which are most interesting we do not know exactly how to apply such measures (p. 503).

Firstly, we can recall our criticism of Berlyne's structuralist approach. There is no *a priori* reason to assume some balance of redundancy is relevant to the aesthetic reactions noted by Attneave. Indeed whether or not we do or do not 'stare for long at a blank canvas', several painters in the past few years *have* produced blank or monochrome pictures. The identification of a traditional aesthetic view with structure assessment based on information theory is highly subjective, and as for its effect on the experience of art the objection by Heyl may be noted again.

Secondly, the identification of structural aspects of form with information theory concepts regardless of aesthetic concomitants has been questioned. Green and Courtis take up the points made by Attneave (1954) in this connexion that '... the information contained in a figure is concentrated along its contours, particularly at those points where the contour changes direction most sharply' (Green and Courtis, 1966, p. 13). By breaking up the figure into a mosaic of coloured patches each element of which could be perceived separately in sequence, Attneave attempted to establish this. Green and Courtis claim that such a procedure, in which a person is compelled to scan the mosaic elements rather than see the whole figure, is not comparable to the process of perception: 'Information theory is concerned with transition probabilities while perception, whether of figures or patterns, is essentially non-sequential, or at least non-linear. A linear sequence may be imposed, but the data no longer have much bearing on problems of perception' (p. 30). They also demonstrate that the results collected by Attneave are essentially an artifact of the particular scanning sequence he imposed upon his respondents.

Since doubts have been cast on the applicability of information theory to figure perception, some comment should therefore be made on Dorfman and McKenna's (1966) paper in which an information measure is related to pattern preference. Here 'grain', the number of white and green cells or squares in a matrix, is the relevant dependent variable. The uncertainty of a particular pattern is calculated in terms of the number of possible patterns of a matrix with so many cells. Thus in a 2×2 matrix in which each cell can be either white or green, there are 16 possible patterns of this sort and the probability of one of these patterns occurring from the possible 16 is what is meant by uncertainty. Uncertainty in this sense is of necessity related to the grain of the matrix, and both are elsewhere arbitrarily identified with complexity. The informational aspect could therefore be left out of the study altogether and the various relations between fineness of matrix grain and preference would still stand. That it is the uncertainty of occurrence of the particular pattern which is affecting preference requires further demonstration. The informational concept does not appear strictly relevant to the finding which is of interest quite apart from it.

The mention of complexity brings us to one important consequence of the attempts to apply information theory to form perception, namely the stimulus it has given to the general attempt to develop objective assessment of the metrics of visual form. Can the complexity, symmetry, and so on, of shapes and designs be measured in order that their attributes be exactly specified for experimental purposes? This work is referred to in a paper by Silver, Landis and Messick (1966) which demonstrates that different individuals are attending to different aspects of, and organizing their experience of, various visual forms in a variety of ways. This finding naturally leads the authors back to the discussion of cognitive style and the conclusion that 'for all their sophistication in devising methods of measuring the informational content in a form, workers in the area of visual form perception seem to have overlooked the fact of individual differences in perception and judgement' (p. 70).

This comment returns us to Green and Courtis's point while dealing with information theory: '. . . it still makes sense to talk about the amount and location of information contained in a figure as an information source. In real life the amount and location of information is a function of the percipient. What has to be measured is not something in the source, but something about the *process* of perceiving' (Green and Courtis, 1966, p. 26).

Concluding Comments

It might seem that I dwell too much on the short-comings of the various approaches. A number of positive points, however, do emerge. It is clear from the papers by Green and Courtis (1966) and Dorfman and McKenna (1966) that in dealing with judgements of, and responses to art, the emphasis can most usefully be put on the processes engaged in by the perceiver, in terms of the characteristic ways in which he orientates himself towards visual material and organizes it as it is being perceived. The correlation between this characteristic process for any individual and his experience and preference for selected types of experimental materials can then usefully be considered. The relation of preference for particular 'objective' parameters of form and colour, which constitute much of so-called 'experimental aesthetics', misses this point since it fails to take into account individual differences in the processing and organization of the material presented for preference judgements.

Child's (1965) study introduces a range of individual difference variables into the study of visual preference and takes a step towards meeting the requirements of the approach just indicated. The use of multidimensional scaling techniques described by

Skager, Schultz and Klein (1966) and also applied to visual form by Silver, Landis and Messick (1966) are highly relevant as well. The latter authors write:

The finding that no one measure of the complexity or geometry of a visual form will serve to describe the dimensions used by individuals is not surprising. It is also not surprising to find that subjects will differ substantially as to the dimensions they use. It is, after all, what would have been predicted from the work on perceptual styles that has been accumulating over the past several years (Silver *et al.*, 1966, p. 70).

Further, not only are such techniques relevant but they should be used in conjunction with the cognitive control approach. Silver *et al.* (1966) conclude: 'Since distinct viewpoints [as shown by their study] did appear, it is important that future research attempts to identify these differences by including measures of perceptual and cognitive styles and, perhaps, of personality and preferences' (p. 71).

Should it be found possible to relate preference to the characteristic way in which a person processes his experience (even if only as a partial explanation), then the problem of 'good' and 'bad' aesthetic judgement in psychological studies will have been by-passed. There is simply no need to establish criteria for correctness of judgement.

However, it would be an over-simplification to anticipate that features of perceptual organization will be the whole answer. An understanding of motivation from at least two points of view will surely be involved. Firstly, the part played by physiological necessity, as proposed by Berlyne (1960 and 1965), must be considered. Secondly, the significance art has for an individual will clearly affect his response to it, and the nature and extent of his contact with it. Expressed differently, a person's *intention* in looking at pictures will play a major part in directing motivation. There can be no doubt that at given times an individual is not concerned with the optimization of pleasurable experience when he seeks out experience of art. The attempt to develop a unified view of a particular school of painting or grasp its philosophical implications are aspects of the response to art going beyond the urge for direct enjoyment.

Finally, the question of the meaning of art to individuals is going to be closely bound up with the type of judgement a person will and is able to make, though this is not to suggest that the meaning of a work of art can be cut off from its structure. The study of the connotations of art (Osgood, Suci and Tannenbaum, 1957) is a step towards one aspect of meaning. The '... consonance and the dissonance of multiple meanings that interlink in the structure of aesthetic experiences' (Gombrich, 1965) require explanation, and have especially attracted the attention of psychoanalytic theorists.

The relevance of what is found in psychological studies of art to theories of art has rightly been treated with caution by non-psychologists concerned with such problems. Of experimental psychological studies of art, Sparshott (1963, p. 45) has commented that they '... are seldom startling and their interpretation is often problematic; but few will wish to philosophize about art in ignorance of them.' It is a reasonable supposition that the extent to which findings become acceptable will be directly related to the degree to which they are integrated with general psychological theory, and ultimately will depend on the judged relevance of such a theory to human experience.

References

AIKEN, H. D. (1955), 'Some notes concerning the aesthetic and the cognitive', *J. Aesthet. art Crit.*, vol. 13, pp. 378–94.

ARNHEIM, R. (1943), 'Gestalt and art', *J. Aesthet. art Crit.*, vol. 2, pp. 71–5. [Reading 10.]

ARNHEIM, R. (1949), 'The Gestalt theory of expression', *Psychol. Rev.*, vol. 56, pp. 156–71. [Reproduced here as Reading 11.]

ARNHEIM, R. (1956), *Art and Visual Perception: A Psychology of the Creative Eye*, Faber and Faber.

ARNHEIM, R. (1967), *Towards a Psychology of Art: Collected Essays*, Faber and Faber.

ATTNEAVE, F. (1954), 'Some informational aspects of visual perception', *Psychol. Rev.*, vol. 61, pp. 262–70.

ATTNEAVE, F. (1959a), *Application of Information Theory to Psychology* Holt.

ATTNEAVE, F. (1959b), 'Stochastic composition processes', *J. Aesthet. art Crit.*, vol. 17, pp. 503–10.

BERLYNE, D. E. (1960), *Conflict, Arousal and Curiosity*, McGraw-Hill.

BERLYNE, D. E. (1965), 'Measures of aesthetic preference', Paper read at the *First International Colloquium on Experimental Aesthetics. Paris, 7 June.* [Reading 5.]

CHILD, I. L. (1962), Mimeographed report of *Cooperative Research Project No. 669, Office of Education, U.S. Department of Health, Education and Welfare*.

CHILD, I. L. (1965), 'Personality correlates of esthetic judgement in college students', *J. Pers.*, vol. 33, pp. 476–511. [Reading 7.]

CHILD, I. L. (1966), 'The problem of objectivity in esthetic value', *Penn. State Pap. in Art Educ.*, no. 1.

DORFMAN, D. D., and MCKENNA, H. (1966), 'Pattern preference as a function of pattern uncertainty', *Canad. J. Psychol.*, vol. 20, pp. 143–53. [Reading 12.]

EHRENZWEIG, A. (1962), 'A new psychoanalytical approach to aesthetics', *Brit. J. Aesthet.*, vol. 2, pp. 301–17. [Reading 4.]

EHRENZWEIG, A. (1967), *The Hidden Order in Art: A Study in the Psychology of Artistic Imagination*, Weidenfeld and Nicolson.

EYSENCK, H. J. (1941), 'A critical and experimental study of color preference', *Amer. J. Psychol.*, vol. 54, pp. 385–94.

EYSENCK H. J. (1961), 'The effects of psychotherapy', in H. J. Eysenck (ed.), *Handbook of Abnormal Psychology*, Basic Books, pp. 697–725.

FARRELL, B. (1963), Introduction to S. Freud, *Leonardo* (trans. by A. Tyson), Penguin Books.

FORGUS, R. H. (1966), *Perception: The Basic Process in Cognitive Development*, McGraw-Hill.

GARDNER, R., HOLZMAN, P. S., KLEIN, G. S., LINTON, H., and SPENCE, D. P. (1959), 'Cognitive control: A study of individual consistencies in cognitive behavior', *Psychol. Issues*, vol. 1, no. 4.

GARDNER, R. W., JACKSON, D. N., and MESSICK, S. J. (1960), 'Personality organisation in cognitive controls and intellectual abilities', *Psychol. Issues*, vol. 2, no. 8.

GOMBRICH, E. H. (1965), 'The use of art for the study of symbols', *Amer. Psychologist*, vol. 20, pp. 34–50. [Reading 6.]

GRANGER, G. W. (1955), 'The prediction of preference for color combinations', *J. gen. Psychol.*, vol. 52, pp. 213–22.

GREEN, R. T., and COURTIS, M. C. (1966), 'Information theory and figure perception: the metaphor that failed', *Act. Psychol.*, vol. 25, pp. 12–36. [Reading 9.]

GREGORY, R. L. (1966), *Eye and Brain*, World University Library.

HEYL, B. C. (1943), *New Bearings in Esthetics and Art Criticism: A Study in Semantics and Evaluation*, Yale University Press.

HOATS, D. L., MILLER, M. B., and SPITZ, H. H. (1963), 'Experiments on perceptual curiosity in mental retardates and normals', *Amer. J. ment. Defic.*, vol. 68, pp. 386–95.

HOGG, J. (1969), 'The prediction of semantic differential ratings of color', *J. gen. Psychol.*, vol. 80, pp. 141–52.

KOFFKA, K. (1915), 'Zur Grundlegung der Wahrnehmungspsychologie', *Zeitsch. fur Psychol.*, vol. 73.

KÖHLER, W. (1924), 'Gestaltprobleme und die Anfänge einer Gestalttheorie', *Rona-Sprio. Jahr.-Ber. ges. Physiol.*, vol. 3.

MUNRO, T. (1963), 'The psychology of art: Past, present, future', *J. Aesthet. art Crit.*, vol. 21, pp. 264–82. [Reading 1.]

NAGEL, E. (1952), 'Wholes, sums and organic unities', *Philosophical Studies III*, vol. 2. Reprinted in D. Lerner (ed.), *Parts and Wholes: The Hayden Colloquium on Scientific Method and Concept*, Free Press and Macmillan, 1963.

NAGEL, E. (1959), 'Methodological issues in psychoanalytic theory', in S. Hook (ed.), *Psychoanalysis: Scientific Method and Philosophy. A symposium*, Grove Press, pp. 38–56.

OSGOOD, C. E., SUCI, G. J., and TANNENBAUM, P. H. (1957), *The Measurement of Meaning*, University of Illinois Press.

PETERMANN, B. (1932), *The Gestalt Theory and the Problem of Configuration*, Kegan Paul.

PIERCE, J. R. (1962), *Symbols, Signals and Noise*, Hutchinson.

PIKE, A. (1967), 'The theory of unconscious perception in music: A phenomenological approach', *J. Aesthet. art Crit.*, vol. 25, pp. 395–400.

SILVER, C. A., LANDIS, D., and MESSICK, S. (1966), 'Multidimensional analysis of visual form: an analysis of individual differences', *Amer. J. Psychol.*, vol. 74, pp. 62–72.

SKAGER, R. W., SCHULTZ, C. B., and KLEIN, S. P. (1966). 'The multidimensional scaling of a set of artistic drawings: perceived structure and scale correlates', *Multivar. behav. Res.*, vol. 1, pp. 425–36. [Reading 18.]

SPARSHOTT, F. E. (1963), *The Structure of Aesthetics*, Routledge and Kegan Paul.

STANILAND, A. C. (1966), *Patterns of Redundancy: A Psychological Study*, Cambridge University Press.

VON SENDEN, M. (1960), *Space and Sight*, Methuen.

WAELDER, R. (1965), *Psychoanalytic Avenues to Art, Psychoanalytical Epitomes*, no. 6, Hogarth Press and the Institute of Psychoanalysis, pp. 16-60. [Reading 3.]

WERTHEIMER, M. (1951), 'Hebb and Senden on the role of learning in perception', *Amer. J. Psychol.*, vol. 64, pp. 133–7.

YOUNG, J. Z. (1964), *A Model of the Brain*, Oxford University Press.

Part Two Motivation and Resolution

There is no reason to assume that the motivation to look at visual art is unified. In part it may be socially motivated, in part a search for novelty, and so on. All components of this motivation, and its subsequent resolution, are of psychological interest. In dealing with art, however, psychologists have tended to look for some hypothesized reaction at the core of the experience of art involving 'the experience of beauty' or 'the aesthetic response'. The three papers in this part are directed towards the problem of the nature of such responses. They present interesting contrasts: Waelder's (Reading 3) discussion of the Freudian position emphasizes the content of art, while Ehrenzweig (Reading 4) rejects this in favour of unconsciously perceived structure; the latter paper rests heavily on introspection in contrast to Berlyne's insistence on observable behaviour (Reading 5).

3 R. Waelder

Psychoanalytic Avenues to Art

Abridged from R. Waelder, *Psychoanalytic Avenues to Art*, *Psychoanalytical Epitomes*, no. 6 (1965), Hogarth Press and the Institute of Psychoanalysis, pp. 16–60. (Copyright The New York Psychoanalytic Institute.)

1. Basic Considerations

The beauty of configurations

Perhaps the simplest form of beauty, a kind of subcerebral stratum in the realm of beauty, is that of certain configurations or Gestalten – pleasing arrangements of colors and shapes, or of sounds or of their sequences in time. Such configurations can probably be studied from more than one point of view. One possible approach is to see them as *patterns of tension and discharge* – either distributed in space as configurations of line, volume, light and shade, or color, or distributed in time, as in a sequence of tones and harmonies. *If* we approach them in this way, psychoanalytic categories become applicable.

Psychoanalysis has tried to see pleasure as a function of tensions, and thus to see a psychic sensation as a function of physiological processes; and while there is as yet no satisfactory psychoanalytic theory along these lines, there are some important experiences and preliminary considerations. In Kantian language, we may speak of *Prolegomena* to a future psychophysiological theory of pleasure, of which a brief review will be attempted in what follows.

Pleasure as function of tension and discharge

In his attempt to see the subjective sensation of pleasure as a function of the 'objective' fact of tension which, at least in principle, is subject to intersubjective verification, Freud thought at first that 'a feeling of tension necessarily involves unpleasure' (1905a, p. 209). He apparently looked at the monumental examples

91

of the great appetites, hunger, thirst, and the desire for copulation, all pressing toward satiation.

But, on the other hand, there was also the patent fact that, except for a very high level of tension, pleasure is felt not only in the final satisfaction which reduces the tensions to zero but also, to a degree, in the state of tension and in the mounting of tension.

Freud tried to give account of this situation by distinguishing between forepleasure and end pleasure, the former accompanying the 'appropriate' stimulation of an erotogenic zone and moderate in degree, the latter 'brought about entirely by discharge' and 'highest in intensity' (1905a, p. 210).

These considerations did not answer the question whether or not, or how, forepleasure could be made a special case of a general theory which describes pleasure of all kinds as a function of tension. At a later time, and with a view toward developing such a general theory, Freud suggested that the *rate of change* may be the decisive factor:

We have decided to relate pleasure and unpleasure to the quantity of excitation that is present in the mind but is not in any way 'bound'; and to relate them in such a manner that unpleasure corresponds to an *increase* in the quantity of excitation and pleasure to a *diminution*. What we are implying by this is not a simple relation between the strength of the feelings of pleasure and unpleasure and the corresponding modifications in the quantity of excitation; least of all – in view of all we have been taught by psychophysiology – are we suggesting a direct proportional ratio: the factor that determines the feeling is probably the amount of increase or diminution in the quantity of excitation *in a given period of time* (1920, pp. 7 ff).

The same idea was repeated in the form of a question (1920, p. 63):

... is the feeling of tension to be related to the absolute magnitude, or perhaps to the level, of the cathexis, while the pleasure and the un-pleasure series indicates a change in the magnitude of the cathexis *within a given unit of time*?

These ideas reflect the influence of Fechner's logarithmic law of sensation. But Freud did not follow this course any further and finally decided that while it was correct to look for the conditions of pleasure and unpleasure in the time curve of tension, the *exact nature of this function was still unknown:*

Pleasure and unpleasure ... cannot be referred to an increase or decrease of a quantity (which we describe as 'tension due to stimulus'), although they obviously have a great deal to do with this factor. It appears that they depend, not on this quantitative factor, but on some characteristic of it which we can only describe as a qualitative one. If we were able to say what this qualitative characteristic is, we should be much further advanced in psychology. Perhaps it is the rhythm, the temporal sequence of changes, rises and falls in the quantity of stimulus. We do not know (1924, p. 160).

Thus, it appears likely that the sensation of pleasure and unpleasure is a function of tension and its changes in time, but we cannot give the exact formula of this function in general terms. We can, however, relate pleasure and unpleasure to tension and its changes in individual instances. Moreover, whatever the exact form of the curve may be, we have reason to believe that its flexibility is limited, i.e. that minute differences in the tension curve can make the difference between pleasure and unpleasure, even intense pleasure. There may be too little as well as too much stimulation. A French proverb says that there is only one step from the sublime to the ridiculous; one could equally say that there is only one step from pleasure to unpleasure through overexcitation or underexcitation.

This seems to apply not only to sexual pursuits on various levels but also to the 'subacute' sensuality of beauty. The fifth-century Greek sculptor Polyclitus is credited with the remark that the quality of a work of art depends on many numerical relationships, with minimal amounts being decisive.

The development of taste

Whatever the relationship of pleasure to tension may be, it is clear that it does not remain forever the same but changes with experience. In the very earliest infancy, pleasure seems to lie in the relief from tension alone. Thereafter, to an ever-increasing extent, stimulations are not avoided but sought out; this is one of the facts that have led Freud to the formulation of a theory which sees life as a struggle between an expansive, tension-seeking life instinct and a restrictive, tension-reducing death instinct.

Whatever the pros and cons of the latter theory, it is unmistakable that, in the realm of the sexual instincts, longer and longer detours on the way to final satisfaction become pleasurable in the course of experience. In sexual life in the narrowest sense of the word, the more experienced adult tends both to prolong and to variegate forepleasure; in this largely consists the *ars amatoria*, the art of loving. The gastronome uses appetizers to whet his appetite; he avoids eating too much of one dish to keep his appetite alive for other courses, and avoids 'filling' dishes altogether. While some nuclear desires remain essentially the same (though admitting of, and perhaps requiring, variety and refinement), others become stale through repetition and attract no more. The *speed of obsolescence*, i.e. the intensity of the need for new stimulation, *varies* enormously with individual and cultural conditions.

2. An Id Approach: A Preserve for the Pleasure Principle

Freud saw in art, above all, an opportunity for the fulfilment, in fantasy, of wishes which in real life are frustrated either by external obstacles or by moral inhibitions. Art, then, is a kind of wild-life preserve in the development from the pleasure principle to the reality principle and serves as a safety valve in civilization. Freud expressed himself on this subject several times, in similar terms, and it seems indicated to quote his statements extensively in view of the fact that they have often been misinterpreted:

Art brings about a reconciliation between the two principles (viz. the pleasure principle and the reality principle) in a peculiar way. An artist is originally a man who turns away from reality because he cannot come to terms with the renunciation of instinctual satisfaction which it at first demands, and who allows his erotic and ambitious wishes full play in the life of phantasy. He finds the way back to reality, however, from this world of phantasy by making use of special gifts to mould his phantasies into truths of a new kind, which are valued by men as precious reflections of reality. Thus in a certain fashion he actually becomes the hero, the king, the creator, or the favourite he desired to be, without following the long roundabout path of making real alterations in the external world. But he can only achieve this because other men feel the same dissatisfaction as he does with the renunciation demanded by reality, and because that dissatisfaction, which results from the replacement of the pleasure principle by the reality principle, is itself part of reality (1911, p. 224).

And shortly thereafter:

In only a single field of our civilization has the omnipotence of thoughts been retained, and that is in the field of art. Only in art does it still happen that a man who is consumed by desires performs something resembling the accomplishment of those desires and that what he does in play produces emotional effects – thanks to artistic illusion – just as though it were something real (1913a, p. 90).

And again:

... art ... an activity intended to allay ungratified wishes in the first place in the creative artist himself and subsequently in his audience or spectators ... The artist's first aim is to set himself free and, by communicating his work to other people suffering from the same arrested desires, he offers them the same liberation. He represents his most personal wishful phantasies as fulfilled; but they only become a work of art when they have undergone a transformation which *softens what is offensive in them, conceals their personal origin and, by obeying the laws of beauty, bribes other people with a bonus of pleasure*. Psychoanalysis has no difficulty in pointing out, alongside the *manifest part* of artistic enjoyment, another that is *latent though far more potent*, derived from hidden sources of instinctual liberation.

... Art is a conventionally accepted reality in which, thanks to artistic illusion, symbols and substitutes are able to provoke real emotions. Thus art constitutes a region half-way between a reality which frustrates wishes and the wish-fulfilling world of the imagination, a region in which, as it were, primitive man's strivings for omnipotence are still in full force (1913b, pp. 187 ff.; italics added).

A decade later he returned to the same motifs:

The realm of imagination was seen to be a 'reservation' made during the painful transition from the pleasure principle to the reality principle in order to provide a substitute for instinctual satisfactions which had to be given up in real life. The artist, like the neurotic, had *withdrawn from an unsatisfactory reality into this world of imagination;* but, unlike the neurotic, *he knew how to find a way back from it* and once more to get a firm foothold in reality. His creations, works of art, were the imaginary satisfactions of unconscious wishes, just as dreams are; and like them they were in the nature of compromises, since they too were forced to avoid any open conflict with the forces of repression. But they differed from the asocial, narcissistic products of dreaming in that they were calculated to arouse sympathetic interest in other people and were able to evoke and to satisfy the same unconscious wishful impulses in them too. Besides this, they made use of the perceptual pleasure of formal beauty as what I have called an 'incentive bonus' (1925, pp. 64 ff.; italics added).

Clearly, these lines were written with the arts of the word – poetry, the drama, the novel – foremost in mind, but they apply also to the nonverbal arts in so far as the *literary content* or the literary associations of a work are concerned, or the memories which it activates.

The theory suggests that, under certain conditions, products of the imagination can 'represent most personal wishes as fulfilled'. Three cases must be distinguished: the respective wishes may have been ousted from consciousness (repressed) as dangerous, or *condemned* as sinful while yet conscious, or merely *frustrated* by external obstacles. Freud's conditions were formulated with the first two cases foremost in mind; they are:

(a) that the goal of the drive be disguised and in some degree modified;

(b) that the product has the merits of 'formal beauty'; and

(c) that the expression of the fantasy is not a purely selfish matter, but that it is communicated to others with a view to its being enjoyed by them, too, and so becomes a social act.

There are also cases in which wishes are not forbidden but merely obstructed. In those cases, the work of art has to create the 'artistic illusion'; and though the wishes are not subject to repression or moral condemnation, they often appear to the adult mind as childish dreams and as escapism of which a mature person has to be ashamed. This kind of censure must also be appeased by the merits of 'formal beauty', by the fact that they are enjoyed in common, and sometimes also by modifications and disguises of the actual goal, although these will be less extensive than in the cases of desires reprehensible or repressed.

These cases may now be considered more closely.

(*a*) *Repressed and condemned wishes.* The first condition – modification and disguise of the goal – is reminiscent of the disguises under which a piece of subversive political writing can pass or outwit censorship, and of the distortions in dreams and in screen memories. The modification which makes the expression of a drive more acceptable has the form of desexualization, which shades over imperceptibly into the second condition, that of beauty as an 'incentive bonus'.

It should be clear from the quoted texts that Freud neither denied nor overlooked the existence of what he called formal beauty, as some of his critics have alleged; nor did he question that it is a source of pleasure (he called it '. . . the manifest part of artistic enjoyment'); nor, finally, did he suggest that this kind of pleasure was itself reducible to instinctual gratification. What he did claim was rather that the 'latent' instinctual gratification was 'far more potent' than the 'manifest part of artistic enjoyment'.

The 'formal beauty' of, say, a female nude makes it possible to consummate, without guilt or shame, the sexual pleasure of the view.

That the quality of beauty does indeed carry the forbidden gratification along somewhat like corrupt politicians ride into office 'on the coat-tails' of a popular national candidate with spotless reputation is shown by the many legal proceedings in which the court has to decide whether a particular publication is or is not pornographic. The experts on one side claim that the respective piece is a work of art and that sexual stimulation, if any, is accidental. The experts on the other side claim that the work in question has little or no artistic merit and is merely prurient.

The degree of desexualization necessary for passage varies according to time, place and circumstances. Where there is none, the product will be classified as a stimulant pure and simple rather than as art. On the other hand, desexualization is *hardly ever complete*, and even in extreme cases there is some remnant of direct gratification. A remark by Sir Kenneth Clark (1956) regarding the nude seems pertinent in this context:

'If the nude,' says Professor Alexander, 'is so treated that it raises in the spectator ideas or desires appropriate to the material subject, it is false art, and bad morals.' This highminded theory is contrary to experience. In the mixture of memories and sensations aroused by the nudes of Rubens or Renoir are many which are 'appropriate to the material subject'. And since these words by a famous philosopher are often quoted, it is necessary to labour the obvious and say that no nude, however abstract, should fail to arouse in the spectator some vestige of erotic feeling, even although it be only the faintest shadow – and if it does not do so, it is bad art and false morals.

The objection to the Freudian theory on the ground that it deals with what is esthetically irrelevant is sometimes presented in this form: that psychoanalytic interpretations of a work of art, by dealing only with the content and not with the quality of execution, are equally applicable to great art and to trash and so do not come to grips with the problem of 'art', i.e. of artifacts of quality. This criticism has been advanced very frequently; the following passage from the 1960 Reith Lectures of Professor Edgar Wind may be quoted as a particularly well-considered expression of it:

Although it is now generally understood that the methods of depth psychology were designed to uncover pre-conceptual types of emotional life, it is not always realized that these types are also pre-artistic. It is no reproach to the psychoanalytic method that, when applied to artistic creation, it tends to wipe out the difference between great art and mawkish art: reduced to the diffuse level of the subliminal, refinements of perception are likely to vanish. On the other hand, if it were clearly stated that it is precisely the infra-artistic kind of impulse that is to be anatomized in psychoanalytic studies, their genuine contribution to artistic psychology might be better defined than it is at present (p. 178).

The statement is correct, at least as far as the id approach to works of art is concerned, which is indeed the one most often found in the literature,[1] except for two facts not considered by Professor Wind: for one, quality – 'formal beauty,' in Freud's language – is indeed part of his theory as a source of pleasure in itself and as the condition under which the 'infra-artistic impulse' can be unleashed; then, if Professor Wind requests that it be 'clearly stated that it is precisely an infra-artistic kind of impulse that is to be anatomized in psychoanalytic studies' in order that 'their genuine contribution to artistic psychology might be better defined', attention must be called to the fact that Freud has done just this. He stated in a paper on Dostoevsky:

Four facets may be distinguished in the rich personality of Dostoevsky: the creative artist, the neurotic, the moralist and the sinner.... The

1. The writings of Ernst Kris (1952) are a conspicuous exception.

creative artist is the least doubtful: Dostoevsky's place is not far behind Shakespeare.... *Before the problem of the creative artist analysis must, alas, lay down its arms* (Freud 1927b, p. 177; italics added).

In his introduction to Marie Bonaparte's study of Edgar Allen Poe, Freud wrote:

Investigations of this kind are *not intended to explain an author's genius,* but they show what motive forces aroused it and what material was offered to him by destiny (1933, p. 254; italics added).

This should clarify the point. But psychoanalysis has actually not remained restricted to the study of the 'material offered by destiny'; as I have already suggested, it can contribute to the understanding of formal beauty and of quality itself by the possibility of a psychoanalytic approach to the beauty of configurations. This will have to be considered again later in another frame of reference.

In the theory under discussion Freud was, of course, speaking of the reaction of the great majority of people; his statement does not exclude that there may be a few – the connoisseurs – for whom this 'manifest' artistic pleasure in 'formal beauty' is more important than the 'latent' content or even, in some cases, the only important thing. In such cases, a *displacement* from content to form has taken place – a process about which more will have to be said later.

(*b*) *Wishes frustrated by external objects.* There is nothing forbidden in the dream of the little office girl that a handsome young boss may fall in love with her and propose marriage to her. True, the wish is a derivative of the forbidden Oedipus fantasy of childhood, and in some cases this origin may sufficiently color it so that the prohibition which adhered to the Oedipus wish may become attached to the derivative as well. But for itself alone, it is an acceptable derivative. However, the fantasy is so rarely realized that it seems childish to entertain it seriously, and an adult has to be ashamed of it; although she may indulge in it in a movie house, in the community wish with hundreds of other spectators, fellows in regression, and with the excuse of the visual qualities or the quality of the performance of the actors which the film may offer. A residue of embarrassment may remain, and conversation upon leaving the movie house may somewhat pointedly be centered around the merits of the acting or the photography, as though to indicate that one was not naïvely engrossed in the story but had enjoyed it only for its formal merits.

Question of esthetic relevance and the aura of a work of art

It may well be held that the pleasure which Freud described, while perhaps decisive for the financial success of a movie, has nothing to do with its esthetic qualities proper and is therefore irrelevant for an esthetic theory. This is, of course, a matter of semantics; if esthetics is defined as that branch of philosophy that deals with the nature of beauty, the enjoyment of literary content is left outside. In that case, Freud's theory would have to be formulated somewhat in the following way: that there is a conscious and an unconscious reaction to art, the former due to its esthetic qualities, the latter to its more or less hidden literary content, and that esthetic merits make it possible for otherwise inadmissible content to pass.

But the reaction to works of art is not merely a matter of esthetics in the narrow sense; a number of other factors enter into the cluster of sensations. Association and fantasies have much to do with it. Medieval art will appeal more strongly in its original environment – as in the churches for which it was made – than in a museum; it will also appeal more strongly in a museum housed in a medieval environment, such as the Musée de Cluny, than in a modern reconstruction of a medieval building set in a modern metropolis, such as the New York Cloisters; and it will appeal more strongly in the latter than in an altogether modern museum building. This we speak of as 'atmosphere'.

There is also a great difference in our responses to the original and to the most faultless replica, not exempting cases in which not even the trained eye can detect the difference without the benefit of laboratory examination. An original piece of Shaker furniture will appeal much more to us than the technically most perfect modern copy; only the former carries the associations of a simple culture in which man and cosmos were still at one, while the latter carries the rather unpleasant and disillusioning associations of an affluent society for which the form of life of men of the past has become a form of luxury and a source of special excitement. The Marxist poet and critic, Walter Benjamin, spoke of the 'aura' of a work of art. In all these instances, we are dealing with associations which are an important part of our response to a work of art even though they may not be called 'esthetic' in a narrow sense.

The development of taste

Pleasing fantasy activities undergo the same development of growing complexity and sophistication that we encountered in discussing the changing taste in configurations. Just as melodies, rhythms or color schemes may become uninteresting or appear childish, so may the literary motifs of yesterday appear naïve today. A simple 'story', dramatically told, about a child who walked down the road and fell into a ditch may be fully satisfying to a child of two or three; he may request to be told it time and again without the slightest alteration, and each time greet the well-known outcome with delight. The same story is not acceptable on a higher level of sophistication. The simple mishap will have to be replaced by misfortunes which have significance for a later age; the road toward it can no longer be unexplained or direct. Motives will have to be invented and detours will have to be added. Perhaps the hero (or victim) will repeatedly circumvent his obstacle, only to meet new ones thereafter. Tension will be built up and only partially released, to be built up again until eventually a happy ending will put an end to all ordeals. And even this may come to appear trite and the story may end inconclusively, with a question mark, or with the indication of a continuing Odyssey.

The reversal of taste which is typical of the development in the oral sphere has its analogy in the literary, the visual and the auditory spheres. Sweetness becomes repellent not only in chocolates but also in landscapes, portraits or melodies. And the development of taste away from the primitive and, in some cases, its actual reversal may become, in literature, music or the visual arts, the hallmark of an élite, just as the development of taste from the sweet to the tart is a sign of adulthood and aspired to for that very reason.

3. An Ego Approach: The Economy of Solutions

Freud's second approach to esthetics

While the id approach to esthetic phenomena is widely known (though often misunderstood and misapplied), the existence of an ego approach is far less known partly, probably, because it came into being before a distinct ego psychology was developed and partly because it appeared in the context not of art but of a psychology of jokes and of the comic in general.[2] According to this theory, the pleasure which we experience in jokes is due to a sudden, unexpected, break-through of sexual or aggressive impulses out of their ordinary confinement, a sudden liberation from the pressures of self-control and a release of inhibitions, i.e. in Freud's words: 'to the momentary suspension of the expenditure of energy upon maintaining repression, owing to the attraction exercised by the offer of a bonus of pleasure' (1925, p. 66).

While part of the pleasure still lies in the satisfaction of desires ordinarily banned from expression – sexual impulses, particularly of the anal and phallic stages, or aggressive impulses – it lies also in the surprise and in the form in which this release has unexpectedly occurred, the way in which the censor has been cheated of his prey. Freud concludes:

All three [forms of comic phenomena] are agreed in representing methods of *regaining from mental activity a pleasure* which has in fact been lost through the development of that activity. For the euphoria which we endeavour to reach by these means is nothing other than the mood of a period of life in which we were accustomed to deal with our psychical work in general with a small expenditure of energy – the mood of our childhood, when we were ignorant of the comic, when we were incapable of jokes and when we had no need of humour to make us feel happy in our life (1905b, p. 236; italics added).

The idea of economy may stand us in good stead when we search for the ego aspect of beauty.

2. Ernst Kris has called attention to the fact that here we have a genuine esthetic theory.

The ego aspect of beauty

The 'ego', in the later psychoanalytic model, is a problem-solving agent. *Quality* of performance lies, first, in the fact that a solution has been found when the task had seemed unsolvable, or would have been unsolvable by ordinary human effort; second, in the perfection of a solution; and finally in its elegance, the economy of means. These are the characteristics that make the beauty of a solution and I suggest that they constitute the ego aspect of beauty.

These characteristics can be seen not only in the arts but in our daily activities. We consider it a 'beautiful' solution of a problem if everything has been achieved that we had set out to achieve and, in particular, if this has been done with a minimum of effort.

The Freudian theory, discussed earlier, of the 'incentive bonus' of 'formal beauty' can be brought to bear on this situation (e.g. the bullfight). There is the secret sadistic excitement and gratification, hidden from oneself or at least from others; there is also the 'formal beauty' which makes its expression possible. The beauty seems to lie in the economy of means – a formal quality which, in this case, can itself be seen as satisfying a fantasy, namely, that of the victory of mind over brute force.

Against this interpretation of the ego aspect of beauty – perfection and economy of means – it may be held that the opposite of Spartan economy, namely, exuberance and delight in ornament, has often been the cause of esthetic pleasure, as, for instance, in flamboyant Gothic and in Baroque. Our hypothesis seems to be based on the appreciation of understatement; but there have been times and cultures that delighted at overstatement.

This is a serious objection, but perhaps not an unanswerable one. The appeal of forms like those of flamboyant Gothic or of Baroque seems to lie partly in the appeal of a *configuration*, a pattern of tension and discharge, and such patterns, as we have seen, can appeal on any level of complexity. Partly this is due to the *content* of a fantasy. The exuberance of Baroque, for instance, conveys a feeling of power and earthly grandeur as is appropriate to the age of the triumphant Counter Reformation and monarchic absolutism. But it does not lie in the perfection and elegance of solutions, i.e. is not 'ego' beauty proper. It may, of course, have the latter quality too, *if* the impression is made with fewer lines than would have seemed necessary.

This aspect of beauty is the more appreciated, the more eye and judgement are trained. For a minority – the connoisseurs – it may become the major, and occasionally the only, source of enjoyment. We then have a shift, partial or total, from id pleasure to ego pleasure.[3]

The development of taste

We noticed in the case of the id aspect of beauty, the satisfaction of fantasy, that there is a process of growing sophistication, from the simple satisfaction of a wish to ever-longer detours. The plain wish fulfilment becomes stale, and more and more obstacles have to be introduced, and tensions build up until they are granted relief – if they are granted it at all. In a similar way, the beauty of scientific theories becomes stale, the satisfaction too complete. Experience shows that nature is not all that simple. The theory of the Pythagoreans, who believed the Universe to be comprehensible in terms of integers, or of the Newtonians, who believed all nature – and perhaps society as well – to be comprehensible in terms of laws of attraction similar to Newton's law of gravitation, seem quite naïve to us. New theories emerge which take account of new facts and new complications; they are also beautiful by reducing the ever-richer canvas of nature to order. But their simplicity is the simplicity of higher order, as it were; their beauty lies in unity in complexity, i.e. in a kind of rhythm between richness and order, complexity and simplicity.

In the case of science, this development is due to growing experience which makes previous theories obsolete, rather than to any boredom and the need for new stimulation – though the latter has a share in letting people look for new facts beyond the known horizons. But in the field of art the same process is entirely

3. In what we call sublimation, we can perhaps distinguish between two types: (a) the displacement of a drive from one subject to another more acceptable one, and (b) the genuine substitution of ego (or superego) pleasure for instinctual pleasure. The latter case is more than a mere displacement of energies; the whole process is raised to another level. We must look upon it as a stimulation of ego activities by instinctual drives, a process the possibility of which seems to depend on native ability. Any displacement of energies in these cases is contingent upon the possibility of this stimulation.

a matter of surfeit, boredom and the need for new stimulation – of the development of taste. The organization of space in a picture may thus develop from the simple to the dynamic as, for instance, from Giovanni Bellini to Poussin and Rubens. And if at a later stage there is an apparent return to simpler patterns, as there often has been, this return is, except for cases in which a tradition was actually lost or wilfully discarded, not a straight resumption of an earlier position; rather, it is conscious archaizing. The geometric simplicity of a Mondrian painting is not the same as that of a Navaho design; its effect is dependent upon the fact that the beholder is familiar with Western art from the fifteenth to the twentieth centuries (see Gombrich, 1960).

4. A Superego Approach: The Transcendence of Nature

The theory of humor

If we can speak of an id aspect and an ego aspect in the impact of art, we may wonder whether there is not a superego aspect, too.

A form of esthetic pleasure that stems from superego operations was indeed outlined by Freud in his paper on humor (1927a). It deals with humor not in the wide sense of the word, which encompasses all comic phenomena including the joke or the cartoon, but only in the narrow sense, in which it refers to the high form of fun which is at once merry and wise and which elicits a mild smile rather than explosive laughter.

Like jokes and the comic, humor has something liberating about it; but it also has something of grandeur and elevation, which is lacking in the other two ways of obtaining pleasure from intellectual activity (Freud, 1927a, p. 162).

Freud places humor, taken in this sense, among the great series of methods which the human mind has constructed in order to evade the compulsion to suffer – a series which begins with neurosis and culminates in madness and which includes intoxication, self-absorption and ecstasy (p. 163).

I should like to illustrate this method with an example which is similar to the one used by Freud in the quoted paper. Like the latter, it is a remark made by a doomed man in one of the last moments of his life. A French aristocrat, at the time of the Terror in the French Revolution, was walking up the steps to the guillotine; he made a wrong step and almost fell. Turning to the spectators, he said with a smile: 'A superstitious Roman would now have turned back.' In the age of classicism, every educated person knew of the Roman trait to which he alluded.

The remark pretended that the speaker was still free to turn back if he so wished, but that he refused to do so because he was not given to superstition and would not take the little mishap as a portent of evil things to come. Had he actually believed that this was the case, he would have been psychotic; but he only pretended to believe it, playfully, and so assumed a higher position above the fate that was about to end irrevocably his physical existence, and refused to succumb mentally to a destiny which he was powerless to avert.

Freud saw the essence of the humorous effect in the fact that the person who 'adopts a humorous attitude towards others . . . (behaves) towards them as an adult does towards a child when he recognizes and smiles at the triviality of interests and sufferings which seem so great to it' (p. 163), and he saw in the assumption of this attitude toward oneself – as shown by the condemned aristocrat in our anecdote – the original form of the humorous attitude. This attitude thus 'consists in the humorist's having *withdrawn the psychical accent from his ego and having transposed it on to his superego*' (p. 164; italics added).

The ability to step back and take a look at oneself from an imaginary observation point – the self-consciousness or the transcendence of oneself, as it has been called in psychoanalysis – is the essence of the superego function. No sense of humor can develop in organisms in which this transcendence of 'platform' is absent, as seems to be the case with animals; or where the cathexis of objects or ideas is so intense that it is not possible to emancipate oneself even temporarily from them in order to assume a detached position toward them as is the case, for instance, with the aggrieved, the fanatic and the paranoid. One does not jest or trifle with holy things.

Humor is thus one of the cases in which man rises above the situation and *preserves his narcissism intact in the midst of disaster*. In Freud's words:

The grandeur of it clearly lies in the triumph of narcissism, the victorious assertion of the ego's invulnerability. The ego refuses to be distressed by the provocations of reality, to let itself be compelled to suffer. It insists that it cannot be affected by the traumas of the external world; it shows, in fact, that such traumas are no more than occasions for it to gain pleasure (p. 162).

There is pleasure in the transcendence of reality, in the triumph over destiny, in the ability to keep one's narcissism intact while the ego perishes. Akin to humor is mellowness, the attitude that W. H. Auden ascribed to Shakespeare's Prospero:

> the powrer to enchant
> That comes from disillusion.

These attitudes have been expressed most often in the arts of the word, from which the examples of this section have been drawn. They are also capable of expression in pictorial art. In the latter case, we are dealing with literary content of a work of art, as in the dreams and illusions discussed in an earlier section.

References

CLARK, K. (1956), *The Nude: A Study of Ideal Art*, Pantheon. (Penguin Edition, 1960.)

FREUD, S. (1905a), 'Three essays on the theory of sexuality', *Standard Edition*, Hogarth Press, 1953, vol. 7, pp. 125–43.

FREUD, S. (1905b), 'Jokes and their relation to the unconscious', *Standard Edition*, Hogarth Press, 1960, vol. 8.

FREUD, S. (1911), 'Formulations on the two principles of mental functioning', *Standard Edition*, Hogarth Press, 1958, vol. 12, pp. 213–26.

FREUD, S. (1913a), 'Totem and taboo', *Standard Edition*, Hogarth Press, 1955, vol. 13, pp. 1–161.

FREUD, S. (1913b), 'The claims of psychoanalysis to scientific interest', *Standard Edition*, Hogarth Press, 1955, vol. 13, pp. 165–90.

FREUD, S. (1920), 'Beyond the pleasure principle', *Standard Edition*, Hogarth Press, 1955, vol. 18, pp. 3–64.

FREUD, S. (1924), 'The economic problem of masochism', *Standard Edition*, Hogarth Press, 1955, vol. 19, pp. 157–70.

FREUD, S. (1925), 'An autobiographical study', *Standard Edition*, Hogarth Press, 1959, vol. 20, pp. 3–74.

FREUD, S. (1927a), 'Humour', *Standard Edition*, Hogarth Press, 1961, vol. 21, pp. 159–66.

FREUD, S. (1927b), 'Dostoevsky and parricide', *Standard Edition*, Hogarth Press, 1961, vol. 21, pp. 175–94.

FREUD, S. (1933), 'Preface to Marie Bonaparte's *The Life and Works of Edgar Allen Poe*', *Standard Edition*, Hogarth Press, 1964, vol. 22, p. 254.

GOMBRICH, E. R. (1960), *Art and Illusion*, Pantheon.

KRIS, E. (1952), *Psychoanalytic Explorations in Art*, International Universities Press.

4 A. Ehrenzweig

A New Psychoanalytical Approach to Aesthetics

A. Ehrenzweig, 'A new psychoanalytical approach to aesthetics', *British Journal of Aesthetics*, vol. 2 (1962), pp. 301–17.

The approach to aesthetics which I am going to discuss is not really new; in fact it was widely practised in classical aesthetics by men like Hogarth. These men searched the structure of a work of art for objective structures that could be made responsible for certain categories of aesthetic feelings: for instance, the feeling of the sublime was related to large awe-inspiring forms or the polar feeling of gracefulness to small and slender structures. In a border problem of aesthetics the witty effect of a good joke was linked with the excessive brevity of its formulation. 'Brevity is the soul of wit,' as Polonius says. But gradually the aestheticians lost heart in their search for the objective justification of aesthetic feelings, perhaps because they failed to find a firm foundation for the most important aesthetic experience, the feeling of beauty itself. Too often the analysis of beauty in works of art served to exclude the revolutionary art of the time – Hanslick's polemics against Wagner are the best-known example. It was only necessary for the rejected unbeautiful type of art to win recognition to discredit the universal validity of the attempted aesthetic laws. This frequent failure in formulating universal criteria of beauty may have contributed to a gradual change in the aim of nineteenth-century aesthetics. It turned away from the analysis of objective structure to the analysis of subjective experience as such. Fechner and Lipps represent turning points in this reorientation of aesthetics towards psychology.

It seems ironical though highly gratifying that Sigmund Freud, himself a psychologist and influenced as an aesthetician by Fechner and Lipps, should have solved a border problem of classical aesthetics in a truly classical manner. In his unjustly neglected book, *The Joke and its Relationship to the Unconscious*, he related the witty effect of a good joke firmly to precisely defined formulations of the joke which correspond to typical techniques of the so-called primary process in the unconscious mind. Freud was led to investigate the structures of a good joke by the disconcerting reaction of some patients to his interpretation of unconscious material. They laughed as though he had told them a good joke. Far from being put out by this unwarranted reaction, Freud began to examine the structure of real jokes and discovered that they expressed a suppressed aggressive or obscene meaning by the same primary-process forms by which a dream would symbolize its hidden phantasy content.

Freud started his review of possible jocular structures with a well-known joke by Heine, cast in the form of a typical dream condensation, one of the most important primary-process forms. Heine condenses two words in a witty way. In the joke a poor man boasts about the familiar way in which he was entertained by a very rich relative. But instead of speaking about his relative's gratifying familiarity, he twists the word and speaks of the 'famillionaire' treatment he had met. The neologism 'famillionaire' is condensed from the words 'familiar' and 'millionaire' and expresses a suppressed meaning; the money-proud man had not really shown genuine friendliness and intimacy but only that superficial and offensive politeness that emphasized his social superiority. The apparent gratification suddenly reveals the poor man's resentment. Telescoped words like 'famillionaire' also occur in dreams. But words are rare in dreams and so the dream usually condenses visual images; a person seen in a dream may combine features belonging to different people or both sexes. Surrealist art in deliberate imitation of dream vision likes to fuse incompatible things, such as pieces of furniture suddenly sprouting human limbs.

There are other primary-process forms shared by dream and joke alike. Displacement is one of them. A dream image might give undue prominence to an unimportant feature and neglect the really significant detail. The dream's subsequent interpretation will then have to give an inconspicuous detail an unsuspected significance and so shift the emphasis back where it belongs. The joke employs the same technique of displacement. Freud tells one of the many Jewish jokes poking fun at the reluctance of Polish

Jews to taking a bath. One Jew meets another in the neighbour-hood of a public bath and asks him: 'Have you taken a bath?' and gets the surprised answer: 'Why, is one missing?' The answer displaces the emphasis from the word 'bath' to the inconspicuous word 'taken', giving it the stronger meaning of 'taken away', 'stolen'. Both the dream and the joke may also express a meaning by the use of the exact opposite. Such con-densations, displacements, representations by the opposite make nonsense of the intended meaning. Our unconscious mind can understand the hidden meaning because, as I will explain in greater detail, the technique of unconscious perception and image making is less differentiated than our conscious language and imagery; it does not differentiate as we would do normally between different categories of things or different meanings of images and words. Freud compared that undifferentiated lan-guage of the dream to old languages which like Latin do not always distinguish between opposite meanings. The Latin word *altus* means high as well as deep. The words 'hospitality' and 'hostility' go back to the same Latin root *host*. The reason why our unconscious mind understands so readily a nonsensical condensation like 'famillionaire', which fuses friendliness and hostility, is its failure to differentiate between opposites. I will later suggest that this gradual dissolution of all precise differen-tiations ultimately approaches an oceanic limit where all dis-tinctions fuse into a single oceanic image.

But first let us continue our account of Freud's success as an aesthetician. His scholarly and exhaustive cataloguing of all possible structures of a joke – I have mentioned only a few – owes nothing to his specific psychoanalytical method. It is an important achievement in itself and could have been emulated by anyone who cared to take a closer look at the manner in which a joke expresses a half-hidden meaning. It is difficult to understand why this achievement has not won wider acclaim. But, of course, Freud went beyond his catalogue and identified the joke's struc-ture as a typical primary-process structure of the unconscious mind. This identification led to the further conclusion that jokes must be formed on the same deeply unconscious level on which dreams are formed. That a new joke is formed spontaneously, that is to say without conscious thought, is evident from a purely behaviouristic observation. If we are lucky and catch a witty person in the act of inventing a really new and pungent joke, we may observe how he will suddenly stop the flow of his conversation. A strained and absent-minded expression will cloud his face for a short while; suddenly the new joke occurs to him and with a sense of liberation he will communicate it as soon as possible as though he was not quite sure of the full impact of his witticism. There is of course a great deal more to be said about the spontaneity and unconscious quality of a new joke. What matters to the aesthetician is the unquestionable success of Freud in conquering at the first assault an old problem of aesthetics and moreover in solving it in a truly classical manner by firmly relating the joke's witty effect to objectively defined structures, here the typical primary-process forms of the unconscious mind.

One could have expected that Freud would continue his incursion into aesthetics and apply his new method to the form problem of art itself. Art was dear to Freud's heart who was himself a master of the German language. His interpretation of the dream had enabled him to transfer, almost wholesale, the entire inventory of dream symbolism to the purpose of a new interpretation of myths, fairy-tales and works of art. But this interpretation concerned only the content, not the form of art. If the symbolism of art welled up from the deep unconscious levels of the dream it was legitimate to expect that the structure of art should carry the imprint of the unconscious mind even more clearly than the relatively shallow joke. Otto Rank, one of the first psychoanalysts to explore the arts, continued in Freud's tracks by searching for primary-process forms in art. He pointed out that the German word for poet, *Dichter*, means a condenser. Myth, folk-lore and art abound in dreamlike apparitions; composite monsters like the Sphinx, chimaera and angels are condensed from animal and human forms. But these frequent intrusions of dreamlike visions did not add up to the exhaustive catalogue of all possible structures which Freud was able to assemble in his analysis of the joke's forms. Apart from the impossibility of compiling a complete catalogue of all possible art forms – nobody has yet succeeded in this – it proved impossible to relate such a catalogue however incomplete to the primary-process forms of dreams. Art form in its often stringent logic and coherence seems a far cry from the nonsensical twists of a joke and of the dream. Half a century has gone by since Freud's book on the joke and psychoanalysis has not made substantial progress in interpreting the form of art. I think we have to accept the failure as definite.

Acceptance of failure does not exclude progress. Often a new interpretation of the failure opens up entirely new fields of knowledge. The most celebrated example for such a re-interpretation is the invention of non-Euclidean geometry which came after centuries of vain attempts at proving all Euclidean postulates. The acceptance of that failure led to a new conception of space which contradicts common sense, but nevertheless explains what otherwise would remain unaccounted for.

The failure of psychoanalysis to discover the unconscious roots of art form can be interpreted in two ways. One can either deny that there exists an unconscious substructure of art – this is what the classical theory of psychoanalysis ultimately did – or else one can assume that the unconscious substructure exists, but for certain reasons cannot be observed consciously. This will be my own approach. The classical psychoanalytical theory of aesthetics summarily disposed of the problem of unconscious art form and attributed the entire aesthetic structure of art to the work of the conscious and preconscious mind, the so-called secondary process. This view reduces the primary process of the unconscious to the role of a purveyor of unstructured raw material, wild and des-tructive phantasies that have first to be tamed and moulded by the secondary process in order to be aesthetically enjoyed. This unconstructive view of the primary process certainly fits the clinical facts of mental illness where the intrusion of unconscious phantasy threatens the patient's sanity. But it does not fit the facts of art and other creative work. Important parts of the structure of art may emerge as from nowhere without the artist's conscious volition and often against his intentions, yet demand to be accepted as an integral part of the composition. Such utterly spontaneous form elements must be conceded roots in the unconscious mind possibly deeper than the levels on which the relatively superficial forms of the joke are shaped. As we have seen, the joke's structure is without doubt the work of the primary process in the deep unconscious. It conveys the characteristically chaotic impression of the primary process with its nonsensical condensations, displacements, representations by the opposite. But the impression of chaos is transient and deceptive. Once we have grasped the joke's half-concealed point its formulation will at once impress us as cogent and neat. Freud, in his detailed survey of jokes, behaves like a true connoisseur and never grows tired of sampling and assessing the relative aesthetic merits of good jokes. My own point will be that the spontaneous elements of art form, such as apparently accidental textures in painting or the inarticulate undulations of primitive melodies, have the same deceptively chaotic look; but they too possess a hidden order and obey some aesthetic discipline if only we can make ourselves sensitive to it. We may have to credit the primary process with playing the same constructive role in the domain of art which Freud concedes to it as far as the joke's spontaneous structure is concerned. That psychoanalytic aesthetics has so far failed to draw this hidden order to the surface may have to be explained by the fact that it rises from mental levels even deeper than those that shape the manifest dream and the joke, and for this reason resists conscious visualization. Our normal common-sense visualization requires a neat juxtaposition of spatial and temporal events and for this reason alone cannot do justice to a different kind of spatial and temporal organization such as is afforded by non-Euclidean geometry. There seem to exist in the structure of a work of art complex relationships that refuse to be caught in the stable and neat grid of common-sense visualization. Incompatible outlines and surfaces permeate and try to crowd themselves into the same point in time and space. In particular, inside and outside space coagulate into something that is inside and outside itself at the same time. In music the neat sequence of tones and chords is burst wide open by systematic serialization. A theme is scrambled up beyond conscious recognition by being played backwards, mirrorwise and in any other arbitrary permutations which refuse to make sense in conscious common-sense experience. These violent twists in the stable order of things must appear chaotic, yet if we accept the testimony of the artists they would obey a different form principle that transcends a purely conscious appreciation. To account for this intuitive order we have to assume an unconscious substructure of art, the form principle of which is inaccessible to common-sense visualization. We cannot see it because it comes from deeper, less differentiated levels than the more superficial primary-process forms of condensation, displacement, representation by the opposite and the like. It may come from an undifferentiated matrix underlying all conscious imagery and image-making where all the nonsensical contradictions and distortions of the primary process are at last resolved.

Recent psychoanalytic researches into the dream and subliminal vision have penetrated into deeper levels where our perception undergoes a fundamental structural change. There is in low-level dreams a characteristic fusion between inside and outside that defies rational comprehension. Geza Roheim, who was originally an anthropologist and who as a psychoanalyst never lost touch with relevance of purely cultural material, summed up in his last book, *The Gates of the Dream*, all that he knew about the dream, myth and art. It is a curious book that does not yet fit easily into the framework of existing theory, written possibly with the courage of an old man who felt no need to heed his audience. Roheim takes the fusion of inside and outside space as part of a basic dream conflict that underlies also the cultural activities of our waking life. The dreamer enters the dream womb through the gates of the dream. In this dream womb all differentiation is dissolved. But the dreamer at the same time leaves the dream womb to rebuild the dream space outside. What concreteness this outer dream space possesses is usually taken from the residual sensations streaming in from the dreamer's body. Roheim's book is full of undifferentiated imagery; he speaks of the dreamer entering his own womb. Entering and leaving the gates of the dream is a single undifferentiated experience. Inside and outside space become one.

Nearer to the centre of psychoanalytic theory are Bertram Lewin's recent researches into the dream screen, which too possesses a curiously undifferentiated space quality. Behind the more concrete images of the dream there is stretched in an uncertain distance an unsubstantial screen that tends to recede from the dreamer or else threatens to engulf him, or do both at the same time. Lewin reports a dream where the dreamer faced

115

an immense wall expanding into the infinite, but while facing this wall he also felt inside the wall.

Perhaps this fusion of inside and outside space will sound less esoteric if you remember the first reaction of art critics to the immense canvases of new American painting. It was said that their enormous expanse forced the spectator into the picture plane which he explored from the inside as it were. At the same time the onlooker felt himself still outside the picture plane, still facing the canvas opposite him. This ambiguity of aesthetic distance, of course, has been an old problem of aesthetics and proves that a measure of spatial undifferentiation is inherent in all aesthetic experience and pertains, as Roheim would have it, perhaps to all creative work.

The gradual dissolution of precise stable space is only one step in the series of gradual undifferentiation. Bertram Lewin while exploring the ineffable dream screen arrived in the end at the totally blank dream, which is filled with an intense emotion that points to the fullness of its symbolism. This full emptiness is another paradox of undifferentiation and the direct result of the failure of our unconscious faculties to organize imagery shaped on these deeper, less differentiated levels of the mind. The emotional fullness of the greatest abstract art which sets it apart from mere decoration is a similar paradox and may be due to a similar failure of our conscious faculties to understand its true portent.

The series beginning with a slight fogginess, increasing vagueness and dreamlike distortion, followed by the dissolution of precise space and time and at last total blankness is characteristic of any descent into lower levels of differentiation. William James, who excelled all other psychologists in his acute introspection, described a similar series of undifferentiation in his celebrated book on the varieties of religious experience. There are first in mystic visions dreamlike distortions and condensations; the vision of a winged angel, half bird, half human, is an example. Then the apparition dissolves into insubstantiality; Peer Gynt on his return from the dream world of the trolls meets with such a frightening intangible monster existing outside normal three-dimensional space. At last there is the true mystic orison, totally empty yet filled with intense experience like a blank dream, most highly prized by the mystics themselves.

The concept of full emptiness has a more sober technical meaning in experiments with subliminal vision. Here we can prove that apparent blankness is consistent with fullness of experience and in certain respects with increased efficiency. By weakening the physiological stimulus in perception, such as shortening the exposure of an image, reducing its brightness and the like, we can induce a kind of perception that is akin to dream perception. By the use of a tachistoscope we can control precisely the duration for which an image is projected on to a screen. The flicking image first becomes vague and incomplete and is easily distorted by the fancies of our imagination. When we cut down the exposure time still further a critical threshold is reached at around 1/100th of a second. Then the faintest flicker disappears and the screen appears blank as far as conscious experience goes. But there exist a number of phenomena which can only be satisfactorily explained if we assume that there persists on a lower level of perception an unconscious type of vision that registers the vanished image. Psychologists call this vision subliminal, i.e. below threshold, but this is only another word for unconscious. Subliminal vision is truly unconscious also because of its connexion with dream imagery. For instance, details of images or whole images that were suppressed by tachistoscopic exposure emerge in later dreams in the guise of typical primary-process structures. Recently a New York psychoanalyst, Charles Fisher, took a new short-cut to make subliminal imagery available in the laboratory. Like Freud, who found a new way to unconscious phantasy by asking his patients to produce ideas by free association, Fisher exposed subliminal images and asked his observers afterwards to draw pictures freely invented by uncontrolled association. Traces of the subliminal images duly showed up in the pictures. For the sake of experimental rigour Fisher mixed truly blank exposures among his slides and significant differences emerged corroborating his findings.

Subliminal imagery also teaches the essential lesson that we must not treat the increasing vagueness and undifferentiation on lower mental levels as structural disintegration due to the failure of perception. In many ways a less differentiated type of perception proves more efficient than our normal common-sense vision. It is for this reason that the artist and creative thinker have to rely to such a large extent on unconscious intuition. Its very ambiguity and lack of detailed differentiation give low-level vision its wider sweep and its capacity for controlling highly complex structures such as occur freely in art. Our normal vision is very restricted in its focus and cannot possibly treat the entire visual field with equal care. Gestalt psychology teaches that our normal vision is compelled to divide the visual field into figure and background areas. The figure patterns stand out plastically from an indistinct background. The details of the ground are lost and fused into vague texture. Every line the artist draws divides the picture plane into something like an inside and outside area, or to use Paul Klee's expression, into endotopic and exotopic surfaces. Paul Klee says that the artist can either emphasize the boundary contrast and keep his attention on one side of the line he draws, that is to say watch only the inside or endotopic part of the picture, or else scatter his attention and make his picture multi-dimensional where inside and outside areas interpenetrate like the voices of musical polyphony. He then shapes inside and outside areas simultaneously, a feat which according to Gestalt psychology is impossible. But this impossibility only pertains to normal common-sense perception which differentiates sharply between figure and ground. When I first wrote on psychoanalytical aesthetics fifteen years ago, I commented on counterchange patterns where the relationship between figure and ground becomes ambiguous; primitive ornaments can often be read as black on white patterns and equally well as white on black patterns because figure and ground are given equally strong emphasis. Modern 'hard-edge' painting too exploits the ambiguity of figure and ground and leaves it uncertain which part of the painting is to be seen as protruding figure and which as receding indistinct background. I concluded that the artist must be able in certain circumstances to rise above the normal compulsion to differentiate sharply between figure and ground and be able to scatter his attention over the entire visual field. It is impossible in art to divide up the painted surface into significant and insignificant areas, such as the figure pattern which matters and an indistinct ground, the details of which are merely vague texturing. Only a bad artist will treat textures as accidental and less significant than the more prominent features of large-scale composition. Every single detail, however small and apparently trifling, has to be firmly related to the all-over structure; this constitutes the enormous complexity of any work of art which defeats our normal powers of vision that cannot take in the whole visual field in a single act of indivisible attention. I concluded, therefore, on the evidence of aesthetic rigour alone that the artist must fall back on unconscious powers of vision that are free from the narrow focus of normal common-sense vision and can scan the entire visual field with impartial equality.

You will understand how gratified I felt when recent experiments with subliminal vision confirmed my hypothesis of an unconscious vision that did not differentiate between figure and ground. Charles Fisher used Rubin's famous double profiles for his experiments. These profiles are typical counterchange patterns where figure and ground become reversible. A square is divided up into two halves by a wavy line running down its middle. Either the right half can be seen as a profile looking to the left, or else the left half can be seen as a profile looking to the right; never both profiles at once owing to the compulsion of normal vision to differentiate the visual field into figure and ground (see Figure 1).

But the subliminal vision is free from this compulsion. When Fisher showed the double profiles subliminally the later, freely associated drawings showed a significant number of patterns that represented two objects and sometimes even two faces looking at each other. Subliminal vision apparently excels normal vision by its scanning power and can search the entire visual field with equal acuity. In a split second it gathers in more details than prolonged conscious examination can in a time perhaps two hundred times longer. The artist who must control the diffuse impact which every single brush stroke has on the all-over structure of his work has to rely on his unconscious sensibilities to scan the complex interrelations concealed in the structure of any work of art.

It was this complexity of artistic structure which made me first assume that there must be a type of vision that can go beyond the narrow focus of normal everyday vision. Let me, therefore, put on record that it was aesthetics which anticipated the experimental findings about subliminal perception. There is

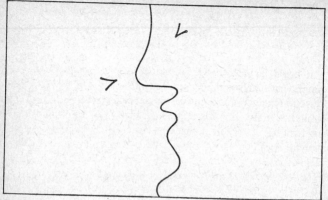

Figure 1.

no such experimental confirmation yet for the existence of a vision free of all spatial and temporal differentiations such as we must infer from other exigencies of aesthetic discipline. A very familiar aesthetic phenomenon, the aesthetic effect of the Golden Section, suggests an unconscious vision free from normal spatial differentiation. The Golden Section rests on a very simple mathematical proportion. We can divide a line, surface or body in such a way that the smaller part relates to the bigger part as the bigger to the undivided whole. But let us try to divide a line in this allegedly so simple way. Comparing the two proportions presents the eye with an insoluble task because the eye movements required for each comparison are quite different. The two unequal parts of the line lie next to each other, but the bigger part is contained within the whole. The best way to compare the two proportions is to repeat the undivided line adjacent to the divided line. Then the eye can compare the proportions in a single sweep. But this explicit way is not the way in which architecture and art usually employ the Golden Section. The related measurements are scattered in a highly complex manner so that the eye is defeated in seeking them out. Again we must assume that there exists a mode of vision, possibly unconscious, that can transcend the common-sense distribution of space and is capable of registering the hidden regularities.

120

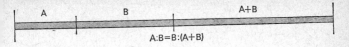

$$A:B=B:(A+B)$$

It could be said that the Golden Section is mathematically simple, but highly complex as a visual fact; it escapes conscious detection unless we take the necessary measurements. Something similar is often said somewhat polemically of serialization in modern music. Mathematically serialization is a very simple permutation of a number of musical elements, such as the twelve semi-tones of the octave, various rhythmical, intensity and pitch values. These permutations in their temporal distribution may be simple enough, but by destroying any vestige of repetition and recognizable pattern, they produce unstructured chaos in our conscious experience. It is easy therefore to dismiss serialization as intellectual exercise without sensual aesthetic merits. Aestheticians have referred to the structural laws of perception in order to reject serialization as chaotic. But the aesthetician should beware of imposing rules on the artist; he is well advised to accept the facts of art however unpalatable and formulate his aesthetic laws accordingly. Because serialization cannot be appreciated on the conscious level we are driven to the conclusion that there must exist an unconscious mode of hearing that does not differentiate musical elements into rigid patterns and so can recognize formal relationships that are scrambled up in every conceivable way. In such an undifferentiated unconscious hearing a theme can be recognized if it is played backwards, mirrorwise and in any other permutation. Then unstructured chaos turns into a complex order in that hidden substructure of art which I am so anxious to press on your attention.

This double aspect of undifferentiation, conscious chaos on the one hand and unconscious discipline on the other, leads us back to the central problem of psychoanalytic aesthetics, the double aspect of the primary process which can be chaotic and destructive in mental illness, but can become highly structured and the instrument of precise control in creative work. The denominator common to these contradictory roles is the structural undifferentiation of low-level imagery.

Conversely, the finer differentiation of conscious vision has a similar double aspect. It may be an impediment in creative work, but for our common-sense orientation in our environment it plays a biologically important role. It immediately selects from the undifferentiated visual field those details that have biological significance and relegates the rest to a receding indistinct background. If the artist undoes this division between figure and ground he certainly regresses to a more primitive, biologically inefficient mode of vision. The child has learned in the course of a long and painful development to acquire a finer differentiation of his environment. For the baby all males are still 'dada' while his mother may have already ascended to the status of an individual distinct in her appearance from all other females. That the child has crude undifferentiated concepts of reality is a well-known fact. What is not sufficiently appreciated is that these undifferentiated concepts correspond to real percepts equally undifferentiated. The baby would really see all males as having the same appearance. Even grown-ups fail to perceive finer differentiations if the biological incentive is not forthcoming. We would fail to pick out individuals from the flies buzzing around the lampshade. All the flies really look the same to us. So do the Chinese, though objectively their appearance may show differences more profound than those distinguishing the European races. Differentiation in percepts, then, is acquired under the pressure of biological need. The Gestalt psychologists assumed first that the basic differentiation between figure and ground was inborn. But even this differentiation has to be learned. The survey by von Senden of cases of people born blind who acquired vision by an operation late in life shows the incredible difficulties encountered by them in organizing the dazzling chaos of undifferentiated colour patches that first meets the eye. Many of these people could not muster the effort needed for learning to fit these patches into patterns, to select the essential figure and to suppress the remainder. If our unconscious vision retains this undifferentiated chaos, it is indeed primitive; yet as we have seen the creative mind uses the same suspension of differentiation for performing highly technical tasks.

It is, of course, quite impossible once we have achieved the finer differentiation of adult vision to put our mind back into the child's undifferentiated mode of vision. This may account for the failure in most psychoanalytic writing to assess properly the far-reaching significance of the undifferentiated matrix underlying our conscious vision. So the undifferentiated structure of the dream-screen has not been fully appreciated, nor do psychoanalytic writers do justice to occasional undifferentiated images that may percolate into surface experience. A recently published psychoanalytic book on man's vision of the world refers to such a case in a casual footnote. A patient dreamt that a man was talking to a chair. The author marvels at a dream image that could not differentiate between a man and a piece of furniture and treats it as a rare intrusion of psychotic imagery into the dream. This interpretation is a far cry from my own which assumes that all dream imagery and indeed all vision rests on an undifferentiated matrix of subliminal vision. Psychoanalytic writing, of course, fully acknowledges the general undifferentiation of primitive concepts that failed to distinguish between opposites and other incongruous meanings. High and low, birth and death are comprised in the same symbol. What is not sufficiently realized is the fact that the unconscious mind expresses these undifferentiated meanings and concepts in actual percepts, lacking the normal organization of space and time so that a man and a chair can coexist in the same shape, or high and low are really seen as the same thing.

Creative thinkers have known that such a vision exists. For instance, the French philosopher Bergson describes the structure of creative intuition in just this way, as a kind of vision in which incompatible things extend into each other and can coexist in time and space. Bergson advises the reader to evoke in himself a state of creativity by trying to visualize such incompatible things occupying the same place within the visual field, things which in the common-sense view would drive each other away.

The abstract concept of the creative thinker succeeds in overcoming the common-sense differences between ordinary, concrete things. It extracts from these different things a common property which is the new abstract concept. What is not sufficiently realized is that this 'seeing together' of concrete things ordinarily held apart again involves a capacity for undifferentiated percepts. The abstract image in the moment of creative insight may appear empty and blank owing to the conscious incompatibility of the imagery. Creative abstraction differs from truly empty generalization in that it is still infested on a lower mental level with the multitude of visions from which it arose in the first place. Empty generalizations can be handled with such smooth facility because they have cut themselves off from their undifferentiated matrix. The need to see concrete things together in a single undifferentiated image is evident as long as science is still struggling to form new abstract concepts. A hypothetical example may help to make this clearer. The modern physicist has to visualize the physical nature of light by two incompatible images or models. It appears either as a wave or else as a stream of solid bodies. The physicist Ernest Hutten once remarked aptly that a future scientist possessing a more advanced power of abstraction might have no difficulty in visualizing a new, more abstract concept that would be neither a wave nor solid body, but both at the same time. Such a truly abstract concept could only be formed by suspending the common-sense differentiation between things of very different appearance. As long as we have not achieved this degree of undifferentiation, it seems as incomprehensible to us as is the undifferentiated world of the child.

Abstraction in art has the same double aspect. It is both primitive undifferentiation and a highly sophisticated achievement. This double aspect is well brought out in Professor Gombrich's well-known paper, 'Meditations on a hobby horse or the roots of artistic form'. Gombrich's comparison between artistic abstraction and childish undifferentiation serves him to poke his gentle fun at the pretensions of much abstract art; but his irony misfires in the face of truly creative abstraction. He points out – in my view correctly – that the modern artist's much-vaunted power of abstraction differs little from the child's weakness in differentiating properly the things around him which makes the child in his play treat a straight stick like a live horse. Nor is it an increased power of abstraction that prompts the drunkard to lift his hat politely to the nearest lamp-post. Alcohol has so weakened his normal powers of differentiation that he cannot keep apart a lamp-post from a human figure. Gombrich does not by this comparison debunk the artist's power of abstraction because, as I have been so anxious to show, creative man can turn primitive weakness into a potent faculty. Sublimation generally transforms primitive crudeness into sublime cultural achievement. When Picasso pares down the naturalistic shape of a bull into a stick-like cipher, he has strengthened not weakened its shape, though his imagination may have regressed to the primitive imagination of the child who accepts a stick for a horse or a bull and many other things beside.

It is perhaps an over-simplification to say that the creative mind 'regresses' to the child's primitive state of undifferentiation. Creative undifferentiation is not so much a passive slipping back to earlier experience as an active undoing of often fundamental organizations of perception. The child has probably never experienced a perception where common-sense space and time are suspended. Active undifferentiation appears to start as soon as creativity stirs in the very young child around the second year of life during the anal stage of libidinous development. Then the child learns to talk, to act as a conforming social being and acquires the basic cultural adaptations. His conscious powers of differentiation also increase greatly and with it his rational orientation in the outside world. But this increase in conscious differentiation is matched in his inner phantasy life by anal imagery of extreme undifferentiation. Freud first drew attention to these anal phantasies. They undifferentiate the child's experience of his own body so that mouth, vagina, anus and any other body opening are confused and excrement, children, genitals and other excrescences of the body are no longer distinguished. This utter lack of differentiation makes anal phantasies less structured and more primitive than the earlier oral phantasies. This loss of structure creates a paradox which so far has not been interpreted. Freud's disciple Abraham, who like Freud was greatly interested in biological speculations, pointed out that a body image that failed to differentiate between the various body cavities and body openings was more appropriate to a primitive animal, far down on the ladder of evolution, possessing only a single body cavity and a single opening to serve for eating, excreting and propagation. It is no more correct to say that the child in the anal stage 'regresses' to such a primitive animal than that the creative mind 'regresses' to such a primitive state of childhood. Both perform active feats of undifferentiation which need not have a correlate in actual earlier experience. Owing to the inbuilt dynamic conflict that underlies all creative work, the child develops in two opposite directions simultaneously. On the conscious level he goes on developing ever finer differentiations among the appearances of the real things around him, while in his unconscious phantasy life he undoes even the most fundamental differentiations of common-sense reality and so creates images that cannot have any possible correlate in rational thought. At last an oceanic limit is reached where all differentiation is suspended altogether. There is no need to explain this oceanic fusion of imagery as a 'regression' to a prenatal state when the child was actually at one with its mother. It may well be a creative suspension of frontiers already set up and so may belong to a much later stage of development.

Artists often assert that for them there is no basic difference between abstract and representational art. Their allegedly abstract imagery is as concrete and real to them as traditional realism. We can understand this. Creative abstraction in art differs from empty ornament and decoration in the same way in which in the domain of science creative abstraction differs from empty generalization. There is still crowded into the new abstract image the medley of undifferentiated imagery that gave it birth in the first place. The first abstract art of mankind, neolithic art, is still close to the undifferentiated matrix of abstraction. A perfectly geometric pot may suddenly sprout two tiny breasts on its otherwise smooth surface to reveal its origin in a vision that did not distinguish a pot from a human form. The nature religion of neolithic man was able to transform a triangular mountain into a representation of the great goddess. In his vision the whole earth itself became the womb of the great mother. This metaphorical interpretation of nature is neither animism nor proof of a poetic disposition, but can be explained from the same oceanic fusion between the outer world and the inner world of phantasy. Nor is the propensity of the poet to metaphor due to clever comparison, but rises spontaneously from an unconscious view that can unite disparate images in a single glance.

I have spoken earlier of our compulsion on a conscious level to organize the visual field into prominent figure and indistinct receding ground. Modern abstract art, true to its intimate relationship with low-level vision, has also weakened this fundamental dichotomy of vision. In traditional art we still have the distinction between deliberate composition on a large scale and the uncontrolled accidental textures and scribbles of the brushwork that fuse into the background. When I first wrote on the psychology of modern art I suggested on the evidence of Kandinsky's and Picasso's work that modern art had enlarged the inarticulate textures of background forms and elevated them into a main structure of the composition. The triumphant entry of American painting into the world of art bore out my diagnosis in a spectacular manner. Pollock and Kline blew up the loops and scribbles of traditional brushwork on a gigantic scale and pushed their undifferentiated structure violently upon our conscious attention. But this onslaught on our conscious sensibilities soon led to a retrenchment. It was only necessary to step back a little and fuse the giant doodles and loops into empty decorative textures serving as a neutral background to pieces of furniture. Most abstract work imitating the pioneers has become little more than empty decoration. This inevitable decadence makes nonsense of any attempt to invest the exuberance of American painting with a permanent depth-psychological panache. However, it so happened that some New York artists welcomed my depth-psychological interpretation of modern art as proof that American painting more than any other type of painting was inspired by unconscious phantasy. Sir Herbert Read in a note to his *Concise History of Modern Painting* also accepts me as a possible theoretician and spokesman of modern action painting. This was certainly not my purpose.

What psychoanalytical aesthetics can teach is that it is not admissible to treat the textures of the background forms in any kind of art as structurally less significant than the more prominent figure patterns of the conscious composition. The scribbles and doodles of the brushwork and of a nervous artistic handwriting only seem accidental and of no consequence. Psychoanalysis generally has put us on our guard against treating any product of the mind as accidental and insignificant. Unconscious symbolism is too easily displaced from the prominent and articulate image to the inconspicuous and inarticulate detail. For our unconscious vision the differentiation between articulate figure and inarticulate background textures does not exist. In an etching by Rembrandt we cannot possibly detach the deliberate composition from the accidental spontaneous scribblings of his handwriting. Obviously both elements arose together in intimate interaction. Only the commercial artist will compose the main structure of his work and then add decorative texture as an after-thought. The scribblings of Rembrandt have no intelligible mean-ing and seem quite chaotic to our conscious analysis. Yet in expressing the artist's personality the common-sense relation between composition and handwriting is almost reversed. The artist's spontaneous and chaotic handwriting is considered far more characteristic of his personality than his more deliberate large-scale forms. It allows the art expert to identify the author of a painting more securely than the study of his more considered composition. Obviously the scribbles of a great artist's hand-writing must possess some order of their own though consciously we are perceiving only inarticulate accidental chaos. We cannot demonstrate this order for inspection, but must infer its uncon-scious existence from its palpable effect on our conscious emo-tional experience.

Psychoanalytic theory will have to accept that the imagery of the primary process can possess an invisible order of its own at least as far as creative work is concerned. The great psycho-analyst and art historian E. Kris prepared the way for recasting our concept of the primary process by suggesting that the creative mind can allow conscious functions to lapse in a controlled regression towards the primary process. But this does not yet mean that the primary process itself is accessible to control and order. More recent psychoanalytic writing suggests that in creative work the boundaries between primary and secondary process become blurred. Most courageously Marion Milner, in her Freud Centenary lecture of 1956, *Psychoanalysis and Art*, put forward the plea that a revision of the concept of the primary process was in the air and that the facts of aesthetics and art called for this revision. What I have tried to do in this paper is to array some of the aesthetic facts that cannot be accommodated within the current framework of psychological theory. The final word has not been spoken. Our descent into deeper levels of mental imagery has only just begun.

5 D. E. Berlyne

Measures of Aesthetic Preference

D. E. Berlyne, 'Measures of aesthetic preference', paper read at the First International Colloquium on Experimental Aesthetics, Paris, 7 June 1965; *Sciences de l'Art*, vol. 3, special number, pp. 9–23.

Discussions of the psychological aspects of art, whether by psychologists, critics, or laymen, depend all too often on implicit assumptions that are prebehaviourist and preoperationist. These assumptions require close scrutiny, both because their validity is questionable and because they stand in the way of attempts to incorporate experimental aesthetics within the framework of modern psychology.

Aestheticians often start out from a view of the communicative function of symbols that is essentially the one that Ogden and Richards put forward in 1923, constituting a formalization of the way in which the ordinary man looks at the matter. It has been criticized by Morris (1946), Osgood (1952), Mowrer (1954) and Skinner (1957), who have offered alternative analyses of signs and symbols in terms of the effects they have on behaviour.

According to this view, certain conscious experiences, which may or may not be elicited by external objects or events, occur in the mind of the communicator, in this case the creative artist, and he creates symbolic patterns that evoke similar experiences in the minds of those with whom he communicates. Under the influence of this kind of theory, aestheticians have become accustomed to looking for the essence of the aesthetic reaction in processes going on inside the subject.

It was only natural therefore to rely on verbal expressions of preference or evaluation as sources of information about these internal processes. These have formed the principal measuring equipment of the experimental aesthetician, being subjected in more recent times to the highly sophisticated procedures for recording and analysing judgements that contemporary scaling techniques have made available.

Verbal reports can be supplemented by recordings of psycho-physiological changes, which afford access to internal reactions that are outside the subject's awareness and thus beyond the scope of his introspection. Now that technological refinements have made it relatively simple to register respiratory, circulatory, electrodermal, electromyographic and electroencephalographic changes, the vast possibilities of these techniques for experimental aesthetics are just beginning to be exploited.

Internal reactions, whether studied through verbal reports or through psychophysiological indices, are presumably related to overt behaviour of some sort, and the sort of overt behaviour that is most clearly relevant is behaviour through which a person exposes his sense organs to aesthetically satisfying patterns. This 'aesthetic behaviour' includes the activities of the creative artist, of the performing artist, of the reader, museum visitor, or listener and of the person who arranges objects in a decorative or aesthetically satisfying way. All of these activities are examples of exploratory behaviour, which has in recent years received intensive experimental study in human beings and in several species of animal. This study has already yielded findings with an obvious bearing on problems of aesthetics (Berlyne, 1960).

I should like to report some of our own experimental results using all three kinds of measure – verbal reports, psychophysiological indices, measures of overt exploratory behaviour – that show the relations both within and between these three types of measure to be quite complicated and cast doubt on some of the tacit assumptions that seem to have been commonly adopted by both experimental and non-experimental aestheticians.

The experiments that I am going to discuss all used the patterns shown in Figure 1. These patterns consist of pairs grouped in categories, each category representing a particular variable. The variables in question are of the kind connoted by words like 'complexity', 'irregularity' or 'incongruity' in everyday speech. Although we have here a collection of logically distinct variables, they have been shown to have similar effects in a variety of experimental situations, so that we can talk about them collectively. They are examples of what I call 'collative' properties of stimulus patterns. They are identical with some of the factors that underly 'form', 'structure' or 'composition' in works of art.

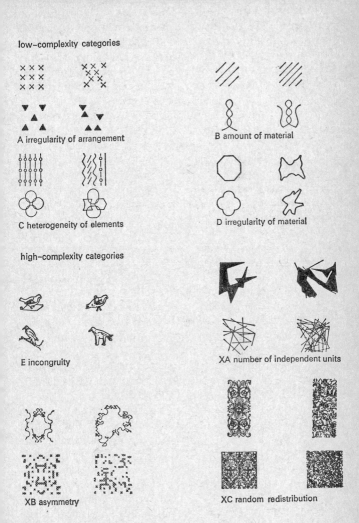

low-complexity categories

A irregularity of arrangement

B amount of material

C heterogeneity of elements

D irregularity of material

high-complexity categories

E incongruity

XA number of independent units

XB asymmetry

XC random redistribution

Figure 1. (From Berlyne, Borsa, Craw, Gelman and Mandell, 1965)

They may be most obviously applicable to the spatial distribution of material in visual art forms, but counterparts can easily be found in sequential media such as literature and music. In each pair shown in Figure 1, the pattern on the left is the one we call the 'less complex' (LC) and the one on the right the 'more complex' (MC) member.

We first used these patterns in a series of experiments studying the effects of complexity variables on duration of exploratory behaviour (Berlyne, 1957, 1958; Berlyne and Lawrence, 1964). Three techniques were employed, and all have given similar results. They consist in (1) allowing a subject to operate a switch to give himself as many tachistoscopic exposures of each pattern as he wishes, (2) observing the length of time for which each pattern is fixated while the two members of a pair are displayed side by side, and (3) allowing the subject control over an automatic projector so that he can inspect each pattern in turn for as long a continuous period as he wishes.

As far as the low-complexity material (the 'non-X categories') are concerned, the results have regularly and decisively shown that the more complex patterns attract more prolonged exploration than the less complex patterns. With regard to the high-complexity material (X categories), which we introduced later because all the patterns of the low-complexity categories are relatively simple, the findings have not been quite so clear-cut. But a number of experiments suggests that there is a decline as complexity becomes more extreme, so that in these categories, the less complex members are generally explored for a longer time. There appears, in other words, to be an inverted U-shaped function linking exploration time with complexity, and as one might expect, the location of the peak varies quite widely from person to person and from population to population.

In all the experiments to which I have just been referring, subjects were exposed to all the patterns in an order determined by the experimenter, although they had control over the duration of exposure to each. Other experiments have been concerned with the somewhat different question of what happens when a subject is allowed to choose which pattern to expose himself to. In an experiment using the same patterns, Hoats, Miller and Spitz (1963) allowed subjects to see both members of a pair for three seconds and then made them choose one of them to look at for an additional period. In these conditions, the subjects, consisting of both normal and retarded subjects, tended significantly to choose less complex patterns. An experiment of our own (Berlyne, 1963) confirmed that adult subjects are likely to choose less complex patterns for continued inspection when they have had something like three or four seconds to see the patterns between which the choice must be made. If, on the other hand, the preliminary exposures are brief, i.e. a half second or one second, they are more likely to choose the more complex patterns.

These findings can be interpreted by assuming that there are two distinct kinds of exploratory behaviour. One, which we call *specific* exploration, is aimed at receipt of information from particular sources and occurs when the subject is in the kind of motivational condition that we call 'perceptual curiosity'. Perceptual curiosity is induced by uncertainty or lack of information, such as results from a brief presentation of a stimulus pattern that does not allow enough time for its characteristics to be identified. In such circumstances, the subject will be more highly motivated to look at the pattern that excited more curiosity, that left the subject with more uncertainty about its nature – namely the more complex one. But if the subject has seen both patterns for long enough to extract the information contained in them, curiosity will play a minor role, if any. The exploration that occurs then will be *diversive* exploration, aimed at stimulation from any source that possesses collative properties to the right degree. In the experiments just mentioned, this evidently means seeking exposure to the less complex patterns. Diversive exploration may seem to have more affinity with aesthetic activities and specific exploration than with scientific or philosophical activities. But this statement is evidently too simple. The motivation factors governing diversive exploration must have a great deal to do with interest in the 'formal beauty' or 'decorative' aspects of art, but curiosity – puzzling out what is in a picture, what it means, how its elements are related – is also an essential element in the psychological effects of art, though more so in some styles than in others. On the other hand, the element of satisfying structure in such fields as science and mathematics has been commented on too often to be overlooked.

In a further line of research, we have been investigating the effects of these variables on indices of arousal. This was undertaken initially because the hypothesis that collative variables increase arousal (a concept that more and more writers are coming to identify with 'drive') formed an essential link in our view of how these variables governed exploratory behaviour. But effects of collative variables on arousal are likely to have still more far-reaching ramifications within the theory of motivation. For example, fluctuations in arousal due to collative variables have evidently a major contribution to make to the so-called emotional aspect of aesthetic appreciation.

An experiment with the galvanic skin response (Berlyne *et al.*, 1963) yielded some indication that the magnitude of the orientation reaction (the transient increase in arousal consequent on the initial impact of a stimulus) is greater with more complex patterns when a subject is specially motivated to attend. A later experiment (Berlyne and McDonnell, 1965), using the electroencephalograph, gave a more conclusive answer to the question. As we can see in Table 1, desynchronization, an index of heightened arousal, was more prolonged when more complex patterns were exposed for three seconds at a time.

Table 1

Mean Duration of EEG Desynchronization (in Seconds) (from Berlyne and McDonnell, 1965)

	Category	Less complex	More complex	F $(1, 258\ df)$	P
A	Irregularity of arrangement	5·8	6·5	6·08	<0·05
B	Amount of material	5·7	6·6	10·17	<0·01
C	Heterogeneity of elements	6·0	6·4	—	N S
D	Irregularity of shape	6·3	6·0	—	N S
E	Incongruity	5·4	6·5	6·28	<0·05
X A	Number of independent units	5·7	6·1	—	N S
X B	Asymmetry	6·0	6·3	—	N S
X C	Random redistribution	5·6	6·2	4·98	<0·05
	All categories	5·8	6·3	24·94	<0·001

Some years ago, an experiment (Berlyne, 1963) was done in which these patterns were rated on a 7-point scale for 'pleasingness' by some subjects and for 'interestingness' by other subjects. As Table 2 reveals, there was a significant tendency for more complex patterns to be rated less pleasing but more interesting. In other words, the patterns that subjects look at for a longer time are not those that they judge more pleasing but, on the contrary, those that they find less pleasing and more interesting. These are also the patterns that, according to our electroencephalographic findings, are more arousing or disturbing. On the other hand, patterns judged more pleasing tend to be the ones to which subjects prefer to expose themselves when given a choice after adequate acquaintance with the alternatives and dissipation of perceptual curiosity.

A doctoral thesis by Day (1965) has recently provided some instructive additional data on these matters. Day asked subjects to rank the patterns (omitting those in category B) for complexity. He found that the material can be divided into four classes – L C non-X, M C non-X, L C X and M C X – representing progressively

Table 2

Mean Ratings for Interestingness and Pleasingness (from Berlyne, 1963)

	Interestingness			Pleasingness		
Category	LI	MI	Wilcoxon's T	LI	MI	Wilcoxon's T
A	3·5	3·5	NS	4·5	3·7	12·5***
B	3·6	3·8	25*	4·4	4·4	NS
C	3·1	3·6	NS	5·0	3·9	10***
D	2·9	3·2	NS	5·1	3·8	35***
E	4·4	5·1	12·5**	4·8	2·6	16***
XA + XB	4·8	4·8	NS	4·4	4·1	NS
XC	5·2	4·5	9***	4·7	3·0	3***
XD	3·6	4·0	NS	4·1	4·1	15·5***
Categories	A–D (LI + MI)	E–XD (LI + MI)		A–D (LI + MI)	E–XD (LI + MI)	
	3·4	4·6	3***	4·3	3·9	7·5***

NS P> 0·05   * P<0·05   ** P<0·02   *** P<0·01

Motivation and Resolution

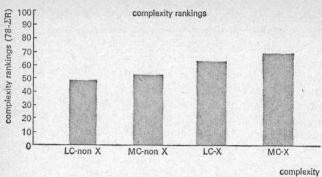

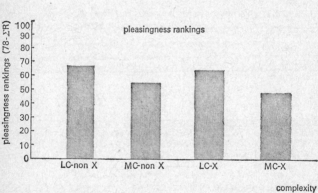

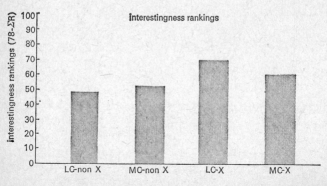

Figure 2. (From Day, 1965)

greater complexity according to the subject's judgements (see Figure 2, upper bar graph).

Other subjects were asked to rank the same patterns either for pleasingness or for interestingness. The results of the pleasingness rankings are shown in Figure 2 (middle bar graph). It will be seen that there are two peaks. This might be considered of minor significance were it not for the strikingly similar picture obtained repeatedly in a number of experiments by Munsinger and Kessen (1964; Munsinger, Kessen and Kessen, 1964). They used a collection of patterns very much like those in our category XB, consisting of randomly constructed polygons with different numbers of angles ranging from three to forty. Figure 3 shows one of their graphs depicting verbally expressed preference as a function of complexity, that is to say, number of angles. Figure 4 shows the function obtained when the dependent variable was rate of key-pressing in a variable-ratio instrumental-conditioning situation, the reinforcing event being the brief appearance of one of the

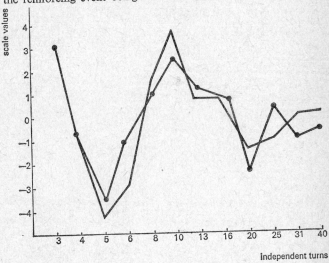

Figure 3. Scale scores of preference for asymmetrical random shapes varying in number of independent turns from 3 to 40. Scores for men and women are shown. (From Munsinger and Kessen, 1964)

polygons. The function relating verbally expressed preference with complexity was also found to be bimodal in an experiment by Terwilliger (1963).

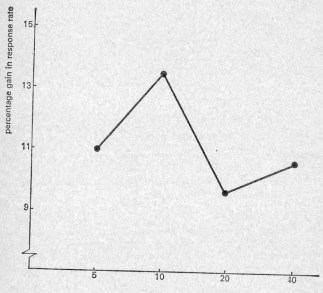

Figure 4. Percentage increase in operant responding to four levels of random shapes. (From Munsinger and Kessen, 1964)

When the electroencephalographic data mentioned earlier are re-analysed, and the mean duration of desynchronization for the four classes of material are compared, the results are as shown in Figure 5. It is evident that the relation borne by this measure of arousal to complexity is the inverse of that borne by judgements of pleasingness. A pattern is found more pleasing the less arousing it is.

Day's interestingness rankings produced the picture shown in Figure 2 (lower bar graph). Judged interestingness is apparently an inverted U-shaped function of judged complexity, which means that it resembles, in this particular respect, the duration of

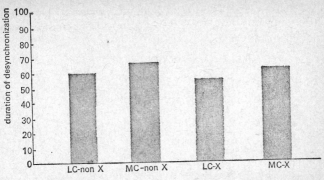

Figure 5. Complexity and duration of EEG desynchronization. (From Berlyne and McDonnell, 1965)

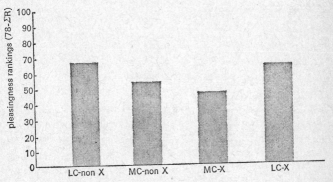

Figure 6. Pleasingness and interestingness rankings.
(From Day, 1965)

exploration. If we rearrange the four classes of stimulus patterns in order of judged interestingness, we obtain the picture displayed in Figure 6, which offers a possible explanation of the bimodality of judgements of pleasingness. Patterns may, it seems, be found pleasing either if they are totally uninteresting, as in the case of simple regular geometrical shapes, or if they are highly interesting, which seems to mean that they possess a great deal of complexity that can readily be organized or assimilated.

At the beginning of 1965 (Berlyne and Peckham, 1966), these phenomena were probed further with the use of Osgood's semantic differential technique. As is well known, this technique requires subjects to rate a stimulus on a 7-point scale whose extremes correspond to a pair of words with opposite meanings. Osgood and his associates have shown, by means of factor analysis, that such ratings enable the 'connotative' or affective meaning of a stimulus to be classified by locating it in a three-dimensional 'semantic space'. The three dimensions represent orthogonal factors, named Evaluation, Potency and Activity.

We selected three of Osgood's scales, each of which has a very high loading in one of the three factors and slight loadings on the other two. The scales were 'ugly–beautiful' (which, apart from being a fairly good measure of the evaluative factor, is of interest because of the frequent use of these two words in connexion with art), 'strong–weak', representative of the potency factor, and 'fast–slow', representing the activity factor. Our visual patterns were paired with each of the three scales in a randomized sequence.

The results are displayed in Figure 7. First of all, there is an impressive similarity, as one might well expect, between ratings on the evaluative dimension and judgements of pleasingness. More surprising is the striking similarity between results pertaining to the evaluative dimension and results pertaining to the potency dimension. Osgood's studies, which have generally used words or verbal formulae as stimuli, have shown these two dimensions to be independent. But in relation to visual patterns such as we are concerned with here, they appear to be closely connected. We must suppose that the subjects judged patterns to be 'strong' or 'weak' according to the extent to which they possessed some quality like 'stability' or 'coherence'. One is, of course, reminded of the concept of 'goodness of configuration' which the Gestalt psychologists developed and related, among other things, to aesthetic value. This kind of property evidently has a large say in determining how 'pleasing' a pattern will be. As for the activity dimension, the picture is quite different. It shows activity to be a curvilinear function of complexity, which, although the coincidence is far from exact, rather resembles the relation between Day's interestingness rankings and judged complexity.

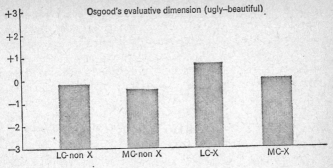

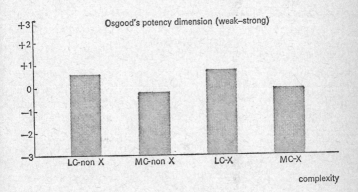

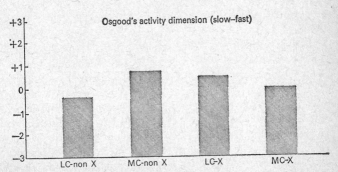

Figure 7. (From Berlyne and Peckham, 1966)

One further technique that we have been trying out is concerned with aesthetic balance and was last used by Puffer at the beginning of the century. It consists in showing the subject a black rectangular panel with one pattern in a fixed position on one side of the centre, subjects being required to adjust the location of a second pattern on the other side until the most pleasing arrangement had been found. Puffer's (1903) findings, as well as those obtained by Pierce in a similar experiment in the 1890s (1894), suggested that the more interesting or attention-attracting patterns tend to be placed nearer the centre than others, as if they had greater 'weight'. For example, lines in 'warm' or long-wave colours were placed closer in, as were larger forms, patterns that change from trial to trial and pictures favouring depth perception. These variables are all ones that can be expected to affect the level of arousal or magnitude of the orientation reaction, which led us to formulate the hypothesis that our more complex patterns would similarly be placed nearer the centre than the less complex patterns. Preliminary experiments, carried out by Miss M. Gassard and Mrs E. Mandell in our laboratory, have obtained some degree of confirmation for this hypothesis. Significant differences in the predicted direction were found with category C (amount of material), in both experiments, and with category D (irregularity of shape) in one experiment (see Table 3). There has, however, been some indication that the trend is reversed in the X categories and that extremely complex patterns, like extremely simple ones, are placed further out. In Miss Gassard's experiment, the interaction between X/non-X categories and more complex/less complex patterns was significant ($P < 0.05$). If these results are corroborated further, and they cannot yet be regarded as fully established the variable that determines how near to the centre a pattern must be placed to achieve aesthetic balance may be identifiable with interestingness.

So we are left with the tentative conclusion that there are at least two distinct kinds of motivational condition of importance to exploratory behaviour, which includes aesthetic behaviour. One of them, corresponding to diversive exploration, inclines the subject to seek out patterns that are judged pleasing or beautiful, which appears to mean that they are relatively lacking in the discomfiting or puzzling properties that make for a steep rise in arousal or an intense orientation reaction. On the other hand, conditions of 'perceptual' or 'epistemic' curiosity bring specific exploratory behaviour or epistemic (knowledge-seeking) behaviour to the fore. Curiosity occurs when the subject finds himself exposed to novel, surprising, ambiguous, problem-raising or otherwise conflict-inducing patterns. It impels him either to seek external stimulation containing the information that he needs to remove his uncertainties and resolve his conflict, or else to engage in ideational processes that will lead to a solution of the problem. He may well deliberately expose himself to troublesome patterns for the sake of the challenges with which they present him, if the difficulty of assimilating them and the satisfaction from overcoming the difficulty are properly balanced. In other words, he will choose those that are maximally interesting. This second kind of motivation plays a part when a work of art is approached as a source of knowledge or a spur to intellectual exertion, as in the historical novel or social problem drama. In subtler ways, it plays a part whenever suspense is manipulated or when appreciation of structure depends on fluctuations in arousal due to alternating conformity with, and defiance of, expectations and transitional probabilities. This last phenomenon is most clearly at work in sequential art forms and has been discussed by Meyer (1956) with reference to music. Its pertinence to other art forms, including those where co-existing elements must be registered in turn, is obvious.

Table 3

Experiments in Aesthetic Balance. L C–M C: Mean Difference in Distance from Centre (in Inches)

Categories	A	B	C	D	X A	X B	X C
Gassard (1963–4)	+0·20	−0·03	+0·57	+1·01*	+0·18	−0·32	−0·41
Mandell (1964–5)	−0·25	−0·30	+0·37*	+0·45*	−0·15	−0·12	+0·18

* $P < 0.05$.

Although it is important to separate these two kinds of motivational condition and the reactions, both external and internal, to which they give rise, it is highly likely that they are intermingled and interacting in most everyday reactions to art. Differences in the relative influence of the one or the other will characterize different personal tastes and different schools of art.

The more general and more important conclusions to be drawn from the work that I have reported are, however, that it is not safe to assume that all so-called measures of aesthetic preference or appreciation are measuring the same thing; that assumptions about the ways in which the various measures are related cannot be trusted without empirical study; and that experimental aestheticians should give a high priority to this empirical study, since these measures constitute the basic instruments on which all their work depends.

References

BERLYNE, D. E. (1957), 'Conflict and information theory variables as determinants of human perceptual curiosity', *J. exp. Psychol.*, vol. 53, pp. 399–404.

BERLYNE, D. E. (1958), 'The influence of complexity and change in visual figures on orienting responses', *J. exp. Psychol.*, vol. 55, pp. 289–96.

BERLYNE, D. E. (1960), *Conflict, Arousal and Curiosity*, McGraw-Hill.

BERLYNE, D. E. (1963), 'Complexity and incongruity variables as determinants of exploratory choice and evaluative ratings', *Canad. J. Psychol.*, vol. 17, pp. 274–90.

BERLYNE, D. E., BORSA, D. M., CRAW, M. A., GELMAN, R. S., and MANDELL, E. E. (1965), 'Effects of stimulus complexity and induced arousal on paired-associate learning', *J. verb. Learn. verb. Behav.*, vol. 4, pp. 291–9.

BERLYNE, D. E., CRAW, M. A., SALAPATEK, P. H., and LEWIS, J. L. (1963), 'Novelty, complexity, incongruity, extrinsic motivation and the GSR', *J. exp. Psychol.*, vol. 66, pp. 560–67.

BERLYNE, D. E., and LAWRENCE, G. H. (1964), 'Effects of complexity and incongruity variables on GSR, investigatory behavior, and verbally expressed preference', *J. gen. Psychol.*, vol. 71, pp. 21–45.

BERLYNE, D. E., and MCDONNELL, P. (1965), 'Effects of stimulus complexity and incongruity on duration of EEG desynchronization', *Electroenceph. clin. Neurophysiol.*, vol. 18, pp. 156–61.

BERLYNE, D. E., and PECKHAM, S. (1966), 'The semantic differential and other measures of reaction to visual complexity', *Canad. J. Psychol.*, vol. 20, pp. 125–35.

DAY, H. (1965), 'Exploratory behaviour as a function of individual differences and level of arousal', Unpublished doctoral thesis, University of Toronto.

HOATS, D. L., MILLER, M. B., and SPITZ, H. H. (1963), 'Experiments on perceptual curiosity in mental retardates and normals', *Amer. J. ment. Defic.*, vol. 68, pp. 386–95.

MEYER, L. B. (1956), *Emotion and Meaning in Music*, University of Chicago Press.

MORRIS, C. R. (1946), *Signs, Language and Behavior*, Prentice-Hall.

MOWRER, O. H. (1954), 'The psychologist looks at language', *Amer. Psychologist*, vol. 9, pp. 660–94.

MUNSINGER, H., and KESSEN, W. (1964), 'Uncertainty, structure and preference', *Psychol. Monogr.*, vol. 78, no. 9 (whole no. 586).

MUNSINGER, H., KESSEN, W., and KESSEN, M. L. (1964), 'Age and uncertainty: developmental variations in preference for variability', *J. exp. child Psychol.*, vol. 1, pp. 1–15.

OGDEN, C. K., and RICHARDS, I. A. (1923), *The Meaning of Meaning*, Harcourt Brace.

OSGOOD, C. E. (1952), 'The nature and measurement of meaning', *Psychol. Bull.*, vol. 49, pp. 197–237.

PIERCE, E. (1894), 'Aesthetics of simple forms. I. Symmetry', *Psychol. Rev.*, vol. 1, pp. 483–95.

PUFFER, E. D. (1903), 'Studies in symmetry', *Psychol. Rev. Monogr. Suppl.*, vol. 4, pp. 467–539.

SKINNER, B. F. (1957), *Verbal Behavior*, Appleton-Century-Crofts.

TERWILLIGER, R. F. (1963), 'Pattern complexity and affective arousal', *Percep. mot. Skills.*, vol. 17, pp. 387–95.

Part Three Cognition and Interpretation

In introducing the previous section the point was made that the motivation to confront art is not necessarily unified. Equally, a number of different processes will be contributing to our experience in this situation. These relate not only to our understanding of the conventions of representation, which are dealt with in the following section, but also to our general cognitive approach to the work of art. The relation between our understanding of symbols and our total experience of a painting is discussed here by Professor Gombrich. He draws on Neisser's (1963) propositions regarding sequential and multiple processes in thought as well as considering the approach developed by Osgood, Suci and Tannenbaum (1957) which we present in Part Seven. In the second paper Professor Child deals with the actual form our experience takes as a result of the way we process our perceptions, and the bearing this may have on our experience of art.

References

NEISSER, U. (1963), 'The multiplicity of thought', *Brit. J. Psychol.*, vol. 54, pp. 1–14.

OSGOOD, C. E., SUCI, G. J., and TANNENBAUM, P. H. (1957), *The Measurement of Meaning*, University of Illinois Press.

6 E. H. Gombrich

The Use of Art for the Study of Symbols

E. H. Gombrich, 'The use of art for the study of symbols', *American Psychologist*, vol. 20 (1965), pp. 34–50.

A psychologist could address a meeting of art historians on the use of symbols for the study of art. An art historian can reciprocate by telling psychologists of the use of art for the study of symbols. If the title I have chosen has an odd and slightly topsy-turvy appearance, it is to express this conviction.

For, thanks partly to the interest which Freud's writings have stimulated in all aspects of symbolism, art historians during the last few decades have also increasingly returned to this field which had previously been neglected, if not despised, by the formalist schools of criticism. A whole branch of studies has sprung up, under the name of iconology, which is devoted to the unriddling of symbols in art (Panofsky, 1939). The Warburg Institute to which I belong can claim to have made its contribution to this development which also found its response and continuation in this country. And from iconology the interest in levels of meaning has spread to the study of literature. In short, emblems and allegories, only recently dismissed as abstruse aberrations, are all the rage, and the hunt for symbols threatens to become another academic industry. Some of you may have seen that amusing satire on this vogue, Frederick C. Crews' (1963) volume, *The Pooh Perplex*, which subjects A. A. Milne's nursery classic to the whole spectrum of interpretations, including 'O Felix Culpa! The Sacramental Meaning of Winnie the Pooh'.

I, too, know the fascination of this game, but it will not concern me tonight. For if we want to make use of art to learn more about the functioning of symbols, we must clearly proceed from the known rather than from the unknown. In fact, I believe that the very pleasures of the symbol hunt have tended to obscure the fact that the vast majority of monuments in our churches and museums do not present this type of riddle. We all recognize the *Statue of Liberty* (Plate 1) without benefit of iconological study, just as we know that if she held a balance instead of a torch, we would call her Justice.

The symbol here would be the mark of identification, not different in principle from a label or a tag. This is indeed the sense of the term we often use when we speak of mathematical symbols or of the symbols used on roadsigns. But if iconology were only concerned with the identification of labels, its psychological interest would be slight. But is it? Not if we follow a different usage that insists that a symbol is more than a sign, whatever 'more' may mean in this context (Castelli, 1958; Knights and Cottle, 1960). This clash over terminology that has much bedevilled discussions is partly due to a divergence of philosophical traditions in Western thought (Bühler, 1934, pp. 185–6). The extension of the term 'symbol' to cover any kind of sign can be traced in the Anglo-Saxon tradition from Hobbes to Pierce, and has led to such coinages as symbolic logic. Against this expansionist tendency, the German Romantics and their French successors (Dieckmann, 1959; Rookmaaker, 1959) stressed the religious connotations of the term and wanted it restricted to those special kinds of signs which stand for something untranslatable and ineffable. It is not my intention to adjudicate between these usages. But I think it might be worthwhile to examine the restrictionists' case in the light of psychology. One of the advantages of the study of art is precisely that it should provide material for such an examination. For it is in the study of art and its history that even the rationalist and agnostic historian has to grapple with the symbol that is called 'more than a sign' because it is felt to be profoundly fitting.

In its most simple way, psychologically, this applies even to the balance of Justice or the torch of Liberty. For these clearly are not just fortuitous identification marks which could be exchanged at will. Their choice is rooted in the same psychological tendency to translate or transpose ideas into images which rules the metaphors of language. It was the idea of *Liberty Enlightening the World* which the Alsatian sculptor Frédéric-Auguste Bartholdi wished to illustrate as a present of the French people to the Americans on the occasion of the first centenary of the Declaration of Independence (Pauli and Ashton, 1948). It was the metaphor of light that suggested the fusion of this image with the beacon or lighthouse – classical antiquity providing a real or fictitious precedent of such a gigantic statue in the *Colossus of Rhodes* representing the sun god, one of the Seven Wonders of the World that lived on in the imagination of the West (Plate 2).

You will not find Bartholdi's name in most histories of nineteenth-century art, and I do not want to make any exaggerated claims for his merits. But in a way the very fact that his name is all but forgotten confirms that the statue has become a real communal symbol, an image that enlists loyalties and mobilizes emotions by itself. It is the symbol arriving passengers crowd to see at New York harbor, not a specimen of nineteenth-century art, or an expression of Bartholdi's personal feelings for his mother, who reputedly posed as his model for the statue. And it is as a symbol that the goddess with the torch held aloft has found her way onto postage stamps and countless similar images. For the spreading of light is a metaphor easily understood as is the balancing of claims that belongs to the Virtue of Justice, or the venomous serpent that belongs traditionally to the Vice of Envy.

The invention of such appropriate emblems or attributes was once a favorite pastime of courtiers and scholars whose job it was to advise the artists on the rendering of these ideas and conceits, and I think we could find no more rapid entry into this strange field than if we imagined ourselves in their company. It need not be virtues or vices we seek to symbolize. It can be anything from an idea to a person. I do indeed remember a parlor game from my childhood of which I was very fond, though I do not think I was particularly good at it. It was a guessing game based on comparisons or metaphors of the wildest kind. We would agree, for instance, that the person to be guessed would be a film star, but you can also play it with victims nearer home, including, for argument's sake, the members of one of your professional committees. The task would be to guess his identity through a series of appropriate emblems or comparisons. The guesser would ask the group in the know such questions as: *If he were a flower, what would he be? Or what would be his emblem as an animal, his symbol among colors, his style among painters? What would he be if he were a dish?* You can imagine what opportunity these questions give to those who are in the know to regress, aggress, or perhaps caress. But the interesting thing is really that provided the field of choice is not too large the task of the guesser is by no means hopeless. Clearly if he started to ask what kind of flower would be the appropriate attribute and were told that it might be a thistle, a whole range of people who are either jovial or shrinking would be ruled out from the start. Should he then be told that among animals his symbol might be a bear, his prickliness would take on a more specific character – very different from the dire possibility of somebody assigning a hyena to that unknown character. If then that bear-and-thistle person is compared among musical forms to a polka rather than a nocturne, there would be another cue to go on.

Clearly the regressive irrationality of these equivalents is no obstacle to their ultimate efficacy as cues. You might indeed compare each of the answers to the indices of letters and numbers on the sides of a very irregular map which combine to plot a position. The psychological category of bear-like creatures sweeps along a wide zone of the metaphorical field, and so does the category of thistly characters, but the two categories are sufficiently distinct to determine an area that can be further restricted by other plottings.

I must leave it to your ingenuity to work out rules and standards of such a game that could be used in a more serious discussion of symbol and metaphor. But some results of such an experiment we can perhaps anticipate. Its interest would not only lie in the frequency of correct scores or guesses, but in the discussions or post-mortems when the guesser has been told the right answer. Sometimes, I remember, we used to say, 'Of course, how silly of me,' but sometimes also there would be violent remonstrations that X could never be a bear, he would surely be rather a wolf. The degree and intensity of assent between players might give you some kind of measure of what we call a common culture. For the conditions of assent are not only similar evaluations of persons; they must include equivalent gamuts of comparisons. Take the illustrations I have chosen. I doubt if they would meet with unqualified assent even here in the American West. I chose the thistle among flowers because it comes to my mind as the prickliest plant – for there are no cacti in Austria where I grew up. Nor is it likely that my bear is your bear – mine, if I examine my mind, is the creature of Aesop's fable; you might easily ask, 'What species of bear?' And as to the polka – the very choice of that cue dates and places me hopelessly and shows that if I were a geometrical shape, I would be a very square square indeed.

One incidental advantage of analysing these post-mortems would be, I think, that we could easily dispose of one of the issues that always come up when symbolism is discussed – the problem of translatability. Those whom I have called restriction-ists always insist that signs are translatable, while the meaning of symbols cannot be put into words. I think this much canvassed distinction rests on a misunderstanding of what is translatable. Even words rarely are. All symbols function within a complex network of matrices and potential choices which can perhaps be explained up to a point, but not translated into exact equivalences unless a happy accident provides one.

You may feel that this discussion of metaphors and matrices has taken us dangerously far away from the use of art for the study of symbols. But in a sense the history of all the arts provides among other things a series of such test performances to which we respond either with incredulity or assent. What else did Elizabethan poets play than the game, *If my mistress were a goddess, which of them would she be?* or, *If my rival were an animal, what would I call him?* Painters could do likewise. The French painter Nattier would paint a rococo beauty in the guise of Hebe, the Olympian waitress who dispenses eternal youth to the Gods (Plate 3), or William Hogarth in eighteenth-century England would portray his critic, Charles Churchill, as a bear clumsily hugging the club of Hercules (Plate 4).

This particular use of metaphor in graphic satire and caricature I have attempted to explore in another paper which grew out of my collaboration with my late friend, Ernst Kris (Gombrich, 1963, pp. 127–42). Today my subject compels me to move nearer to the center of the origins of artistic symbolism, the field of religious art – and most of the art with which we art historians deal is religious in content. I remember overhearing a sophomore at a college who complained about some lectures – they may have been mine – 'It's terrible. The professor shows one Madonna after another.' But it is one of the permanent gains of iconology that we now see why you cannot, for instance, discuss that miraculous achievement of fifteenth-century Flemish realism, *The Adoration of the Lamb* by the brothers van Eyck (Plate 5), without trying to enter into its meaning (Panofsky, 1953). What else, then, is the lamb of God on the altar than a traditional metaphor originally chosen by a culture which could watch every day the difference between the behavior of a lamb or a kid being taken to the altar for slaughter ? Van Eyck's Madonna is, indeed, another such center of symbolic references, for in the cult of the Virgin the link between word and image can best be studied. Her praise is sung in countless hymns and litanies which largely draw their imagery from the Hebrew love songs enshrined in the Bible that were transposed from the profane to the sacred.

Behind van Eyck's Virgin enthroned we can read quotations from these scriptural praises: 'She is fairer than the sun, brighter than all the stars, like the radiance of eternal light, God's mirror without blemish' (Baldass, 1952, p. 272). Clearly the white lilies and red roses of her crown are likewise the traditional metaphors for the Virgin's purity and love (Panofsky, 1953, pp. 446, 448). There are humbler types of devotional images in which all these metaphors and comparisons are literally illustrated and neatly labeled for our contemplation. Plate 6 from a French Book of Hours of 1505 shows the Virgin in the center whom God the Father addresses in the words of the Song of Songs. All around her are the symbols of her praise: *Electa ut sol* (choice as the sun); *pulchra ut luna* (fair as the moon); *porta coeli* (the gate of heaven); *plantatio rosae* (the rose garden); *exaltata cedrus* (the exalted cedar); *virga Jesse floruit* (the rod of Jesse flowered); *puteus aquarum viventium* (the well of living waters); *hortus conclusus* (a garden inclosed) – fully to quote only those on the left side. On the right we still find the star of the sea, the lily among thorns, the fair olive, the tower of David, the mirror without blemish, the fountain of gardens, the city of God (Mâle, 1908, p. 223).

I have chosen this example to remind you that art was once the servant of symbolism and not symbolism the servant of art. The images of the past in our churches and museums were commissioned and fashioned to proclaim the holiness of the supernatural or the greatness of the ruler. It is not easy, perhaps, for the modern psychologist to make this adjustment, for he has learned to look at art in the contemporary context where it serves such different social ends, for instance, as a release of the artist from social pressures or as a status symbol for the collector. In these contexts the overt and interpretable meaning of any painting or sculpture has almost ceased to matter, because what we are asked to assent to is not the metaphor but the claim that 'here is art'. Hence the historian is likely to talk at cross purposes with the esthetician or psychologist if he concentrates on the social meaning of symbols. Yet it was this meaning which once mattered, if images were to form the focus of worship and the reminders of power. And it was the transcending primacy of meaning that led to the importance also of form.

It is one of the stock accusations against the study of symbols in art that it leads to a concentration on content and a disregard of the one thing that matters in art, the beauty and harmony of forms. I would not deny that such traps exist for the unwary, but if many were caught this was due, perhaps, to insufficient analysis rather than to insensitivity. It is those who introduced the distinction between form and content who prepared the trap for themselves and for others. For why should we assume that forms cannot symbolize? Take the two images of the Virgin – clearly the print (Plate 6) is a rather humble product, an accumulation of symbols without great artistic pretensions, while van Eyck's Virgin (Plate 5) is a masterpiece. But is it not a masterpiece precisely also because it commands our assent far beyond the individual symbols of lilies, roses, or rays? 'She is lovelier than the sun,' says the text, and she is. Who ever said that beauty itself could not be a fitting symbol?

We here come across another distinction that has worried the restrictionists. What is characteristic of ordinary sign systems is what Karl Bühler (1934, pp. 42–8) called the principle of abstractive relevance; by this he meant the irrelevance of certain features within sign systems. There are notoriously infinitely many ways of writing the letter 'a', or even of drawing a rose. They will signify the same as long as certain invariant relationships are observed. The same is true of signs such as traffic signs where it is the color that counts and not the shape or height, of flags where the pattern matters but not the size or the material.

Yet even in our utilitarian civilization we pay some regard to our choice of form where ceremonial and solemn occasions preserve more archaic traditions. The flag should be presented and saluted in a worthy manner; we adjust our voice and our vocabulary to a suitable hush or drone when we think that the occasion demands it, and even pay attention to the form of lettering when the meaning of the text seems to preclude a casual scrawl. This exercise of choice from a range of possible tones or forms is usually treated under the heading of expression: we express awe in hushed tones, and our sense of occasion in writing diplomas on imitation parchment. But of course the choice of suitable lettering or material also falls under the category of symbolism, at least if we take this term in the expansionist sense. I remember an advertisement of a duplicating machine for business circulars which recommended its products on the very valid ground that each copy would look like a top copy, a personal letter. Every recipient should thus feel flattered at this sign or symbol of respect – though by now the trick is so general that it annoys more than it pleases.

It is clear, once more, why such a sign that is reinforced by its shape and material cannot be translated into a mere word, even less so, than can other words. You can type out a copy of a diploma, but you cannot even translate the true meaning of imitation parchment into discursive speech – for the exact relevance of its choice depends on a whole cluster of associations or potential contexts.

What is marginal and even occasionally comical as a survival in our civilization presents for the historian the true soil from which grew what we call art. In closed societies which are still ruled by awe it is a matter of course that the symbols of faith and power must not be profaned by unworthy presentation. We all remember how the holiness of the text leads to the elaboration of the script and that proliferating richness of initials we admire in medieval art. For the holy only the most precious may serve, and only the greatest care and love can fashion the vessel for such an awesome content. It is not, I believe, an illicit expansion of meaning if we call beauty here a symbol of divinity and power – nor need we worry too much in this context what is meant by beauty; we can take the medieval definition *quod visum placet* (what delights the eyes) and assume that glowing colors, sparkling jewels and intricate symmetries meet that definition. For one of the uses of art for the study of symbols is precisely the possibility of testing the assertion that such an idea of beauty is fairly widespread and occurs independently in various cultures. It is true that in the symbols of religion and power this visual aspect is much reinforced by the knowledge that the material is precious and the workmanship rare and expensive. There is an element of sacrifice here, and also of sheer display of wealth in what is called conspicuous waste. Gold shows this confluence of meanings which makes it the natural choice for the rendering of the divine, for its radiance is not only pleasing and precious, but also the nearest approximation to light, that widespread metaphor for the good and the holy (Gombrich, 1963, pp. 15–16). It is true, also, that certain cultures recognize a degree of holiness that must not even be profaned by these tributes. The real name of God must not even be written in letters of gold. It is here that the symbol sometimes rejects the services of art, but for our present context this is a marginal problem. For wherever art does enter the service of symbolism, the division between content, form, and material becomes artificial.

If God is thus represented on van Eyck's altar-piece (Plate 5) in regal and priestly splendor as a dignified man with the papal crown, it is clearly impossible to separate the content of the symbol from the manner of its presentation. To van Eyck and his sponsors the doctrine was clear that God is not a man with a beard, but that among all sensible things of which man can have experience here on earth, a beautiful and dignified fatherly ruler of infinite splendor is the most fitting metaphor our mind can grasp (Anthropomorphism, 1913). The Church warns the faithful not to take any of these symbols literally but only as sensible analogues to higher meanings. The esthetician and the psychologist might do worse than study the implications of this doctrine from their own points of view. For they seem to me superior to the traditional approach which scrutinizes symbols for the degree of likeness they exhibit with the so-called referent or *denotatum*. This likeness, or 'iconicity', is supposed to allow us to regard the symbol as a representative or a presentation of what it signifies (Langer, 1942; Morris, 1946; Schaper, 1964). Theology, if I understand its doctrines aright, asks us to consider only that a dignified man is perhaps the least unlike experience of the divine we mortals are able to select among a gamut of possible choices. But is this not true of all symbolization? We call van Eyck's paintings 'iconic signs' of gold, pearls and radiance, but even the painter's magic skill in representation only succeeds because he selects from his limited medium of ground pigments those mixtures that most closely approximate the appearance of light and of sparkle.

I must be careful here, for I am moving dangerously close to the subject of my book on *Art and Illusion* (Gombrich, 1960), which I do not want to harp upon. But I think that the problem under discussion is in a way the obverse, the mirror image of the question I tried to tackle in that book. There I aimed at drawing attention to the fact that all so-called representations or iconic signs are in need of interpretation, and that we are too easily misled into taking this problem for granted. We say this is a seascape, or this the image of a man, without often pausing to ask how we know and what this implies. Where ordinary symbolism is concerned, as I said, we may sometimes have neglected the opposite procedure. We have concentrated on problems of interpretation and have still to explore the potential value to us of works of art of which we know the meaning. How far, for instance, is van Eyck's formal treatment of the figure of God the Father (Plate 5) here typical of symbols of highest power? For of course it is not only the splendor that distinguishes this figure from others, but also its stillness, its frontality, all the formal characteristics which we experience as hieratic – a word that really derives from *hieros*, holy. Even a medium which cannot represent splendor in the way van Eyck's technique allowed him to do can symbolize the holy through this hieratic symmetry and immobility – whether you think of the fresco of the *Trinity* by Masaccio, another of the great pioneers of realism, or of a humble French woodcut of the next generation (Plate 7). Indeed, the meaning of this rigid immobility is so obvious in its context that it seems redundant to spell it out.

I have been sometimes taken to task by critics and estheticians for operating too freely with the concept of understanding a work of art (Stolnitz, 1964). I was even accused of equating the word 'understanding' with that translation into conceptual terms that leads away from the artistic quality of the work. But this is far from my intention. On the contrary, I would think that it is only through art that some of us can still recapture the meaning of certain symbols and understand their import as well as their translatable significance. As a historian, I also know that this confidence is sometimes misplaced. Even forms and colors depend on contexts and traditions in their meaning, and what strikes us as hieratic in one context may have lacked distinctive significance in another style where all figures are rigid. It is for this reason that our attempts to stand in front of a slide and explain or evoke the confluence of meanings are bound to look artificial. But this technical difficulty does not diminish my conviction that we can become so familiar with a given idiom of form that we understand and appreciate the artist's choice. Even the agnostic historian can thus learn what the symbols of religion once meant to the community. Most people who have been to Chartres share this conviction. It is not an irrational one.

Let me try to substantiate this bold claim by an illustration from the realm of music. Countless composers through the ages have written liturgical music, notably Masses in which the recital of the creed forms a central part. Once more the meaning of the words, the interpretation of the symbolism presents no problem to the historian. But it is precisely because this meaning and context is so rigidly determined that a study of these compositions conveys to us something of the meaning the text has for the faithful. I recommend to those of you who like music a systematic comparison of how such great masters as Bach, Haydn, Mozart and Beethoven develop and orchestrate the identical words of the creed. How they select from the range of available sounds, harmonies and rhythms strains of hieratic majesty to reinforce and elucidate the words *Credo in unum Deum*; how frequently contrapuntal and intellectual complexities appear in the composition of the dogmatic assertion about the Second Person of the Trinity being 'begotten, not made, and consubstantial with the Father'; and how the character of the music changes to tenderness and sweetness with the words 'who for us men and for our salvation came down from heaven' introducing the central mystery: 'and was incarnate by the Holy Ghost of the Virgin Mary.' These

159

words often call forth the most unexpected and mysterious resources of the master's style. The sorrow of the passion, the silence of the entombment, the jubilation of the resurrection are all expected to be reflected in the music, and so they are in a very precise sense.

Reflecting can here mean any number of devices – from the tradition of using an ascending scale to depict Christ's ascension to the mysterious sounds in the archaic Dorian mode that Beethoven uses in the *Missa Solemnis* to proclaim the miracle of the Incarnation. Here as often our terminology shifts between the music depicting or expressing the meaning of the words, but I have always felt it might be better to reserve the term 'expression' for the spontaneous symptoms that indicate an emotion. It is a commonplace of esthetics that the confusion of these two levels has wrought havoc in critical discussion. The composer's mood and even his innermost beliefs are private and for ever inaccessible to us. What we understand is not him, but his work, his choice, that is, of musical metaphors that reflect the majesty of the *Sanctus* or the sweetness of the *Benedictus* to all who have learned to assess the significance of his choices. And whatever the private beliefs of either the composer or the listener, the music can still convey the untranslatable meaning of the text.

Would the sound alone carry the meaning? Surely this is a wrong question. Not every ascending scale means the ascension of Christ; it only can mean it in the appropriate context. The classic formulation for the art of poetry here comes from Pope's *Essay on Criticism* that sums up the wisdom of an old critical tradition (Gombrich, 1960, ch. 11): *The sound must seem an echo to the sense;* an echo, not a carrier.

Let me quote you the whole stanza that both teaches and demonstrates this doctrine:

> 'Tis not enough no harshness gives offence,
> The sound must seem an echo to the sense:
> Soft is the strain when Zephyr gently blows,
> And the smooth stream in smoother numbers flows;
> But when loud surges lash the sounding shore,
> The hoarse, rough verse should like the torrent roar.
> When Ajax strives some rock's vast weight to throw
> The line, too, labours, and the words move slow...

The speed of the verse is slowed down by deliberate phonetic obstacles, and so it reflects or underscores the meaning of the words where the hero hurls the heavy rock; the liquid consonants depicting and denoting the smooth stream stand in obvious contrast to the tongue twisters describing the storm.

The sound alone, of course, does not do this unaided. Read the verse to anyone who does not know English and all he will hear is an even stream of gibberish. I know, for I was once the unwilling subject of such an experiment when a Hungarian friend of mine recited to me reams of his favorite native poetry because he thought their pure sound alone would delight me. Had I understood the discursive symbols, I might also have grasped the way the sound echoed the sense. It just does not work the other way round.

I believe the study of known symbols in artistic contexts, be they in painting, music or poetry, might indeed elucidate to the psychologist what forms, colors, rhythms, or sounds are felt to go with what meanings. They might direct his attention to the old doctrine of *decorum* which is precisely concerned with the search of such fitting or appropriate matches.

It is still my conviction that such an investigation would tend to confirm Osgood's idea of what he calls the semantic differential. That it would be possible in principle to plot gamuts of color, or sound, or of shapes along the coordinates of Osgood's semantic space with its dimensions of active and passive, good and bad, potent and weak, though we may find in the process that the convenience of three dimensions is rather too dearly bought and that his coordinates do not necessarily represent the optimal way of plotting all feeling tones. There may be other ways in which the study of artistic symbols might draw attention to features neglected in Osgood's (Osgood, Suci and Tannenbaum, 1957) classic study on *The Measurement of Meaning*. One of them is precisely the relation between sound and sense in our reaction to words. In his original study, at any rate, Osgood asked his subjects to plot ideas on his 7-point scales to find, as you remember, whether snow is more wise than foolish or sin more opaque than transparent. I am sure I am not the first to wonder whether the actual sound of the word does not influence this rating. What you call a truck is called a lorry in England. I would propose the hypothesis that a truck would be rated as heavier, darker, more active, but less friendly than a lorry, which to me conveys something slightly lighter, brighter, and a bit less efficient than the dark, sharp, monosyllabic truck.

Whatever the fate of my particular hypothesis, the consensus of artists and critics is strong that artistic media are all potentially suitable to reflect or echo the sense, however vaguely and in whatever indeterminate a form. For indeterminacy, as we see by now, is no obstacle. One form or sound might prove an appropriate echo to several meanings and command assent among the participants of the game.

For surely Osgood's findings can be fitted quite effortlessly into that guessing game I described and that we might now call 'multiple matrix matching'. You remember, after all, that it was not only matrices from the world of things that could be used as cues or pointers – animals, flowers or dishes – but also colors, shapes, sounds or tastes. None of these, of course, can be said to have an intrinsic meaning, but they can interact through their very multiplicity and generate meaning within suitably narrow contexts.

In referring to an interaction of independent matrices, I am alluding to the terminology recently advocated by Arthur Koestler (1964) in his wide-ranging book on *The Act of Creation*. I am not sure I can agree with Koestler in his generalizations which subsume every artistic or scientific discovery under this type of fusion. I am more interested in my present context in the effect of such fusions on the beholder, the receiver of this multiple kind of message. For remember, in the work of art the matrices are not neatly separated for stepwise decoding as they were in our guessing game. They are telescoped and condensed into one. The effect of this simultaneity can be dramatic. The sudden deflection of attention from one level of meaning to another creates a shock which is certainly worth investigating in psychological terms. The most suggestive treatment of this question I have come across is an article by Ulric Neisser (1963). Basing himself on his work with computers, the author proposes to replace some of the older distinctions between mental activities by the two types of information processing he calls sequential and multiple processing. Ordinarily, he writes, there is a main sequence in progress in human thought, dealing with some particular material in step-by-step fashion. The main sequence corresponds to the ordinary course of consciousness, consciousness being intrinsically single. But this main sequential operation of what might be called logical thought is normally accompanied by a complex orchestration of multiple operations which are, in the nature of things, infinitely richer though less precise than the well-focused sequential process. Neisser discusses the difficulty of multiple response or multiple conscious activity, and proposes fields of research. Maybe he would find the study of art of some use. For consider Pope's advice that the sound should prove an echo to the sense in its most precise application – the simple punning device of onomatopoeic sound painting. Take the way Ovid, in the *Metamorphoses*, tells the story of the wicked peasants who refused a refuge to the pregnant Latona, the mother of Apollo and Diana, and who were turned into frogs as a punishment. 'But even under water,' Ovid ends his tale, 'they still try to curse' (*Quamvis sint sub aqua, sub aqua maledicere tentant*). We have been following the main sequence and focusing our conscious attention on the meaning of the words which step by step unfold the story. Suddenly one of the words not only signifies along the main sequence, it also paints the sound of the quacking; we are hit, as it were, from an unexpected angle; the word becomes transparent, and we hear the frogs quacking. If you want a high-sounding term for this humble sound you might call it 'extrasystemic redundancy' – redundancy being normally confined to the channel of communication to which we are asked to attend, we suddenly get this whiff of immediate confirmation from an unexpected direction. Multiplicity is mobilized and forced into consciousness with all that feeling of richness and elusiveness that goes with the abandonment of the main sequence. We are a little closer, I hope, to a psychological account of the experience of the ineffable that the restrictionists claim to be the hallmark of symbol: the feeling that it is more than a sign, because it vouchsafes us a glimpse into vistas of meaning beyond the reach of convention and logic.

I have once before in this context quoted the passage from the first page of Dickens' novel, *Great Expectations* (Gombrich, 1948), but I still know of no better description of this dreamlike and regressive attitude to signs than this masterly evocation:

As I never saw my father or my mother, and never saw any likeness of either of them (for their days were long before the days of photographs), my first fancies regarding what they were like, were unreasonably derived from their tombstones. The shape of the letters on my father's gave me an odd idea that he was a square, stout, dark man, with curly black hair . . .

It is almost a pity, is it not, to dissect this convincing account of a child's imaginings, but all we need say, perhaps, is that the child experienced the conventional signs as profound. Remember Bühler's principle of abstractive relevance. Ordinary letters just do not signify beyond their meaning as letters, at least they are not ordinarily used to portray what they name. Hence, in dealing with letters, the grown-up person of our culture hardly attends to their shape or font. We may shut a book and not know what font it was printed in, though we may have scanned thousands of characters. Jerome Bruner (1957) has called this principle of economy in ordinary perceptual situations the mechanism of 'gating'. Where we cannot derive more information or do not need it, we shut the gates and go on to other business. I would guess that gating is a typical operation of what Neisser calls the 'main sequence', the sequential process of logical thought. Dickens' child hero would not and could not gate; he could not accept what one of Bühler's students, Julius Klanfer in an unpublished Vienna dissertation, aptly called the sign limit. The sign or symbol must yield the information he so desperately needs, something of the appearance and looks of his father whom he never saw. For of course it is not any configuration of letters to which the child responds in this regressive way, but the most important symbol in his little universe, his father's name.

I suppose it could be argued that what we call the esthetic response in front of works of art involves a certain refusal to gate. The image is open, as it were, and we are free to look for further and further echoes of the sense in an indeterminate level of sound or form. But of course this refusal is only a relative one. We all can distinguish between sanity and insanity in criticism – or at least we hope we can. There are the constraints of tradition, of medium, of genre, and of culture that apply reins to the historian's and the critic's fancy. He knows, or thinks he knows, that the Grand Pyramid does not embody in its measurements a compendium of the world's subsequent history, that Shakespeare's plays are not to be read as cyphers referring to the authorship of Francis Bacon, and that Jerome Bosch's paintings are not cryptograms of a nudist sect, of which the existence in his time and city has never been documented (Bax, 1956). No doubt his insistence on these and similar sign limits makes him something of a spoilsport. For where should we be allowed to dream if not in front of works of art? We may grant these critics that the intensity of the experience is not necessarily proportionate to the clarity of understanding. In fact, we know that the archaic, the remote, the unintelligible even, exerts a fascination all of its own because we are not tied to any sequential discipline. Historically, it may well be true that it was the images and symbols of which the true meaning was forgotten that most aroused the imagination. That marvelous tag from Tacitus, *Omne ignotum pro magnifico*, applies certainly to the study of symbols.

The most handy example here is the impression made by the symbols and images of ancient Egypt, once their true significance had been lost in the mists of the past. The Greeks and Romans, no less than their heirs in the Renaissance, were convinced that the weird images known as hieroglyphs, that is as sacred signs, contained some deep revelation that the Egyptian priests had recorded in esoteric fashion (Gombrich, 1948).

What is interesting to the psychologist in this particular episode is the attempt to rationalize the faith in the profundity of these signs. Marsilio Ficino, the influential Neoplatonic philosopher of the Renaissance, writes that it was for a profound reason that the Egyptian priests chose images rather than individual letters when writing of divine mysteries, for God has knowledge of things not through a multiplicity of cognitive steps, but as an integral and immutable idea. It is in this context that Ficino introduces what might be called the paradigm of all mystical symbols, the serpent biting its own tail (Plate 8). For this image which stands for time can tell us in a flash what discursive argument could only enumerate, such as the proposition that time is swift, that time in its turning somehow joins the beginning to the end, that it teaches wisdom, and brings and removes things.

I am not sure that I understand all these propositions and

many more which the mystic wants to find in the enigmatic image that has been handed down to him as a key to revelation (Boas, 1950).

But at least it is easy to see the connexion between this attitude and Neisser's multiple processes. In contemplating this particular image, of course, sequential thought is baffled to distraction when it tries to think its implication to the end. Start with the head and follow the feed of the serpent which devours its own body, and you will soon come to the impasse of what happens when it reaches its own neck.

It is this kind of paradox that is to spur the mystic on to transcend the limits of logic and ascend to a realm where the law of contradiction no longer applies. In this respect, the mystical symbol differs from the artistic symbol. Its principle might perhaps be described as that of deliberate dissonance against that consonance of meanings I tried to elucidate in the artist's treatment of the sign. The mystic's sign is often monstrous, abstruse, dissonant and perhaps even repellent because it wants to proclaim that the true ineffable mystery lies beyond it, not in it. It is not a sensuous analogue, but a challenge to leave the world of the senses. Its inadequacy as an image is a guarantee of its divinity.

It is this conception of the symbol that was taken over by the Romantic philosophy of art. Characteristically, its adoption was due to a student of ancient myth and religion, Friedrich Creuzer, whose approach stems in direct line from the Neoplatonic interpretation of hieroglyphs (Dieckmann, 1959). To Creuzer, writing around 1800, the mysterious and remote images of most ancient civilizations were such adumbrations of the mystery – groping, perhaps, in their esoteric monstrosity, but charged with profound meaning which challenged our understanding. It was Creuzer who first contrasted this early and mystical approach to the divine with the artistic triumph of Greece which Winckelmann, the prophet of eighteenth-century classicism, had taught him to see as a true act of artistic incarnation – the creation of visible shapes for the gods. For Creuzer and his contemporaries a statue such as the *Apollo Belvedere* (Plate 9) is more than a symbol of the sun god; it is a manifestation or realization of the god in human shape, a true find and fitting symbol that commands assent among all right-minded people.

Creuzer's distinction gained currency through its embodiment in Hegel's esthetics. In Hegel's view of history as a dialectical progress upwards, the Egyptian sphinx represents the enigmatic and inadequate symbol of the mystics, the Greek god the true consonance of form and meaning, while the Christian faith leads again to a divorce between the two. I am not known as a particular friend of Hegel's constructions, but I happen to think that there is something interesting in this distinction. Not that the images of the ancient Orient really correspond to Hegel's Romantic conception of the inadequate symbol, but it is true, I believe, that the classic conception of art is incompatible with the mystical symbol, its aim being the consonance of meanings. The tradition that started in Greece looked for the open sign where, perhaps, it can indeed be found, in the expressiveness of the human physiognomy. Not that our fellow beings are to us like open books, but we do look at the human countenance and gesture without gating, and feel that the sensuous and the meaningful can here for once be fused into an indissoluble unit (Gombrich, 1963, pp. 45–55). Thus the classical conception of art replaced the serpent by the god. In the painting and sculpture of this tradition, symbolization thus merges with characterization. When a Renaissance handbook for artists recommends a symbol for time it translates the concept into a personification of 'Old Father Time' (Plate 10); the symbol of the serpent only survives as his identification mark (Panofsky, 1939, ch. 3).

Perhaps Hegel was not even so far from the truth when he sensed the impermanence of this solution. For if it is ever true that familiarity breeds contempt, it is in this field of art. The perfectly characterized human symbol may lack precisely that strangeness that proclaims its transcendent meaning. Thus attempts were not lacking during the Renaissance and after to import the mystical conception of the dissonant symbol into art; but however interesting these complexities are for the iconologist, artistically they remained rather barren.

And yet, as you know, art has increasingly shied away from the consonant and satisfying to exploit the challenge of the enigmatic, the contradictory and unresolved for its own psychological ends. What it thus loses in clarity it hopes to gain in richness, in that plenitude of meaning that embodies all the ambiguities and ambivalences that orchestrate our experience.

It is thus, perhaps, no accident that the idea or conception of the symbol that conquered twentieth-century psychology and criticism derived through Romanticism from the mystical tradition of dissonance. There is indeed a line that links Freud's use of the term in the *Interpretation of Dreams* with the Romantic tradition of Schubert and Volkelt, and with the approach of German culture historians to the symbols of myth and anthropology.

Remember that Freud's dream symbols are also enigmatic, monstrous and opaque; they are in fact the masks that our unconscious wishes must don in order to pass the censor; their meaning is only accessible to the initiated. What they share with the mystic tradition is not only their character as revelations of an otherwise unknowable realm. Like their predecessors, they also embody the irrational, antilogical character of that realm where contradictions are fused and meanings are merged. The plenitude of meaning of each symbol is practically infinite in its overdetermination which excludes the idea of a sign limit. It is free association, not meditation, which will reveal to the dreamer these infinite layers of significance behind the apparent absurdity of the manifest content.

There is no difficulty, however, in subsuming Freud's concepts of symbolism under the ancient idea of metaphor. If you accept my formulation that the symbol represents the choice from a given set of matrices of what is least unlike the referent to be represented, that variety of objects which can stand for sexual organs or acts need cause us no surprise. The set or matrix in Freud is of course frequently the memory traces of recent conscious impressions which stand in the foreground of the manifest dream content and both represent and mask its deeper meaning – deeper here standing for another matrix closer to biological functions and drives.

There is no doubt that Freud's discoveries have enabled us to look deeper both into the consonance and the dissonance of multiple meanings that interlink in the structure of artistic symbols. They have allowed us to push the sign limit even further back, to ask fresh questions about the motives that made man select certain metaphors rather than others and to divine the reasons that make for the unconscious appeal of certain forms; they have added a fourth dimension to the semantic space whose depth has not, perhaps, been plumbed by Osgood's workers.

But as far as I can see, Freud nowhere encouraged or sanctioned the view that it is this dimension that presents the true or essential meaning of art. On the contrary, his whole conception of art and of culture postulated the fusion of this matrix with overt and communal meanings. He, less than anybody, welcomed a development that made the dream symbol into the standard of art. For he was convinced of its unintelligibility to all who had no access to the dreamer's associations (Gombrich, 1960, p. 31).

It was only in the system of Carl Gustav Jung that the Freudian conception of the symbol regressed, as it were, to its origins in Neoplatonic mysticism. This is achieved, if I understand these dark matters, by fusing the transcendent realm of religious traditions with the ineffable content of the collective unconscious that talks to us in riddles – but riddles for which the key is somehow provided (Jacobi, 1959).

The more one studies these mystical interpretations, the more one is struck by the unwillingness of man to accept the human condition which is grounded in the use of signs. The longing for immediacy, the faith in some direct communion with other minds, if not with spiritual beings, manifests itself in that leap across the sign limit that promises escape from the fetters of reason.

As a rationalist, I do not believe in this escape road, but I do not think that any psychological study of art can be worth its salt that cannot somehow account for this experience of revelation through profundity. I do not pretend that I have done that tonight, or that I shall be able to do it tomorrow; but I hope I have convinced you that if we are to make progress in this direction, we must not neglect the historical dimension; we must remember that art, as we know it, did not begin its career as self-expression, but as a search for metaphors commanding assent among those who wanted the symbols of their faith to make visible the invisible, who looked for the message of the mystery. Nobody who remembers the enigmatic hieroglyphs of our contemporary art can overlook the continued force of this longing. But to probe the use of that art for the study of symbols, you do not need to call in a historian.

Cognition and Interpretation

References

ANTHROPOMORPHISM (1913), in *Catholic Encyclopedia*, Encyclopedia Press, vol. 1, pp. 558–9.

BALDASS, L. (1952), *van Eyck*, Phaidon Press.

BAX, D. (1956), 'Het Tuin der Onkuisheiddrieluik van Jeroen Bosch gevolgd door Kritiek op Fraenger', *Verhandelingen der Koninklijke Nederlandse Akademie van Wetenschappen, Letterkunde*, Amsterdam, new series, part 63, 2, pp. 1–208.

BOAS, G. (ed. and trans.) (1950), *The Hieroglyphics of Horapollo*, Pantheon.

BRUNER, J. S. (1957), 'On perceptual readiness', *Psychol. Rev.*, vol. 64, pp. 123–52.

BÜHLER, K. (1934), *Sprachtheorie*, Fischer, Jena.

CASTELLI, E. (ed.) (1958), *Umanesimo e Simbolismo*, Milanesi, Padua.

CREWS, F. C. (1963), *The Pooh Perplex*, Dutton.

DIECKMANN, L. (1959), 'Friedrich Schlegel and Romantic concepts of the symbol', *Germanic Review*.

GOMBRICH, E. H. (1948), 'Icones symbolicae', *J. Warburg Courtauld Instits.*, vol. 11, pp. 163–92.

GOMBRICH, E. H. (1960), *Art and Illusion*, Pantheon.

GOMBRICH, E. H. (1963), *Meditations on a Hobby Horse*, Phaidon Press.

JACOBI, J. (1959), *Complex, Archetype, Symbol*, Pantheon.

KNIGHTS, L. C., and COTTLE, B. (eds.) (1960), *Metaphor and Symbol*, Butterworths.

KOESTLER, A. (1964), *The Act of Creation*, Hutchinson.

LANGER, S. K. (1942), *Philosophy in a New Key*, Harvard University Press.

MÂLE, E. (1908), *L'Art Religieux de la Fin du Moyen Âge en France*, Colin, Paris.

MORRIS, C. (1946), *Signs, Language and Behavior*, Prentice-Hall.

NEISSER, U. (1963), 'The multiplicity of thought', *Brit. J. Psychol.*, vol. 54, pp. 1–14.

OSGOOD, C. E., SUCI, G. J., and TANNENBAUM, P. H. (1957), *The Measurement of Meaning*, University of Illinois Press.

PAULI, H., and ASHTON, E. B. (1948), *I Lift my Lamp: The Way of a Symbol*, Appleton-Century.

PANOFSKY, E. (1939), *Studies in Iconology*, Oxford University Press.

PANOFSKY, E. (1953), *Early Netherlandish Painting*, Harvard University Press.

ROOKMAAKER, H. R. (1959), *Synthesist Art Theories*, Swets and Zeitlinger, Amsterdam.

SCHAPER, E. (1964), 'The art symbol', *Brit. J. Aesthet.*, vol. 4, pp. 228–39.

STOLNITZ, J. (1964), 'Review of E. H. Gombrich, *Meditations on a Hobby Horse*', *Brit. J. Aesthet.*, vol. 4, pp. 271–4.

7 I. L. Child

Personality Correlates of Esthetic Judgement in College
Students

I. L. Child, 'Personality correlates of esthetic judgement in college students',
Journal of Personality, vol. 33 (1965), pp. 476–511.

Esthetic judgement is used here as in a previous paper (Child,
1964) to mean the extent to which, when a person judges the
esthetic value of works of art, his judgements agree with an appropriate external standard of their esthetic value. The external
standard used here is provided by the judgement of experts.

Many hypotheses about esthetics, whether stated in philosophical or psychological terms, would suggest that esthetic
judgement should be related to other personality characteristics.
Observational test of these hypotheses should make an important contribution to scientific study of esthetic value.

Method

Subjects

Ss for this study were 138 young men, one a graduate student
and the rest undergraduates at Yale University. They were obtained as paid Ss for a psychological research project described as
concerned with personality and preferences, some through a
bulletin board used mainly to secure Ss for experiments connected with elementary psychology courses and some through the
student employment bureau. Opportunity to earn money appeared to be the main incentive, but interest in taking part in
psychological research was probably significant for many. Most
Ss did not know that their reactions to art were to be investigated;
but since the research continued through a considerable period of
time, some may have signed up after learning from others that it
was concerned with reactions to art. Thus the samples may be
somewhat biased in the direction of including an above-normal
number of students with a definite interest in art.

Procedure

Each *S* made an appointment for the first of two evening group sessions. This first session, three hours in length, was followed, generally one week later, by a second group session. In signing up, each student also committed himself to participate at a later time in a single hour's individual session, ordinarily conducted within a week or two after the second group session. In the group sessions the students were given various tests and questionnaires, and these were supplemented in the individual session by some procedures which could be administered to only one person at a time.

At the beginning of the first group session the students were informed that the research was especially concerned with reactions to art and with aptitudes, skills and other characteristics that might be related to those reactions. They were told that the research was concerned with generalizations about variables and that all the information obtained about them as individuals would be used in a manner to guarantee anonymity.

Measures of esthetic judgement

The measure of esthetic judgement was suggested by that of the English esthetician Margaret Bulley (1951). As used here, the method consisted of presenting pairs of works of art in the form of projected slides, with the *S* instructed to attempt to judge 'which of the two works of art is better esthetically – that is, is the better work of art.' The *S* was asked to express an esthetic judgement of his own if he had one; if he had no such judgement, then he was to judge which of the two works of art must be the one a group of experts agreed to be the better.

The pairs of slides in this study were especially prepared. A number of assistants, mostly graduate students in art or history of art but some older people with a background in art, selected the pairs. They were instructed to form pairs of works of art, the two works to be of the same subject matter or type and if possible also of the same style, but yet in the opinion of the selector to differ decidedly in esthetic value. To prevent the initial pairs from representing the esthetic judgement of only one or a few people, diversity among the selectors was sought within the limits necessarily imposed by the fact that they were all obtained in a brief period in a single community. Pairs were selected by twenty-four people altogether, including people from widely scattered places of origin; about a third of the pairs, however, was selected by a single full-time assistant.

All pairs selected and made into slides were then shown to fourteen judges who each independently indicated which work in each pair they considered to be better. These judges were mostly students in the School of Art at Yale; some were graduate students in history of art, and some were older people in the New Haven area with similar qualifications. Their judgements were made quite rapidly; each pair was projected on a screen for only about 20 seconds, and the judgement had to be recorded within this time. Of about 3360 pairs prepared and judged, there were about 1270 on which the fourteen judges were unanimous or only one or two judges disagreed with the original selector. Out of these pairs, 120 were chosen at random to constitute a relatively easy test of esthetic judgement.

On this test, items were scored for agreement with evaluation by the expert judges, yielding scores which ranged from 44 to 104 out of 120 possible agreements, with a mean of 74. The alpha coefficient was $0 \cdot 87$; this is an estimate of the mean of all possible split-half reliability coefficients (Cronbach, 1951) and indicates very satisfactory reliability.

Results are generally based on 138 cases. For some variables, as will be indicated, fewer cases are available. The principal reason is the introduction partway through the study of a more difficult test of esthetic judgement consisting of 120 pairs on which the expert judges were not so well agreed. In order to include this measure within an unchanged testing time, some other measures had to be dropped. The difficult test turned out to have a much lower alpha coefficient ($0 \cdot 45$) than the easier test and to correlate with the latter highly enough ($+0 \cdot 75$) to suggest it may not be measuring anything different. Results obtained with it are available for anyone interested (Child, 1962b), but will not be reported here.

Hypotheses, Measures and Results

Background in art

It is hard to imagine a plausible explanation of variation in esthetic judgement which would not lead one to expect that esthetic judgement would be positively correlated with amount of background in art. The principal reason for measuring background in art, therefore, is to permit statistical control of it.

Assessment of background in art was made through an interview conducted at the end of the individual session with each *S*. For the first fifty-nine *S*s the interview was somewhat variable because several interviewers were involved and attention was given primarily to standardizing other procedures in the individual session. The last seventy-nine *S*s were all interviewed by one person who followed a very uniform plan of inquiry. The interview was always recorded in writing, as nearly verbatim as possible, while it was being conducted.

After all interviews had been completed, two judges working independently read these records and rated four background variables, listed in Table 1. Some variables could not be rated for some of the early *S*s. Table 1 shows the intercorrelations of these variables (each measured by pooled ratings of the two judges), and in the diagonal appears the interjudge correlation for each variable. The number of *S*s for whom each variable was rated is given in the right-hand column.

The correlations of these variables with the measure of esthetic judgement are also given in Table 1; these correlations are all positive, and two are very high. Esthetic judgement is very substantially correlated with amount of formal education in art and with amount of experience looking at art in galleries, books and magazines. It is significantly correlated, but not very highly, with pursuit of art-related hobbies such as sketching, sculpting, or photography with some art-related interest, and with family attitude toward art. The multiple correlation of esthetic judgement with all four background variables together is $+0.59$.

These findings give no satisfactory basis for estimating the relative importance of various causal influences that might underlie them. The one background variable least under the individual's control, family attitude toward art, shows the smallest correlation

Table 1

Intercorrelations of Background Variables (in the Diagonal, Interjudge Correlations Corrected by the Spearman–Brown Formula) and Relation to Esthetic Judgement

	1	2	3	4	Esthetic judgement	N
1. Education in art	0·89	0·57	0·42	0·22	0·49**	138
2. Experience in galleries, etc.		0·89	0·46	0·36	0·49**	138
3. Art-related hobbies			0·86	0·26	0·21*	126
4. Family attitude toward art				0·88	0·18*	132

*$= P < 0·05$ (i.e. probability is less than 0·05 that so large a correlation, either positive or negative, would occur by chance if true correlation is zero).

**$= P < 0·01$

with esthetic judgement. This would suggest that the higher correlations are largely produced by the fact that the esthetic judgement score and amount of background are both influenced by degree of basic esthetic sensitivity and interest; but this evidence is not very substantial. What the Ss said in the interviews, however, does make it very clear that background in art is obtained partly through a person's own initiative and is thus a product of, as well as an influence on, his esthetic sensitivity and interest in art. At the extreme, for example, one student reported that he seeks out art galleries in any city he visits, while another who lives in a suburb of New York City said that he had never been to an art gallery because there are none near his home.

For every relation between esthetic judgement and any variable described in later sections the effect of statistical control of these four art background variables by the technique of partial correlation has been looked at. Application of statistical control here runs the risk of eliminating much of the true relation between variables. This is likely in so far as visits to galleries, art courses, etc., have been chosen or avoided because of prior characteristics, rather than being formative influences imposed upon the individual by external forces. Hence priority will be given to the simple correlation between esthetic judgement and each of the other variables; the partial correlation (with the four measures of art background controlled) will be given afterward in all instances where it is relevant because of being appreciably larger or smaller than the simple correlation.[1]

Skill in perception of visual form

The hypothesis explored here is that esthetic judgement in the visual arts depends in part upon skill in perception of visual form. For this purpose several tests were used which seem to challenge a person to perceive visual form under conditions making it difficult for him to do so.

Four tests – Dotted Outlines, Hidden Digits, Mutilated Words, and Picture Perception – were adapted in an identical manner from the tests Thurstone (1944) describes under these names. His stimuli were used, but they were projected on a screen at a group session for 15 seconds each, with the S recording his own response. These tests call for seeing a letter, number, word or simple picture despite fragmentation of its form or blending of its elements into a diffuse field of similar elements. The score for each of these tests was the number of items for which a correct percept was given.

A Hidden Figures test was drawn directly from Thurstone's monograph, except that a speed measure was added by having the fast Ss write down the time at which they finished. This test requires the S to search in a complex geometrical pattern for a simple pattern presented separately and also embedded within the complex pattern. Speed was so highly correlated with number correct that the two were pooled to yield a single score. Number of incorrect responses was treated as a separate score as was the number of odd, grotesquely wrong responses.

Finally, the Psychological Corporation Test of Spatial Relations was used, with the time limit reduced from 30 to 15 minutes so that few would finish. The fact that this test requires 3-dimensional understanding of 2-dimensional representation is what made it desirable to include in this section, even though it

1. The partial correlation may also differ from the simple one because of difference of sample; all four measures of art background are available for only 122 out of the total 138 Ss, and the partial coefficients are calculated for only these 122 Ss. While the simple coefficients were calculated for these 122 Ss, it does not seem worthwhile to present them here.

may be more a test of imagery manipulation than of perception. Two measures were used: number of correct and number of incorrect responses.

The relation of all these measures to esthetic judgement is shown in Table 2. The two correlations contrary to prediction,

Table 2
Relation of Esthetic Judgement to Skill in Perception of Visual Form

Perceptual measure	Correlation with esthetic judgement	
	Simple N = 138	Art background controlled N = 122
Dotted outlines	+0·04	+0·01
Hidden digits	+0·07	−0·06
Mutilated words	+0·06	−0·04
Picture perception	+0·22*	+0·18
Hidden figures: speed and number correct	(−0·03)	(−0·01)
Hidden figures: number incorrect	−0·14	−0·20*
Hidden figures: number of odd responses	−0·07	−0·10
Spatial relations: number correct	(−0·01)	(−0·01)
Spatial relations: number incorrect	−0·14	−0·20*

* = $P < 0.05$
( ) = Correlation in direction opposite to prediction.

both close to zero, are in parentheses. Most correlations are in the predicted direction. Only one is statistically significant, though two others become significant when art background is controlled. The evidence suggests that there is a consistent tendency for esthetic judgement to be positively related to skill in perception of visual form, but not that the relation is very important.

The evidence in Table 2 suggests that esthetic judgement may especially tend to be related to successful avoidance of incorrect visual perceptions. This would fit with the idea that a very general critical attitude toward one's visual experience may to some degree be involved in, or result from, the development of esthetic sensitivity.

Finding human meaning in ambiguous stimuli

The esthetic value of representational art seems to depend partly upon whether such non-representational elements as form and color, considered for their human meaning, are appropriately used in relation to the subject matter represented. And the same elements when used in abstract art have, for at least some viewers, similar human meaning. These considerations suggest the hypothesis that esthetic judgement in visual art depends partly upon a tendency to look for, and skill in finding, human meaning in ambiguous or non-representational stimuli.

One test employed to measure this tendency was Barron's Ink-blot Test (Barron, 1955) modified in three ways. (1) The inkblots were presented by projection on a screen before a group for 20 to 25 seconds, with the Ss instructed to write down the first thing they saw. (2) The test followed other measures of originality and was described as a test of visual originality. (3) Instead of a threshold measure, the score was the number of inkblots to which a person gave a human movement response. The inkblots were presented in order of increasing likelihood to evoke human-movement responses as reported by Barron for his standardization group. Responses were scored twice, once by a lenient standard, and once by a stricter standard for deciding whether a movement response had been made. The two scores showed correlations of $+0.13$ and $+0.17$ with esthetic judgement. These correlations are in the expected direction, and the second is significant; but they do not suggest any very important relationship.

Attempts were also made to measure the accuracy with which a person judged appropriate connotative meaning in visual stimuli. The stimuli used were abstract paintings as projected on a screen. The tasks were to report emotional meaning and masculinity-femininity of the stimuli. The tests initially devised seemed unsatisfactory, and those later substituted were not sufficiently better. The inconclusive results are reported elsewhere (Child, 1962b, pp. 42–4). The only conclusion justified is that they provide no further evidence in support of the hypothesis that esthetic judgement is related to the finding of human meaning in ambiguous stimuli.

Questionnaire measures of cognitive style

Esthetic judgement must depend upon an interest in, or at least a toleration of, those aspects of experience relevant to it. People differ greatly one from another in their orientation toward various aspects of experience, and the label *cognitive style* has come to be applied to such variations. Questionnaires were used to explore the possible relation of esthetic judgement to a number of variables of cognitive style. The hypotheses that guided the selection of the particular variables will be presented one by one as the variables are discussed.

Two published questionnaires – the Myers–Briggs Type Indicator (Myers, 1962) and the Independence of Judgement scale (Barron, 1953) – and an unpublished questionnaire by David Singer on regression in the service of the ego were among those used. New questionnaires also were devised for this project, incorporating some items taken directly or adapted from already published questionnaires. Two separate instruments were made up, in which items that represented several variables, including items from Barron and Singer, were intermingled. Each item appeared as a statement to which the *S* was to respond on a 4-point scale: agreeing with (or accepting) the statement *v.* not agreeing with it, and doing so either slightly or decidedly. Each variable for which items were especially prepared was balanced with respect to direction of items, an equal number being phrased so that agreement would represent the positive and the negative end of the variable. The score on each variable was a simple count of the number of items on which the *S* had responded in a manner indicative of the positive end.

The internal consistency of each variable (except those derived from the Myers–Briggs test, for whose reliability see Stricker and Ross, 1963) has been assessed by a split-half coefficient of correlation, corrected by the Spearman–Brown formula, with positive and negative items distributed equally between halves. These reliability coefficients are given in Table 3. With one exception they are moderately satisfactory for present purposes; they are too low to permit any very accurate statement about a

Table 3
Relation of Esthetic Judgement to Questionnaire Measures of Cognitive Style

Variable	No. of items	Reliability (corrected split-half coefficient)	N	Correlation with esthetic judgement	
				Simple	Art background controlled[1]
Tolerance of complexity	20	0·55	138	+0·23**	+0·21*
Tolerance of ambiguity, ambivalence and unrealistic experience	36	0·64	138	+0·13	+0·15
Scanning	20	0·54	138	+0·29**	+0·19*
Sharpening	20	0·52	138	+0·06	−0·02
Narrowness of equivalence range	20	0·38	138	+0·14	+0·10
Flexibility	20	0·52	138	(−0·06)	(−0·15)
Field independence	20	0·53	79	+0·13	+0·06
Independence of judgement	22	0·51	138	+0·25**	+0·22*
Regression in the service of the ego	25	0·52	49	+0·29**	+0·20
Extroversion v. introversion (MBTI)[2]			138	−·202*	−0·29**
Intuition v. sensation (MBTI)[2]			138	+0·36**	+0·21*
Perception v. judgement (MBTI)[2]			138	+0·22**	+0·18

* = P < 0·05 ** = P < 0·01 ( ) = Correlation in direction opposite to prediction.
1. With art background controlled, Ns of 138 fall to 122; Ns of 79 and 49 are unchanged.
2. Reliability of the MBTI variables was not assessed in this study, but Stricker and Ross (1963) report values from 0·75 to 0·84 for college men.

single individual but high enough to permit relationships among variables to be tested.

1. Tolerance of complexity. Works of art are complex stimuli whose full appreciation requires recognition of their complexity and willingness to look at them in several ways. A sufficient degree of toleration of cognitive complexity should therefore be required for the development of esthetic judgement.

In an effort to measure general tolerance of complexity, twenty items were used. To indicate their character, the six which have the highest correlation with total score on all twenty are given here; the sign preceding each item indicates whether agreement ($+$) or disagreement ($-$) was scored as indicative of tolerance of complexity.

$+$ 1. In so far as the study of philosophy makes one doubt one's basic beliefs, it should be encouraged.

$+$ 2. Those religions are to be most respected which impose no uniform beliefs on their members.

$-$ 3. The man who truly loves a woman must regard her as the best in the world in every important respect.

$-$ 4. People fall very naturally into distinct classes such as the strong and the weak.

$-$ 5. Most of our social problems would be solved if we could somehow get rid of the immoral, crooked and feeble-minded people.

$+$ 6. No one can be sure of conquering one's difficulties; will power is not enough.

Tolerance of complexity has a significant positive correlation ($+0.23$) with esthetic judgement, which remains almost as high ($+0.21$) when art background variables are partialed out. The hypothesis leading to its measurement is thus confirmed.

2. Tolerance of ambiguity, ambivalence and unrealistic experience. Works of art may be said to be by definition unrealistic; many works of art present a variety of more compelling reasons to term them unrealistic. They may also be regarded as inherently ambiguous, and an appreciative attitude toward a work of art is often ambivalent (involving, for example, both suffering and enjoyment). Esthetic judgement might therefore be expected to be positively related to general tolerance for ambiguity, ambivalence, and unrealistic experience.

In a previous study (Child, 1962a), esthetic preference (amount of agreement between a S's personal preferences and experts' judgements of esthetic value) was found to be positively related to a twenty-item measure of tolerance for ambiguity and ambivalence. This measure was for the present study enlarged to thirty-six items in an effort to measure three components separately, but the three were found to be so highly correlated that they were merged into a single score after all. The six items most highly correlated with total score follow:

+ 1. The expert ski jumper should enjoy the sport all the more if it remains a source of tension and even alarm.

+ 2. It would be exciting to arrive in a new city for the first time and find it enshrouded in a heavy fog.

+ 3. It is fun to get a new view of yourself – as in mirrors which show you your own profile, or in a frank account of other people's opinions of you.

− 4. Clouds that are frankly clouds and cover the whole sky are preferable to the little floating ones that leave you never knowing whether the next moment will be bright or dull.

− 5. Even if you were an expert in all the relevant languages, it would be disquieting to be in a multilingual group where you would never know which language to use next.

+ 6. Optical illusions and other experiences that put you in conflict about what is real and what isn't are on the whole quite enjoyable.

This measure, too, had moderately satisfactory reliability, as shown in Table 3. It was correlated with esthetic judgement in the direction predicted, and the correlation is not reduced by statistical control of art background. But it is low and not statistically significant. Only because of the very high correlation found in the previous study must we conclude that the evidence still supports the presence of a genuine relation here.

3. Scanning. A third measure was of scanning, a concept derived from Gardner *et al.* (1959). The upper end – high scanning – is defined as a tendency toward broad deployment of attention so that one is acutely aware of what is occurring outside the main focus of attention and notices changes in background stimulation, unusual events of any kind, and also the possibly trivial elements in the events whose important aspects one is principally concentrating on. The lower end represents narrow focusing of attention so that little is noted outside the activity or event one is principally concentrating on, and even there little is noticed except the aspects most important or central to one's purposes or interests.

The variable of scanning seems likely to be related to adequacy of attention to art, and hence competence of judgement about it, on two separate grounds. One is that thorough grasp of a complex work of art involves the ability to attend simultaneously to various aspects of its stimulus value. The second is that interest in art seems most likely to develop in scanners, since objects of art are constantly present as a part of one's environment from early childhood but may be reacted to solely for their practical significance except by the scanner. Chinaware and tableware, for example, are necessarily reacted to by everyone in eating, but who will notice their form and decoration? Magazines inform and influence everyone, but which readers notice the composition of their pages? Young children early learn that the front door is an essential part of a house; who among them will notice the specific shape of the door or of the space to which it leads? Perhaps the answer to each question is the person who has a general alertness to a variety of aspects of the world around him, who notices things unimportant to the dominant interest of the moment as well as things central to it – in short, the scanner.

Here are the items most highly correlated with the total score on twenty scanning items:

+ 1. After having a date with a girl, I could describe pretty accurately the color and style of her clothes.
+ 2. I am very sensitive to the emotional attitudes people sometimes want to convey but are unwilling to state openly.
− 3. When I am concentrating on one thing, I am really oblivious to everything else that's happening.
+ 4. I seem to notice unusual noises sooner than other people do.
− 5. I rarely notice the color of people's eyes.
+ 6. Going down a street, I usually notice what the billboards and signs say.

The expectation of a relationship to esthetic judgement was confirmed by the substantial correlation of +0·29. Partialing out of art background leaves this figure much lower but still significant.

4. Sharpening. The concept of sharpening is also derived most directly from Gardner *et al.* (1959). For present purposes a high degree of sharpening was defined as a keen awareness of differences, both at the time of occurrence and in later recall, among the various related or similar experiences occurring at different times – at the extreme, a sense of uniqueness about every experience. The lower end (leveling) is represented by keen awareness of similarities among various related or similar experiences occurring at different times – at the extreme, a great exaggeration of the similarities and a fusing of memories, a blurring of the boundaries between them.

Sharpening should be related to esthetic judgement on the supposition that intense involvement in any work of art, and hence understanding of it, is favored by attention to the uniqueness of the experience obtained through contemplating it.

This expectation was not confirmed. While the correlation was in the predicted direction, it was extremely low. (To save space, sample items will not be given for variables yielding negative results.)

5. Narrowness of equivalence range. Narrowness of equivalence range is also derived from Gardner *et al.* (1959). In constructing questionnaire items, narrow range of equivalence was defined as a tendency to react distinctively even to stimuli which are only slightly different. Broad equivalence range, the opposite end of the scale, was defined as a tendency to react to stimuli in an identical manner even when the difference between them is considerable. An attempt was made to distinguish this dimension from sharpening *v.* leveling in two ways: (1) sharpening *v.* leveling has to do exclusively with response to events spread out in time, while narrowness of equivalence range may refer to response to a set of objects present at a single time; (2) narrowness of equivalence range refers more to the degree to which one acts on differences, while sharpening *v.* leveling refers more to the degree of awareness of differences.

The reason for expecting that narrowness of equivalence range would be related to esthetic judgement was essentially the same as for sharpening. In a different way the upper end of this variable also refers to absorption in or enjoyment of the uniqueness of a specific experience as against reacting to it primarily in terms of generality or similarity to other experience. Such an approach would be expected to favor thorough understanding of a work of art. This expectation, too, was not appreciably confirmed; the correlation with esthetic judgement was again in the predicted direction but small and not statistically significant. The reliability of this measure is lower than any of the others, and significant results would be surprising.

6. *Flexibility*. The notion of cognitive flexibility was also immediately suggested by recent writings on cognitive style (Gardner *et al.*, 1959). A high degree of flexibility was defined as ability to change one's perceptual orientation when conditions make it appropriate, ability to shift the main focus of attention radically when doing so is adaptive, and toleration or liking of circumstances which call for exercise of this ability. Low flexibility was defined as the opposite: rigidity in the main focus of attention and set, and dislike or avoidance of circumstances calling for flexibility.

The basis on which a correlation with esthetic judgement was expected for flexibility is that an esthetic mode of responding to objects is a somewhat distinctive way of considering objects to which other responses are required by the exigencies of everyday life, and that ability to take and enjoy an esthetic attitude would be favored by general flexibility of cognitive approach. This expectation was also not confirmed. Here is the one instance among the results given in Table 3 where the correlation was of opposite sign to what was predicted, but it was extremely low.

7. *Field independence*. Field independence – a concept derived from Witkin *et al.*, (1954) – was defined as ability to maintain a set, to focus selectively on what one intends to do, and to obtain new perceptual structuring despite irrelevant attention-demanding stimulation and despite irrelevant well-determined structure of the perceptual field; and a liking for situations calling for such

ability. The perceptual organization obtained in the experience of a work of art must be supplied partly by the viewer's own discovery of forms or structures not immediately and easily apparent; the perception or understanding of these forms often comes only as a result of careful, close search. On these grounds a positive relation to esthetic judgement was expected.

The dimension of field independence had seemed initially an unlikely one to measure usefully by questionnaire. But encouraging results with other variables measured by questionnaire led to the addition of twenty items on it in time for the last seventy-nine *S*s. Again, however, there was no significant confirmation of this prediction, though the sign of the correlation was positive.

8. Independence of judgement. Independence of judgement is a particularly interesting aspect of cognitive function in relation to esthetic judgement. On the one hand, goodness of esthetic judgement as measured here might be thought to be a function primarily of the extent to which one has sought out and accepted the judgement of experts on esthetic values; on this basis esthetic judgement should be negatively correlated with general independence of judgement. On the other hand, goodness of esthetic judgement might be thought to derive to a greater extent from one's observing works of art carefully and formulating one's own judgement about them, so that the careful observer tends to arrive independently at judgements of value similar to those which experts have arrived at largely by the same process; on this basis a positive correlation between esthetic judgement and general independence of judgement would be expected. The latter hypothesis prompted an attempt to measure independence of judgement.

For this variable a questionnaire measure has been developed and validated by Barron (1953). *S*s in Asch's experiments who under social pressure had either yielded to the judgements of others or else had maintained their own independent judgement answered questionnaire items which Barron thought might be correlated with conformity *v.* independence. The scale for independence of judgement consists of sixteen items giving the best discrimination between yielders and non-yielders. Unlike the measures described earlier, the items here need have no direct or obvious relevance to the variable, since their inclusion is justified empirically rather than rationally. Here are the six items most highly correlated with total score:

— 1. What the youth needs most is strict discipline, rugged determination, and the will to work and fight for family and country.
— 2. The happy person tends always to be poised, courteous, outgoing and emotionally controlled.
— 3. If young people get rebellious ideas, then as they grow up they ought to get over them and settle down.
+ 4. Some of my friends think that my ideas are impractical, if not a bit wild.
— 5. I must admit that I would find it hard to have for a close friend a person whose manners or appearance made him somewhat repulsive, no matter how brilliant or kind he might be.
+ 6. The unfinished and the imperfect often have greater appeal for me than the completed and polished.

The prediction was decidedly confirmed, with a highly significant positive correlation which was only slightly lowered by partialing out art background. Agreement with expert judgement, for such people as served as Ss here, apparently grows out of independence more than it does out of conformity.

9. Regression in the service of the ego. The concept of regression in the service of the ego is derived from recent psychoanalytic writings on ego psychology and its application to the psychodynamic meaning of art. The concept has appeared especially in discussions of creativity but is applicable also to appreciation of the arts. The idea as presented by Kris (1952) and Schafer (1958) may be summarized by saying that creation or enjoyment of the arts involves in part a controlled regression from more mature forms of cognitive activity to less mature forms, with the ego functions remaining intact and in command, so that a positive use of the less mature functions can be made in the interest of the more mature ones. It seems likely that just such an ability to fuse the more infantile with the more mature might be involved in the ability to enter fully into a work of art and to integrate it into one's general cognitive functioning.

Questionnaire items on regression in the service of the ego, prepared by David Singer for unpublished research of his own, became available for only the last forty-nine *S*s. Singer's questionnaire included a few items referring to the arts; to ensure conceptual independence these were replaced for present use by new items not referring to the arts. The six items most highly correlated with total score follow:

+ 1. Unusual but unimportant aspects of a situation or object often intrigue me, occupying my attention and imagination for a time.
− 2. I get little pleasure or fun out of playing with words or language – as by talking nonsense, baby-talk, or in a foreign accent – and seldom do that sort of thing.
+ 3. I sometimes have daydreams in which I become a heroic type of figure – either all-powerful, all-knowing and successful or someone who has sunk to the lowest depths of depravity, weakness, and suffering.
+ 4. I find it easy when playing with very young children to get into their world and try to experience things as they do.
+ 5. I sometimes just let my thoughts wander aimlessly, and find myself daydreaming and thinking about all sorts of unusual and unrelated things.
− 6. I can detect in myself no strong anti-social impulses of the sort which, under certain circumstances, might lead to crime.

The expectation of a correlation with esthetic judgement was fulfilled, with a coefficient of $+0.29$. Regression in the service of the ego is sufficiently associated with art background so that the partial correlation falls to $+0.20$ and with only forty-nine cases is no longer statistically significant.

10. Jungian measures of cognitive orientation. Jung, in his *Psychological Types* (1923), suggested variables of cognitive functioning somewhat akin to some of those discussed recently in connexion with the concept of cognitive style or cognitive control; his variable of introversion *v.* extroversion has received most attention. The Myers–Briggs Type Index (Myers, 1962) is a questionnaire designed to measure these Jungian variables. It was used in a preliminary study (Child, 1962a) primarily to test the common belief that introverts, because of their more reflective and thoughtful response to stimuli, would tend to be higher than extroverts on esthetic preference. This hypothesis was not confirmed, but two of the other Jungian dimensions measured by the questionnaire did turn out to be appreciably related to esthetic preference. The same questionnaire was therefore administered to the Ss in the present investigation.

Here, in contrast to the preliminary study, there was some evidence of a relation to introversion. Esthetic judgement showed a correlation of -0.22 with the dimension of extroversion v. introversion, and with art background variables partialed out this rose to -0.29. These highly significant correlations are in a direction which confirms the original prediction. However, there is now reason to doubt whether it should have been predicted. Stricker and Ross (1964), in a careful review of the meaning of the Myers–Briggs variables, find no evidence to justify the belief that the full Jungian variable of extroversion–introversion is measured by the E–I score; rather, this appears to resemble other 'extroversion–introversion' scales in measuring interest and proficiency in social relations, especially as expressed in talkativeness.

For the dimension of intuition v. sensation, the findings of the preliminary study were confirmed by a marked correlation of $+0.36$ with esthetic judgement, which falls to $+0.21$ when art background is controlled. A relation of esthetic judgement to the dimension of perception v. judgement was confirmed to some extent by a correlation of $+0.22$; this correlation also drops somewhat, to $+0.18$, when art background variables are statistically controlled. (The Myers–Briggs questionnaire also yields a score called feeling v. thinking; its correlation with esthetic judgement, $+0.08$, does not appear in Table 3 since no prediction was made about it.)

The suggestion of a connexion between goodness of esthetic judgement and tendency toward intuition and toward perception as these are defined by the authors of the test seems quite reasonable. Intuition is supposed to represent an interest in the *possibilities* of experience and relatively free access to unconscious aspects of current experience. Perception is supposed to represent a preference for perceiving an object rather than making a judgement about it. Stricker and Ross's review (1964) of the Myers–Briggs test, however, leaves the meaning of these two scores and hence of these findings very uncertain.

Behavioral measures of cognitive style

Behavioral measures of cognitive style are extremely time consuming. Several minutes or more may be required to get information which, as a sample of the domain to be covered, may be less than the equivalent of one questionnaire response. Behavioral measures are therefore inefficient for an exploratory survey such as that undertaken here. Yet they are so important on other grounds that a small set of them were included. The generally negative results do not seem important enough to present here, but they are available in a mimeographed report (Child, 1962b).

One of the techniques employed showed results so different from the others it will be reported here; the fact that it stood out in a surrounding of negative results (including one correlation significant at the 5 per cent level in the direction not predicted) should be kept in mind, however, as a possible reason for skepticism. This exceptional technique consisted of having the *S* put on aniseikonic lenses and report what he saw. Previous use of this technique as a measure of tolerance for unrealistic experience is summarized by Gardner *et al.* (1959). The particular lenses used here were ones which, for a person tolerant of the novel experience, create a gradient in size across the visual field from left to right, perceivable either as a gradient in size among objects retaining their normal apparent distance or as a gradient in distance among objects retaining their normal apparent size. The *S* was seated in a standard place in the experimental room where the location of objects was kept fairly although not absolutely standardized. He was instructed to put on the lenses and then report what he saw, having been forewarned that they lead some people to see things rather differently from usual, either immediately or after a while, but that some people continue to see things quite the same as usual. The *E* noted the *S*'s comments and the time when they were made. Then about $1\frac{1}{2}$ min after the *S* had put on the lenses the *E* instructed him to hold his hands up in front of him but not touching each other and to report anything further that he observed. In a subsequent $\frac{1}{2}$ min or so the *E* noted any further spontaneous comments and if necessary asked the *S* how things now looked.

For the first fifty-nine Ss an over-all rating was made of the extent to which the individual showed a recognition and acceptance of the perceptual changes the lenses might produce. This measure had a highly significant correlation of $+0.40$ with esthetic judgement. However, the various aspects of response to the lenses seemed somewhat separable; and in dealing with the data obtained from the entire body of 138 Ss a more detailed analysis of four variables in the response was made. First rated was the extent to which the S reported novelty in perception during the initial period before his attention was called to his hands. Response varied all the way from the very common report of no change to reporting the room and furniture as markedly distorted. The second rating was of the S's response to looking at his hands. Although reporting one hand as decidedly larger than the other was most common, variation was found all the way down to reporting no change from their usual appearance. The third rating was of the maximum distortion reported in the appearance of the room and furniture, whether this maximum was reached before looking at one's hands or in the period afterward. Finally, a fourth rating was made, possible only for those people who did report some decided distortion of the physical environment; it was a rating of the direction in which the effect was reported. This was made initially because of the possibility that Ss varied from seeing an appropriate distortion all the way to seeing an opposite distortion as a form of struggle against the effects produced by the lenses. In the course of making this fourth rating, however, it become apparent that the variation was rather in the extent to which people described the effect in terms of the changed appearance of a single relatively isolated element in the visual field, such as the table in front of and below their eyes, as against reporting the effect in terms of the total visual field.

Each of the first three measures, applicable to all of the Ss, was correlated with esthetic judgement in the direction to be predicted from its being considered as a measure of tolerance of unrealistic experience. The effect obtained while looking at the hands yielded a nonsignificant correlation of $+0.13$. The effect on perception of the physical environment up to the point of looking at the hands yielded a correlation of $+0.22$ ($P<0.05$). The maximum effect obtained in perception of the physical environment yielded a correlation of $+0.31$ ($P<0.01$). Adding together the ratings on these three variables, the correlation of this total score with esthetic judgements was $+0.29$; partialing out the art background variables raises this value to $+0.32$. The fourth rating, applicable only to the fifty-eight Ss who reported substantial distortion, yielded a correlation of $+0.41$ ($P<0.01$) with esthetic judgement, which drops very substantially to $+0.23$ ($P>0.05$) when art background is controlled. The tendency here is for Ss high in esthetic judgement to report the direction of effect that seems dependent on attention to the total visual field.

Other variables of personality

In this section results are reported that were obtained with a variety of other measures. Some, as indicated, were included in the study to determine their relation to esthetic judgement. Others were included for purposes not relevant to this paper but showed unpredicted relations with esthetic judgement.

1. Social extroversion v. introversion. The questionnaires constructed especially for the present research included twenty items on social extroversion *v.* introversion previously used by Child (1962a). (The Myers–Briggs scale as described by Myers (1962) was intended to measure the intellectual or cognitive aspects of extroversion *v.* introversion.) The items were mainly derived from earlier questionnaires, most directly from the Maudsley Personality Inventory (Eysenck, 1956), and were deliberately balanced so that there would be an equal number of items in each direction. The following six items showed the highest correlation with total score:

 − 1. I am inclined to keep in the background on social occasions.
 − 2. The presence of the opposite sex makes me feel shy.
 + 3. Other people probably regard me as a lively person.
 + 4. I am rather a talkative person.
 − 5. I am inclined to be rather quiet when in a large group.
 − 6. I could be quite happy even if circumstances prevented me from having many social contacts.

Social extroversion might be thought to be negatively correlated with goodness of esthetic judgement – because of a popular stereotype of the socially isolated pursuit of beauty in an ivory tower, however, rather than from the view of art implied in this paper. As in the previous study (Child, 1962a), such an expectation was not confirmed. The correlation was very small and was in fact in the opposite direction, a tendency toward extroversion being correlated $+0.13$ with esthetic judgement.

2. Anxiety. Anxiety, or essentially what in some questionnaire usage has been called neuroticism, was measured by twenty items which had also been employed in preliminary research (Child, 1962a). Like the items on extroversion, these were drawn largely from previous questionnaires, though more modification and invention were required here to provide for a set containing an equal number of items stated in each direction. The six items most highly correlated with the twenty-item total were:

+ 1. I often experience periods of loneliness.
− 2. I spend very little time worrying over possible misfortunes.
− 3. My mood is pretty steady, not characterized by frequent ups and downs.
+ 4. My feelings are rather easily hurt.
+ 5. I often find that I have made up my mind too late.
+ 6. There are quite a few subjects on which I am rather touchy.

The variable of anxiety was included in the research without any expectation about a relation to esthetic judgement, but evidence of a slight positive relationship was found. The correlation was $+0.18$; statistical control of art background variables did not change this value, and it is significant at the 5 per cent level. This finding is consistent with other results if interpreted tentatively in relation to regression in the service of the ego. The person with greater interest in esthetic values may be one who is more able to face and recognize unpleasant emotions and undesirable states in himself, and he may express this tolerance in his answers to questionnaires as well as in his willing exploration of the unpleasant as well as the pleasant in the world of art.

3. Variables in temperament. When this research was begun, it seemed likely that the dimension of temperament described by Sheldon (1942) as cerebrotonia might be relevant in the same way that intellectual introversion seemed to be. In fact, this variable as described by Sheldon has a good deal in common with the concept of intellectual introversion. In some earlier research by Child (1950), Sheldon's concepts of viscerotonia, somatotonia and cerebrotonia were used to formulate questionnaire items intended to yield scores on all three of these variables. In that research, however, items successful in measuring cerebrotonia (by Sheldon's criterion of relation to physique) were the same as items measuring one of the other two dimensions, rather than forming a cluster of their own. As in Child (1962a), therefore, an attempt was made here to measure only viscerotonia and somatotonia, with the lower end of each representing some of the characteristics Sheldon groups together under the label of cerebrotonia.

Child (1962a) found viscerotonia to be negatively correlated with esthetic preference. Somatotonia was not found to be related in either direction. In the present research the results for viscerotonia are in the same direction as before, though not of large magnitude; esthetic judgement shows a correlation of -0.19 ($P < 0.05$) which, when art background is partialed out, rises to -0.21. For somatotonia there is this time a suggestion, not significant, of a relationship in the predicted direction, with a correlation of -0.15; but this is diminished by -0.07 by taking art background into account.

4. Scholastic aptitudes. In Child (1962a), esthetic preference was found to be somewhat related positively to verbal aptitude measures by the C.E.E.B. Scholastic Aptitude Test but not related to mathematical aptitude. This relationship could be tested with most of the present Ss; a few had not taken this test, and several Ss whose native language was probably not English were omitted. The verbal score was correlated $+0.17$ with esthetic judgement ($N = 129$, P approx. 0.05), a value which rises to $+0.24$ when art background is controlled. With mathematical aptitude the correlation is almost zero (-0.01, $N = 129$). These results agree closely with those of the earlier study.

5. Masculinity–femininity. The dimension of masculinity $v.$ femininity seems eminently worth exploring in any study of behavior related to the arts because of the seemingly contradictory ways in which sex differences appear to enter into such behavior. On the one hand, artistic creativity has been and continues to be displayed primarily by men. Artistic appreciation and criticism, too, have been very largely masculine pursuits. On the other hand, there is a belief common in the United States that interest in or participation in the arts is essentially feminine and somewhat threatening to the male sense of self-esteem. Also, psychoanalytic interpretation of the arts often postulates greater bisexuality or less rigid sex-typing in people participating in the arts. To this issue of great interest the research here, because of the uncertain meaning of the measuring instruments used, makes only an inconclusive negative contribution.

One measure was a questionnaire comprising items which tend to discriminate between the sexes, drawn from Gough's Masculinity–Femininity Test (Gough, 1952). All the items of Gough's test were embedded in one of the personality questionnaires already mentioned. Since they included an excess of items for which a positive response was scored as feminine, enough were eliminated in scoring so as to produce a balanced set – twenty-eight items, fourteen scored in each direction. This questionnaire has been used as a measure of more-or-less conscious sexual identification (Miller, Swanson et al., 1960). It does not in the present research, however, promise to be a good measure of anything, as its internal consistency is very low; a split-half correlation, corrected, has the value of only $+0.25$. As then might be expected, it shows no relation to esthetic judgement ($r = +0.02$, with the higher end of the measure representing femininity, as is also true for the other measures of masculinity-femininity).

A second measure of masculinity v. femininity was provided by the Franck Drawing Completion Test,[2] which has been used as a measure of unconscious or latent sexual identification (Franck and Rosen, 1949; Miller, Swanson et al., 1960). The S is presented with thirty-six incomplete drawings, each to be quickly completed in whatever way he pleases. The test was introduced to the Ss of the present research as a test of originality (not a standard mode of introducing it). It was then scored by the

2. I am very grateful to the copyright holder, Mr S. S. Dunn of the Australian Council for Educational Research, Melbourne, for permission to reproduce this test for use in the present research, and to Dr Leonard Lansky of the University of Cincinnati for his generous assistance in providing information and scoring manuals.

manual prepared by Franck (n.d.), based on classifying a person's completion of an item as more closely resembling responses typical of men or of women. Interjudge agreement in using the manual was very satisfactory (uncorrected r of $+0.78$ for the first fifty-nine Ss, $+0.70$ for the other seventy-nine). The measure shows no evidence of a relation to esthetic judgement ($r = -0.04$).

Two other measures were ratings of the masculinity–femininity of visual material produced by the Ss – that is, of the degree to which their drawings were in themselves masculine or feminine in connotative meaning. First, this approach was applied to the drawing completions the Ss produced on the Franck test. The individual items were rated on a 3-point scale, and a person's score was obtained by adding his item scores. Interjudge agreement for the Ss' scores was extremely poor; interjudge correlations were 0.11, 0.05 and 0.04, yielding a corrected reliability coefficient of only 0.18 for the pooled rating. The item-to-item internal consistency of the Ss' scores obtained from the pooled ratings of the three judges, however, was very good, with a corrected split-half coefficient of 0.77. This measure is nearly independent of the two already described, with a correlation of $+0.11$ with the Gough score and $+0.15$ with the Franck score. (These two had a correlation of $+0.13$ with each other.) It too shows no significant relation to esthetic judgement ($r = -0.10$).

Finally, this same rating procedure was applied to a single abstract drawing the S was required to produce during 5 minutes of a group session, as a task intended to measure originality. (For this measure, $N = 116$.) There was some agreement among judges (interjudge correlations of 0.70, 0.42 and 0.34), but subject consistency could, of course, not be assessed. This measure had no significant correlation with the questionnaire measure ($+0.11$), a significant correlation with the rated masculinity–femininity of drawing completions ($+0.19$, $P < 0.05$), and a significant correlation of $+0.22$ ($P < 0.05$) with the score of tendency to resemble women in drawing completions made. Thus it shows a little more sign than do any of the other three measures of representing something in common among them. But it too gives no evidence of being related to esthetic judgement ($r = -0.07$).

This study thus provides no evidence that esthetic judgement is related in either direction to a dimension of masculinity–femininity. For lack of sufficient knowledge about the meaning of the measures used, it is impossible to judge whether this is satisfactory negative evidence.

6. *Originality*. Ratings of originality were made on the *S*s' responses to three tests already described: the Barron Inkblot Test, the Franck Drawing-Completion Test and the 5-minute Abstract Drawing. In addition, the New Uses of Common Things Test (see Guilford *et al.*, 1954) was given in a one-item, 5-minute version; the *S*s were required to write down as many and as varied uses as they could for 'a book', and these responses also were rated for originality. Interjudge agreement on most of these ratings was not very good, and the intercorrelations among these four possible measures of originality were low and insignificant. Two of the six coefficients were negative, and the highest was $+0\cdot15$.

The principal conclusion we can draw is that no general dimension of originality has been satisfactorily measured by these tests. Only one of them has a significant correlation with esthetic judgement, and that is not impressively high (drawing-completion originality, $+0\cdot19$).

7. *Color preferences*. During the individual session all 138 *S*s were given a color-preference test based on that devised by Barrett and Eaton (1947) but considerably modified. The *S* was presented with pairs of small patches of colored paper, each pair mounted on a black 3×5 in card. The two patches were always approximately of the same hue but differed in one of three ways: one was a 'hue' and the other a 'tint' of it; or one was a 'hue' and the other a 'shade' of it; or one was a 'tint' and the other a 'shade'. There were twenty-four pairs to represent each of the three kinds of choice, presented in mixed order. The *S* was not told how the colors in a pair differed and was asked only to express his immediate preference within each pair. Each *S* was later given the Ishihara Test, and the records of eight who showed some sign of color deficiency were deleted in treating the results from the color-preference test (and also other measures which were specifically concerned with color), so that *N* is

130. Scores on this test showed some correlation with the esthetic judgement scores: preference for hues over tints, $+0.17$; for hues over shades, -0.15; and for tints over shades, -0.32. The last value is highly significant. With art background controlled, these correlations remain nearly as high: $+0.18$, -0.12 and -0.29.

What these findings indicate most definitely is a tendency for persons with higher esthetic judgement scores to choose shades over tints more frequently than do persons with lower scores. This finding of a relationship between simple sensory preferences and esthetic judgement seems very surprising. But it is of great importance if it is generally valid.

In an effort to begin clarification of this finding, an additional color-preference test was devised to be used with the last group of Ss. Instead of presenting contrasts within the framework of artists' classification of colors, it presented contrasts defined in relation to the psychological dimensions of hue, saturation and brightness; contrasts were presented for choice along each of the three dimensions, separately on a black background and on a white. Only for preferences along the brightness dimensions was there an indication of a relation to esthetic judgement. Preference for the color of lower brightness, of two patches on a black background, had an insignificant correlation of $+0.13$ with esthetic judgement; for colors on a white background the corresponding correlation had the significant value of $+0.30$ ($N = 47, P < 0.05$). When art background variables are partialed out, this correlation falls to $+0.28$, not quite at the 5 per cent significance level. These results in themselves are not impressive. There is, however, reason to believe that the relationship suggested is genuine. An additional thirty-two Ss not included in the 138 of the main study were given this new color-preference test and the esthetic-judgement test. Their tendency to prefer the color of lower brightness was correlated with the esthetic-judgement score $+0.20$ when a black background was used and $+0.35$ with a white background. Only the larger of these is approximately significant at the 5 per cent level, but they agree in direction with the previous correlations. They also agree with the statistically more decisive finding of a preference for shades in the test applied to all Ss in the main study. The largest and most consistent way that shades differ from hues and tints is in having lower brightness, i.e. value, in the terminology of the Munsell color system; this difference is especially pronounced when a shade is paired with a tint, and it was for that comparison that the most decisive evidence of a relation to esthetic judgement was found.

For *S*s such as were used in this study, then, esthetic judgement appears to be positively correlated with a tendency to prefer colors of lower brightness. The speculations that might be based on this finding will be of greatest interest when combined with further pertinent observations.

8. Other visual preferences. With the first fifty-nine *S*s, a test of visual preferences was used as an additional measure possibly relevant to masculinity–femininity. The stimuli consisted of twenty pairs of abstract paintings used for a measure, briefly mentioned earlier, of judgement of sexual connotative meaning. The pairs were so selected that, in the selectors' opinion, one member would be definitely masculine in connotative meaning and the other definitely feminine. They were presented without mention of this characteristic and embedded in forty other pairs with less decided sexual connotation. The *S* was asked to record his personal preference for one painting in each pair. A count was made of the number of pairs on which the *S* preferred the more masculine painting. As this score showed no tendency to be related to either of the measures of masculinity–femininity adapted from previous research (the Gough and Franck tests), it was one of the measures chosen for subsequent elimination to make way for inclusion of the difficult esthetic-judgement test. The elimination was unfortunate, for this preference measure yielded interesting results which cannot be confirmed until the measure is used in further investigation. Most important for present purposes is the fact that in these fifty-nine *S*s preference for the more masculine painting was correlated $+0.29$ ($P < 0.05$) with esthetic judgement. Such a relationship may have something to do with the sexual element in the choices made. Or it may have to do more specifically with strength or power (which clearly characterized the masculine paintings), if people high in esthetic judgement are likely to prefer strength in painting.

Another measure based on visual preferences was the Barron–Welsh Art Scale (Barron and Welsh, 1952) administered in the individual session. The S was given a pile of cards on each of which was printed a different abstract drawing. He was asked to divide them into those he liked and disliked (and in our procedure was asked to adopt a cutting point which would make the division approximately equal). The drawings were of two kinds: those liked more by artists than non-artists, those liked more by non-artists than by artists. The score represented the S's tendency to make the choices more characteristic of artists. This measure had been found to be positively correlated with indices of originality (Barron, 1958). It might thus have been reported on earlier in the section on originality. In our data the Barron–Welsh Scale is not appreciably correlated with the measures of originality described in that section; the correlations vary from -0.01 to $+0.10$. It is therefore reported on here. Quite possibly, however, it is a better index of a general dimension of originality than those other measures, which were found to be hardly appreciably correlated with each other. The Barron–Welsh Art Scale was found to be significantly correlated with esthetic judgement ($r = +0.18$, $P < 0.05$). This correlation may well be connected entirely with a common relation to variables of art background; for when these are controlled, it drops to $+0.09$. The relationship seems remarkably low in view of the way the Art Scale was developed.

Finally, with other purposes in mind, a measure was obtained of relative preference for Baroque v. Classical Art. These terms are used here as defined by Wölfflin (1932), with 'Classical' meaning 'High Renaissance', not 'Ancient'. Pairs of contrasting works were presented for choice with no statement about the nature of the contrast. These pairs were based on the illustrative examples given by Wölfflin. A surprisingly high degree of internal consistency was found; the corrected split-half correlation was $+0.62$. The measure of preference for Baroque over Classical showed an entirely unexpected correlation of $+0.22$ ($P < 0.01$) with esthetic judgement, which drops to $+0.14$ when art background is partialed out. This finding has several possible interpretations; a choice among them would depend on further study. One is that the Baroque member of most pairs presented tends to be the one which our experts would consider esthetically better (whether the reasons lie in Wölfflin's biased selection of examples or in style prejudices of our experts). Another is that the Baroque works are more complex or less like present-day art and therefore require, in comparison with Classical, more background or interest in art in order to be understood and thus potentially liked.

Partial Replication of the Study

As a demonstration of personality measurement and hypothesis testing, some of this study was replicated in an introductory course in psychology for undergraduate men in Yale College. The replication differed from corresponding parts of the original study in the following ways:

(1) The Ss consisted of all students present in class on the relevant days instead of being restricted to volunteer employees; participation was as a part of the course, though anonymity was preserved by having students enter code numbers instead of names.

(2) For purposes not germane to this article, half the Ss were instructed to make an esthetic judgement, while the other half were to express a personal preference in response to each pair of slides. This variation was introduced by having the instructions appear on each student's mimeographed forms instead of being given orally. No students were told how the pairs of slides had been formed. Results are reported separately for the groups given different instructions.

(3) Eighty pairs of slides were used, of which only twenty-eight pairs had been among the 120 used in the main study. The alpha coefficient of internal consistency was 0·73 for Ss making esthetic judgements and 0·78 for those expressing personal preferences.

(4) Art background was measured by questionnaire instead of by interview. The questionnaire was given many weeks after the rest of the data were collected and on a day when a number of students were absent. In giving partial correlation coefficients, therefore, the simple coefficient is also given for the smaller sample for which partialing out of art background is possible. Art background was measured by seven items dealing with

experience largely subject to a person's own voluntary choice (art education in secondary school and college, experience looking at art in museums, magazines and books); four items on experience not likely to be subject to his own choice (art education in primary school, art interests of close relatives); four items asking for over-all rating of background in four other arts (literature, music, drama and dance); participation in group hobbies of artistic nature (one item); participation in individual hobbies of artistic nature (one item); and an over-all self-rating of art background relative to that of fellow students. These six variables were all partialed out.

(5) Personality measurement differed in several details. Some of the personality variables were represented by a larger number of items. An attempt was made to measure cerebrotonia separately from viscerotonia and somatotonia, and this involved some alteration of items to represent the latter two. Tolerance of Ambiguity, Tolerance of Ambivalence and Tolerance of Unrealistic Experience were more independent of one another than in the main study, and so have been kept separate; Tolerance of Ambiguity, however, has too low an internal consistency to expect it to be correlated with anything else, and Tolerance of Ambivalence also has low internal consistency. The items used for the personality variables predicted to be related to esthetic judgement were embedded in a single questionnaire along with items included for entirely different purposes. Results obtained with these other items will also be reported, to permit comparison.

The results are given in Table 4. In general, they confirm and extend the findings of the main study. First appear six variables of art background; their correlations with the esthetic measures confirm the previous but unilluminating findings of a positive relationship. For the next eleven variables listed in the table a prediction can clearly be made either from hypotheses already presented in this paper or from statistically significant findings of the main study. For nine of these eleven variables the direction of relationship to esthetic judgement found in this replication is consistently the predicted one; for the other two variables the very small correlation shifts direction according to which cases are included or whether the correlation is simple or partial. With the students who were asked to express a personal preference instead of an esthetic judgement, all eleven variables yield a correlation consistently in the predicted direction. On the whole, the relationships remain but are smaller when art background is partialed out. Several of the correlations reach high levels of statistical significance; especially striking and consistent results are obtained for Tolerance of Complexity and for Independence of Judgement. For only three out of the eleven variables are there no statistically significant correlations; one of these (Somatotonia) is the single variable included here because of an original theoretical prediction despite that prediction's having been tested and not significantly confirmed in the main study. Putting together the two studies, we must conclude for the population sampled that somatotonic tendencies are perfectly compatible with esthetic sensitivity.

Clearly Table 4 confirms the corresponding results of the main study and shows that these personality variables are correlates of esthetic preference as well as of esthetic judgement. It creates somewhat more doubt than does the main study about whether these very consistent relations would hold true if art background were perfectly controlled. With respect to magnitude of relationship between these personality measures and esthetic judgement or preference, these results are very impressive. When the rather low reliability of the measures is taken into account, the significant correlations are of a magnitude which suggests a very close relationship.

For the last four variables in Table 4 there was no predicted relationship to esthetic sensitivity, and none makes any compelling appearance here. The most convincing correlation is the negative one between Crowne and Marlowe's (1960) Social Desirability Scale and esthetic preference. A common view, not adopted in this paper, is that agreement with experts' esthetic judgement is likely to reflect principally a desire to make the socially desirable responses. From this view can be predicted a positive correlation between social desirability and esthetic sensitivity. That prediction is directly contradicted by the significant negative correlation of social desirability with esthetic preference, and less decisively by its low negative correlation with esthetic judgement.

Table 4
Correlations Obtained in Partial Replication of Study

Variable	Alpha coefficient of internal consistency: Entire sample 137 Ss	Correlation with esthetic Judgement 84 Ss with information on art background		Correlation with esthetic preference Entire sample: 139 Ss	88 Ss with information on art background	
		Simple	Art background controlled		Simple	Art background controlled
Art background						
1. Background subject to choice		0·48**			0·44	
2. Background not subject to choice		0·12			0·30	
3. Background in other arts		0·14			0·19	
4. Art-related hobbies, group		0·29			0·42	
5. Art-related hobbies, individual		0·34			0·33	
6. Over-all rating		0·52			0·45	

Personality variables for which correlation was predicted

7. Tolerance of complexity	0·42	0·24*	0·40**	0·33*	0·21*	0·27**	0·20
8. Tolerance of ambiguity	0·16	0·17	0·24*	0·14	0·12	0·16	0·02
9. Tolerance of ambivalence	0·33	0·22*	0·32**	0·23*	0·05	0·03	0·03
10. Tolerance of unrealistic experience	0·50	0·20*	0·20	0·13	0·32**	0·30**	0·16
11. Scanning	0·60	0·16	0·15	0·01	0·18	0·14	0·07
12. Independence of judgement	0·54	0·26**	0·33**	0·13	0·32**	0·28**	0·12
13. Regression in the service of the ego	0·62	0·31	0·17	0·07	0·16	0·19	0·04
14. Anxiety	0·70	0·15	0·12	0·11	0·27**	0·23*	0·08
15. Viscerotonia	0·34	−0·16	−0·16	−0·11	−0·22*	−0·13	−0·09
16. Somatotonia	0·33	−0·13	(0·02)	−0·11	−0·09	−0·11	−0·16
17. Cerebrotonia	0·22	0·08	0·02	(−0·07)	0·16	0·13	0·11

Personality variables for which correlation was not predicted

18. Superego	0·56	−0·16	−0·22*	−0·09	−0·06	−0·17	−0·19
19. Sexual guilt	0·66	−0·13	−0·17	−0·05	−0·03	−0·09	−0·08
20. Hostility guilt	0·60	−0·05	−0·16	−0·14	0·07	0·08	0·12
21. Social desirability	0·74	−0·13	−0·16	−0·15	−0·21*	−0·21*	−0·28*

* = $P < 0.05$
** = $P < 0.01$
( ) = Correlation in opposite direction to prediction.

Summary and Discussion

We have described a method of measuring esthetic judgement by determining extent of agreement with expert opinion on the relative esthetic value of the two works of art presented in each of a number of slide pairs. After measuring esthetic judgement in 138 male university students working as paid *S*s in psychological research, we have reported the relation of their esthetic judgement to a number of other variables.

First, we find that esthetic judgement is related to amount of background in art. We have no way of assessing to what extent this reflects an influence of background on esthetic-judgement score and to what extent it reflects a tendency for people with better esthetic judgement to be more interested in art and thus obtain more experience with it. Since background in art might conceivably be an influence both on esthetic judgement and on the other variables to which we relate esthetic judgement, we have in every case determined the partial correlation between variables, with art background statistically controlled. Many of the relationships we report remain statistically significant, and some become even more so, when art background is thus removed as a possible joint cause; some are greatly diminished. From this one study it would be premature to draw any conclusions about which relationships exist only by virtue of a common relation with art background and which exist independently of variations in art background.

Second, for several groups of measures we fail to find consistently the significant relations to esthetic judgement that various hypotheses might reasonably have led one to expect. These are as follows:

(a) Skill in perceiving visual form. Here we find a predominance of correlations in the predicted direction, but none are large and few are even barely significant statistically.

(b) Skill in perceiving human meaning in ambiguous stimuli. Results with different measures are contradictory in direction and none are statistically significant.

(c) Masculinity *v.* femininity. Several measures used showed no sign of relation to esthetic judgement; on the other hand, their value as measures of masculinity–femininity may be doubted.

(d) Originality. Several behavioral measures of originality showed little correlation with each other or with esthetic judgement.

(e) Behavioral measures of cognitive style other than ones classified under the more specific headings above. Correlations of several measures with esthetic judgement were small and sometimes in the opposite direction from that predicted. There was one outstanding exception where results were so striking and consistent as to suggest strongly a genuine and substantial relationship to esthetic judgement: reaction to putting on aniseikonic lenses. This result indicates a positive relation of esthetic judgement to a behavioral measure of tolerance for unrealistic experience.

For none of these groups of measures is it true that the measures used are a well-established set known to give reliable and valid coverage of a group of intercorrelated variables. Thus we are unable to view the results as providing strong evidence that esthetic judgement is not importantly related to the aspects of behavior referred to. All we conclude is that our evidence is against any important relation of esthetic judgement to these aspects of behavior as we have been able to measure them.

Third, for a number of aspects of cognitive style as measured by questionnaires, significant relations with esthetic judgement were found. Esthetic judgement showed tendencies to be positively related to the following questionnaire measures:

(a) Tolerance of complexity (accompanied by non-significant correlations in the same direction for tolerance of ambiguity, ambivalence and unrealistic experience).

(b) Scanning.

(c) Independence of judgement.

(d) Regression in the service of the ego.

(e) Intuition rather than sensation.

(f) Perception rather than judgement.

The positive ends of these variables, taken together, suggest a person of actively inquiring mind, seeking out experience that may be challenging because of complexity or novelty, ever alert to the potential experience offered by stimuli not already in the focus of attention, interested in understanding each experience thoroughly and for its own sake rather than contemplating it superficially and promptly filing it away in a category, and able to do all this with respect to the world inside himself as well as the world outside. The consistency of this picture is marred somewhat by the lack of significant findings with some additional questionnaire measures which would be consistent with this general picture. However, the results obtained are very impressive. They are in general agreement with the results of the more limited preliminary investigation reported by Child (1962a), which used different subjects and a measure of esthetic preference rather than esthetic judgement. They also are strikingly similar in some respects to the picture of personality correlates of creativity which has emerged from the Berkeley studies of more *v.* less creative people in several professions (Barron, 1958; MacKinnon, 1962). Finally, they are for the most part strongly confirmed by a partial replication of this part of the study, which extends the findings to esthetic preference as well as esthetic judgement.

Fourth, a relation to esthetic judgement was found for several measures that cannot confidently be fitted into the pattern just described. Some perhaps do properly form a part of it, and some may be entirely separate correlates of esthetic judgement.

(a) Anxiety, as measured by a questionnaire, shows a positive relation to esthetic judgement. This finding too is confirmed to some extent by the replication. For persons high in esthetic judgement, a high anxiety score may reflect not an unusually high level of anxiety but an unusually high willingness to be aware of anxiety and report it. (This interpretation is consistent with the substantial correlation of $+0.50$ between anxiety and regression in the service of the ego for the forty-nine Ss of the main study for whom the latter measure is available, and a corresponding correlation of $+0.37$ for the several hundred Ss involved in the replication.)

(b) A negative correlation between esthetic judgement and viscerotonia (love of comfort and relaxation) is perhaps consistent at a temperamental level with the picture of an actively inquiring mind interested in challenges. Such an interpretation might equally call for a positive relation with somatotonia, which was not found. At any rate, the result with viscerotonia agrees with results on esthetic preference and viscerotonia obtained in an earlier study (Child, 1962a). The replication tends to confirm the negative relation of viscerotonia to both esthetic judgement and esthetic preference, but suggests little relation for cerebrotonia.

(c) A small but significant positive correlation between esthetic judgement and verbal aptitude agrees with the findings of the earlier study but seems to have no distinctive bearing on the general interpretation offered here.

(d) Esthetic judgement was found to be positively related to several measures of visual preferences: preference for colors of lower brightness ('shades'), preference (on the Barron–Welsh test) for abstract designs liked by artists, and preference for Baroque over Classical art. What the person of better esthetic judgement prefers in each case may possibly be said to have in common a relative lack of obvious unity, structure or meaning. This seems clear in the case of Baroque style compared with Classical. It also seems clear in the case of the Barron–Welsh test, where the designs preferred by artists are asymmetrical and chaotic in comparison with the generally simple geometrical figures preferred by non-artists. The results on color preferences may have a similar meaning if, as Knapp (1958) suggests in another context, more somber colors have less tendency to impel attention and are thus more challenging to the viewer.

This study has dealt with individual differences within only one particular group: men students at a particular university. Whether the results can be extended to other groups cannot be known except when other groups are studied in some similar way. The results of this study provide hypotheses for the study of other groups.

Of special importance is the general pattern into which a number of findings fall, suggesting that good esthetic judgement is in large measure an outcome of a general cognitive approach to the world, an approach involving search for complex and novel experience which is then understood and evaluated through relatively autonomous interaction of the individual with objects providing such experience. The esthetic value of works of art, on this hypothesis, would be a function of their aptness for engaging and rewarding the attention of a person whose cognitive approach to the world is of this character.

References

BARRETT, D. M., and EATON, E. B. (1947), 'Preference for color or tint and some related personality data', *J. Pers.*, vol. 15, pp. 222–32.

BARRON, F. (1953), 'Some personality correlates of independence of judgement', *J. Pers.*, vol. 21, pp. 287–97.

BARRON, F. (1955), 'Threshold for the perception of human movement in inkblots', *J. consult. Psychol.*, vol. 19, pp. 33–8.

BARRON, F. (1958), 'Psychology of imagination', *Sci. Amer.*, vol. 199, p. 50.

BARRON, F., and WELSH, G. S. (1952), 'Artistic perception as a possible factor in personality style', *J. Psychol.*, vol. 33, pp. 199–203.

BULLEY, M. H. (1951), *Art and Everyman*, Batsford, vol. 1.

CHILD, I. L. (1950), 'The relation of somatotype to self-ratings on Sheldon's temperamental traits', *J. Pers.*, vol. 18, pp. 440–53.

CHILD, I. L. (1962a), 'Personal preferences as an expression of aesthetic sensitivity', *J. Pers.*, vol. 30, pp. 496–512.

CHILD, I. L. (1962b), 'A study of esthetic judgment', Mimeographed report of Co-operative Research Project No. 669, Office of Education, U.S. Department of Health, Education and Welfare.

CHILD, I. L. (1964), 'Observations on the meaning of some measures of esthetic sensitivity', *J. Psychol.*, vol. 57, pp. 49–64.

CRONBACH, L. J. (1951), 'Coefficient alpha and the internal structure of tests', *Psychometrika*, vol. 16, pp. 297–334.

CROWNE, D., and MARLOWE, D. (1960), 'A new scale of social desirability independent of psychopathology', *J. consult. Psychol.*, vol. 24, pp. 349–54.

EYSENCK, H. J. (1956), 'The questionnaire measurement of neuroticism and extraversion', *Rivista di Psicologia*, vol. 50, no. 4, pp. 113–40.

FRANCK, K. (no date), *Franck Drawing Completion Test: Preliminary Manual Containing Direction for Scoring, Norms, Scoring Key*, Australian Council for Educational Research.

FRANCK, K., and ROSEN, E. (1949), 'A projective test of masculinity–femininity', *J. consult. Psychol.*, vol. 13, pp. 247–56.

GARDNER, R., HOLTZMAN, P. S., KLEIN, G. S., LINTON, H., and SPENCE, D. P. (1959), 'Cognitive control', *Psychol. Issues*, vol. 1, no. 4, monogr. 4.

GOUGH, H. G. (1952), 'Identifying psychological femininity', *Educ. psychol. Measmt*, vol. 12, pp. 427–39.

GUILFORD, J. P., KETTNER, N. W., and CHRISTENSEN, P. R. (1954), 'A factor-analytic study across the domains of reasoning, creativity and evaluation: I. Hypotheses and description of tests', *Univer. Southern Calif. Rep. Psychol. Lab.*, no. 11.

JUNG, C. G. (1923), *Psychological Types*, Harcourt Brace.

KNAPP, R. H. (1958), 'Achievement and aesthetic preference', in J. W. Atkinson (ed.), *Motives in Fantasy, Action, and Society*, Van Nostrand, pp. 367–72.

KRIS, E. (1952), *Psychoanalytic Explorations in Art*, International Universities Press.

MACKINNON, D. W. (1962), 'The nature and nurture of creative talent', *Amer. Psychol.*, vol. 17, pp. 484–95.

MILLER, D. R., SWANSON, G. E., in collaboration with ALLINSMITH, W., MCNEILL, E. B., ALLINSMITH, B. B., ARONFREED, J., BEARDSLEE, B. J., and LANSKY, L. M. (1960), *Inner Conflict and Defense*, Holt.

MYERS, I. B. (1962), *The Myers–Briggs Type Indicator Manual*, Educational Testing Service, Princeton.

SCHAFER, R. (1958), 'Regression in the service of the ego: The relevance of a psychoanalytic concept for personality assessment', in G. Lindzey (ed.), *Assessment of Human Motives*, Grove, pp. 119–48.

SHELDON, W. H. (1942), *The Varieties of Temperament*, Harper.

STRICKER, L. J., and ROSS, J. (1963), 'Intercorrelations and reliability of the Myers–Briggs type indicator scales', *Psychol. Rep.*, vol. 12, pp. 287–93.

STRICKER, L. J., and ROSS, J. (1964), 'Some correlates of a Jungian personality inventory', *Psychol. Rep.*, vol. 14, pp. 623–43.

THURSTONE, L. L. (1944), 'A factorial study of perception', *Psychometr. Monogr.*, no. 4 University of Chicago Press.

WITKIN, H. A., LEWIS, U. B., HERTZMAN, M., MACHOVER, K., MEISSNER, P. B., and WAPNER, S. (1954), *Personality through Perception*, Harper.

WÖLFFLIN, H. (1932), *Principles of Art History*, Holt.

Part Four **Representation and Reality**

No single book relating psychological findings and visual art has made such an impact as Professor Gombrich's *Art and Illusion* and these readings, in dealing with the problem of representation in painting, would be incomplete without presentation of the book's position. In his paper, 'Visual discovery through art', Gombrich clarifies some of the arguments put forward in the book and extends his consideration to the interaction between and experience of the visual arts and reality. Green and Courtis, like Gombrich, utilize the concept of 'schemata' and consider the nature of figure perception in the context of both 'real' objects and graphic representation.

Reference
GOMBRICH, E. H. (1960), *Art and Illusion*, Phaidon.

8 E. H. Gombrich

Visual Discovery Through Art

E. H. Gombrich, 'Visual discovery through art', *Arts Magazine*,
November 1965.

1

Not all art is concerned with visual discovery in the sense in
which I propose to use these terms. Our museums show us a
dazzling and bewildering variety of images which rival in range
the creations of the living world of Nature. There are whales
among these images as well as humming-birds, gigantic monsters
and delicate trinkets, the products of man's dreams and night-
mares in different cultures and different climes. But only twice on
this globe, in ancient Greece and in Renaissance Europe, have
artists striven systematically, through a succession of generations,
step by step to approximate their images to the visible world and
achieve likenesses that might deceive the eye. I realize that most
critics' admiration for this discovery has considerably cooled off
in this century. Their taste has veered towards the primitive and
the archaic. There are good and interesting reasons for this preference, to which I hope to return in a different investigation, but
taste is one thing, history another. The ancient world certainly
saw the evolution of art mainly as a technical progress, the conquest of that skill in *mimesis*, in imitation, that was considered the
basis of art. Nor did the masters of the Renaissance differ here.
Leonardo da Vinci was convinced of this value of illusion as was
the most influential chronicler of Renaissance art, Giorgio Vasari, who took it for granted that in tracing the evolution of a
plausible rendering of nature he was describing the progress of
painting towards perfection. It goes without saying that in Western art this evolution did not come to an end with the Renaissance. The process of the conquest of reality through art continued, at a varying pace, at least as far as the nineteenth century,

and the battles fought by the Impressionists were fought over this issue – the issue of visual discoveries.

One thing stands out from this story and demands a psychological explanation. It is that this imitation of visual reality must be a very complex and indeed a very elusive affair, for why should it otherwise have taken so many generations of gifted painters to learn its tricks? It was to explain this puzzle that I set out, in my book on *Art and Illusion*,[1] to explore the relation between visual perception and pictorial representation. It is five years since this book came out, and more than ten years since I began writing the lectures on which it was based. It may be time to take stock once more and present some afterthoughts. Not that I see any reasons to repudiate the results of my investigation, such as they were. In fact, the reader who has worked through that rather groping presentation may have to put up with some recapitulations here. But I think that today I can render some of my explanations less elusive by anchoring them more firmly in an experience that is accessible to anyone. If I were to start the book today I would pivot the argument on the distinction between *recall* and *recognition*.

For the relevance of recognition to art, I can quote venerable authority, an authority, moreover, who wrote at a time when naturalistic paintings were still an object of wonder. Aristotle, writing in the fourth century B.C., discusses in his *Poetics* why 'imitation' should give man pleasure, why we enjoy looking at the perfect copies of things we find painful to behold in reality. He attributes this pleasure to man's inborn love of learning, which, as he politely concedes, is not confined to professional philosophers. 'The reason why we enjoy seeing likenesses is that, as we look we learn and infer what each is; for instance, that is a so-and-so.' The pleasure, in other words, is one of recognition. Naturalistic painting enables us to recognize the familiar world in the configurations of paint arranged on the canvas. Unlike Aristotle and his contemporaries, we may be so used to this experience that it no longer offers us a thrill. But most of us still feel the pleasure of recognition when the situation is reversed and we suddenly exclaim in front of a real scene, 'this is a so-and-so', a Whistler, perhaps, or a Pissarro.

1. The A. W. Mellon Lectures in the Fine Arts, 1956, New York (Bollingen Series) and London (Phaidon Press), 1960.

Clearly, as historians we must approach this second experience through the first. For if Whistler or Pissarro had not been enabled to create on their canvases recognizable images of the visible world, we would not in our turn have been able to recognize their images in nature.

2

But though recognition is clearly an act of remembering, it must not be confused with that other aspect of memory: our power of recall. The difference is easily demonstrated with a little experiment which also introduces us to its bearing on art. Take paper and pencil and draw anything from memory with which you think you are utterly familiar; the design of the chairs in your study or the shape of an animal you know very well. Even without paper and pencil we can check our power of recall if we ask ourselves such simple but awkward questions as to describe exactly how the horns of a cow are related to its ears.

Looking at the painting of a cow by the modern primitivist Jean Dubuffet (Plate 11) you will discover that he has shirked this issue. His *Cow with the Subtile Nose* does not boast any ears I can discover. His *Cow with the Fine Teats* (Plate 12) certainly makes up for this deficiency, but is the relationship right? Surely not. And here is the important paradox to which I must draw immediate attention. Even where we find it hard to recall, we know when we *recognize*, and say, in Aristotle's words, 'this is a so-and-so.' And failing to recognize, we claim the right to criticize and to say, 'but cows don't look like this.'

It so happens that Dubuffet's curious creatures are not really primitive, but rather over-sophisticated pictures. He wants to 'show the appearance of objects as they have been impressed on the man's brain when his attention or consciousness did not intervene, or at least intervened only vaguely, or not more than in the daily life of any ordinary man who is normally preoccupied with all sorts of other things at the moment his eyes light upon any object' (Selz, 1962, p. 102).

We shall discover that there is a fallacy here. The man in the street may not be able exactly to recall a cow, but what he sees when he meets a cow is a very different matter. One thing is sure.

Our difficulties of recall have nothing to do with the fact that we are men in the street, or streets, and not farmers in the fields. Take the *ex voto* of an Austrian peasant (Plate 13). In this genuinely naïve picture, too, the animal is hard to recognize. Is it a cow or is it a goat? And yet, the peasant who painted this would know not only how to recognize cows and goats, he would even recognize every individual cow of his herd. He would also, of course, immediately recognize in a picture what he cannot recall, and so can we if we look at a painting by the most famous specialist in cattle painting, the Dutch seventeenth-century artist, Paul Potter (Plate 14). It proves, if proof is needed, how immediate and effortless is recognition.

There is another paradox here connected with the first: the paradox that confused Dubuffet, and not only him. Recognition is easy, it is almost automatic, but, perhaps because of its automatic quality, largely unconscious. Not unconscious, to be sure, in the Freudian sense, but in the sense of those automatic processes to which we need not and often cannot attend. We do not know how and why we recognize a correctly drawn cow, but we soon notice if something is amiss in a real or pictured cow. If the transition from cows to people is not too offensive, let me refer to the difficulties portrait painters so often experience. Troublesome relatives of their sitters will insist that there is still something around the mouth that is not right, that they still cannot quite recognize Uncle Jimmy. Yet they are rarely willing or able to say why the mouth looks wrong to them. Maybe the painter will succeed in satisfying them by working through a period of trial and error, until, at least, the mouth looks 'right'. Unlike the exasperated painter, I tend to believe that the relatives probably knew what they were talking about. It is genuinely disturbing to feel an element of strangeness unsettling a familiar sight. We tend to notice at once if something in our room has been shifted, though few of us could ever recall, let alone draw, the contents of our rooms.

This is the point at which art educators often start a little sermon. They have become quite expert in creating in us a sense of guilt for failing to use our eyes and never noticing the wonderful variety of the visible world which we so lazily take for granted. I am all for making people use their eyes, but unless the sermon is carefully phrased it really makes little psychological sense. The teacher whose pupil fails to attend to the lesson has a right to scold him; but he would not get far if he asked him to attend to everything around him, the flies on the ceiling, the hum of the traffic or the play of light on the desk. It is the essence of attention that it is selective. We can focus on *something* in our field of vision, but never on *everything*. All attention must take place against a background of inattention. A heightened awareness of reality as such is something mystics may dream about, but cannot realize. The number of stimuli that impinge on us at every moment – if they were countable – would be astronomical. To see at all, we must isolate and select. The true miracle, it seems to me, is not that we do not notice everything, but that we still store so many impressions that recognition of the familiar is guaranteed.

It is clear that the distinction between the familiar and the unfamiliar must be of utmost biological importance, not only to man, but even to the animal. Insects and birds must recognize their homeground and regard with suspicion any changes that may betoken danger. Whether they also have a power of recall is perhaps an idle question. Ours, as we have seen, is rather imperfect. But we have developed an instrument to overcome this disability, an instrument we retain largely in our grasp, namely, the symbol.

For though what we call reality is too rich and too varied to be reproducible at will, symbols can be learned and recalled to a surprising extent. The same person who could perhaps not recall the appearance of his own right hand may reproduce for you any number of Shakespeare's sonnets or cricket and basketball scores. The power of recall of symbols varies of course enormously, but thanks to their economy of elements, symbols are much more amenable to availability in storage. Think of music, perhaps the extreme example. Most people in our culture can recall a great variety of tunes at will; indeed, tunes will keep running through their heads and be whistled and hummed as a kind of mood music accompanying many of their waking hours.

Whatever can be coded in symbols can then be retrieved and recalled with relative ease. The tricks of how to draw this or that – a cat for instance – of which I speak in my book at some length, can really be described as such simple methods of coding. The need for schema is the need for a code.

There are many styles in the history of art that operate with ready-made memorizable codes alone, styles in which the artist learns from his masters how to represent a mountain or a tree, or the Ox and Ass at the manger according to a well-proven formula (Plate 15). Indeed, the majority of artistic traditions operate in some such way. An older psychological art theory, including that of my teacher Emanuel Loewy, described these schematic images as 'memory images'. I now think that this description confuses cause and effect. It is not likely that anybody ever remembers reality in precisely that way, but images of this schematic kind admirably serve as codes that are aids in memorizing.

Of course, it is open to us, within limits, to codify and thus to memorize whatever we especially wish to recall. In inspecting a house we may think of buying, we will sketch a schematic diagram as an *aide-memoir*, only to find to our annoyance that the diagram occasionally has superimposed itself on our memory of the place. We have to return to modify and enrich it.

Something of this kind can always be done in case of need. Once you have noticed, for argument's sake, that you do not know enough about the relationship of those horns and ears of the cow, you can check and verbalize this information, or better still, enter it onto your schema and you are safe; safe, that is, until the next person asks you an awkward question about its nostrils – and the number of such potential questions is virtually unlimited.

Clearly, an expert cattle painter such as Potter would have been able to meet most of them head-on. He knew about cows, he could paint them by heart, and paint them so correctly that recognition accepted them as familiar and convincing.

In my book on *Art and Illusion*, I chose for this process of approximation to nature the psychological formula of 'schema plus correction'. The evolution of naturalistic art can be seen in terms of this formula. I cannot expect this solution to be accepted by the reader before I have answered a question that may have irked him for some time: Is there not a fundamental difference between the so-called 'conceptual' styles that operate with a re-membered code and those periods of naturalism to which Potter belonged? Is not the secret of Potter quite simply that he drew cattle from nature, even though he may later have used these sketches for his studio paintings? Is not all naturalism grounded on the discipline of drawing from the model or motif? And if these artists really trained themselves to observe and to draw what they saw in front of their eyes, what relevance has the distinction between recall and recognition to their type of art?

The answer must be one which every art teacher would give who has had to teach the traditional skills of representation – if such are still around. It is that the difference between drawing from memory and drawing from life is, strangely enough, only one of degree. Max Liebermann somewhere quotes his teacher as saying, 'What you cannot paint from memory you cannot paint at all.' It is true that in painting from the motif you have the inestimable advantage of easy comparison between your work and your model. You can always pause to see whether you recognize your motif in your picture or your picture in the motif. But though such comparisons will make it easier for you to spot mistakes, the example of the portrait painter I have mentioned shows that a feeling of discrepancy is one thing, the invention of a fitting code another.

There are many reasons for this difficulty, some of which I analysed at some length in my book. I also quoted Sir Winston Churchill, who rightly emphasized that even in painting from nature we must use our memory as we change fixation from motif to canvas. This would even be true of an artist copying a picture. But in painting from nature, more formidable psychological problems intervene. For psychologically it does not make much sense to say that we 'copy' what we see in the visible work. What we see extends in depth, while our painting surface is flat. The elements of what we see differ in color. To invent a code of color combinations distributed on a plane for the variety of experience in the real world is, of course, the achievement of naturalism. It is an achievement simply because, as I said several times in my book, the real world does not look like a flat picture, though a flat picture can be made to look like the real world. The reason for this paradox is discussed in psychology under the heading of the *constancies*. The name covers the totality of those stabilizing tendencies that prevent us from getting giddy in a world of fluctuating appearances. As a man comes to greet us in the street, his image will double in size if he approaches from twenty yards to ten. If he stretches out his hand to greet us, it becomes enormous. We do not register the degree of these changes; his image remains relatively constant and so does the color of his hair, despite the changes of light and reflection.

Even the amateur photographer knows something about this effect. He has learned how disappointingly small an object may look in his picture if he fails to move close enough for it to fill most of the field of vision. Painters, of course, have learned to break down the constancies by measuring the apparent size of an object against the brush held at arm's length. The novice who tries this simple technique for the first time is in for surprises if he knows how to watch his visual experience. And yet he would be mistaken if he inferred from this surprise effect that the methods he is taught only represent a 'convention', a fortuitous code that differs from the way we really see the world. Arguments of this kind frequently have been used by critics of mathematical perspective. I believe them to be as misleading as is Dubuffet's claim that we never really see a cow in the way Potter represents it. Both these criticisms fail to take into account that we know very well when a picture looks 'right'. A picture painted according to the laws of perspective will generally evoke instant and effortless recognition. It will do so to such an extent that it will in fact restore the feeling of reality, including – and this is most important – the constancies.

I am afraid I somewhat muffed this decisive point in my book by taking a poor example. I am all the more glad to be able to reproduce here the brilliant demonstration of this fact which originally convinced me of the crucial relevance of this transformation. It comes from the book *Color* by Ralph Evans (Plate 17).

All Evans has done is duplicate the image of the lamp post in the background nearer the picture's lower edge and to do the same with the last of the row of posts. The effect is surprising indeed. Even with the illustration we must have recourse to measurement to convince ourselves that the lamp post in the background is *really* so small and that the row of posts *really* diminishes to such an extent. The constancies operate even in a photograph. Yet nobody would deny for a moment that we have no difficulty in recognizing the familiar appearance of a suburban street when looking at the picture. Perspective diminution, however surprising, results in recognition. It is a valid instrument, and Vasari was right when he regarded perspective as a genuine discovery.

3

And yet there remains a question which Vasari failed to ask because he took the answer for granted. If only the tricks of naturalistic painting result in convincing images that make for effortless recognition, how can we explain the fact that most cultures are quite happy with schematic representations?

A humorous contemporary drawing, done in a medieval schematic style, which an unknown reader of my book kindly sent me from Australia, not only poses this question afresh, but may also contain the germ of an answer (Plate 16). The caption tells us (as the King watches with exasperation while his meal slides from the table to the ground): 'It's the way they drew these wretched tables.'

To us, at least, the medieval convention suggests in fact that the table is tilted and that nothing could stand on it. If we could find out when this feeling first arose and when this kind of criticism would have been understood, we would be a long way nearer an explanation of why artists felt that the schema was in need of correction. Once this process was set in motion, the rest may have been a matter of trial and error, of taking thought and trying again. *Ce n'est que le premier pas qui coûte.*

In my book I have tried to sketch an answer to this question as far as the beginnings of the Greek revolution are concerned. I shall try here to apply it briefly to the Renaissance, leaving it to another occasion to fill in the outlines. My answer was that the purpose of art that led to the discovery of illusionistic devices was not so much a general desire to imitate nature as a specific demand for the plausible narration of sacred events.

Perhaps we should still distinguish here between various forms of pictorial narration. One may be called the pictographic method. Here the sacred event is told in clear and simple hieroglyphs which make us understand rather than visualize it. Within the context of such a style, it may be argued, the 'conceptual method' of drawing a table surface produces no discomfort. The hieratic figures of the Three Angels represented on the Romanesque tapestry as partaking of Abraham's meal (Plate 20) may look pictographic to our eyes, but the scene as such is impressive in its solemn consistency. It is only where the artist aims more visibly at telling us not only *what* happened but *how* it happened that the conceptual method becomes vulnerable to criticism. The rise of naturalism, in other words, presupposes a shift in the beholder's expectations and demands. The public asks the artist to present the sacred event on an imaginary stage as it might have looked to an eyewitness. There is some evidence, I think, that this demand was in fact insistent around the time of Giotto's revolution. It is, of course, generally agreed that Giotto in his Biblical narratives aimed at such a dramatic evocation. We know that at first the effect of his art was stunned surprise at the degree of lifelikeness the master's brush could achieve. But if I am right, it was this very success that made certain remaining inconsistencies in the spatial framework of his narratives more obtrusive. In front of his rendering of the Feast of Herod (Plate 21), an irreverent wit might easily have asked whether the dishes were safe on that table. I do not know whether such a joke was cracked, nor even whether such criticism of Giotto's method was in fact voiced. But, clearly, the invention of perspective three generations later eliminated this potential discomfort. Its rapid spread throughout Europe suggests at least that it met an existing demand. The closer the code came to the evocation of a familiar reality the more easily could the faithful contemplate the re-enactment of the story and identify the participants.

It is true that if this was the purpose it soon became overlaid by technical interest. The rendering of depth, of light, of texture and facial expression was singled out for praise by the connoisseur, and the problems of the craft became aims in themselves. But these aims, to repeat, were only achieved by a long process of trial and error that was guided by the critical scrutiny of paintings that failed to pass the 'recognition test'. The motive force we may imagine as underlying the growth of naturalism is not the wish to imitate natural appearances as such, but to avoid and counter the critic's impatient questions: 'What does this onlooker feel?'; 'What sort of fabric is his cloak?'; 'Why does he throw no shadow?'

Plate 1. F.-A. Bartholdi, *The Statue of Liberty*, 1886,
New York Harbor

Plate 2. J. B. Fischer von Erlach, *The Colossus of Rhodes* (reconstruction), 1721

Die der Sonnen gewidmete Wünder-Statua,
Colossus zu Rhodis, welche unter dem Carischen Fürsten —
Theagones ungefehr, im Jahr der Welt 3600, durch Charem —
Lyndium von 70 Ellen höhe aus Ertz gegoßen und aufgerichtet.

Ta.VIII.

veilleux Colosse de Rhodès dedié
eil, qui fût jetté en bronze par Care Lyndien,
gouvernement de Theagone Prince de Carie,
l'an du monde 3600 Il avoit 70. aûnes de haut.
Plin: L: 2 cap 62 et L: 34 c: 7. Strab L: 2.

Plate 3. Jean-Marc Nattier, *The Duchess of Orleans as Hebe*, 1774, Stockholm National Museum

Plate 4. William Hogarth, *The Bruiser* (Charles
Churchill), 1763

Plate 7. *God the Father*, 1487, from a Lyons Missal

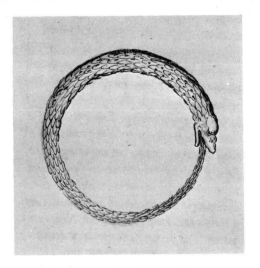

Plate 8. Attributed to Albrecht Dürer, *The Hieroglyph of Eternity*, circa 1512

Plate 9. *The Apollo Belvedere,* Rome, Vatican

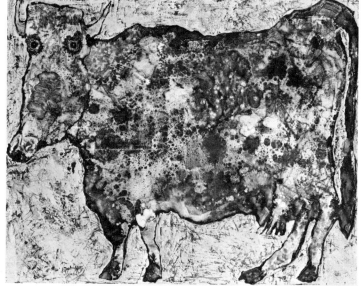

Above left: Plate 10. *Father Time*, 1615, from V. Cartari, *Imagini degli Dei Antichi*, Padua

Below left: Plate 11. Jean Dubuffet, *The Cow with the Subtile Nose*, Museum of Modern Art, New York

Below: Plate 12. Jean Dubuffet, *The Cow with the Fine Teats*, Mr and Mrs Harry Sherwood Collection, Los Angeles

Above left: Plate 13. Anonymous Austrian *Ex Voto*

Below left: Plate 14. Paul Potter, *The Bull*,
Mauritshuis, The Hague

Below: Plate 15. German fourteenth century,
Nativity, The Warburg Institute, London

Plate 20. *Abraham and the Three Angels*,
Halberstadt Cathedral, Vienna

Plate 22. Melanesian wood shield, British Museum

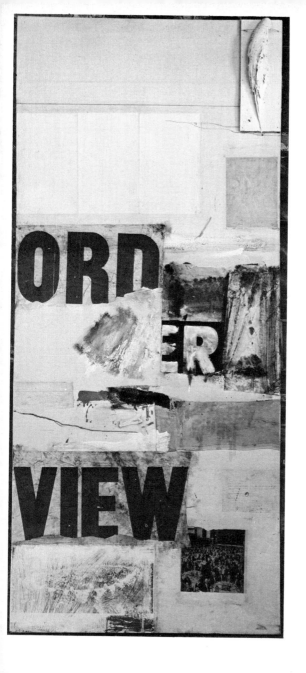

Left: Plate 24. Robert Rauschenberg, *Hazard,*
Collection : Mr Wolfgang Hahn, Cologne-Lindental,
Germany

Below: Plate 25. Lawrence Gowing, *Parabolic
Perspective,* Tate Gallery

Plate 26. Claude Lorrain, *Narcissus and Echo*,
National Gallery

Plate 27. Richard Wilson, *Dinas Bran Castle*, National Museum of Wales, Cardiff

Plate 28. (a) Prelate; (b) Outdoor type exercising;
(c) On parade; (d) Business man; (e) Woman on
floor; (f) Woman reclining; (g) Woman walking;
(h) Office boy. Reproduced by permission of
Haro Hodson

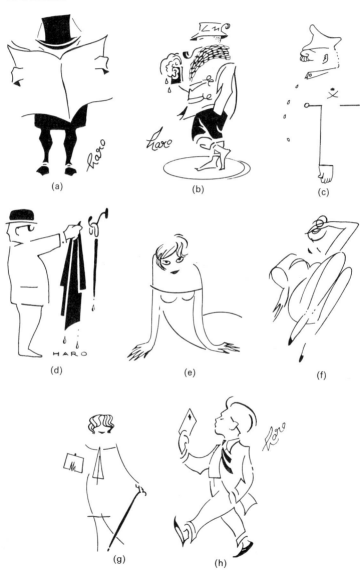

(a)

(b)

(c)

(d)

(e)

(f)

(g)

(h)

Once we describe the rise of naturalism in terms of such scrutiny, it also becomes clear that there are rival functions of the image which do not elicit this kind of question at all. Even within the context of a sacred art, it may be didactic clarity that is demanded of artists designing images that should above all be as legible from afar as are Byzantine mosaics. Today there are such functions of the image as advertising (favoring some 'striking' effect) or diagrams and pictographic roadsigns (Figure 1) which are better served by a reduction of naturalistic information. Accordingly, the poster and the pictographic illustration have gradually 'evolved' away from nineteenth-century illusionism.

4

I think that in strictly definable contexts such as these, the term 'evolution' is more than a loose metaphor. Indeed, the schematic process I have sketched out here could be presented in almost Darwinian terms. The fitting of form to function follows a process of trial and error, of mutation and the survival of the fittest. Once the standard of either clear or convincing images has been set, those not conforming will be eliminated by social pressure.

Figure 1. Pictographic roadsign from *Design Quarterly*

There is a real Darwinian parallel here which should not be overlooked. For the evolution of convincing images was indeed anticipated by nature long before human minds could conceive this trick. I am referring to the wonders of protective coloring and mimicry, of deterrent and camouflaging forms in plants and animals. As we have all learnt at school, and as we can see with amazement in zoological displays, there are insects that look exactly like the leaves of the tree which is their habitat (Plate 18). There are caterpillars which, when they freeze into immobility, look deceptively like twigs; there are mammals which are so colored that their dappled or striped skin merges surprisingly with the play of light in their native forest; there are harmless insects which deceptively imitate the shape and color of dangerous species and thus manage to increase their chances of survival.

The art historian and the critic could do worse than ponder these miracles. They will make him pause before he pronounces too glibly on the relativity of standards that make for likeness and recognition. The eye and the brain of the bird from which protective coloring must hide the butterfly surely differs in a thousand ways from ours. And yet we can only assume that for both the bird and for us the butterfly and the leaf have become indistinguishable. The naturalistic style of these butterflies deceives a great range of predators including ourselves. Thus, in comparing earlier the bewildering variety of shapes in art with that of living creatures, I had a little more in mind than a mere illustration of multiplicity. For might it not be argued that the shapes of art are also arrived at through adaptation to various functions? I have spoken of the evolution of naturalistic styles in the animal world. Clearly nature is not always naturalistic in that sense. The evolution of some forms and colorings are explained by scientists as deterrents or attractents in a more general sense. Take the 'eyes' we frequently see on the wings of moths (Plate 19). If we can believe the prevailing hypothesis, these have a deterrent effect on predators (see Tinbergen, 1953, pp. 94–5). If you paint them out, the moths so treated are more likely to be eaten than those able suddenly to display these pairs of threatening eyes. It has been suggested that it is not accidental that the threatening shape takes this particular form. Maybe predators are attuned from birth to the danger of this particular stimulus. A pair of large, watching eyes would signify a predator dangerous to them. But these, we might say, are not naturalistic in the same sense in which the imitated leaf is. They are rather in the nature of generalized, schematic – but expressive – images. They represent, if you like, the Expressionist style of nature.

We may assume that evolution in art as well as in nature could also approximate other specifications than that of effortless recognizability. Maybe the immensely disquieting and expressive forms of those tribal styles we call 'primitive' also evolved step by step towards awe-inspiring or terrifying configuration (Plate 22). Admittedly, there was nobody around to express and formulate these standards. They may also have been less easy to formulate. One might imagine that it was merely felt that certain masks, images or ornaments were charged with more potency, more *mana* than others, and that those features that made for their magic power survived and increased in the course of time.

And yet, I do not want to overstress the parallelism between human art and the creativity of nature. The comparison seems to me as illuminating for what the two processes may have in common as for their differences. In the evolution of natural forms that extend over geological epochs, we have learnt to beware of the teleological fallacy. Nature does not set itself aims. Man does. Admittedly, he does so to varying degrees. It is fashionable to doubt this, too. We are constantly warned against indulging in parochial pride, and against seeing our culture as superior to other varieties. I confess that I am an unrepentant parochial. I believe that the birth of critical rationalism in Greek culture gave mankind a new tool towards the shaping of its own destiny that other cultures lack. We call it science. The evolutionary series of Greek and Renaissance painting differ from other evolutions precisely through the admixture of science. The science of anatomy, the science of projective geometry and of optics were called in to hasten the experimentation towards recognizable images. In the end, as we know, science overtook art in this respect through the evolution of photography, the color film and the wide screen.

Maybe it is only in these periods of directed research that we can legitimately speak of 'visual discovery'. Indeed, what is usually described in these terms differs quite significantly from the unconscious process I have tried to characterize so far. It differs so much that it might appear at first sight to contradict and disprove my description of the processes of recognition and recall. For contrary to what this description would make us

227

expect, there are visual discoveries which the public at first refused to accept as convincing.

The standard examples are the discoveries of the Impressionists, the methods of *plein air* painting which concentrated on colored reflections and colored shadows. These, we are told, did not at first look convincing. The public had to learn to see them by attempting their verification. Sympathetic observers noticed to their surprise that having looked at Impressionist paintings, they, too, could recognize these colored shadows in nature. The whole process seemed to be reversed. In fact, it was mainly this experience that led to the dismissal of Vasari's theories of learning as naïve, and to an increasing stress on visual relativism that I should like to criticize in my turn.

5

It is vital to my whole approach that I be allowed to specify a little more closely in psychological terms what is going on when, as the saying goes, the artist 'teaches us to see'. In the remaining sections, I should like to give you at least a sketch of a tentative answer, knowing full well that it cannot be the whole story.

We must here return to the fact that recognition is largely unconscious and automatic. Even so, both logically and psychologically, this task of recognition is far from simple. For in fact, the stimuli can hardly ever be identical with those received before. A different angle of vision, a change in illumination transforms the stimuli – and yet the impression of familiarity is not necessarily affected. Psychology discusses some of the stabilizing mechanisms involved here under the heading of the constancies with which we are already familiar. But the stability of recognition reaches beyond them. Take the most mysterious of all: our ability to recognize a familiar face in a crowd. There is nothing more mobile to our senses than the human physiognomy, for every slight shift in its configuration has a strong expressive meaning. And yet, we also establish a framework of identity in change that is recognized through all the transformations of expression. It is the same face that now 'looks happy', now morose. It remains the same face even throughout the relentless transformations wrought on it by time and age. Familiarity is not to be confused with identity.

I have chosen the example of facial recognition because it may serve best to bring home even to the skeptic the plasticity of our visual experience. What we 'see' is not simply given, but is the product of past experience and future expectations. Thus, it may happen that we meet an old friend after many years and receive a shock – he has changed so much, we would hardly have recognized him. But after an hour, we do recognize the earlier face in the altered features, memory and impression merge again and we 'see' the old friend once more through, or across, the signs of age. Indeed, try as we may, we can hardly recover the first impression of strangeness, we no longer see him as unfamiliar.

And yet, the recognition of faces also teaches another lesson. The framework is more easily upset than we might expect. The unrecognizable disguise is not the mere fancy of old-fashioned dramatists. Change the hairstyle of a girl, or add or subtract a beard, and recognition will be disproportionately difficult, as I have learned to my embarrassment when my students turned up thus transformed. Obviously, recognition demands some anchorage. Even in trying to remember the participants of a class, we look for some method of 'coding' these faces for recognition. Miss Smith is the girl with the ponytail; Mr Jones, the boy with the moustache. Subsequent learning relies on this mark of identity that determines the *Gestalt*.

We return here to the example of the portrait painter and his difficulty in achieving a likeness that is recognized as such by the sitter's relatives. Clearly, what is required is the choice of a code that coincides with the way these critics 'see' the sitter. I have insisted that their criticism may well be more valid than the painter is inclined to admit. But we may now add that the painter's own version may also win through. He may be able to persuade the relatives of the validity of his own vision; looking at the sitter, they may suddenly recognize the portrait in him. Art has imposed a fresh vision on a face.

The most extreme case of this exploitation of the instability of vision is portrait caricature. It is also the most instructive, because the caricaturist need not be a great artist to seize upon those invariants which are all we generally remember of the appearance of politicians or actors. In distilling this framework into a simple code, he shows us the formula and helps the public figure to secure recognition. But the caricaturist can also transform his victim. He can single out characteristic invariants which we have yet never used for recognition, and in thus focusing our attention on these features, he teaches us a fresh code (Plate 23). We then say that the caricaturist has made us see the victim differently – we cannot help thinking of the caricature whenever we meet the man.

It is in this direction that I propose to look for a solution to the problem of visual discovery in art. Its most striking effects presuppose a degree of plasticity in the way we 'see' the world which leaves recognition unaffected. This must be connected with the wealth of cues at our disposal for coding our visual experience. The painter, like the caricaturist, can teach us a new code of recognition, he cannot teach us to 'see'.

6

Having stated the direction in which I think we have to go, I should like to proceed a little more slowly and to introduce a number of distinctions I failed to make in my book.

I am afraid as a first step I must slightly reduce the importance generally attached to the artist and painter in this process of discovery. It is true, of course, that, being professionally concerned with visual experience, artists have played a conspicuous role in the discovery of unexpected features in the visible world. But there is no intrinsic reason why such discoveries need be coded in paint and not in words. Our colored shadows are a case in point. As early as 1793, Goethe sent the German physicist and writer Lichtenberg a section of his color theory dealing with the phenomenon of colored shadows. Lichtenberg replied in a most interesting letter, in which he said that ever since receiving Goethe's paper he had been running after colored shadows as he ran after butterflies as a boy. Lichtenberg discusses the general failure to notice these things 'because in our judgements which are based on visual impressions, sensation and judgement interpenetrate to such an extent that after a certain age it becomes hardly possible to separate them. ... It is for this reason that bad portrait painters lay in the entire face all over with pink flesh color. They are unable to realize that there could be blue, green, yellow and brown shadows in a human face.'

I feel we would get further in our study of visual discoveries if we made some distinction between change of interest and change of perception. Lichtenberg's interest, once aroused, led him to notice things he had not noticed before. In itself, there is not much of a problem here. It can and does happen all the time. If you want to buy new curtains, you will probably notice curtains and their features that you would otherwise overlook. If you read about facial asymmetry, you will become aware of deviations from symmetry which you had never noticed. Some of these fluctuations are superficial and transitory, others more permanent. If fashion arouses interest in vintage cars, old cars will acquire a new look; if collectors should make news by paying high prices for a particular type of dustbin, we would begin to look at dustbins on our way to the office.

Clearly, art is a frequent source of such novel interests. Contemporary artists such as Rauschenberg have become fascinated by the patterns and textures of decaying walls with their torn posters and patches of damp (Plate 24). Though I happen to dislike Rauschenberg, I notice to my chagrin that I cannot help being aware of such sights in a different way since seeing his paintings. Perhaps if I had disliked his exhibition less, the memory would have faded more quickly. For emotional involvement, positive or even negative, certainly favors retention and recognition.

And yet, I would think, this experience of noticing things because artists have drawn attention to motifs still differs from visual discoveries at least in degree.

I recently experienced the surprise of such a discovery. It may sound trivial enough as I describe it, but it will show that this function of art is not confined to representational painting. Our kitchen floor at home happens to have a simple black-and-white checkerboard pattern. As I was taking a glass of water from the tap to the table, I suddenly noticed the delightful and interesting distortions of this pattern visible through the bottom of the glass. I had never seen this transformation before, though I must have made this same movement hundreds of times. And suddenly I recognized the pattern and knew why I saw it now. I had visited an exhibition of the paintings of Lawrence Gowing, a painter who shares my interest in perception and was experimenting with abstracts. I had looked with interest at one of the paintings in which the illusion of space and light in a forest is created through the systematic distortion of a checker pattern (Plate 25). It was a classic case of what might be called inverted recognition – the recognition not of reality in a painting but of a painting in reality. Clearly it was interest that had triggered it off. Without it, I might have taken a hundred or thousand more glasses from the tap to the kitchen table without noticing the appearance of the floor through the bottom of the glass – without noticing, not really without seeing. For of course I must have seen the pattern before, if we mean by 'seeing' that the stimuli must have reached my retina and my visual cortex. But I had attended to these as little as I attend to millions of other impressions that impinge as I move through the world.

I must draw attention to the difference between this and the former example, although it is only a difference of nuance. Rauschenberg may have created an interest in old billboards as possible motifs of artistic attention, but it would be stretching usage beyond common sense if I said in this instance that I had never seen billboards before. But this would be true of the pattern Gowing enabled me to arrest and to see. Moreover, he also enabled me to discuss and recall it. I suppose we might say his painting had unwittingly provided a symbol in which this fleeting impression could be coded and had thus isolated it from the stream of 'preconscious' or 'subliminal' perception. I thus experienced the thrill and shock of recognition when I encountered the configuration of the painting in this unexpected context, though I was not immediately aware of the cause of this isolation.

To probe a little deeper into this kind of visual discovery, we should, I think, investigate the effect of isolation from context, not only through art but also through other agencies. For isolation will easily break up familiarity and thus transform the experience. Take the example of our familiar room. Anybody who has ever moved house can tell how unfamiliar that old room can look when emptied of furniture. Not only unfamiliar, but strikingly different. Its very size seems to have changed. The once pleasant and cozy place seems to have shrunk into a small, stark cell. Admit the demolition firm, break down the walls and visit the foundation for a last time, and they will look tiny in relation to the total landscape. What was once a comfortable framework for your actions, as you moved from the easy-chair to your book-shelf is now a speck on the terrain. The context completely trans-forms the experience. Yet, it would be quite misleading to say you had never looked at your room before or never knew its real size. Your experience of familiarity was as real as is that of your unfamiliarity.

As far as images are concerned, the most convincing demon-stration of this effect of context comes not, perhaps, from art but from photography. We all know that not all snapshots look convincing. Some isolate the phase of a movement from its con-text and look surprisingly unreal in consequence. Others give such a steep foreshortening that they look surprising and almost un-believable. Does it make sense then to say that this is what we really see in such situations? Yes and no. Interaction of cues can restore familiarity. We have the technical means now to put this surprising fact to the test. In Cinerama, the temporal and spatial context so closely simulates the experience of the real world that, far from finding steep foreshortening unrealistic, we tend to duck or blink as the object appears to approach us so closely.

One answer to the question of how the same image can be both verifiably correct and yet unfamiliar surely lies in the effect of isolation. Here we can return to those famous colored shadows of the Impressionists. In the sixth chapter of Zola's novel *L'Oeuvre*, the painter's rather simple-minded wife ventures to criticize him for painting a poplar quite blue. He makes her look at the motif and notice the delicate blue of the foliage. It was true, the tree was really blue, and yet she did not quite admit defeat; she blamed reality: there could not *be* blue trees in nature.

Was she so stupid? Her experience of familiarity, like that of everyone, was grounded on a knowledge of invariants, on what Hering called, a bit misleadingly, 'memory color'. Psychologists – since the time of Goethe and of Lichtenberg at least – use artificial means for eliminating this mechanism, breaking down the inter-action of cues and isolating the sensation as far as this can ever be done. They use what is called a reduction screen for defeating the constancies and demonstrating, for instance, the degree to which an illuminated surface changes its appearance as we tilt or

233

move it in relation to the light source. Naturalistic painters have always used reduction in one way or another to break down the constancies. They tend to isolate and half close their eyes for this very purpose. But obviously, if they restore the context we do not experience surprise. The correct placing of the right values results in recognition. But there are both technical and artistic limits to this restoration, and hence the shock of incredulity.

If this shock results in interest, however, we can all be made to hunt for colored shadows or other effects seen in paintings, as Lichtenberg did. We shall not need a reduction screen; interest and attention will do the isolating for us. And here the isolation really can lead to transformation – or, to use a more emotive word, to the transfiguring of reality.

7

And yet, even this is not the whole story. For something more interesting might intervene to assist transformation through isolation. Briefly, isolation tends to increase ambiguity. In real life, it is the interaction of innumerable cues that generally allows us to find our way through the world with comparative ease. Yet it is a well-known fact that in certain situations we cannot tell whether an unfamiliar object seen in isolation is large and distant or small and close-by, or whether an unevenly shaded area is hollow and lit from the left or protruding and lit from the right. Clearly, in reducing the richness of nature to suit his code, the painter will always increase the ambiguity of his individual stroke or mark. A line can stand for anything from a match to a distant horizon. In what are called 'conceptual' styles, every effort is made to reduce or eliminate these ambiguities and to secure the intended reading. Naturalistic styles mobilize all available means for the mutual clarification of cues and any obtrusive ambiguity counts as a fault to be eliminated. The master of the life class will draw attention to any passage that is not clear, any line that is not recognized for what it stands for. But once art has become emancipated from its purpose of illustration and evocation, this ambiguity acquires a new interest. From Impressionism to Cubism, the exploration of isolation and ambiguity has drawn increasing attention to the instability of the visible world. Once again these lessons can be recalled in real-life situations – most easily in conditions of reduced visibility: in mist, in flickering light or in unfamiliar situations. But increasing experience with the unexpected ambiguity of visual cues in paintings will alert us to the unsuspected ambiguity of visual cues in real life and thus lead to fresh discoveries. In recognizing such pictures in nature we learn about the complexity of vision as such.

Once again, painting has no monopoly here. I remember an unsettling experience of this kind that was elicited by a psychological experiment. I had just attended a demonstration of that intriguing visual teaser, Adelbert Ames's 'revolving trapezoid', in essence a flat, foreshortened window-frame that turns on its axis but looks stubbornly as if it swayed to and fro. As I walked cross-country, I happened to see a broken farm gate propped up in an inaccessible pond. It reminded me of the trapezoid and I suddenly realized that I could not tell its real shape, or position either. There was a moment of slight anxiety as I woke up to the fact that the same applied to distant trees or countless other configurations in my surroundings. The passing shock has helped me to understand why we prefer to ignore this instability in our readings of the world.

Yet, it is clear that if it were not for this instability it would make no sense to say that the painter can impose his vision on our world. He does it at those vulnerable points where coding is more or less optional. What is involved here is perhaps best illustrated with the help of a well-known textbook example of ambiguity, the notorious old 'rabbit or duck' figure I used in my book (Figure 2). Clearly, in this most simple of cases we can elicit alternate readings depending on captions of a verbal description – but it might be even more effective to impose one of these readings through visual means.

I have not made any experiments, but I would predict that you could bring about a transformation merely by changing the visual context, either spatially, by drawing a duckpond or rabbit warren around the blot, or temporally, by showing a subject, a series of pictures of rabbits, before projecting the ambiguous image; in which case, what we call mental set will surely do the trick and determine the reading.

It would be fascinating to go on from here and watch the

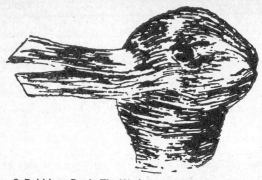

Figure 2. Rabbit or Duck, The Warburg Institute, London

final transition from interpretation to suggestion. In our blot, there is still an objective anchorage for the reading of either rabbit or duck. You might systematically reduce this anchorage and still make your subjects project an expected image, provided their initial conviction and desire is strong enough. For there is a natural transition here from interest to mental set, and thence to projection. The hungry rabbit catcher will scan the field for his quarry with such intensity that a clod of earth or a clump of leaves may tempt him, unless he has learned to hold his imagination in check. The degree to which a hunt or search can reorganize and transform cues was brought home to me – if I may continue my autobiography – when I was preparing this paper and looking in a library for a book with suitable illustrations of mimicry and protective coloring. Running my eyes along a line of miscellaneous books, I suddenly thought I had got it; I 'saw' a book with the odd but promising title *Deceptive Beetles* – obviously some treatise on insect camouflage. Alas, as I looked more closely the title turned out to read *Decisive Battles*. I felt pretty silly, but I could not help wondering about the flexibility of the preconscious mind. Beetles to battles is not a surprising transformation; it involves the misreading of only two letters out of seven. But, it was almost disturbing, that in this joy of false recognition, my preconscious had changed 'decisive' into 'deceptive' to keep the promise of a book on mimicry.

Have I moved too far away from art? Not, I hope, if this extreme example of my folly illustrates the end of the spectrum, as it were, between perception and projection. I do not know if it is ever possible to separate the two completely. In scanning the world with interest roused by past experience, the previous impression and the incoming sensations tend to coalesce like two drops of water forming a larger drop. When paintings have aroused our interest in certain configurations, we may look for anchorage and confirmation and use every hint in a visual experience to find there what we sought. This may go for the 'conformist' as well as for the 'progressive'. The first will find his prejudices confirmed and recognize only the familiar code in the familiar world; this is what the innovators always complained of. But the other experience may be equally possible. The wish to find confirmation of some new experiment may make the progressive suggestible and may thus facilitate the artist's task of modifying his code. The premium in self-esteem that may be offered to those who can share a new way of seeing should not be overlooked as a determinant.

The experience of visual discovery I have tried to stalk is probably a compound of these elements. I especially mean the experience in which the normal relationship of recognition and recall is reversed, so that we genuinely recognize pictorial effects in the world around us, rather than the familiar sights of the world in pictures. The road to this experience led from interest to isolation and from isolation to increased ambiguity. In discovering through this experience an alternative reading of an isolated set of impressions, we receive a kind of minor revelation through recognition. Is this the thrill of learning of which Aristotle speaks?

I have so far steered clear of esthetics, and it would be out of place to introduce it now. But we can be sure, I think, that this revelation is experienced as a new kind of beauty. It is well known that it was the admiration for the effects of Claude Lorrain, his symbols of serenity and idyllic peace (Plate 26), that first led the English connoisseurs of the eighteenth century to discover the beauties of what they called picturesque landscape nearer home. Richard Wilson learned from Claude's code how to isolate and represent the beauties of his native Wales (Plate 27). In this momentous development that had its influence on the rise of

Romantic nature worship in poetry no less than in art, new interests and new visual experiences were no doubt intertwined in a way that is hard to disentangle. Wilson probably wished to see Wales in Claude's terms. But the very word 'picturesque' shows that one element involved was the thrilling and unexpected encounter with beloved pictures in what had previously looked like a familiar reality of the kind that is unconsciously recognized but not consciously recalled.

There is no reason to doubt that this process can and does go on. The world of visual experience is infinite in its variety and richness. Art can code reality correctly and yet paradoxically we have no cause to fear that artists need ever stop revealing to us new facets of this inexhaustible experience.

References

SELZ, P. (1962), *The Work of Jean Dubuffet*, The Museum of Modern Art, New York.

TINBERGEN, N. (1953), *Social Behaviour in Animals*, London.

9 R. T. Green and M. C. Courtis

Information Theory and Figure Perception: The Metaphor that Failed

Excerpt from R. T. Green and M. C. Courtis, 'Information theory and figure perception: the metaphor that failed', *Acta Psychologica*, vol. 25 (1966), pp. 12–36.

[Introduction

In the section of their article preceding this excerpt Green and Courtis point out that two of the fundamental principles of information theory are not met in the attempt to apply the theory to figure perception. The first principle is that members of the ensemble of possible items have known probabilities of occurrence, a requirement imposed on figure perception by breaking the figure into a mosaic of elements and imposing an arbitrary scanning sequence of these elements on the perceiver. The second principle is that the probabilities of occurrence of members of the ensemble are *objective*, while in the application to figure perception the assumption that subjective probabilities mirror objective probabilities is not necessarily valid.

In the first of three demonstrations they show that the technique of breaking a figure into a mosaic of elements and requiring the perceiver to guess whether a particular element is figure or ground does not demonstrate, as has been asserted (Attneave, 1954), that errors necessarily collect at the corners of the figure. Further, they show that the number and location of such errors depend upon the particular scanning sequence imposed in the situation. A second demonstration shows that Attneave's claim that maximum information is carried at the points of maximum curvature of the figure is an artifact of the situation he used. Their third demonstration is also directed at the question of what aspects of a figure convey information, and makes the point that 'A reasonable conclusion to draw from this exercise is that points of maximum curvature carry little information *per se*. Only when *direction* is indicated does the figure take shape, and this function may be performed by various parts of the contour, not necessarily those parts encompassing corners.' (Editor)]

Cartoon Drawings

To pursue this line of thought we may turn to the practices of professional cartoonists. There are three distinct styles in current use. The simplest of these is the line drawing of heavy contours, with little attempt to introduce tonal quality. *Peanuts*, *Popeye* and *Donald Duck* are fair examples in this genre. Then, in a more sophisticated vein, comes the chiaroscuro drawing with careful, often delicate, shading to form a pattern of light and shade more in line with a photographic rendering. The *Rip Kirby*, *Carol Day* and *Gun Law* strips are familiar examples of this kind of treatment. Most sophisticated of all, and relatively rare, is a disjointed 'patchwork' style in which shape is conveyed by cunningly contrived strokes and patches, contours being indicated rather than drawn. Haro Hodson is the outstanding exponent of this technique (see Plate 28, a–h).

A comparison of these three styles may throw some light on figure perception in its natural habitat. The task confronting a cartoonist is to represent in black and white some more or less familiar part of our visual world in a recognizable form. A photograph does the job exactly, and the chiaroscuro style is an approximation to this. For this reason it is the least interesting of the three techniques in the present context. It is when the cartoonist aims for a more economical style that we begin to see how complexity may be reduced without loss of vital features – how an impression may be conveyed without supplying all the material. In simple line drawings subtleties of light and shade are ignored or only crudely indicated. A set of conventions is adopted whereby a heavy contour, plus several special features, is used to facilitate recognition of the figure represented. A face, for instance, is conventionalized in terms of eyes, nose, mouth and ears placed within a clear-cut boundary. Expressions are conveyed by eye-brows, shape of eyes and mouth, and an occasional line around the mouth, nose or forehead to indicate the bringing into play of particular muscle groups. With this simple equipment a skilled cartoonist may convey a vast range of facial expressions, some remarkably subtle in their overtones.

These simple line drawings seem to support Attneave's contentions about the location of information, but even at this stage there is more going on than meets the eye. There is a selection process involved whereby certain contours are pressed into service, while others, just as clear on a photograph, are dispensed with. Attneave's cat would be drawn by a competent cartoonist using far less of the contour to convey an impression just as realistic.

Even the contours that are used to do not consistently obey the Attneave formula. Points of rapid curvature such as the end of a chin, nose, finger, knuckle, angle of jaw or dome of the forehead are often left out, although perceptually they are not missing. The cartoonist suggests them and the percipient supplies them. It is this economy of line that is regarded as one of the hallmarks of the gifted draughtsman.

This selection process becomes even more obvious when we come to consider the 'patchwork' style. Large and important sections of the illustration are deliberately omitted by the artist in such a way that they are as perceptually present as the sections actually drawn. This is a remarkable achievement which will repay closer inspection. Somehow the artist manages to convey a sense of spatial relationships in parts of the figure that are objectively empty, homogeneous and unstructured. How is this paradox possible?

The answer seems to be that the artist picks out some salient features of the figure to be represented and draws these with such fidelity that the percipient is compelled to complete the figure according to the prescription suggested by the features presented. By presenting a partial cue of unique precision the artist forces the percipient to draw on his own resources to 'make sense' of what he sees. He is obliged to structure certain parts of the empty field according to the demands made by the partial cue, completing the figure to meet the prescription supplied by the artist.

There is an obvious connexion here with Street's (1931) Gestalt completion figures, the difference being that a Street figure is designed to confuse the percipient. The relevant partial cues are disguised by arbitrary fragmentation and concealed among other patches that are irrelevant or misleading (see Figure 1, a and b). In both cases, however, the role of past experience is crucial. The raw sensory data of a Street figure can be organized into a meaningful percept only if it can be made to fit into a schema already

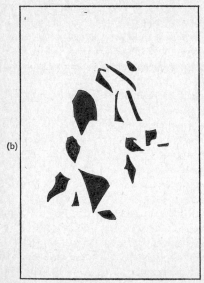

Figure 1. (a) Street
Gestalt completion
figure, a train;
(b) Street Gestalt com-
pletion figure, a man
crouching with camera

built up as a result of commerce with the object represented. There is usually a period during which the percipient searches the display for the partial cues that will enable him to identify the schema into which all the patches may be fitted. He can be aided in this by being told 'It's a train', or completely frustrated by having the figure presented in the wrong spatial orientation or being given a misleading set. Presented upside down, or with the spurious information 'It's a face', the random patches remain random and cannot be made to cohere into a meaningful percept.

With Hodson's figures the task is made easier, and the percept is formed almost instantaneously. The partial cues are chosen for their compelling quality and are not concealed by irrelevant or misleading cues. The only way to reduce the figure to meaningless elements is to turn it upside down.

Some of Hodson's comments (private communication) are relevant in this connexion. When asked to describe how he came to develop his special style he referred back to an earlier interest in writing poetry that conveyed its message indirectly. The message was never stated, only hinted at in such a way that the reader was obliged to state the message for himself. By means of this elliptical style Hodson aimed to convey the sort of message that loses its impact if an attempt is made to state it directly. Classical mime uses a similar artifice. The quintessence of a story that would seem banal if stated directly is conveyed with a disarming simplicity by gestures alone.

In his drawings Hodson is intent on making the percipient 'do the work', as he puts it. He aims to structure the field in such a way that the percipient is obliged to supply the missing parts. Obliged, in fact, to see something that is not there. A nose is often missing, presumably because it so rarely carries vital information, and because we know where it belongs anyway. By way of analogy Hodson refers to his fascination with trapeze artists who 'draw curves in space that aren't there'.

Sometimes a whole face is left almost blank, and yet we feel we know exactly what expression the sporting type in Plate 28b is wearing as he downs his pint. In Plate 28c we see the sergeant major's shapeless chin lost in rolls of invisible fat, and the wooden expression of the faceless businessman stares out from Plate 28d.

243

The women in Plate 28e, f and g have no contours to their faces at all, yet the bone structure and set of the facial muscles are plain enough. Plate 28g is especially remarkable for the sparseness of the cues the percipient is given to work on and the amount that has to be perceptually filled in. Nevertheless, the implied posture obliges us to see the missing arm, shoulders, chest cage and foot, along with the faintly simpering expression. Plate 28h is worth including for the apparently arbitrary way in which Attneave's second principle has been flouted. Some points of maximum curvature, such as the shoulders, elbows, nose and forehead, have been drawn, while others equally sharp, such as fingertips, lower lip, cuffs and back of the collar have been left to the imagination. Ankles are drawn, but wrists are not.

Hodson is not unique in this. He has simply developed a particular attribute of the cartoonist's craft to the point where we may become aware of the demands that are made of us. Any cartoonist worth his salt tries to make us 'do the work' and see with conviction something that is only hinted at in the actual display.

When it comes to deciding what parts to leave out there seem to be few hard and fast rules. The newspaper being read by the prelate in Plate 28a, for instance, has lost its bottom corners while retaining the upper ones. There seems to be no special reason for this – the upper corners may be removed without making nonsense of the picture. Possibly the lines chosen help to make the top edge of the newspaper loom over the percipient, emphasizing the angle at which it is being held. Such judgements have an intuitive quality that defy exact formation, and it may be that a line is left in because it keeps the balance of the composition – which is an aesthetic principle, not necessarily in line with the principles of economy and the compelling partial cue.

Discussion

It may be thought that the habits and idiosyncracies of cartoonists provide a somewhat laboured and homely way of discussing the refined technicalities of information theory. All this loose talk about partial cues sounds less untidy when referred to the concept of redundancy. But this is precisely the point. There are in fact two languages in vogue using a common vocabulary to conceal their fundamental differences. It is misleading to talk about the information content of a figure and the location of information within a figure as if this were the same kind of information introduced by Wiener, Weaver and Shannon. There can be no objective transition probabilities from element to element when the elements are undefined, perhaps undefinable, and in any case unique to the person perceiving the figure, along with the scanning sequence and transition probabilities.

To use the language of information theory in this context is to employ a metaphor. Metaphors can be exciting, illuminating and useful, but metaphors they remain. Unless we are very careful we shall find ourselves trying to roll back the frontiers of science with a bulldozer. This would be unprofitable as well as faintly ridiculous – like having a close shave with Occam's razor.

There are times when Attneave (1959) seems almost to concede this point. Drawing on the distinction between metrical and structural information first put forward by MacKay (1950), it is suggested that the metron content can be inferred from the logon content. In the case of figure perception this is alleged to obviate the difficulties associated with defining the 'grain' of the stimulus array, and the logon content '... will almost certainly be proportional to information-in-bits, to a first approximation, once any particular grain is specified' (Attneave, 1959, p. 83). In other words, the amount of selective information is inferred from some other measure. This idea might pass muster if specifying the grain were the only bar to obtaining a measure of selective information. Since, however, the scanning procedure is of crucial importance we are left with a model that has scant bearing on the problem of figure perception as it normally occurs.

In the model it still makes sense to talk about the amount and location of information contained in a figure as an information source. In real life the amount and location of the information is a function of the percipient. What has to be measured is not something in the source, but something about the *process* of perceiving. Attneave (1959, p. 83) still talks as if the model were more than a metaphor. 'It may be demonstrated (for instance, by the guessing game technique) that angles and intersections are regions of high informational content in the visual field.' This discovery, we have seen, is an artifact of the task imposed.

245

As it so happens, information often is concentrated at the corners of a figure because distinctive features commonly involve sharp changes in the direction of the contour. But this is fortuitous. For any particular figure among a given set of figures the distinctive features may or may not be provided by corners – to discriminate between a set of snakes, for example, it would be necessary to rely on such cues as length or girth or position of head in relation to the coils. These cues, be it noted, are not even contour cues in the simple sense; they are cues based on spatial relationships. Just as a circle with a dot in the centre is discriminable from a circle with a dot off centre, and a circle with a dot at 12 o'clock is discriminable from one with a dot at 10 o'clock.

If we are going to borrow a language from another discipline we would probably do better to draw on game rather than information theory. By using this conceptual framework we can direct our attention to the process of perception as it occurs in its natural environment – the human ethology of perception, so to speak. Our efforts would be more gainfully directed if we considered how information (loose sense) is utilized by the percipient, instead of trying to measure the amount and locus of information (technical sense) in the display. What we might profitably concern ourselves with is defining, analysing, and eventually understanding the perceptual strategies and categories actually used by percipients. Doubtless, Kelly (1955) and Bannister (1962) would be only too ready to accord perception a place of this kind under the general rubric of personal construct theory.

Binder (1955) and Bruner (1957a, b) have already gone some way towards establishing a bridgehead in this territory without having seen through the metaphor or abandoned the pseudo-language cribbed from information theory. Nevertheless, they are on the right track and are not hopelessly committed to the concepts or mathematics of information theory. Provided that the terminology is handled with more circumspection this approach need not suffer from the fatal flaws inherent in the application of information theory to the problems of figure perception. The guessing game then falls naturally into place as one of the available techniques for investigating search procedures and perceptual strategies, along with a number of others reviewed by Binder.

As a final exercise we can construct a general model of the game as it is played naturally. This is not intended as an *ex cathedra* pronouncement on the nature of figure preception. The aim is simply to offer a convenient framework within which fruitful research may proceed.

In real life two distinct stages may often be distinguished. In seeking to identify a particular person at a distance we first have to establish any candidate as belonging to the required class, for example, human female. At this stage we direct our attention to those attributes that are most *typical* of members of this class (skirt, long hair, etc.). Having established that we are dealing with a member of the required class we turn our attention to those features most *unique* to the individual we wish to identify (the characteristic pose, profile, article of dress, etc.). So the locus of information will be a function of the task and will change with it – not a fixed attribute completely inherent in the figure itself. Similarly, the locus of information will be a function of the percipient, depending on how well and in what capacity he happens to know the particular person he is trying to identify.

The schema that we use to classify the candidate as a human female is a *general* one, and that to identify the individual a *special* one. At either stage the percipient is engaged in a kind of hypothesis-testing game in which the information (loose sense) is matched against the various schemata to allow acceptance, rejection or modification of the hypothesis, and further direct the search procedure. Oldfield (1954), although more concerned with the Bartlett type of recall phenomena than with figure perception, puts forward some interesting suggestions as to just how such schemata might be subjected to an encoding process by the organism cum computer. In this connexion it is worth noting that Bartlett's (1932) account of remembering as a process of reconstruction within schemata provides a far closer and more illuminating parallel for the perceptual process than does information theory, a point made by Vernon (1957).

In any event the search procedure will be determined largely by the percipient rather than by the display, and will almost certainly be independent of the grain or mosaic of the display, even assuming that such a grain could be specified. In genuine figure perception, information (loose sense) is gathered in localized blocks corresponding to the fixation points associated with saccadic eye movements. This much has long since been established by Buswell (1935), who also noted the two main stages of the perceptual process in the same study. Leeper (1935) put forward some similar ideas.

This account of the perceptual process echoes the controversy between Gibson and Gibson (1955) and Postman (1955) concerning the role of experience in learning to perceive. The view being put forward here is more in line with Postman's enrichment theory, with its emphasis on the central importance of meaning as a factor shaping our percepts, than with the Gibsons' view that perception becomes more veridical as stimulus differentiation takes place. In fact it is necessary to go back to Titchener's (1915) context theory, with its blunt distinction between sensation and perception, to see how easy it has become these days to overlook simple facts in an attempt to clothe our ignorance with a spurious 'scientific' air. This is not to say that the Gibsons' views are utterly irrelevant. It is quite possible that their account of perceptual learning applies during the earliest stage of development, before being supplemented by a more sophisticated process as meaningful concepts begin to shape our percepts.

Garner (1962) deals at some length with the problems of applying information measurements to pattern perception, but very wisely he makes a distinction between meaning as structure and meaning as signification. Roughly speaking, this runs parallel to the distinction between pattern perception and figure perception. Figures are meaningful in that we have learned their significance and can refer them to an object or event in the real world. Patterns may have predictable structures, but do not in general look like a familiar object. Perhaps the easiest way of illustrating the main feature of the distinction is to turn Figure 2 upside down. To quote Garner (1962, p. 142): 'Thus meaning as structure can be quantified, and the information concepts are quite appropriate for its quantification. On the other hand, meaning as signification cannot be quantified other than to say that it exists or does not exist.'

Garner, however, has still failed to appreciate the full extent of the difficulties inherent in applying information theory even to pattern perception. He tends to overlook a number of problems in

Figure 2. The distinction between a pattern and a figure

this area because he is more often concerned with structural information in language sequences than with pattern perception. In his chapter on pattern perception, whether he is talking about discrimination, redundancy, noise or 'goodness' of form, the problems associated with defining the alphabet of signs, the grain of the array, the subjective nature of the transition probabilities involved, and the scanning sequence are all unresolved. In particular, the last of these is almost completely ignored. There are points at which Garner comes close to openly recognizing the subjective nature of the 'information' being measured. For instance, in dealing with the problem of the variables involved in redundancy he states:

There are many experiments in which a proper analysis of the amount and form of redundancy requires careful consideration of the variables as the subject sees them. . . . If the total constraint for the subject is lower due to his seeing fewer variables, then, clearly, the redundancy which we would assume to be operating for any fixed number of selected stimuli would also be lower. It is necessary, in other words, to use a considerable amount of good judgement in applying these principles and concepts to an actual experimental problem (1962, p, 186).

Or again, (1962, p. 189): 'In other words, redundancy increases the discriminability of the stimuli actually used, but this increased discriminability can be of value *only if it is perceived*' (author's italics).

Fundamentally there is no way out of this dilemma. Information theory is concerned with transition probabilities, while perception, whether of figures or patterns, is essentially non-sequential, or at least non-linear. A linear sequence may be imposed, but the data no longer have much bearing on problems of perception. Garner appreciates the difficulty, but seems to suggest that it might be overcome, at least with regard to patterns.

With two-dimensional geometric patterns, the problem is more complex because of the several directions of movement possible on the plane surface. With a time sequence of stimuli, for example, there is no doubt about which stimulus comes after any given stimulus; but with filled cells on a matrix, each stimulus has eight adjacent stimuli, if each cell is considered a stimulus. Perhaps this fact suggests the possibility that as a first-order analysis, we could use a multi-variate analysis of patterns of cells on a matrix, in which each cell is predicted from the eight adjacent cells. Attneave (1954) has suggested a more restricted procedure of this sort, by having subjects guess along horizontal rows whether the next cell will be black or white. Thus Attneave converted the two-dimensional problem into a uni-dimensional problem so that it could be handled more easily (1962, p. 205).

Unfortunately, once the problem is cast in these terms it is no longer the same problem. Pattern perception may involve a kind of guessing game, but not the kind used by Attneave. To see just how far this hope of Garner's falls short of reality it is necessary to take in turn each of the four requirements already discussed. It then becomes apparent that not only is it impossible to meet all four requirements – in a genuine perceptual task it is not possible to meet any one of them.

The personal, idiosyncratic nature of the scanning sequence, and the subjective nature of the transition probabilities involved have already been dealt with. Defining the alphabet of signs and the elements of the mosaic pose difficulties quite as intractable.

An abstract picture or design can be broken up into half-inch squares, or whatever mosaic the experimenter decides, but this is not how it is *seen* by the percipient. A three-colour reproduction of the display will provide a 'natural' grain and alphabet, in that there is a definite number of dots each of which can have only one of three possible colour values, but even if the display is blown up sufficiently for the subject to resolve each dot and discern its colour, this still has nothing to do with pattern perception. Viewed under normal conditions a mixture of red and blue dots is seen as a shape of purple, which is not included in the alphabet of signs as already specified. By blowing up the display to create a discriminable mosaic the experimenter has destroyed the quality of the percept. And the same argument holds, of course, for the spatial relationships between the parts of the display. The quality that makes a pattern into a pattern is lost when elements are presented in isolation, just as surely as the quality of signification is lost if a meaningful picture is presented in this way. Perception of a sequence of relationships between points is a very different process from that of the perception of simultaneous relationships between parts. If the Gestalt school said this ages ago this is no excuse for imagining that the facts will disappear simply by muttering the hermetic formulae of information theory.

Perhaps it is to Miller (1962) that credit should go for dealing the most grievous blow. Up to now we have been considering arguments against only the misapplication of information theory to figure and pattern perception, tacitly allowing that language sequences provide legitimate material for an analysis of this kind. Miller (1951), originally one of the foremost exponents of information theory applied to language, has since revised his earlier views in a most courageous and forthright manner. As he says (1962, p. 761), 'In the course of this work I seem to have become a very old-fashioned kind of psychologist. I now believe that mind is something more than a four-letter, Anglo-Saxon word – human minds exist and it is our job as psychologists to study them.' Without going into the arguments in detail it is sufficient to note that language is not just a set of transition probabilities. As soon as we look for meaning in a language sequence (and this is what language is all about) we discover that the transition probabilities are a function of the reader and the situation in which he finds himself. 'Give me the sheet' has two entirely different meanings to the sailor and the housewife. Moreover, a word sequence can occur for the first time and yet be entirely predictable. 'The boy spoke a triangle' is an unusual and unexpected sequence, but if it is suggested that the same kind of sentence construction can be applied in respect of a regular four-sided figure, then the sequence 'The boy spoke a square', although never encountered hitherto, is perfectly predictable.

So two of the cardinal requirements of information theory are lost; transition probabilities are no longer objective, even in principle, and the alphabet of signs is not one of letters or words, but of meaning units, which are again peculiar to the individual. What is transmitted may be regarded by an engineer as simply a string of words, or letters and spaces for that matter, but what is *communicated* is a set of meanings. To use Miller's terminology – the essential property of language is not to be found in Markov chains but in syntactic constituents. It is easy to overlook this crucial distinction in print because of the absence of speech melody in the channel. Both the sender and receiver of the written message use speech melody to carry the meaning, but the melody itself is not transmitted – it is re-created by the receiver according to a set of rules external to the message itself. Miller and Isard (1963) and Marks and Miller (1964) have taken pains to show the importance of syntactic and semantic rules, but the influence of the speech melody has yet to be systematically investigated. Which leaves information theory right back where it started – a mathematical tool in communication engineering, particularly useful for dealing with the technical problems of channel capacity.

Attneave (1959, p. 83) tacitly concedes the main point when he says: 'We should constantly bear in mind, however, that the subject need not perceive objects in accordance with the experimenter's descriptive system; indeed, it is from just these discrepancies that we acquire a new knowledge about the nature of perceptual processes. One such set of discrepancies gives rise to the important distinction between "bits" and "chunks".' The distinction between 'bits' and 'chunks' is where the metaphor is obliged to reveal its limitations. To gloss over this distinction is to miss the point, and possibly, the bus.

References

ATTNEAVE, F. (1953), 'Psychological probability as a function of experienced frequency', *J. exp. Psychol.*, vol. 45, pp. 81–6.

ATTNEAVE, F. (1954), 'Some informational aspects of visual perception', *Psych. Rev.*, vol. 61, pp. 183–93.

ATTNEAVE, F. (1955), 'Symmetry, information and memory for patterns', *Amer. J. Psychol.*, vol. 68, pp. 209–22.

ATTNEAVE, F. (1957), 'Physical determinants of the judged complexity of shapes', *J. exp. Psychol.*, vol. 53, pp. 221–7.

ATTNEAVE, F. (1959), *Applications of Information Theory to Psychology*, Holt.

ATTNEAVE, F., and ARNOULT, M. D. (1956), 'The quantitative study of shape and pattern perception', *Psychol. Bull.*, vol. 53, pp. 452–71.

BANNISTER, D. (1962), 'Personal construct theory: a summary and experimental paradigm', *Acta Psychol.*, vol. 20, pp. 104–20.

BARTLETT, F. C. (1932), *Remembering*, Cambridge University Press.

BINDER, A. (1955), 'A statistical model for the process of visual recognition', *Psych. Rev.*, vol. 62, pp. 119–29.

BRUNER, J. S. (1957a), 'On perceptual readiness', *Psych. Rev.*, vol. 64, pp. 123–52.

BRUNER, J. S. (1957b), 'Going beyond the information given', *Contemporary Approaches to Cognition*, Harvard University Press.

BUSWELL, G. T. (1935), *How People Look at Pictures*, University of Chicago Press.

CHERRY, E. C. (1957a), 'On the validity of applying information theory to experimental psychology', *Brit. J. Psychol.*, vol. 41, pp. 176–88.

CHERRY, E. C. (1957b), *On Human Communication*, Chapman & Hall.

CRONBACH, L. J. (1955), 'On the non-rational application of information measures in psychology', in Quastler (ed.), *Information Theory in Psychology*, Free Press, Glencoe.

GARNER, W. R. (1962), *Uncertainty and Structure as Psychological Concepts*, Wiley.

GIBSON, J. J., and GIBSON, E. J. (1955), 'Perceptual learning – differentiation or enrichment?', *Psych. Rev.*, vol. 62, pp. 32–41.

GRANT, D. A. (1954), 'The discrimination of sequences in stimulus events and the transmission of information', *Amer. Psychol.*, vol. 9, pp. 62–8.

HOCHBERG, J. E., and MCALISTER, E. (1953), 'A quantitative approach to figural "goodness"', *J. exp. Psychol.*, vol. 46, pp. 361–4.

KELLY, G. A. (1955), *The Psychology of Personal Constructs*, Norton, 2 vols.

LEEPER, R. W. (1935), 'The development of sensory organization', *J. genet. Psychol.*, vol. 46, pp. 41–75.

MACKAY, D. M. (1950), 'Quantal aspects of scientific information', *Phil. Mag.*, vol. 41, pp. 289–311.

MARKS, L. E., and MILLER, G. A. (1964), 'The role of semantic and syntactic constraints in the memorisation of English sentences', *J. verb. Learn. verb. Behav.*, vol. 3, pp. 1–5.

MILLER, G. A. (1951), *Language and Communication*, McGraw-Hill.

MILLER, G. A. (1962), 'Some psychological studies of grammar', *Amer. Psychol.*, vol. 17, pp. 748–62.

MILLER, G. A., and ISARD, S. (1963), 'Some perceptual consequences of linguistic rules', *J. verb. Learn. verb. Behav.*, vol. 2, pp. 217–28.

OLDFIELD, R. C. (1954), 'Memory mechanisms and the theory of schemata', *Brit. J. Psychol.*, vol. 45, pp. 14–23.

POSTMAN, L. (1955), 'Association theory and perceptual learning', *Psych. Rev.*, vol. 62, pp. 438–46.

SHANNON, C. E., and WEAVER, W. (1949), *The Mathematical Theory of Communication*, University of Illinois Press.

STREET, R. F. (1931), *A Gestalt Completion Test*, Columbia University Press.

TITCHENER, E. B. (1915), *A Beginner's Psychology*, Macmillan.

TODA, M. (1956), 'Information receiving behaviour in man', *Psych. Rev.*, vol. 63, pp. 204–12.

VERNON, M. D. (1957), 'Cognitive inference in perceptual activity', *Brit. J. Psychol.*, vol. 48, pp. 35–47.

WEINSTEIN, M., and FITTS, P. M. (1954), 'A quantitative study of the role of stimulus complexity in visual pattern discrimination', *Amer. Psychol.*, vol. 9, p. 490 (abstract).

WIENER, N. (1948), *Cybernetics*, Wiley.

Part Five Expression and Gestalt Theory

The choice to illustrate Gestalt psychology and to deal with the problem of expression simultaneously reflects my feeling that it is in dealing with this aspect of art (though of course expression is not limited to art) that the Gestalt position is most stimulating. It is not the only psychological approach to attempt to do this, and in the second of these papers Professor Arnheim reviews some other attitudes. Gestalt theory itself is insufficiently rigorous (and is not on its own in this) to generate a clear-cut set of propositions about art. On many occasions Arnheim's extensive writings reflect the spirit of the approach rather than its somewhat obscure letter. This section, then, in addition to representing Gestalt theory and the problem of expression may also be seen as reflecting Arnheim's own approach to the psychological problems of art.

10 R. Arnheim

Gestalt and Art

R. Arnheim, 'Gestalt and art', *Journal of Aesthetics and art Criticism*, vol. 2 (1943), pp. 71–5.

There are styles in science just as in art. The Gestalt theory is such a new style of science. It came about, negatively, as a protest against what is now called the atomistic approach: the method of explaining things by adding up local effects, qualities and functions of isolated elements. It came about, positively, as the scientific expression of a new wave of *Naturphilosophie* and romanticism in Germany, which revived in a strongly emotional way the feeling of the wonderful secrets of the organism, the creative powers of natural forces as opposed to the detrimental effects of a rationalism which praised the emancipation of the brain from vitality and from the elementary tasks of life as the highest achievement of culture. Gestalt theory has a kinship to certain poets and thinkers of the past, the nearest in time being Goethe.

Gestalt theory, created mainly by three men, Max Wertheimer, Wolfgang Köhler, and Kurt Koffka, uses as its method in psychology, physics, biology, sociology, etc., the description of the structural features, the whole-qualities of 'systems', i.e. of those natural things or happenings in which the character and function of any part is determined by the total situation. The method, however, must be understood as deriving from a more basic attitude which respects the simple, strong and spontaneous reactions of children, primitive people and animals, as something which, on any level of mental and cultural development, the human being should preserve – an attitude which refuses to reserve the capacity of synthesis to the higher faculties of the human mind, but emphasizes the formative powers and, if I may say so, the 'intelligence' of the peripheral sensory processes, vision, hearing, touch, etc., which had been reduced by traditional theory to the task of carrying the bricks of experience to the architect in the inner sanctuary of mind. From this attitude results a strong sympathy with, and an intimate understanding of, the artist. For through his eyes and ears, the artist directly grasps the full meaning of nature's creations, and, by organizing sensory facts according to the laws of 'Prägnanz', unity, segregation and balance, he reveals harmony and order, or stigmatizes discord and disorder. It is not accidental that a product of art, a melody, was used as the first example of a whole, whose structure can be explained neither by the qualities of its single elements, nor by the relations between these elements. Moreover, whoever has made experiments with the Gestalt method knows that, in order to create conditions which will bring about certain crucial effects, a sensitivity akin to the artist's must operate with respect to the conditions under which the structural features of, say, visual figures come out clearly, are maintained or changed. One has to 'see' the phenomenon long before one can formulate it scientifically. Whether it is true of science in general or not, the productive Gestalt scientist has to be something of an artist. And 'blindness' (as opposed to such insight) is one of the favorite terms of the Gestalt vocabulary.

Let me now discuss an example of the application of Gestalt theory to the psychology of art. It seems that, with a more adequate approach to the psychology of perception, it is possible to deal more successfully with an intricate, but basic problem of artistic representation. If we assume, as it used to be, that perception is based on a sum of sensations produced by the millions of punctiform receptors in the retinae of the eyes, a puzzling paradox arises. It would then be logical to expect that, the more elementary the psychological level of a human being, the more closely his drawings ought to stick to what would correspond psychologically to the image projected on the retinae by the lens; and, on the other hand, only from people more developed mentally would one expect elaboration and transformation. On the contrary, we find in fact that children and primitives tend to draw in simple patterns; realism appears only as the late product of a long cultural evolution. The fact cannot be explained by manual inability, because even though a child is unable to trace a perfect circle, we can show that he meant to draw a circle. The child's drawing is essentially different from what we would get if we asked a skilled draftsman to draw a realistic picture of a nude not with his hand, but with his foot. The current theory is that a child 'draws what he knows rather than what he sees'. This theory implies the paradox that the more undeveloped creatures elaborate their sensations through higher mental processes. Furthermore, any attempt to explain the origin of such 'knowledge' faces again the problems which the theory was meant to solve: how can the simple shapes of children's drawings be derived from the complex and everchanging pattern of a human head or body as projected on the retinae? By abstraction? If we remember that in logic, abstraction is defined as the setting aside of some elements of particular phenomena and retaining others, we realize that no elimination of parts can ever lead from the 'projective picture' to those simple shapes.

A more adequate approach is possible if we understand that the content of perception is not identical with the sum of qualities corresponding to the projective picture. Rather it seems that productive perception – in the sense of an activity which allows us to understand, identify, remember and recognize things – is a grasping of basic structural features, which characterize things and distinguish them from others. There is a tendency in the organism to produce simple shapes wherever circumstances allow it to do so. Optical experiments have shown that when the influence of external stimuli is subdued, for instance by reducing the size of the stimulus, the intensity of lighting or the time of exposure, the subjects report that they see things of a more simple, more regular, sometimes more symmetrical shape than those really exposed to them. But even when the precision of the stimulus does not permit such manifest modification, perception consists in organizing the sensory material under the patterns of simple, 'good' Gestalten.

The artist may think here of the saying attributed to Cézanne, that nature can be seen as cubes, spheres, cones, etc. The philosopher may be reminded of Kant's epistemological 'categories'. With respect to Kant there is, however, one important difference. Gestalt theory does not hold that the senses carry amorphous material on which order is imposed by a receiving mind. It emphasizes instead that 'good shape' is a quality of nature in general, inorganic as well as organic, and that the processes of organization active in perception somehow do justice to the organization outside in the physical world. Wolfgang Köhler, in his early book on the physical Gestalten – which he calls 'eine naturphilosophische Untersuchung' – has shown that a tendency toward the production of simple forms can be observed in many physical systems or fields, because the interacting forces do their best to create a state of balance. A case in which balance leads to complete symmetry is observed when a drop of oil falls into a glass of water. Mechanical forces become active, pushing and pulling, until the oil is collected in a circular shape in the middle of the water surface. They will do so not because of a longing for beauty, but because only under these conditions will all the forces involved balance each other in such a way that a state of rest is obtained. Similar processes are likely to occur in the physiological field of vision when stimuli interfere with its balance. Areas stimulated by light of different amplitude and wave length are adjusted, as to their shape, contours, color, etc., to the most stable organization possible under the given circumstances.

The discovery of this elementary relationship between perception and balance should be welcome to the theory of art. Balance was generally considered as something added by the artist to the image of the objects. Why he does so was not quite clear. Balance arouses pleasure, but justifying balance only as a source of pleasure seemed somewhat distasteful and humiliating to many. By describing the tendency towards balance as a basic effort of the organism to assimilate stimuli to its own organization and by showing that balance is, quite in general, a state sought for by physical forces wherever they interact in a field, the artist's striving for balance is revealed as just one aspect of a universal tendency in nature. From this point of view, pleasure appears as a psychological correlate of balance, not as its cause.

The extreme case of the oil drop should not induce us to think of balance only in connexion with closed systems at rest. One would have a hard time to find in art corresponding cases of total symmetry, which would express a state of complete inactivity. Without activity there is no life and therefore no art. What I mean by balance based on activity will become clearer if I use as an example the human body which is at balance with its surroundings as to temperature when the amount of heat constantly drained off from the body by the colder environment just equals the constant surplus of heat production in the body. More than simply an analogy is intended when we assert that something similar happens: for instance, in a painting where the eccentric position and irregular shape of masses express the dynamical situation of the subject represented as well as of the artist's soul, but are distributed in such a way that the active masses balance each other.

This leads me to a second topic, which seems to promise a particularly fruitful application of Gestalt principles. The theory of expression, in its traditional form, does not seem to do justice to what happens when we look at or listen to a work of art. If expression were nothing but an empirical connexion between what we see, say, in a person's face and what we know about our own state of mind at the time when our own face displays a similar pattern, then no inner kinship would exist between the two correlated features, i.e. physical pattern and psychological state. The relationship between a doleful face and a sad mood is then at best explained as a causal relationship. Wertheimer has drawn attention to the fact that neither past experience nor logical conclusions are necessary for an understanding of the elementary features of expression. Their meaning is perceived at least as directly and spontaneously as the shape and color of an object, by means of what has been termed the 'tertiary qualities' of sensory phenomena. Kindliness or aggression, straightshooting determination or hesitation, are expressed in the curves of the physical movements (or traces of movements) which accompany such mental attitudes. A geometry of expressive features is anticipated which would describe their characteristics with as much scientific precision as our present geometry is able to describe the difference between a straight line and a circular curve. The underlying idea is that the dynamical characteristics of, say, timidity are identical whether we trace, e.g. as to time and direction, the walking curve of the timid man who approaches the private office of his boss or whether we translate into a graph the succession of his psychological impulses, inhibitive and propulsive, with respect to his aim. This theory of isomorphism (identity of form) between psychological and physical processes scientifically corroborates the common observation that we call the movements of a dancer mournful not because we have often seen sad persons behave in a similar manner but because the dynamical features of mourning are physically present in these movements and can be directly perceived. Therefore the theory of expression in art must not necessarily start from the attitudes of the human body and explain the flaming excitement of Van Gogh's trees or El Greco's clouds through some sort of anthropomorphic projection, but should rather proceed from the expressive qualities of curves and shapes and show how by representing any subject matter through such curves and shapes expression is conveyed to human bodies, trees, clouds, buildings, vessels, or whatever other things. What science is trying here to assert and to prove against the opposition of well-established traditional theories may sound familiar to many a good painter or sculptor who does his job with some consciousness. This, however, as far as I see, does not tell against Gestalt theory, but in favor of it.

11 R. Arnheim

The Gestalt Theory of Expression

R. Arnheim, 'The Gestalt theory of expression', *Psychological Review*,
vol. 56 (1949), pp. 156–71. (Reprinted in R. Arnheim, *Towards a
Psychology of Art: Collected Essays*, Faber and Faber, 1966.)

What is the exact location and range of the territory covered by
the term 'expression'? Thus far, no generally accepted definition
exists. In order to make clear what is meant by expression in the
present paper, it is therefore necessary to indicate (a) the kind of
perceptual stimulus which involves the phenomenon in question
and (b) the kind of mental process to which its existnece is due.
This delimitation of our subject will show that the range of
perceptual objects which carry expression according to Gestalt
theory is unusually large and that expression is defined as the
product of perceptual properties which various other schools of
thought consider non-existent or unimportant.

(a) In present-day usage, the term 'expression' refers primarily
to behavioral manifestations of the human personality. The
appearance and activities of the human body may be said to be
expressive. The shape and proportions of the face or the hands,
the tensions and the rhythm of muscular action, gait, gestures
and other movements serve as objects of observation. In addition,
expression is now commonly understood to reach beyond the
observed person's body. The 'projective techniques' exploit
characteristic effects upon, and reactions to, the environment.
The way a person dresses, keeps his room, handles the language,
the pen, the brush; the colors, flowers, occupations he prefers;
the meaning he attributes to pictures, tunes, or inkblots; the
story he imposes on puppets; his interpretation of a dramatic
part – these and innumerable other manifestations can be called
'expressive' in that they permit conclusions about the personality
or the temporary state of mind of the individual. Gestalt psychologists extend the range of expressive phenomena beyond this

limit. For reasons which will be discussed, they consider it indispensable to speak also of the expression conveyed by in-animate objects, such as mountains, clouds, sirens, machines.

(b) Once the carrier of expression is determined, the kind of mental process must be indicated which is charged with producing the phenomenon. It is the contention of Gestalt psychology that the various experiences commonly classified under 'perception of expression' are caused by a number of psychological processes which ought to be distinguished from each other for the purpose of theoretical analysis. Some of these experiences are partly or wholly based upon empirically acquired knowledge. The mere inspection of many half-smoked cigarettes in an ashtray would suggest no connexion with nervous tension to a visitor from a planet inhabited by non-smokers. The letters EVVIVA GUERRA and EVVIVA DON PIO scribbled all over the walls of an Italian village will reveal the mentality of the natives only to someone who happens to know that these words pay homage to a champion cyclist and the village priest. For the purpose of the present paper, the use of past experience for the interpretation of per-ceptual observations will be excluded from the field of expression and referred to the psychology of learning. We shall be concerned only with instances in which, according to Gestalt psychology, sensory data contain a core of expression that is perceptually self evident. The way a person keeps his lips tightly closed or raises his voice or strokes a child's head or walks hesitatingly is said to contain factors whose meaning can be understood directly through mere inspection. Instances of such direct expression are not limited to the appearance and behavior of the subject's own body. They are also found in such 'projective' material as the stirring red of a woman's favorite dress or the 'emotional' character of the music she prefers. In addition, inanimate objects are said to convey direct expression. The aggressive stroke of lightning or the soothing rhythm of rain impresses the observer by perceptual qualities which according to Gestalt psychology must be distinguished theoretically from the effect of what he knows about the nature of these happenings. It is assumed, however, that practically every concrete experience combines factors of both kinds.

Procedures and Findings

What is expression, and what enables the observer to experience it? By means of which perceptual factors and in what way do stimulus configurations evoke such experiences in the onlooker? During the last twenty-five years or so, numerous experimental investigations have been devoted to the phenomena of expression, but hardly any of them have tried to answer our questions. Limited as they were to the connexion between how a person behaves and what happens in him psychologically, they centered upon the certainly important problem: to what extent are observers, untrained or trained, gifted or average, capable of getting valid information about a person's temporary state of mind or his more permanent psychical constitution from an inspection of his face, voice, gait, handwriting, etc?

This is true for the various matching experiments which are conveniently summarized by Woodworth (24, pp. 242–56) and by Allport and Vernon (1, pp. 3–20). Similarly, in the field of the projective techniques psychologists have looked for correlations between personality traits and reactions to environmental stimuli. Almost invariably, these stimuli contain factors of the kind which concern the present paper. However, thus far, little explicit discussion has been devoted to the question why and how the given percepts provoke the observed reactions. There is evidence that the whole structure of a face rather than the sum of its parts determines expression (2). But which structural features make for what expression and why? In the Rorschach test, the typical reactions to color are probably based on expression. But why are emotional attitudes related to color rather than shape? Ernest G. Schachtel has done pioneer work in this field, pointing out, for instance, that responses to colors and to affect-experiences are both characterized by passive receptivity (19). On the whole, however, questions of this kind have been answered thus far by summary and scantily supported theoretical assertions.

A few remarks are in order on the investigations which have tested the accomplishments of observers. A glance at the results reveals a curious contrast. One group of experimenters reports essentially negative findings. Another, consisting mainly of Gestalt psychologists, asserts that observers judge portraits, handwritings and similar material with a measure of success that clearly surpasses chance. Pessimistic generalizations have been drawn from the studies of the first type. The subject of expression is sometimes treated with the buoyant unkindness that distinguished the early behavioristic statements on introspection. This attitude has not encouraged research.

The main reason for the conflicting results can be found in differences of approach. The investigators of the first type asked: how validly can the bodily expression of the average person or of a random member of a particular group of people be interpreted? In other words, they focused on the important practical question of the extent to which expression can be relied upon in everyday life. On the other hand, the Gestalt psychologists preferred the common scientific procedure of purifying as carefully as possible the phenomenon under investigation. They searched for the most favorable condition of observation. A major part of their efforts was spent in selecting and preparing sets of specimens which promised to demonstrate expression clearly and strongly (2, p. 8).

Some of the factors which may account for the often disappointing results obtained in experiments with random material are the following.

(a) Everyday observation suggests that the structural patterns of character, temperament, mood are not equally clear cut in all people. While some individuals are pronouncedly depressed or lighthearted, strong or weak, harmonious or disharmonious, warm or cold, others strike us as indefinite, lukewarm, fluid. Whatever the exact nature of such indefiniteness, one would expect the corresponding faces, gestures, handwritings to be equally vague in form and therefore in expression. When one examines material of this kind, one notices in some cases that the decisive structural features are not sharply defined. In other cases, factors which are clear cut in themselves add up to something that shows neither harmony not conflict but a lack of unity or relatedness, which renders the whole meaningless, inexpressive. Many telling examples can be found among the composite faces made up by the summation of unrelated parts for experimental purposes. If observers can cope with such material at all, they do so presumably by guessing what these artifacts are meant to mean rather than by having the experience of live expression.

(b) The presence of a portrait photographer's camera tends to paralyse a person's expression, and he becomes self-conscious, inhibited, and often strikes an unnatural pose.

(c) Candid shots are momentary phases isolated from a temporal process and a spatial context. Sometimes they are highly expressive and representative of the whole from which they are taken. Frequently they are not. Furthermore, the angle from which a shot is made, the effect of lighting on shape, the rendering of brightness and color values, as well as modifications through retouching, are factors which make it impossible to accept a random photograph as a valid likeness.

(d) If for purposes of matching experiments a number of samples is combined at random, accidental similarities of expression may occur, which will make distinction difficult, even though every specimen may be clear cut in itself. Further reasons for the lack of consistent results are discussed by Wolff (23, p. 7).[1]

The conclusion seems to be that the recognition of expression has been proven to be reliable and valid under optimal conditions. For the average face, voice, gesture, handwriting, etc. the results are likely to be less positive. However, in order to establish this fact trustworthily, the additional obstacles created by unsuitable experimental conditions will have to be reduced.

Associationist Theories

What enables observers to judge expression? The traditional theory, handed down to our generation without much questioning, is based on associationism. In his essay on vision, Berkeley

---

1. Since there is no reason to expect that every photograph will reproduce essential features of expression, it would be interesting to know by which criterion the photographs for the Szondi test (18) have been selected. If an integral feature of the test consists in establishing the reactions of people to the personalities of homosexuals, sadistic murderers, etc., two questions arise. (a) Is there a complete correlation between these pathological manifestations and certain clear-cut personality structures? (b) Are the latter suitably expressed in the photographs? These problems are avoided if the test is meant simply to investigate people's responses to a given set of portraits, whatever their origin.

(4, para. 65) discusses the way in which one sees shame or anger in the looks of a man.

> Those passions are themselves invisible: they are nevertheless let in by the eye along with colours and alterations of countenance, which are the immediate object of vision, and which signify them for no other reason than barely because they have been observed to accompany them: without which experience, we should no more have taken blushing for a sign of shame, than of gladness.

Darwin, in his book on the expression of emotions, devoted a few pages to the same problem (7, pp. 356–9). He considered the recognition of expression to be either instinctive or learned. 'Children, no doubt, would soon learn the movements of expression in their elders in the same manner as animals learn those of man,' namely, 'through their associating harsh or kind treatment with our actions.'

> Moreover, when a child cries or laughs, he knows in a general manner what he is doing and what he feels; so that a very small exertion of reason would tell him what crying or laughing meant in others. But the question is, do our children acquire their knowledge of expression solely by experience through the power of association and reason? As most of the movements of expression must have been gradually acquired, afterwards becoming instinctive, there seems to be some degree of *a priori* probability that their recognition would likewise have become instinctive.

In Darwin's view, the relationship between expressive bodily behavior and the corresponding psychical attitude was merely causal. Expressive gestures were either remnants of originally serviceable habits or due to 'direct action of the nervous system'. He saw no inner kinship between a particular pattern of muscular behavior and the correlated state of mind.

A variation of the associationist theory contends that judgements of expression are based on stereotypes. In this view, interpretation does not rely on what belongs together according to our spontaneous insight or repeated observation but on conventions, which we have adopted ready-made from our social group. We have been told that aquiline noses indicate courage and that protruding lips betray sensuality. The promoters of the theory generally imply that such judgements are wrong, as though information not based on first-hand experience could never be trusted. Actually, the danger does not lie in the social origin of the information. What counts is that people have a tendency to acquire simply structured concepts on the basis of insufficient evidence, which may have been gathered first-hand or second-hand, and to preserve these concepts unchanged in the face of contrary facts. While this may make for many one-sided or entirely wrong evaluations of individuals and groups of people, the existence of stereotypes does not explain the origin of physiognomic judgements. If these judgements stem from tradition, what is the tradition's source? Are they right or wrong? Even though often misapplied, traditional interpretations of physique and behavior may still be based on sound observation. In fact, perhaps they are so hardy because they are so true.

Empathy

The theory of empathy holds an intermediate position between the traditional and a more modern approach. This theory is often formulated as a mere extension of the association theory, designed to take care of the expression of inanimate objects. When I look at the columns of a temple, I know from past experience the kind of mechanical pressure and counterpressure that occurs in the column. Equally from past experience I know how I should feel myself if I were in the place of the column and if those physical forces acted upon and within my own body. I project my feelings into the column and by such animation endow it with expression. Lipps, who developed the theory, stated that empathy is based on association (16, p. 434). It is true, he also says, that the kind of association in question connects 'two things belonging together, or being combined by necessity, the one being immediately given in and with the other.' But he seems to have conceived of this inner necessity as a merely causal connexion, because immediately after the statement just quoted he denies explicitly that the relationship between the bodily expression of anger and the angry person's psychical experience could be described as an 'association of similarity, identity, correspondence' (p. 435). Like Darwin, Lipps saw no intrinsic kinship between perceptual appearance and the physical and psychological forces 'behind' it. However, he did see a structural similarity between physical and psychological forces in other respects. After discussing the mechanical forces whose existence in an inanimate object is inferred by the observer through past experience, Lipps writes the following remarkable passage:

And to [the knowledge of these mechanical forces] is furthermore attached the representation of possible internal ways of behavior of my own, which do not lead to the same result but are of the same character. In other words, there is attached the representation of possible kinds of my own activity, which in an analogous fashion, involves forces, impulses, or tendencies, freely at work or inhibited, a yielding to external effect, overcoming of resistance, the arising and resolving of tensions among impulses, etc. Those forces and effects of forces appear in the light of my own ways of behavior, my own kinds of activity, impulses, and tendencies and their ways of realization (16, p. 439).

Thus Lipps anticipated the Gestalt principle of isomorphism for the relationship between the physical forces in the observed object and the psychical dynamics in the observer; and in a subsequent section of the same paper he applies the 'association of similarity of character' even to the relationship between the perceived rhythm of musical tones and the rhythm of other psychical processes that occur in the listener. Which means that in the case of at least one structural characteristic, namely rhythm, Lipps realized a possible inner similarity of perceptual patterns and the expressive meaning they convey to the observer.

The Gestalt Approach

The Gestalt theory of expression admits that correspondences between physical and psychical behavior can be discovered on the basis of mere statistical correlation but maintains that repeated association is neither the only nor the common means of arriving at an understanding of expression. Gestalt psychologists hold that expressive behavior reveals its meaning directly in perception. The approach is based on the principle of isomorphism, according to which processes which take place in different media may be nevertheless similar in their structural organization. Applied to body and mind, this means that if the forces which determine bodily behavior are structurally similar to those which characterize the corresponding mental states, it may become understandable why psychical meaning can be read off directly from a person's appearance and conduct.

It is not the aim of this paper to prove the validity of the

Table 1
Isomorphic Levels

A. *Observed person*

I. State of mind	psychological
II. Neural correlate of I	electrochemical
III. Muscular forces	mechanical
IV. Kinesthetic correlate of III	psychological
V. Shape and movement of body	geometrical

B. *Observer*

VI. Retinal projection of V	geometrical
VII. Cortical projection of VI	electrochemical
VIII. Perceptual correlate of VII	psychological

Gestalt hypothesis.[2] We shall limit ourselves to pointing out some of its implications. Only brief presentations of the theory are available so far. However, Köhler's (12, pp. 216–47) and Koffka's (10, pp. 654–61) remarks about the subject are explicit enough to indicate that isomorphism on only two levels, namely the psychical processes which occur in the observed person and the corresponding behavioral activity, would be insufficient to explain direct understanding of expression through perception. In the following an attempt will be made to list a number of psychological and physical levels, in the observed person and in the observer, at which isomorphic structures must exist in order to make the Gestalt explanation possible.

2. For that purpose, observations of infants are relevant. Even in his day, Darwin was puzzled by the fact that young children seemed directly to understand a smile or grief 'at much too early an age to have learnt anything by experience' (7, p. 358). According to Bühler (6, p. 377), 'the baby of three or four months reacts positively to the angry as well as to the kind voice and look; the 5- to 7-month-old baby reflects the assumed expression and also begins to cry at the scolding voice and threatening gesture' on the basis of 'direct sensory influence.' Further evidence will have to come from detailed demonstrations of structural similarities (cf. p. 284).

Let us suppose that a person A performs a 'gentle' gesture, which is experienced as such by an observer B. On the basis of psychophysical parallelism in its Gestalt version it would be assumed that the tenderness of A's feeling (Table 1, level I) corresponds to a hypothetical process in A's nervous system (level II), and that the two processes, the psychical and the physiological, are isomorphic, that is to say, similar in structure.

The neural process will direct the muscular forces which produce the gesture of A's arm and hand (level III). Again it must be assumed that the particular dynamic pattern of mechanical action and inhibition in A's muscles corresponds structurally to the configuration of physiological and psychical forces at the levels II and I. The muscular action will be accompanied with a kinesthetic experience (level IV), which again must be isomorphic with the other levels. The kinesthetic experience need not always take place and is not strictly indispensable. However, the structural kinship of the experienced gentleness of his gesture and the equally experienced gentleness of his mood will make A feel that his gesture is a fitting manifestation of his state of mind.

Finally, the muscular forces of level III will cause A's arm and hand to move in, say, a parabolic curve (level V); and again the geometric formation of this curve would have to be isomorphic with the structure of the processes at the previous levels. An elementary geometrical example may illustrate the meaning of this statement. Geometrically, a circle is the result of just one structural condition. It is the locus of all points that are equally distant from one center. A parabola satisfies two such conditions. It is the locus of all points that have equal distance from one point and one straight line. The parabola may be called a compromise between two structural demands. Either structural condition yields to the other.[3] Is there any possible connexion between these geometrical characteristics of the parabola and the particular configuration of physical forces to which we attribute gentleness? One may point to the kind of physical process that produces parabolic patterns. In ballistics, for instance, the parabolic curve

3. One can express this also in terms of projective geometry by saying that the parabola as a conic section is intermediate between the horizontal section, namely the circle, and the vertical section, the straight-edged triangle.

of a trajectory is the result of a 'compromise' between the direction of the original impulse and the gravitational attraction. The two forces 'yield' to each other.[4]

At this point the description must shift from the observed person A to the observer B. B's eyes receive an image (level VI) of the gesture performed by A's arm and hand. Why should this image produce in B the impression that he is observing a gentle gesture? It may be true that the geometrical pattern of the gesture as well as the configuration of muscular forces which has created this pattern can both be characterized structurally as containing compromise, flexibility, yielding. But this fact in itself is not sufficient to explain the direct experience which B is said to receive by his perceptual observation. It becomes clear at this point that the Gestalt theory of expression is faced not only with the problem of showing how psychical processes can be inferred from bodily behavior, but that the primary task consists in making plausible the fact that the perception of shape, movement, etc., may convey to the observer the direct experience of an expression which is structurally similar to the organization of the observed stimulus pattern.

A's gesture is projected on the retinae of B's eyes[5] and, by

4. One of the principles on which the analysis of handwritings is based indicates that the script pattern reflects dynamic features of the writer's motor behavior, which in turn is produced by a characteristic configuration of muscular forces. The same isomorphism of muscular behavior and resulting visible trace has found applications in the technique of drawing. Langfeld (15, p. 129) quotes Bowie (5, pp. 35 and 77–9) concerning the principle of 'living movement' (*Sei Do*) in Japanese painting: 'A distinguishing feature in Japanese painting is the strength of the brush stroke, technically called *fude no chikara* or *fude no ikioi*. When representing an object suggesting strength, for instance, a rocky cliff, the beak or talons of a bird, the tiger's claws, or the limbs and branches of a tree, the moment the brush is applied the sentiment of strength must be invoked and felt throughout the artist's system and imparted through his arm and hand to the brush, and so transmitted into the object painted.'

5. At this stage a number of factors may interfere with the adequate projection of decisive characteristics of body A on the receptor organ of B. In our specific example it will depend, for instance, on the angle of projection, whether or not the perspective retinal image will preserve the essential structural features of the parabolic movement or transform it into a stimulus trace or unclear or clearly different structure. (In photographs and motion-pictures such factors influence the kind of expression obtained

way of the retinal images, on the visual cortex of B's cerebrum (level VII). Correspondingly, B perceives A's gesture (level VIII). Is there a possible similarity of the geometrical structure of the stimulus configuration and the structure of the expression which it conveys to the observer? We may go back to our mathematical analysis of the circle and the parabola. Simple experiments confirm what artists know from experience, namely that a circular curve looks 'harder', less flexible, than a parabolic one. In comparison with the circle the parabola looks more gentle. One could try to explain this finding by assuming that the observer knows, through past experience, the geometrical characteristics of such patterns or the nature of the physical forces which frequently produce them. This would take us back to the associationist theory. Along Gestalt lines another explanation suggests itself.

The projection of the perceptual stimulus on the visual cortex can be assumed to create a configuration of electrochemical forces in the cerebral field. The well-known Gestalt experiments in perception suggests that retinal stimulations are subjected to organizational processes when they reach the cortical level. As a result of these processes the elements of visual patterns are being grouped according to Wertheimer's rules. Furthermore, any visual pattern appears as an organized whole, in which some predominant elements determine the over-all shape and the directions of the main axes, while others have subordinate functions. For the same reasons, modifications of objective shape and size are perceived under certain conditions.

It will be observed that all these experimental findings focus upon the effects of the strains and stresses which organize the cortical field. Is there any reason to assume that only the *effects* of these dynamic processes, namely the groupings, the hierarchies of structural functions and the modifications of shape and size, are reflected in perceptual experience? Why should not the strains and stresses of the cortical forces themselves also have their psychological counterpart? It seems plausible that they represent the physiological equivalent of what is experienced as expression.

---

from the reproduction of physical objects.) Similar factors will influence the veracity of other perceptual qualities which carry expression.

Such a theory would make expression an integral part of the elementary processes of perception. *Expression, then, could be defined as the psychological counterpart of the dynamic processes which result in the organization of perceptual stimuli.* While concrete verification is obviously far away, the basic assumption has gained in concreteness since Köhler and Wallach (14) have explained phenomena of perceptual size, shape and location through the action of electrochemical forces. The future will show whether the theory can be extended to cover the phenomena of expression.

It is possible now to return to the question of how the perception of shape, movement, etc., may convey to an observer the direct experience of an expression which is structurally similar to the organization of the observed stimulus pattern. We referred previously to the constellations of physical forces which will induce an object to pursue a parabolic path. The physicist may be able to tell whether the example from ballistics is invertible. Will a parabolic pattern, such as the one projected on the cortical field, under certain conditions set off a configuration of forces which contains the structural factors of 'compromise' or 'yielding'? If so, isomorphism of the cortical forces and those described as levels I–V could be established.

This brings the description of isomorphic levels to an end. If the presentation is correct, the Gestalt-theoretical thesis would imply that an observer will adequately gauge another person's state of mind by inspection of that person's bodily appearance if the psychical situation of the observed person and the perceptual experience of the observer are structurally similar by means of a number of intermediate isomorphic levels.

Expression as a Perceptual Quality

The definition which was given above suggests that expression is an integral part of the elementary perceptual process. This should not come as a surprise. Perception is a mere instrument for the registration of color, shape, sound, etc. only as long as it is considered in isolation from the organism, of which it is a part. In its proper biological context, perception appears as the means by which the organism obtains information about the

275

friendly, hostile or otherwise relevant environmental forces to which it must react. These forces reveal themselves most directly by what is described here as expression.

There is psychological evidence to bear out this contention. In fact, the observations on primitives and children cited by Werner (21, pp. 67–82) and Köhler (13) indicate that 'physiognomic qualities', as Werner calls them, are even more directly perceived than the 'geometric-technical' qualities of size, shape or movement. Expression seems to be the primary content of perception. To register a fire as merely a set of hues and shapes in motion rather than to experience primarily the exciting violence of the flames presupposes a very specific, rare and artificial attitude. Even though the practical importance of, and hence the alertness to, expression has decreased in our culture, it cannot be maintained that a basic change has taken place in this respect. Darwin (7, pp. 359–60) noted that people sometimes observe and describe facial expression without being able to indicate the features of form, size, direction, etc., which carry it. In experimental work, one notices that even with the object directly in front of their eyes, subjects find it a hard and uncomfortable task to take note of the formal pattern. They constantly fall back upon the expressive characteristics, which they describe freely and naturally. Everyday experience shows that people may clearly recall the expression of persons or objects without being able to indicate color or shape. Asch observes: 'Long before one has realized that the color of the scene has changed, one may feel that the character of the scene has undergone change' (3, p. 85). Finally, there is the fact that the artist's, writer's, musician's approach to their subject is principally guided by expression.[6]

Generalized Theory

Thus far, the phenomenon of expression has been discussed essentially in its best-known aspect, namely, as a physical manifestation of physical processes. However, some of the foregoing considerations implied that expression is a more universal phenomenon. Expression does not only exist when there is a mind

6. This has led to the erroneous notion that all perception of expression is esthetic.

'behind' it, a puppeteer that pulls the strings. Expression is not limited to living organisms, which possess consciousness. A flame, a tumbling leaf, the wailing of a siren, a willow tree, a steep rock, a Louis XV chair, the cracks in a wall, the warmth of a glazed teapot, a hedgehog's thorny back, the colors of a sunset, a flowing fountain, lightning and thunder, the jerky movements of a bent piece of wire – they all convey expression through the various senses. The importance of this fact has been concealed by the popular hypothesis that in such cases human expression is merely transferred to objects. If, however, expression is an inherent characteristic of perceptual factors, it becomes unlikely this non-human expression should be nothing but an anthropomorphism, a 'pathetic fallacy'. Rather will human expression have to be considered a special case of a more general phenomenon. The comparison of an object's expression with a human state of mind is a secondary process (cf. p. 278). A weeping willow does not look sad because it looks like a sad person. It is more adequate to state that since the shape, direction and flexibility of willow branches convey the expression of passive hanging, a comparison with the structurally similar psychophysical pattern of sadness in humans may impose itself secondarily.

Expression is sometimes described as 'perceiving with imagination'. In doing so Gottschalk (9) explains that 'something is perceived as if it were actually present in the object of perception, although literally it is only suggested and not actually there. Music is not literally sad or gay or gentle; only sentient creatures or creatures with feeling, such as human beings, could be that.' If our language possessed more words which could refer to kinds of expression as such, instead of naming them after emotional states in which they find an important application, it would become apparent that the phenomenon in question is 'actually present in the object of perception' and not merely associated with it by imagination.

Even with regard to human behavior, the connexion of expression with a corresponding state of mind is not as compelling and indispensable as is sometimes taken for granted. Köhler (12, pp. 260–64) has pointed out that people normally deal with and react to the expressive physical behavior in itself rather than being conscious of the psychical experiences reflected by such behavior. We perceive the slow, listless, 'droopy' movements of one person as against the brisk, straight, vigorous movements of another, but do not necessarily go beyond the meaning of such appearance by thinking explicitly of the psychical weariness or alertness behind it. Weariness and alertness are already contained in the physical behavior itself; they are not distinguished in any essential way from the weariness of slowly floating tar or the energetic ringing of the telephone bell.

This broader conception has practical consequences. It suggests, for instance, that the phenomenon of expression does not belong primarily under the heading of the emotions or personality, where it is commonly treated. It is true that the great contributions which the study of expression has in store for these fields of psychology are thus far almost untapped. However, the experience of the last decades shows that little progress is made unless the nature of expression itself is clarified first.[7]

Secondary effects

Strictly speaking, the phenomenon of expression is limited to the levels V–VIII of Table 1. That is, the term 'expression', as used in this paper, refers to an experience which takes place when a sensory stimulus affects the visual cortex of an observer's brain. The processes which may have given rise to the stimulus as well as those which the cortical stimulation provokes in other brain centers are supplementary.

Once perceptual stimulation has taken place, a number of secondary happenings may follow.

(1) The observer B may deduce from the expression of A's bodily behavior that particular psychical processes are going on in A's mind; that is, through the perception of level V the observer gains knowledge about level I. The observation of a gentle gesture leads to the conclusion: A is in a gentle mood. This conclusion may be based on an isomorphic similarity between the

7. Once this is done, it will be possible and necessary to approach the further problem of the influences which the total personality exerts upon the observation of expression. To Vincent van Gogh, cypress trees conveyed an expression which they do not have for many other people. Cf. Koffka (10, p. 600).

observed behavior and a state of mind known or imaginable to the observer. In other cases, the conclusion may rely on past experience. Yawning, for instance, conveys the direct expression of sudden expansion; but the connexion between yawning and fatigue or boredom is discovered by learning. The same seems to be true for the spasmodic outbursts of sound which we call laughter and which in themselves are so far from suggesting mirth that they remain permanently imcomprehensible to the chimpanzee, who otherwise 'at once correctly interprets the slightest change of human expression, whether menacing or friendly' (11, p. 307). It is important to realize that an expression may be correctly perceived and described, yet the inferences derived from it may be wrong. If, in an experiment, 80 per cent of the observers agree on an 'erroneous' attribution, it is not sufficient to dismiss the result as an instance of failure. The high amount of agreement represents a psychological fact in its own right. The reliability of the observer's responses to a perceptual stimulus is a problem quite different from the validity of such responses, i.e. the question whether the observers' diagnosis is 'true'.

(2) The observed expression may bring about the corresponding state of mind in B. In perceiving A's gentle behavior, the observer himself may experience a feeling of tenderness. (Lipps speaks of 'sympathetic empathy' as distinguished from 'simple empathy', 16, p. 417.)

(3) The observed expression may provoke the corresponding kinesthetic experience, e.g. a feeling of relaxed softness. The effects described under (2) and (3) may be instances of a kind of 'resonance' based on isomorphism. Just as a sound calls forth a vibration of similar frequency in a string, various levels of psychological experience, such as the visual, the kinesthetic, the emotional seem to elicit in each other sensations of similar structure.

(4) The perceived expression may remind B of other observations in which a similar expression played a role. Thus past experience is considered here not as the basis for the apperception of expression; instead, the direct observation of expression becomes the basis for comparison with similar observations in the past.

The Role of Past Experience

While there is no evidence to support the hypothesis that the central phenomenon of expression is based on learning, it is worth noting that in most cases the interpretation of the perceived expression is influenced by what is known about the person or object in question and about the context in which it appears. Mere inspection will produce little more than over-all impressions of the forces at work, strong and clear cut as such an experience may be. Increasing knowledge will lead to more differentiated interpretations, which will take the particular context into account. (As an example, one may think of the expression conveyed by the behavior of an animal whose habits one does not know and the changes that occur with closer acquaintance.) Knowledge does not interfere with expression itself, it merely modifies its interpretation, except for cases in which knowledge changes the appearance of the carrier of expression, that is, the perceptual pattern itself. For instance, a line figure may change its perceptual structure and therefore its expression if it is suddenly seen as a human figure. A lifted eyebrow is seen as tense because it is perceived as a deviation from a known normal position. The expression of Mongolian eyes or Negro lips is influenced, for a white observer, by the fact that he conceives them as deviations from the normal face of his own race.

In Gestalt terms, past experience, knowledge, learning, memory are considered as factors of the temporal context in which a given phenomenon appears. Like the spatial context, on which Gestaltists have concentrated their attention during the early development of the theory, the temporal context influences the way a phenomenon is perceived. An object looks big or small depending on whether it is seen, spatially, in the company of smaller or larger objects. The same is true for the temporal context. The buildings of a middle-sized town look tall to a farmer, small to a New Yorker, and correspondingly their expression differs for the two observers. Mozart's music may appear serene and cheerful to a modern listener, who perceives it in the temporal context of twentieth-century music, whereas it conveyed the expression of violent passion and desperate suffering to his contemporaries against the background of the music they knew. Such examples do not demonstrate that there is no intrinsic connexion between perceptual patterns and the expression they convey but simply that experiences must not be evaluated in isolation from their spatial and temporal whole-context.

Knowledge often merges with directly perceived expression into a more complex experience. When we observe the gentle curve of a coachman's whip while being aware at the same time of the aggressive use of the object, the resulting experience clearly contains an element of contradiction. Such contradictions are exploited by artists; compare, in motion pictures, the uncanny effect of the murderer who moves softly and speaks with a velvety voice.

Finally, the perceptual experience of expression can be influenced by the kind of training which in artistic and musical instruction is known as making students 'see' and 'hear'. By opening people's eyes and ears to what is directly perceivable, they can be made to scan the given sensory pattern more adequately and thus to receive a fuller experience of its expression. A neglected or misled capacity for responding perceptually can be revived or corrected.

The role of kinesthesia

Frequently people feel that another person, whom they are observing, behaves physically the way they themselves have behaved before. They get this impression even though at that time they probably did not watch themselves in the mirror. It may be that they compare their own state of mind as they remember it from the former occasion with the expression conveyed by the bodily behavior of the other person and/or with the state of mind reflected in that behavior. Probably the kinesthetic perception of one's own muscular behavior plays an important part in such situations. If muscular behavior and kinesthetic experience are isomorphic, it becomes explainable why at times one is so keenly aware of one's own facial expression, posture, gestures. One may feel, for instance: right now, I look just like my father! The most convincing example is furnished by actors and dancers, whose bodily performance is created essentially through kinesthetic control. And yet their gestures are understandable to the audience visually. This suggests that there is a valid correspondence between bodily behavior and the related kinesthetic perception.

The problem of what enables an infant to imitate an observer who smiles or shows the tip of his tongue belongs in the same category. Of particular interest is the fact that the blind express their feelings – even though imperfectly – in spite of their inability to observe expression in others visually. The blind also understand certain gestures on the basis of their own kinesthetic experiences.

> The blind man, like the person who sees, is aware of the gestures he makes when under the influence of various emotions. He shrugs his shoulders and raises his arms to express his disdain and amazement. The same gestures recognized by him in a statue will evoke within him the same sentiments (20, p. 320).

Isomorphism would seem to account also for the fact that it often suffices to assume a particular posture (levels III and IV) in order to enter into a corresponding state of mind (level I). Bending the head and folding the hands is more than an accidentally chosen posture of praying, which derives its meaning merely from tradition. The kinesthetic sensation which accompanies this posture is structurally akin to the psychical attitude called devotion. 'Bowing' to a superior power's will is a mental condition so directly related to the corresponding bodily gesture that its common linguistic description uses the physical to describe the psychological. Rituals not only express what people feel but also help them to feel the way the situation requires. By straightening our backbones we produce a muscular sensation which is akin to the attitude of pride, and thus introduce into our state of mind a noticeable element of bold self-sufficiency.[8]

Even the 'practical' motor activities are accompanied more or less strongly by structurally corresponding states of mind. For instance, hitting or breaking things normally seems to evoke the emotional overtone of attack. To assert merely that this is so because people are aggressive would be an evasion of the problem. But if the dynamic character of the kinesthetic sensation which accompanies hitting and breaking resembles the emotional dynamics of attack, then the one may be expected to evoke the other –

8. James's theory of emotion is based on a sound psychological observation. It fails where it identifies the kinesthetic sensation with the total emotional experience instead of describing it as a component which reinforces and sometimes provokes emotion because of the structural similarity of the two.

by 'resonance' (cf. p. 279). (This kinship makes it possible for aggressiveness, wherever it exists, to express itself through such motor acts.) Probably this parallelism holds true for all motor activity. Muscular behavior such as grasping, yielding, lifting, straightening, smoothing, loosening, bending, running, stopping seems to produce mental resonance effects constantly. (In consequence, language uses all of them metaphorically to describe states of mind.) The psychosomatic phenomena of pathological 'organ-speech' ('I cannot stomach this!') may be considered the most dramatic examples of a universal interdependence. The range and the importance of the phenomenon are not acknowledged as long as one studies expression only in motor activities that are not, or not any more, serviceable. It seems safe to assert that all motor acts are expressive, even though in different degrees, and that they all carry the experience of corresponding higher mental processes, if ever so faintly. Therefore, it is inadequate to describe expressive movements as mere atavisms, the way Darwin did. They are physical acts which take place because of their inner correspondence with the state of mind of the person who performs them. To use one of Darwin's examples: a person who coughs in embarrassment is not simply the victim of a meaningless association between a state of mind and a physical reaction, which was or can be serviceable under similar circumstances. Rather does he produce a reaction which he experiences to be meaningfully related to his state of mind. The bodily accompaniment completes the mental reaction. Together they form an act of total psychophysical behavior. The human organism always functions as a whole, physically and psychically.

This view permits an application to the theory of art. It highlights the intimate connexion of artistic and 'practical' behavior. The dancer, for instance, does not have to endow movements with a symbolic meaning for artistic purposes, but uses in an artistically organized way the unity of psychical and physical reaction which is characteristic for human functioning in general.

In a broader sense, it is the direct expressiveness of all perceptual qualities which allows the artist to convey the effects of the most universal and abstract psychophysical forces through the presentation of individual, concrete objects and happenings.

While painting a pine tree, he can rely on the expression of towering and spreading which this tree conveys whenever it is seen by a human eye, and thus can span in his work the whole range of existence, from its most general principles to the tangible manifestations of these principles in individual objects.

An illustration

It has been pointed out in the beginning that experimenters have been concerned mostly with the question whether and to what extent observers can judge a person's state of mind from his physical appearance. In consequence, the psychological literature contains few analyses of perceptual patterns with regard to the expression they convey. As an example of the kind of material which is badly needed in this field, Efron's study on the gestures of two ethnic groups (8) may be cited. He describes the behavior of Eastern Jews and Southern Italians in New York City by analysing the range, speed, plane, co-ordination and shape of their movements. A comparison of these findings with the mentalities of the two groups would probably produce excellent illustrations of what is meant by the structural similarity of psychical and physical behavior. Among the experimental investigations, Lundholm's early study (17) may be mentioned. He asked eight laymen in art to draw lines, each of which was to express the affective tone of an adjective given verbally. It was found, for instance, that only straight lines, broken by angles, were used to represent such adjectives as exciting, furious, hard, powerful, while only curves were used for sad, quiet, lazy, merry. Upward direction of lines expressed strength, energy, force; downward direction, weakness, lack of energy, relaxation, depression, etc. Recently Willmann (22) had thirty-two musicians compose short themes, meant to illustrate four abstract designs. Some agreement among the composers was found concerning the tempo, meter, melodic line and amount of consonance, chosen to render the characteristics of the drawings. Subsequently the designs and compositions were used for matching experiments.

Because of the scarcity of pertinent material, it may be permissible to mention here an experiment which is too limited in the number of cases and too subjective in its method of recording and evaluating the data to afford a proof of the thesis we are discussing. It is presented merely as an example of the kind of research which promises fruitful results.[9] Five members of the student dance group of Sarah Lawrence College were asked individually to give improvisations of the following three subjects: sadness, strength, night. Rough descriptions of the dance patterns which resulted were jotted down by the experimenter and later classified according to a number of categories. Table 2 presents the findings in an abbreviated form. The numerical agreement is high but obviously carries little weight. As a point of method, it may only be mentioned that instances of disagreement cannot be

Table 2
Analysis of Dance Movements Improvised by Five Subjects

	Sadness:	Strength:	Night:
Speed:	5: slow	2: slow 1: very fast 1: medium 1: decrescendo	5: slow
Range:	5: small, enclosed	5: large, sweeping	3: small 2: large
Shape:	3: round 2: angular	5: very straight	5: round
Tension:	4: little tension 1: inconsistent	5: much tension	4: little tension 1: decrescendo
Direction:	5: indefinite, changing, wavering	5: precise, sharp, mostly forward	3: indefinite, changing 2: mostly downward
Center:	5: passive, pulled downward in body	5: active, centered	3: passive 2: from active to passive

taken simply to indicate that there was no reliable correspondence between task and performance. Sometimes, the task allows more than one valid interpretation. For instance, 'strength' expresses

9. The data were collected and tabulated by Miss Jane Binney, a student at Sarah Lawrence College.

itself equally well in fast and in slow movement. 'Night' is less directly related to one particular dynamic pattern than sadness or strength.

Most tempting is the comparison between the movement patterns and the corresponding psychical processes. Such comparison cannot be carried through with exactness at this time mainly because psychology has not yet provided a method of describing the dynamics of states of mind in a way which would be more exact scientifically than the descriptions offered by novelists or everyday language. Nevertheless, it can be seen from our example that the dynamic patterns of expressive behavior permit relatively concrete and exact descriptions in terms of speed, range, shape, etc. Even the crudely simplified characterizations given in the table seem to suggest that the motor traits through which the dancers interpreted sadness reflect the slow, languishing pace of the psychological processes, the indefiniteness of aim, the withdrawal from the environment, the passivity – all of which distinguish sadness psychologically. The fact that expressive behavior is so much more readily accessible to concrete scientific description than the corresponding psychical processes deserves attention. It suggests that in the future the study of behavior may well become the method of choice, when psychologists undertake the task of reducing emotions and other psychical processes to configurations of basic forces. Already the analysis of handwriting has led to a number of categories (pressure, size, direction, proportion, etc.) which invite a search for the corresponding psychological concepts.

Our example will also show why it is fruitless to dismiss the phenomena of expression as 'mere stereotypes'. If it can be demonstrated that the dynamics of psychical and physical processes are structurally interrelated and that this interrelation is perceptually evident, the question of whether and to what extent the performance and its interpretations are based on social conventions loses importance.

References

1. G. W. ALLPORT and P. E. VERNON, *Studies in Expressive Movement*, Macmillan, 1933.
2. R. ARNHEIM, 'Experimentell-psychologische Untersuchungen zum Ausdrucksproblem', *Psychol. Forsch.*, vol. 11 (1928), pp. 2–132.
3. S. E. ASCH, 'Max Wertheimer's contribution to modern psychology', *Soc. Res.* vol. 13 (1946), pp. 81–102.
4. G. BERKELEY, *An Essay Toward a New Theory of Vision*, Dutton, 1934.
5. H. P. BOWIE, *On the Laws of Japanese Painting*, Elder, 1911.
6. C. BUHLER, 'The social behavior of children', in C. Murchison (ed.), *A Handbook of Child Psychology*, Clark, 1933, pp. 374–416.
7. C. DARWIN, *The Expression of the Emotions in Man and Animals*, Appleton, 1896.
8. D. EFRON, *Gesture and Environment*, King's Crown, 1941.
9. D. W. GOTTSHALK, *Art and the Social Order*, Chicago University Press, 1947.
10. K. KOFFKA, *Principles of Gestalt Psychology*, Harcourt Brace, 1935.
11. W. KÖHLER, *The Mentality of Apes*, Harcourt Brace, 1925.
12. W. KÖHLER, *Gestalt Psychology*, Liveright, 1929.
13. W. KÖHLER, 'Psychological remarks on some questions of anthropology', *Amer. J. Psychol.*, vol. 50 (1937), pp. 271–88.
14. W. KÖHLER and H. WALLACH, 'Figural after-effects. An investigation of visual processes', *Proc. Amer. phil. Soc.*, vol. 88 (1944), pp. 269–357.
15. H. S. LANGFELD, *The Aesthetic Attitude*, Harcourt Brace, 1920.
16. T. LIPPS, 'Aesthetische Einfühlung', *Z. Psychol.*, vol. 22 (1900), pp. 415–50.
17. H. LUNDHOLM, 'The affective tone of lines', *Psychol. Rev.*, vol. 28 (1921), pp. 43–60.
18. D. RAPAPORT, 'The Szondi test', *Bull. Menninger Clin.*, vol. 5 (1941), pp. 33–9.
19. E. G. SCHACHTEL, 'On color and affect', *Psychiatry*, vol. 6 (1943), pp. 393–409.
20. P. VILLEY, *The World of the Blind*, Duckworth, 1930.
21. H. WERNER, *Comparative Psychology of Mental Development*, Harper, 1940.
22. R. R. WILLMANN, 'An experimental investigation of the creative process in music', *Psychol. Monogr.*, vol. 57 (1944), no. 261.
23. W. WOLFF, *The Expression of Personality*, Harper, 1943.
24. R. S. WOODWORTH, *Experimental Psychology*, Holt, 1939.

Part Six Metrics of Visual Form and the Response to Art

The hope that the 'unity' and 'diversity' of a picture will one day be measurable has often been expressed, and such measurement has been attempted by Birkoff (1933) among others. The assumption that measurement is relevant has been carried to extremes in the study of proportion – as by Ghyka (1946). More recently research into the metrics of visual form has intensified, stimulated by, but not necessarily dependent upon, information theory. There are serious problems in evolving such metrics, though there are now many experiments correlating proposed metrics with the picture preferences of animals, children, adults and sub-normals. They have an important bearing on the study of determinants of picture preference, and we have illustrated the approach here with a paper by Dorfman and McKenna. Further, the use of the computer in generating pictures varying systematically on several dimensions is becoming increasingly relevant as we see in Noll's paper.

BIRKOFF, G. D. (1933), *Aesthetic Measure*, Harvard University Press.
GHYKA, M. (1946), *The Geometry of Art and Life*, Sheed and Ward.

12 D. D. Dorfman and H. McKenna

Pattern Preference as a Function of Pattern Uncertainty

D. D. Dorfman and H. McKenna, 'Pattern preference as a function of pattern uncertainty', *Canadian Journal of Psychology*, vol. 20 (1966), pp. 143–53.

This study tested the hypothesis that level of preference for patterns is a function of uncertainty defined in terms of matrix grain. In Experiment 1, 100 women served as Ss. Preference data were obtained by the method of paired comparisons. The results showed a reliable curvilinear relation between preference level and fineness of matrix grain. These findings agreed with results obtained by Munsinger and Kessen (1964) where uncertainty was defined in terms of the co-ordinality of the patterns. The Ss were then separated according to their most preferred level of uncertainty. The results showed that each S has a preferred level of uncertainty and that preference for other levels of uncertainty decreases as the distance increases from this preferred level. Experiment 2 confirmed these results on eighteen art majors.

Several authors (e.g., Attneave, 1959; Berlyne, 1960; Munsinger and Kessen, 1964) have suggested that pattern preference depends upon the uncertainty of patterns being judged. Munsinger and Kessen (1964) have recently obtained evidence supporting this hypothesis with a class of patterns whose uncertainty was manipulated by varying the number of turns of each pattern. They found a curvilinear relation between the number of turns and level of preference. In addition, there was an unexpectedly high preference for figures of very few, and very many, turns. In constructing their patterns, K random points were plotted in a $N \times N$ matrix and the points were connected randomly into a polygon of K sides or turns, where turn is defined as a contour side of the polygon. The number of turns was approximately equal to the number of points. One can represent each of these points by two numbers or coordinates, each number varying from 1 to N. Consequently, this manipulation of the number of turns has been termed the manipulation of co-ordinality (Attneave, 1957, 1959).

Another way of manipulating the uncertainty of a set of patterns is to vary the matrix grain used to construct the patterns. It should be noted that Munsinger and Kessen held matrix grain constant in their manipulation of uncertainty. This study was undertaken to determine if the general findings of Munsinger and Kessen (1964) on the number of turns may be extended to matrix grain. Studies on matrix grain are particularly important because the matrix grain is basic to the computation of information or uncertainty. In fact, a pattern may not be said to contain any determinate number of bits of information until its grain (the size of its smallest elements) is specified (Attneave, 1959). A second major goal of this study was to investigate certain detailed predictions of the Dember–Earl theory of pattern preference (1957) with respect to individual differences. Since the group-preference function is an average of a number of individual-difference functions, their theory would be of particular interest in the present study.

Experiment 1

Method

Subjects. Ss were 100 girls enrolled in Introductory Psychology. They were given extra credit for participating in the experiment.[1]

Apparatus. Two Viewlex projectors were used to present pairs of patterns on 2 in × 2 in slides. An attachment to the projectors permitted the projection of two patterns simultaneously and side by side.

Stimuli. The patterns were constructed on 11 in × 11 in pieces of cardboard. The patterns consisted of a matrix of painted and un-painted cells with the matrix employed in construction not visible in the completed pattern. They were made by covering the white cells of the matrix with brisket paper and applying green water colour with a spray gun. After the paint dried, the brisket paper was removed. The method was quite efficient and produced excel-

1. Seventy-five of the Ss had been given other preference tasks immediately preceding this task, for example, Graves Design Test, Rectangle and Painting Preferences.

lent results. The patterns were then photographed and made into 2 in × 2 in slides. Green rather than black paint was used because pilot research showed that coloured patterns were more pleasing and appeared easier to evaluate.

Six $N \times N$ matrix grains were used with N equal to 2, 4, 6, 8, 10 or 12. Each cell in a matrix grain was made either green or white, with the probability of a white or green cell set at 0·50 and determined by a table of random numbers. The green was approximately 5G 5/8 in the Munsell notation. Four sets of patterns were constructed. Each set contained six patterns, one instance of each matrix grain. Figure 1 shows a set of six patterns constructed in this fashion. Over all, there were therefore twenty-four patterns, six matrix grains, and four instances of each grain. Adopting the Shannon–Wiener measure of information, this resulted in six classes of patterns, each class having an uncertainty of 4, 16, 36, 64, 100 or 144 bits of information. The pattern space of each matrix grain consisted of the set of all possible patterns generated from the matrix, with all patterns being equally probable in this case. As an example of how the uncertainty measure was computed, consider the 2×2 grain. There are sixteen possible patterns which can be generated from this grain. Since the probability of a painted and unpainted cell is 0·50, each pattern is equally probable and has an information measure of 1/16. The average information or uncertainty of the total class is also 1/16 by the formula $H = -\log_2 p$ for equiprobable alternatives (Attneave, 1959).

Procedure. The method of paired comparisons was used to obtain subject preferences. Ss were given all possible pairs of patterns within each set of patterns and were asked to choose the pattern they preferred of the pair. Paired-comparisons data were obtained on the four sets of patterns in succession. Order of presentation of the sets of patterns and pattern location on the screen were randomized across Ss. The instructions were as follows: 'You will be shown sixty pairs of patterns, a pair at a time, side by side on the screen. Each pair will be exposed for only 7 seconds, no longer. With L representing the pattern on the left and R representing the pattern on the right, check either L or R with an X alongside each number for the pattern you prefer. There are no right or wrong answers. Just designate the pattern you

Figure 1. Six patterns, each constructed from a different matrix grain.

prefer of the pair. If you have any questions, raise your hand.'

The Ss were tested in groups of two to ten and their responses were recorded on response sheets given to them. The stimuli were projected in pairs on a screen on the front wall of the room in which they were seated. As noted in the instructions, each pair was exposed for 7 seconds.

Results and discussion

The total percentage of times that each subject chose a particular matrix grain was obtained for the six matrix grains, and these percentages were rank-ordered. The mean ranks for the six matrix grains averaged over all subjects are presented in Figure 2. As can be seen, the results show a mild curvilinear relation between the uncertainty of each class and mean rank. A Friedman analysis of variance performed on these data showed a highly significant χ_r^2 ($\chi_r^2 = 57 \cdot 35$, $df = 5$, $p < 0 \cdot 001$). In order to test for curvilinearity, a normalizing transformation was performed on the ranks (Fisher and Yates, 1963) which permitted a trend analysis of the data.[2] The coefficients used for the trend analysis were corrected for unequal intervals. The analysis revealed a highly significant non-linear trend ($F = 5 \cdot 60$, $df = 4/495$, $p < 0 \cdot 001$) and a moderately significant linear trend ($F = 5 \cdot 90$, $df = 1/495$, $p < 0 \cdot 05$). Figure 2 shows an inverse linear trend between mean rank and uncertainty level as well as a non-linear (curvilinear) trend.

Since the ranks were based upon four sets of matrix grains, there is an assumption that preferences obtained for one set of patterns correlate with preferences obtained for other sets of patterns. To test this assumption, a coefficient of concordance (W) was computed for each subject over the four sets of patterns. The average W was $+0 \cdot 551$, and there were fifty-nine significant Ws among the 100 Ws computed ($\alpha = 0 \cdot 05$). The probability of obtaining fifty-nine significant Ws by chance among a sample of 100 is very low ($z = 9 \cdot 63$, $p < 0 \cdot 001$). It should be noted that one would not expect perfect concordance in this experiment since there are probably some unique pattern preferences irre-

2. The applicability of such a transformation was noted by Dr B. J. Winer in a personal communication. Fisher and Yates (1963) state that such a transformation allows normal-curve statistics on ranked data such as analysis of variance.

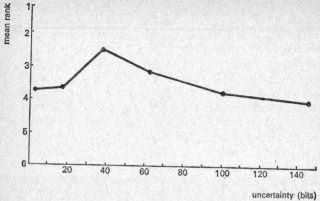

Figure 2. Mean rank as a function of the uncertainty of each pattern class

spective of matrix grain, and preferences may change over trials.

Although particular trends may exist for the group data, there may be some consistent individual differences which merit consideration. Dember and Earl (1957) have suggested that each subject has his own preferred level of complexity, and that preference for other levels of complexity will decrease as the distance of a pattern increases from this preferred level. If degree of complexity is defined in an *a priori* fashion as fineness of matrix grain, their hypothesis should have implications for the present data.

Table 1

Analysis of Variance of Transformed Ranks as a Function of Uncertainty[1]

Source	df	MS	F
Subjects (Ss)	99	0·000	
Uncertainty (U)	5	4·332	5·66**
Linear[2]	(1)	4·514	5·90*
Non-linear	(4)	4·286	5·60**
U × Ss	495	0·765	

*p <0·05   **p <0·001

1. The expected MS for subjects is 0·00 with no ties.
2. The coefficients were corrected for unequal intervals.

On the basis of this hypothesis, the subjects were separated according to their most preferred level of uncertainty among the six possible levels. Figure 3 shows the data of the subjects combined into subgroups according to their most preferred level of uncertainty. Twelve of them had ties at the first rank and were therefore excluded. As can be seen, the data provide good support for the Dember–Earl hypothesis. A Friedman analysis of variance performed on these data showed highly significant effects in all six groups ($p < 0.001$, $df = 4$, in all cases). The null hypothesis was that the set of ranks in each of the five classes (excluding the most preferred class) represented a random sample from a rectangular distribution. Figure 3 shows that the order predicted by Dember and Earl (1957) held in all groups except that in the groups from whom 100 and 144 bits were most preferred, there was a slight rise in preference for the class having the lowest level.

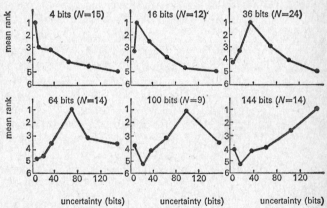

Figure 3. Mean rank as a function of uncertainty, where each group of *S*s is separated according to the most preferred level of uncertainty

Although these data may be accounted for by the assumption that subjects have preferences with respect to matrix grain, it may also be argued that unsophisticated subjects have no preferences with respect to matrix grain and that they simply adopted an arbitrary strategy for making orderly judgements. A second experiment was performed to answer this criticism.

Experiment 2

If art majors were asked to evaluate these patterns, one would expect that they would be more likely to have criteria for making judgements of pattern preference. This experiment was performed to determine if art majors give the same general results as non-art majors on these patterns. In order to make the task resemble as closely as possible a situation where art majors customarily express preferences, the original patterns were shown rather than slides.

Method

Subjects. Ss were eighteen female art majors enrolled in Introductory Psychology. They were given extra credit for participating in the experiment.

Stimuli. The cardboard patterns constructed in Experiment 1 for slide production were used in this experiment.

Procedure. Ss were run in groups. The set of twenty-four patterns was placed in a random order along the ledge of a blackboard with $1\frac{1}{2}$ inches between patterns. Ss sat in a group facing the patterns and were asked to rank them in order of preference. The rankings were recorded on dittoed sheets provided to the Ss for this purpose, and no time limit was placed upon the task. The instructions were as follows: 'You are to rank order in terms of preference the twenty-four paintings which are before you. First, put a 'one' before the painting which you prefer the most. Next, put a 'two' before the painting that you now prefer the most among those remaining, and continue in this fashion until all of the paintings have been ranked. Finally, make sure that you do not assign a given number to more than one painting. Any questions? Okay, you have as much time for the task as you like, and after you finish, give me your paper and you can leave.' The patterns were designated by numbers from 1 to 24 placed above each pattern.

All Ss entered the testing room at the same time and the patterns were observable from the time of their entrance to the time of their exit. To give some indication of the length of time of the task, the instructions took about 5 minutes. Some Ss left as soon as 10 min after instructions and some remained as long as 30 min.

Results and discussion

Figure 4 presents the mean ranks for the six matrix grains averaged over subjects. These results show a fairly large curvilinear relation between the uncertainty of each class and mean rank.

Table 2

Analysis of Variance of Transformed Ranks as a Function of Uncertainty with Art Majors as Subjects

Source	df	MS	F
Subjects (Ss)	17	0·000	
Uncertainty (U)	5	2·539	3·19*
Linear	(1)	0·319	<1
Non-linear	(4)	16·822	21·15**
U × Ss	85	0·795	

*$p < 0.05$ **$p < 0.001$

A Friedman analysis of variance performed on these data gave a significant ($\chi_r^2 = 226·59$, $df = 5$, $p < 0·001$). To test for curvilinearity, the normalizing transformation on the ranks (Fisher and Yates, 1963) was used. The trend analysis (Table 2) showed a significant non-linear trend ($F = 21·15$, $df = 4/85$, $p < 0·001$), but no linear trend as in Experiment 1. As for individual differences, subjects were separated according to their most preferred level of uncertainty and these results are shown in Figure 5. Although the number of art majors was rather small for purposes of classifying into subgroups, the data do appear to support the hypothesis proposed by Dember and Earl (1957). A Friedman analysis of variance by ranks performed on five of the six subgroups showed a significant χ_r^2 ($p < 0·001$, $df = 4$, in all cases). No analysis was performed on the 100-bits subgroups since it contained only one subject. This particular subject (see Figure 5) conformed perfectly to the order predicted by Dember and Earl. It might be noted that, in this particular case, the probability of getting such an order by chance is 0·041.

In summary, the data on art majors also show the curvilinear

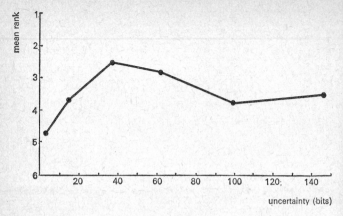

Figure 4. Mean rank as a function of the uncertainty of each pattern class for art majors

relation between preference and matrix grain. The results obtained on individual differences in Experiment 1 were also found in this experiment. While these data do support the hypothesis of a curvilinear relation between mean rank and pattern uncertainty, the importance of individual differences must also be emphasized. Although Munsinger and Kessen (1964) did consider the importance of individual differences in their theory, they evaluated only the group results in their research. These data show that group results are the average effect of a set of subjects with *wide* individual differences, some of whose data are curvilinear and some of whose data are essentially linear with respect to the relation of preference level and uncertainty (see Figures 3 and 5). Averaging the diverse data of these subjects gave the curvilinear results shown in Figures 2 and 4. As noted earlier, Munsinger and Kessen (1964) obtained some evidence of high preference for very few and very many turns in addition to their over-all curvilinear result. It is possible that this preference for extremes observed in their group data may have been the result of a fair number of subjects whose most preferred pattern contained either very few or very many turns. The Dember–Earl analysis performed in this paper might be useful in such preference studies in which conclusions are drawn from group data.

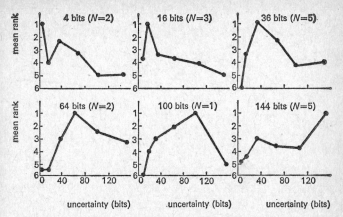

Figure 5. Mean rank as a function of uncertainty, where each group of *S*s is separated according to the most preferred level of uncertainty. The *S*s are all art majors

One final study of interest is that of Vitz (1964) who studied the relation between uncertainty and preference level in terms of ratings of pleasantness in an auditory task. Unlike these data and those reported by Munsinger and Kessen (1964), he did not obtain a non-monotonic relation, but a monotonic relation between uncertainty and preference level. At present, no clear explanation exists for the divergent results obtained by Vitz (1964).

References

ATTNEAVE, F. (1957), 'Physical determinants of the judged complexity of shapes', *J. exp. Psychol.*, vol. 53, pp. 221–7.

ATTNEAVE, F. (1959), *Applications of Information Theory to Psychology*, Holt.

BERLYNE, D. E. (1960), *Conflict, Arousal and Curiosity*, McGraw-Hill.

DEMBER, W. N., and EARL, R. W. (1957), 'Analysis of exploratory, manipulatory and curiosity behaviors', *Psychol. Rev.*, vol. 64, pp. 91–6.

FISHER, R. A., and YATES, F. (1963), *Statistical Tables for Biological, Agricultural, and Medical Research*, Hafner.

MUNSINGER, H., and KESSEN, W. (1964), 'Uncertainty, structure and preference', *Psychol. Monogr.*, vol. 78, no. 586.

VITZ, P. O. (1964), 'Preferences for rates of information presented by sequences of tones' *J. exp. Psychol.*, vol. 68, pp. 176–83.

13 A. M. Noll

Human or Machine: A Subjective Comparison of Piet
Mondrian's *Composition With Lines* (1917) and a
Computer-Generated Picture

A. M. Noll, 'Human or machine: a subjective comparison of Piet Mondrian's *Composition with Lines* (1917) and a computer-generated picture',
Psychological Record, vol. 16 (1966), pp. 1–10.

A digital computer and microfilm plotter were used to produce a
semi-random picture similar in composition to Piet Mondrian's painting *Composition with Lines* (1917). Reproductions of both pictures
were then presented to 100 subjects whose tasks were to identify the
computer picture and to indicate which picture they preferred. Only
28 per cent of the *S*s were able to correctly identify the computer-
generated picture, while 59 per cent of the *S*s preferred the computer-
generated picture. Both percentages were statistically different (0·05
level) from selections based upon chance according to a binomial test.

Piet Mondrian's *Composition with Lines*

In 1914 the Dutch painter Piet Mondrian (1872–1944) introduced
a horizontal–vertical theme into his paintings which later cul-
minated in the black-and-white painting *Composition with
Lines* (1917). This abstract painting has been described by a prominent French critic and writer as 'the most accomplished' of
Mondrian's series of paintings based upon the horizontal–
vertical theme (Seuphor, 1962). These paintings are said to incorporate masculinity and femininity by symbolizing the masculine
as vertical (the upright trees of a forest) and the feminine as horizontal (the sea) with each complementing the other (Seuphor).
Mondrian sought to indicate the plastic function of the sea, sky
and stars through a multiplicity of crossing verticals and hori-
zontals (Mondrian, 1945). *Composition with Lines*, reproduced
in Figure 1, consists of a scattering of vertical and horizontal
bars which, at first glance, seem to be randomly scattered
throughout the painting. With further study, however, one real-

izes that Mondrian used considerable planning in placing each bar in proper relationship to all the others. Conceivably, Mondrian followed some scheme or program in producing the painting although the exact algorithm is unknown.

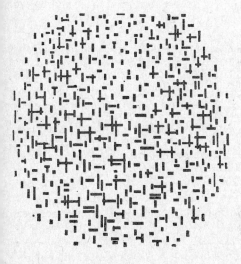

Figure 1. *Composition with Lines* (1917) by Piet Mondrian. (Copyright Rijkmuseum Kröller-Müller)

If Mondrian's *Composition with Lines* is studied carefully, some interesting observations about its over-all composition can be made. The more evident of these are: (a) The outline of the painting is a circle that has been cropped at the sides, top and bottom; (b) The vertical and horizontal bars falling within a region at the top of the painting have been shortened in length; and (c) The length and width of the bars otherwise seem to be randomly distributed.

303

'Computer Composition With Lines'

Many pictures can be thought of as consisting of series of connected and disconnected line segments. Since two points determine a line, such pictures can be described numerically by the Cartesian coordinates of the end points of the lines. Thus, a picture can be uniquely transformed into numerical data which are then inversely transformable back into the original picture.

Digital computers perform arithmetic operations with numerical data under the control of a set of instructions called a program. If this numerical data were the coordinates of end points of lines, then the computer could be programmed to numerically specify a picture. This numerical data could then be used to position and move the beam of a cathode ray tube to trace out the desired picture. In this manner, and as depicted in Figure 2, an IBM 7094 digital computer has been programmed to generate pictures using a General Dynamics SC–4020 Microfilm Plotter. The picture drawn on the face of the cathode ray tube is photographed by a 35-mm camera which is also under the control of the microfilm plotter.

The microfilm plotter is presently limited to producing black and white pictures composed of connected and disconnected line segments. Mondrian's *Composition with Lines*, a black and white painting composed of vertical and horizontal bars, was a type picture that the microfilm plotter was capable of reproducing with suitable programming of the computer. The computer picture thus generated, called 'Computer composition with lines', is shown in Figure 3.

The vertical and horizontal bars in 'Computer composition with lines' were produced as a series of parallel line segments that were closely enough spaced to slightly overlap each other. Although Mondrian apparently placed his bars in a very orderly manner, the computer was programmed to place the bars randomly within a circle of radius 450 units so that all locations were equiprobable. The choice between vertical bar or horizontal bar was equally likely, and the widths of the bars were equiprobable between seven and ten lines; the lengths of the bars were equiprobable between ten and sixty points.

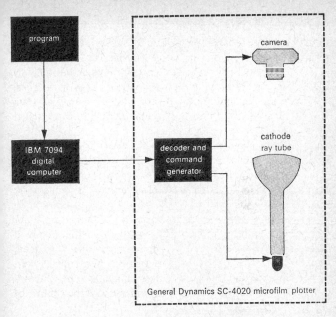

Figure 2. Block diagram of method for producing computer pictures

If a bar fell inside a parabolic region at the top of the picture, the length of the bar was reduced by a factor proportional to the distance of the bar from the edge of the parabola. A trial-and-error approach was used to ensure that the effect of the picture was reasonably similar to Mondrian's *Compositon with Lines*.

Human or Machine

After the computer had produced its version of the Mondrian painting, two pictures similar in composition, but one painted by a human and the other generated by a machine, were available. Subjective tests were then administered in which the Ss were shown reproductions of both pictures and indicated their preferences and also which picture they thought was produced by the machine. The remainder of this paper describes these subjective tests and their results.

305

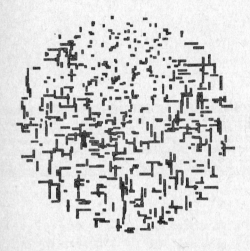

Figure 3. 'Computer composition with lines' (1964) by the author
in association with an IBM 7094 digital computer and a General
Dynamics SC–4020 microfilm plotter. (Copyright Michael Noll, 1965)

Method

Procedure

The photographic print of the computer-produced microfilm and
the photograph of Mondrian's painting had clues to their identity
since the quality of the two photographs was somewhat different.
Since only differences in the designs or patterns of the two pictures were desired, the two photographs were copied xerographically to be identical in quality. These copies were arranged in two
pairs so that the computer picture was alternately labeled 'A' or

306

'B'; the order of presentation was counter-balanced. An example of a picture pair as given to the *S*s is shown in Figure 4.

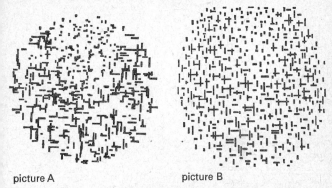

picture A   picture B

Figure 4. Picture pair as presented on separate sheets to subjects. The original microfilm and Mondrain photograph were copied xerographically and then reproduced so that both pictures were identical in quality. (Copyright Michael Noll, 1965, and Rijkmuseum Kröller-Müller)

In addition to the two pictures, each *S* was also given three separate questionnaires: a background questionnaire, an identification questionnaire, and a preference questionnaire. The background questionnaire was given first to each *S*, and informed him that he was about to participate in 'an exploratory experiment to determine what esthetic factors are involved in abstract art.' The *S* then wrote his name and job classification on the questionnaire, and checked appropriate boxes for his sex (male, female), age (under 30, 30–45 over 45), and over-all feeling towards abstract art (strongly like, like, indifferent, dislike, strongly dislike). In those cases in which *S*s stated that they liked some and disliked other abstract art, they were instructed to mark the indifferent category. The job classification information was used to classify each *S*'s job as either technical or non-technical.

The identification questionnaire was worded: 'One of the pictures is a photograph of a painting by Piet Mondrian while the other is a photograph of a drawing made by an IBM 7094 digital computer. Which of the two do you think was done by the computer?' The *S* then checked appropriate boxes on the questionnaire for picture 'A' or for picture 'B' and also gave written reasons for his choice. The preference questionnaire asked the *S* to check appropriate boxes to indicate which picture he 'most strongly liked or preferred' and also to give reasons for his choice.

The order of presentation of the identification and preference questionnaires was counter-balanced. The *S*s were not given the last questionnaire until the other two were completed.

Subjects

A total of 100 *S*s participated in the tests. All of the *S*s had education beyond grade school, ranging from high school to postdoctoral, and all but two *S*s were employees of Bell Telephone Laboratories. Of the fifty *S*s who were given the preference sheet first, fourteen were non-technical (one male and thirteen females) and thirty-six were technical (twenty-eight males and eight females). Of the fifty *S*s who were given the identification sheet first, seventeen were non-technical (all females) and thirty-three were technical (twenty-seven males and six females). Note that the technical group consisted primarily of males, while only one male was considered non-technical. This occurred because the non-technical people at the laboratories are clerks, typists, stenographers and secretaries; females usually perform these types of jobs. However, the technical people include engineers, physicists, and chemists (all usually males) and a lesser number of technicians and computer programmers (usually male and female). The *S* grouping reasonably represents an approximation of the population at Bell Telephone Laboratories.

Results

Table 1 gives the percentages of *S*s who preferred the computer picture and who correctly identified the computer picture. A chi-square test indicated that the questionnaire order did not statistically affect the preferences or identifications, and for this reason questionnaire order is not shown in the table. A binomial test was performed with each cell entry, and an asterisk indicates those entries statistically different (0·05 level) from selections based upon chance. Of the 100 Ss in the experiment, 59 per cent preferred the computer picture while only 28 per cent were able to correctly identify the computer picture.

Perhaps the Ss' preferences would be affected by the knowledge that one of the pictures was generated by a computer. For this reason, the first fifty Ss were given the preference questionnaire first while the second fifty were given the identification questionnaire first. A chi-square test was then performed with the contengency table relating preference and questionnaire order. The test strongly indicated no association between preference and questionnaire order ($\chi^2 = 0$, $df = 1$). Since there was only one degree of freedom, Yates' correction was used in computing χ^2 (Walker and Lev, 1953). Thus the Ss' preferences were not affected by knowledge that one of the pictures was generated by a computer.

Table 1

Percentage Preferences and Percentage Correct Identifications

	Total number of subjects	Preferred computer picture	Correct identification
All Subjects	100	59%*	28%*
Job classification:			
Technical	69	59%	35%
Non-technical	31	58%	13%
Age:			
Under 30	61	69%*	18%*
30 to 45	31	48%	42%
Over 45	8	25%	50%
Sex:			
Males	56	55%	37%
Females	44	64%*	16%*
Abstract Art Assessment:			
Strongly like and like	34	76%*	26%*
Indifferent	46	52%	26%*
Strongly dislike and dislike	20	45%	35%

*Indicates statistical significance at the 0·05 level according to binomial test.

Chi-square was computed for the table relating identification and questionnaire order, and these two factors were also not associated ($\chi^2 = 0.24$, $df = 1$).

A chi-square test was also performed for the contingency table relating preference and identification for all Ss, and, as might be expected from the preceding, preference and identification were independent ($\chi^2 = 0.213$, $df = 1$). The results of the chi-square tests are summarized in Table 2.

Table 2

Summary of Chi-Square Tests

	Preference			Identification		
	χ^2	df	Result	χ^2	df	Result
Questionnaire order	0.000	1	not significant	0.240	1	not significant
Abstract art assessment	5.452	1	significant ($p < 0.02$)	0.000	1	not significant
Job classification	0.008	1	not significant	149.798	1	significant ($p < 0.001$)
Sex (technical subjects only)	1.768	1	not significant	0.906	1	not significant
Identification	0.213	1	not significant			

The effects of the Ss' abstract art attitudes were determined by considering those Ss 'strongly liking' and 'liking' abstract art as one group, with all other Ss as another group. The results of chi-square tests showed that art attitude and preference were associated at the 0.02 level ($\chi^2 = 5.452$, $df = 1$) while art rating and identification were independent ($\chi^2 = 0.000$, $df = 1$). The Ss 'strongly liking' and 'liking' abstract art preferred the computer picture better than 2 to 1 while the other Ss were evenly divided in their preferences. This possibly occurred because those Ss liking abstract art might have been more accustomed to the randomness found in many abstract paintings and would therefore prefer the more random of the two pictures, namely, the computer picture.

It was expected that a larger proportion of the Ss with technical training would correctly identify the computer picture because of their possible knowledge and familiarity with computers. This indeed occurred as indicated by a chi-square test ($\chi^2 = 149 \cdot 798$, $df = 1$) on the contingency data relating identification and job classification and this association was significant at the $0 \cdot 001$ level. However, preference and job classification were independent ($\chi^2 = 0 \cdot 008$, $df = 1$). As shown in Table 1, 25 per cent of the technical Ss and only 13 per cent of the non-technical Ss were able to identify the computer picture. Apparently, the non-technical Ss very strongly thought that computers would produce mechanical, orderly pictures, and hence a large percentage of the non-technical Ss were fooled into incorrectly identifying the Mondrian as being the computer picture. The technical Ss, however, were somewhat more sophisticated and as a group tended to disregard the differences in randomness between the two pictures with the result that their identifications were closer to pure guessing.

Unfortunately, the non-technical group contained only one male, and therefore the possibility arises that the association between preference and job classification was a result of the preponderance of females in the non-technical group. To determine if the sexual imbalance between the two groups was affecting the judgements, chi-square tests were made for the contingency tables relating sex with preference and sex with identification for only the technical Ss. The results indicated that these factors were independent ($\chi^2 = 1 \cdot 768$, $df = 1$, and $\chi^2 = 0 \cdot 906$, $df = 1$, respectively.) Since there was no reason to suspect that sex would matter for the non-technical group if sex were insignificant for the technical group, it seemed reasonable to conclude that the sexual imbalance between the two groups did not affect the preferences or identifications. However, the two groups were unbalanced with respect to other factors, such as education, and hence further tests would be required to determine more definitely the causes of the differences in identification ability between the two groups.

In general, the reasons given by the Ss for both their preferences and identifications supported most of the preceding conclusions. The computer picture was described as being 'neater', more 'varied', 'imaginative', 'soothing' and abstract' than the Mondrian. One S even found some golden rectangles in the random designs within the computer picture. In general, the non-technical Ss strongly associated randomness with human creativity and therefore incorrectly identified the Mondrian as the computer-generated picture.

The knowledge that one of the pictures was produced by a computer did not bias the *S*s for or against either picture, as mentioned previously. However, the *S*s in this experiment had very little or no artistic training and also were quite accustomed to the impact of technology upon many different fields. These *S*s therefore probably were less prejudiced against computers as a new artistic medium than artistic *S*s would have been. If artists and *S*s from a non-technological environment had been similarly tested, the results might have been different.

Discussion and Conclusion

Mondrian has been widely acclaimed as the 'greatest Dutch painter of our time' (Bradley, 1944) and, as one of the 'most influential masters of painting' (Lewis, 1957). However, a computer-generated random pattern was preferred over the pattern of one of Mondrian's paintings. Furthermore, the majority of the *S*s participating in the experiment were unable to identify correctly the computer-generated picture. Some questions now arise concerning the conclusions to be drawn from these results.

Both patterns were conceived by humans, although certain features of the computer-generated picture were decided by a programmed random algorithm. The computer functioned only as a medium performing its operations under the complete control of the computer program written by the programmer–artist. As stated before, the programmer–artist working with the computer produced a pattern that was preferred over the pattern of one of Mondrian's paintings. This would seem to detract from Mondrian's artist abilities. However, artistic merit is not generally accepted as something that can be determined by a jury. The experiment was designed solely to compare two patterns that differed in elements of order and randomness. It is only incidental that the more orderly pattern was painted by Piet Mondrian while the preferred random pattern was produced with the assistance of a digital computer.

The randomness introduced by the computer was in the form of a mathematical algorithm for computing sequences of uncorrelated numbers. Thus, the 'randomness' is completely deterministic, and the resulting pattern is mathematically specified in every detail. The writing of the computer program was done in an objective manner incorporating appropriate mathematical formulas. All of this indicates that no attempt was made to communicate any emotions on the part of the programmer to the final computer pattern. Therefore, the experiment compared the results of an intellectual, non-emotional endeavor involving a computer with the pattern produced by a painter whose work has been characterized as expressing the emotions and mysticism of its author. The results of this experiment would seem to raise some doubts about the importance of the artist's milieu and emotional behavior in communicating through the art object. But then again, many present-day estheticians do not subscribe to such definitions of art, and some even question whether art can be attributed any defining properties (Weitz, 1956).

Since xerographic copies of a photograph of the Mondrian painting were used as stimuli in the experiment, any artistic effects due to the size or painting techniques were eliminated. The subjective comparisons hence were only on the basis of differences between the two patterns. Also, only one particular painting by Mondrian and only one particular random realization by the computer were used.

Clearly, the computer picture was more random than the Mondrian. Further programming of the computer, however, has indicated that more elaborate schemes can be used to produce a picture that even more closely resembles the Mondrian. Undoubtedly, an indistinguishable pair could finally be obtained, but performing experiments similar to those reported in this paper would not then be very revealing.

The experiments and techniques reported in this paper should suggest many novel and interesting investigations of artistic perception and esthetics. For example, experiments are presently in progress to determine such things as the preferred range of randomness in the bar positions of Mondrian-like pictures and whether statistically identical pictures are equally preferred. Computer-generated pictures are mathematically and statistically specified in an objective manner and should be quite useful as stimuli in such investigations.

313

References

BRADLEY, J. (1944), 'Greatest Dutch painter of our time', *Knickerbocker Weekly*, vol. 3, no. 51, p. 16.

LEWIS, D. (1957), *Mondrian*, Wittenborn.

MONDRIAN, P. (1945), 'Toward the true vision of reality', *Plastic Art and Pure Plastic Art*, Wittenborn.

SEUPHOR, M. (1957), *Piet Mondrian*, Abrams.

SEUPHOR, M. (1962), *Abstract Painting*, Abrams.

WALKER, H. M., and LEV, J. (1953), *Statistical Inference*, Holt, Rinehart and Winston.

WEITZ, M. (1956), 'The role of theory in aesthetics', *J. Aesthet. art Crit.*, vol. 15, pp. 27–35.

Part Seven The Dimensions of Aesthetic Experience

Our response to a particular area of art is not random. Implicitly or explicitly we organize our experience, judging pictures to be similar or dissimilar in whatever respects we consider relevant. The various kinds of difference we respond to can be represented in a dimensional structure through factor analytic and multidimensional scaling techniques. They can show the way different groups differ in this structure as well as the way individuals differ. The paper by Skager, Schultz and Klein (Reading 18) and the work by Tucker (see Reading 15) consider pictures from this point of view, while Wright and Rainwater (Reading 16) and Kansaku (Reading 17) do the same for colour connotations. The effort to distinguish people into various 'types' on the basis of their characteristic response to art is criticized by Gregson (Reading 14).

14 R. A. M. Gregson

Aspects of the Theoretical Status of Aesthetic Response Typologies

R. A. M. Gregson, 'Aspects of the theoretical status of aesthetic response typologies', *Psychological Reports*, vol. 15 (1964), pp. 395–8.

Aesthetic response typologies are criticized for their imprecision and lack of theoretical parsimony. An alternative approach which subsumes reported characteristics of aesthetic choices under one model, related to stochastic learning theory, is advanced.

The diversity of verbal or evaluative choice responses to material designated *fine art* or *aesthetic* by E was noted early by psychologists (Binet, 1903; Bullough, 1908; Valentine, 1919) and led to the construction of response typologies as nominal scale classifications. More recent attempts to obtain similar most-economical classifications by factor analysis of subjective value spaces (Burt, 1939; Eysenck, 1941; Guilford and Holley, 1949; Tucker, 1955 [cf. Osgood *et al.*, 1957, for comment on Tucker]) essentially replicated the phenomenological and behavioural structure of such typologies. In the relatively neglected state of psychological aesthetics such descriptive typologies have been left uncontested as empirical and theoretical summaries of value response patterns. We question and reject aesthetic typologies on the grounds that they are probably artifactual, certainly not parsimonious, and theoretically obsolescent; we propose a fresh approach to the problem.

Aesthetic response typologies have not been generally subjected to any rigorous analysis, and on close examination exhibit some oddly restrictive characteristics. The early typologies all follow the pattern of Binet (1903) who classified Ss according to their ostensive reasons for liking pictures. The reasons were classified after being obtained in an open-sided situation and are in part a reflection of the linguistic repertoire of S and any prior training in art appreciation which may have been given. The method leads to difficulties, typologies are forced to include a separate category – a rag-bag – for miscellaneous or unclassifiable responses (Valentine, 1919), and the categories are not mutually exclusive. If no one typology can be taken as correct to the exclusion of all others, we require rules to convert from one to another. But there is no unequivocal way of working from one typology to another; Bullough gives rudimentary equivalences between his system (given first) and Binet's (given second) as follows: *objective = descriptif + érudit, physiological = observateur + émotionnel, associative = observateur + émotionnel + érudit*, and *character = émotionnel + observateur*. Such relations between the two systems, or any two similarly derived systems, are empirically useless because they cannot be worked in reverse; they are also ambiguous in a sense which is fundamentally crucial: they may mean that *descriptifs* are *objective* but some *érudits* are *objective* and some *associative*, or they may mean that any one individual is at some times in one response category and some times in another, or that any individual gives value responses which are so complex as to contain elements which may be characterized as belonging to more than one type. We need not consider the later classifications because they raise precisely the same logical issues, and the problems arise in part because the typologies are not mapped at least into an ordered vector space (Coombs, Raiffa and Thrall, 1954).

While there is no adequate evidence on the reliability or stability of these typologies, indications are given by Burt (1933) that the transition probabilities between response types, where such response types are regarded as states of S, may be non-zero. He observes that the associative type comes more plainly to the surface with children. He also notes that some Ss apparently adopt an ordering between types of response, for S may use one type of description as evidence of approval, another of disapproval; in short S employs a two-level response system, reasons for liking are used as value levels, evaluation takes place both within and between levels, so the proper mapping of any one S's response system, for positive evaluations alone, must be multivariate and probably lexicographic (Gregson, 1963). Because evaluations are complex in this way, it can be argued, if a rigorous isomorphism between theory and choice behaviour is demanded, that the factor analyses of later workers cited above are irrelevant, the partial agreement between studies being artifactual and a consequence of forcing Ss to give responses within the framework of a data collection protocol which impoverishes the logical structure of their value space, and thus makes it amenable to factor analysis by obscuring the characteristic form of aesthetic evaluations.

Evaluative responses which are more than simple choices involve rationalization, recording choices between complex aesthetic stimuli implies tapping S's verbal repertoire and concept structure. Rationalizations are intrinsically so complex, even if collected on a forced-choice protocol with such mutually exclusive grounds as are implicit in 'give the most important reason for your choice from among the following: colour, form, mood tone, tonal values, connotations, abstract v. realistic, historical period', that the number of alternative classificatory schemes is intractably large. In this context we take any rule for allocating evaluative responses to equivalence classes which exhaustively partition the possible or available responses to be a classificatory scheme by definition; if one equivalence class is put into one–one correspondence with an element in a typology, the rule becomes a response typology. If the equivalence classes are defined by reference to the alternatives of the forced-choice protocol, we have predetermined our typology except for the possibility of empty response classes. All that remain as variables to distinguish S groups or different time samples of the same S group are parameters of the distribution of response probabilities over the alternatives of the protocol, which we may express as the response information (Garner and Hake, 1951), but we have no concept of response equivocation because the task is itself response-defined and not stimulus-defined.

A way to avoid these problems is to abandon the typology as a classificatory basis, and replace it by the matrix probabilities between evaluative criteria. Any S, at one point in time, is describable as being in one response state, or in an ordered set of response states (the ordering being a mapping of his preference between criteria) which is representable by a vector in n space. At the next instant in time he may or may not have shifted in his usage of evaluative response criteria, but the total set of criteria within which he can move or which he can order remains invariant. The typology as an explanatory or intervening hypothesis

319

is abandoned; the response criteria are defined in terms of the extension of a forced-choice paradigm, and estimates are sought of the total set of transition probabilities between response states, and the over-all probability of being in any one specific response state.

If transition probabilities are constant, the matrix operationally defines a Markov chain process, and methods of stochastic learning theory are applicable for choice sequence description or estimation of parameters. The estimate of the *a priori* probability of a S's using a particular criterion to explain his evaluations is obtained directly from a sample of independent responses at one point in time. Successive matrix multiplication of the transition probabilities by the vector of response category probabilities should lead to a stable estimation of the asymptotic relative frequencies of the different criteria in a homogeneous adult population. Togrol-Birand (1957) has offered evidence that these frequencies should be estimated from social class or educational demographic analyses in the first instance.

The effects of social learning or art appreciation education could be postulated to modify the transition probabilities between response states. Some states would be modified in the direction of minimal input and maximal output transition probabilities; others which are considered desirable by educationalists would have their input transition probabilities maximized. Estimates of the pattern of such modifications may be based on ratings by educationalists of the relative desirability of different forms of aesthetic response or a content analysis of their theories in the first instance. A more direct method which is preferable is also available. If we assume that the rank order in which an S places the total set of response categories at a point in time is correlated with the transition probabilities between his present most preferred response category and each of the other categories taken in turn, we can use part or all of his ranking to derive estimates of his transition probabilities over part of the matrix, and further we can use modal orderings of categories as generators of most likely paths or cycles through the matrix of response states. Of particular interest are paths which terminate, for their existence depends on whether or not there exist response categories in which the output transition probabilities are nearly zero.

If such categories exist, they would be an artifactual basis for the reported typologies. This matrix approach is economical of postulates because it has a structure similar to contemporary learning theory models; typologies explain nothing that cannot be deducted from such a model, given stochastic changes in responses over time. Evidence that criterion shifts do occur, and occur readily, was advanced by Evans (1939) anecdotally as grounds for increasing the complexity of her typology. We have recently shown that such shifts can be induced experimentally (Gregson, 1964a), although the way in which Ss make such shifts may not be explicable in terms of one response-shift strategy (Gregson, 1964b).

We conclude that aesthetic response typologies reflect a naïve and early form of theorizing and can be replaced by a single theory which has testable consequences, allows for parameter estimation, and integrates experimental aesthetics into preference and learning theory instead of leaving it out on a limb.

References

BINET, A. (1903), *Étude Expérimentale de l'Intelligence*, Ancienne Librairie Schleicher, Paris.

BULLOUGH, E. (1908), 'The perceptive problem in the aesthetic appreciation of single colours', *Brit. J. Psychol.*, vol. 2, pp. 406–62.

BURT, C. L. (1933), *How the Mind Works*, Allen & Unwin.

BURT, C. L. (1939), 'Type factors in aesthetic judgements', *Character & Pers.*, vol. 7, pp. 238–54 and 285–99.

COOMBS, C. H., RAIFFA, H., and THRALL, R. M. (1954), 'Some views on mathematical models and measurement theory', *Psychol. Rev.*, vol. 61, pp. 132–44.

EVANS, J. (1939), *Taste and Temperament*, Cape.

EYSENCK, H. J. (1941), 'The general factor in aesthetic judgments', *Brit. J. Psychol.*, vol. 31, pp. 94–102.

GARNER, W. R., and HAKE, H. (1951), 'The amount of information in absolute judgments', *Psychol. Rev.*, vol. 58, pp. 446–59.

GREGSON, R. A. M. (1963), 'Some possible forms of lexicographic evaluation', *Psychometrika*, vol. 28, pp. 173–83.

GREGSON, R. A. M. (1964a), 'Additivity of value in the representation of aesthetic choices', *Aust. J. Psychol.*, vol. 16, pp. 20–32.

GREGSON, R. A. M. (1964b), 'A study in the psychometrics of substitution choices', *Univer. Canterbury, Dept. Psychol. Res. Rep.*, no. 5.

GUILFORD, J. P., and HOLLEY, J. W. (1949), 'A factorial approach to the analysis of variance in aesthetic judgments', *J. exp. Psychol.*, vol. 39, pp. 208–18.

Osgood, C. E., Suci, G. J., and Tannenbaum, P. H. (1957),
The Measurement of Meaning, University of Illinois Press.

Togrol-Birand, B. A. (1957), 'Aesthetic evaluation of works of art by artists and laymen'. Paper read at XVth Int. Congr. Psychol., Brussels.

Tucker, W. T. (1955), 'Experiments in aesthetic communications', Unpublished doctoral dissertation, University of Illinois.

Valentine, C. W. (1919), *The Experimental Psychology of Beauty*, Nelson.

15 C. E. Osgood, G. J. Suci and P. H. Tannenbaum

A Report on 'Experiments in Esthetic Communication' by W. T. Tucker

Excerpts from C. E. Osgood, G. J. Suci and P. H. Tannenbaum, *The Measurement of Meaning*, University of Illinois Press, 1957, pp. 69 and 290–95.

Although it is by no means the only fruitful approach, esthetics can be studied as a form of communication. The message in this case is the esthetic product itself – the musical composition as performed, the painting as viewed, the poem or essay as read, or even the advertisement as seen in a national magazine. Like ordinary linguistic messages, the esthetic product is a Janus-faced affair; it has the character of being at once the result of responses encoded by one participant in the communicative act (the creator) and the stimulus to be decoded by the other participants (the appreciators). Esthetic products differ, perhaps, from linguistic messages by being more continuously than discretely coded (e.g. colors and forms in a painting can be varied continuously whereas the phonemes that discriminate among word-forms vary by all-or-nothing quanta called distinctive features). They also differ, perhaps, in being associated more with connotative, emotional reactions in sources and receivers than with denotative reactions. It also seems likely that the individual variations in both encoding and decoding – in the ways creators express intentions and in the ways appreciators derive significances – are much greater than in language *per se*. But nevertheless, to the extent that the creators of esthetic products are able to influence the meanings and emotions experienced by their audiences by manipulations in the media of their talent, we are dealing with communication.

It is precisely because the semantic differential taps the connotative aspects of meaning more immediately than the highly diversified denotative aspects that it should be readily applicable to esthetic studies. Indeed, [. . .] the semantic differential had its origins in an essentially esthetic context – studies of color-music synesthesia (Odbert, Karwoski and Eckerson, 1942). To date, applications of the instrument in the field of esthetics have been modest in scope. One fairly extensive study of the factor structure of esthetic judgements (in the visual arts) has been undertaken; a series of studies on the connotative meanings of colors, in both abstract art forms and in advertised products, has been done; and a number of more remote studies on interactions of music with dramatic productions and on pictorial and cartoon symbolism can be reported. Again, these researches have more value as illustrations of the potential usefulness of the measuring technique than they do as contributions to a 'science of esthetics', if we may use such a term.

There are, of course, many people who shudder at the thought of bringing a quantitative measuring instrument into the domain of esthetics, who are dismayed at any attempt to make a science out of art. It is necessary to draw a sharp distinction between study of the process of esthetics as a kind of human communication and the creation of esthetic products. Whereas the latter should, and undoubtedly will, remain in the domain of art, the former is a perfectly legitimate area of scientific study, and any instruments, quantitative or otherwise, which facilitate this study are to be welcomed.

Factorial Studies on the Structure of Esthetic Judgements

Problem

To apply the semantic differential technique effectively in the study of esthetics, it is first necessary to determine the major factors or dimensions underlying esthetic meanings. The particular instruments used, the specific scales selected, etc. depend upon such analysis. The factors operating in esthetic judgements may be the same as those that appear in ordinary semantic judgements of linguistic signs, or they may be quite different; the factors operating for visual art objects may differ from those for musical or poetic objects, although it would be hoped that this would not be the case. Restricting his attention to the visual arts (painting), Tucker (1955) first studied the factor structures apparent in the judgements of both artists and non-artists – hypothesizing that there would be differences between these groups. To demonstrate differences, however, he found it necessary to analyse separately the judgements of representational as compared with nonrepresentational (abstract) paintings. Using a reduced sample of scales, selected on the basis of his factor work, Tucker then undertook to investigate which artistic techniques are related to which semantic factors.

Method

Tucker's methods have been briefly described in connexion with the generality of semantic factors [see pp. 68–70 of *The Measurement of Meaning*]. The forty scales finally used in his factor studies were selected in a variety of ways: from the spontaneous comments of art students when viewing large numbers of slides, from the comments of visitors to an art exhibition, and from the previous factor studies of Osgood and Suci (particularly to include reference scales for the factors they had isolated). The complete list is given in Table 1. The paintings finally chosen as the objects for judgement included seven representational paintings and four nonrepresentational paintings or abstracts. These stimuli were presented on projected slides to thirty-three non-artists (juniors and sophomores in the College of Commerce) and ten artists (graduate students and faculty members of the Art Department). The subjects were allowed one minute to view the picture (without making judgements); then the stimulus was removed and all judgements about it were made on the usual graphic form of the differential. The D^2 method of factoring was used to get at the structuring of esthetic judgements.

Results of factor analyses

The judgements of both artists and non-artists, when analysed over *all eleven paintings*, generated three major factors which were quite comparable in nature to those originally obtained by Osgood and Suci for verbal concepts. For artists, an *activity factor* (characterized by scales like *active–passive*, *vibrant–still*, and *dynamic–static*) accounted for 46 per cent of the variance; an *evaluative factor* (characterized by scales like *ordered–chaotic*, *controlled–accidental*, *clear–hazy*, and *pleasant–unpleasant*) accounted for 17 per cent; and a *potency factor* (characterized by scales like *hard–soft*, *masculine–feminine*, and *formal–informal*) accounted for 10 per cent of the variance. The non-artists showed essentially the same factors, but in more nearly equal weights. When the judgements on representational paintings were analysed separately, an even closer approximation to the Osgood–Suci results on verbal materials was obtained, for both artists and non-artists. The data for representational paintings judged by non-artists are given as Table 1.

On the other hand, when the judgements on abstract paintings were factor analysed separately, artists and non-artists displayed completely different structures. The judgements of abstract paintings by artists are accounted for by a single, overwhelming evaluative factor which reflects 79 per cent of the total variance.

Table 1

Factor Loadings for Non-artists on Seven Representational Paintings (Tucker Study)

Scale	Factor I (Activity)	Factor II (Evaluation)	Factor III (Potency)
hot–cold	0·64	−0·08	0·00
pleasant–unpleasant	−0·02	0·59	−0·60
lush–austere	0·64	−0·16	−0·23
vibrant–still	0·91	−0·08	0·29
repetitive–varied	−0·81	−0·48	0·29
happy–sad	0·34	0·38	−0·71
chaotic–ordered	0·55	−0·84	0·00
smooth–rough	−0·57	0·83	0·00
superficial–profound	0·18	−0·72	−0·58
passive–active	−1·00	0·00	0·00
blatant–muted	0·80	−0·26	0·11
meaningless–meaningful	−0·33	−0·79	0·28
simple–complex	−0·66	0·55	−0·48
relaxed–tense	−0·57	0·39	−0·54
obvious–subtle	−0·23	0·80	0·01
serious–humorous	−0·22	−0·05	0·97
violent–gentle	0·41	−0·37	0·69
sweet–bitter	−0·32	0·23	−0·67
static–dynamic	−0·78	0·19	−0·53
clear–hazy	−0·04	0·85	0·38
unique–commonplace	0·50	0·22	0·72
emotional–rational	0·67	0·09	0·40
ugly–beautiful	0·12	−0·51	0·42

Scale	Factor I (Activity)	Factor II (Evaluation)	Factor III (Potency)
dull–sharp	−0·53	−0·34	−0·74
sincere–insincere	0·18	0·80	0·34
rich–thin	0·56	0·35	0·46
bad–good	−0·33	−0·77	−0·27
intimate–remote	0·09	0·45	−0·46
masculine–feminine	0·31	0·13	0·76
vague–precise	−0·04	−0·84	−0·43
ferocious–peaceful	0·39	−0·46	0·58
soft–hard	−0·39	0·09	−0·84
usual–unusual	−0·52	−0·16	−0·70
controlled–accidental	0·00	0·80	0·34
wet–dry	−0·37	−0·89	0·35
strong–weak	0·37	0·46	0·81
stale–fresh	−0·45	−0·54	−0·51
formal–informal	−0·58	−0·40	0·24
calming–exciting	−0·54	0·26	−0·55
full–empty	0·60	0·31	0·52

Judging from other research (particularly studies by Suci on political and ethnic judgements), this suggests that artists have highly polarized and emotional reactions to abstract paintings which collapses the semantic space about a dominant single dimension. All scales of judgement tend to rotate toward this dominant dimension of evaluation; if an abstract is liked it is also *smooth*, *dynamic*, *vibrant*, *serious*, *intimate*, and so on through the favorable poles of the various scales. It also suggests that artists have explicitly worked out and agreed upon systems of evaluation; otherwise individual differences in scale allocation would wash out such a dominant factor. The situation for non-artists judging abstract paintings is quite the reverse. Here, what could best be described as semantic chaos results. Although two factors accounted for a large part of the variance, the factors made no semantic sense whatsoever. The graphic plot of the variables in terms of the two factors was a nearly homogeneous circle, and the factors could have been placed equally well in any orientation. In other words, when non-artists judge a set of abstract paintings, there is very little structuring of the judgements – as if they had no frame of reference for the task.

Relation of artistic techniques to semantic judgements

What uses of color and form by artists are correlated with what types of semantic judgement? To answer this question, Tucker first studied the encoding operations of student artists and then the decoding operations of non-artist viewers of their work. In the first part of the experiment, fifty-two art students at the University of Georgia served. Each student was asked to create an abstract pastel appropriate to one of the following phrases: *extreme activity*, *extreme passivity*, *extreme chaos*, *extreme orderliness*, *extreme strength*, *extreme weakness* – these terms, of course, representing the poles of the three major factors found in representational paintings. The students, without exception, were enthusiastic over this problem. In general, paintings made to represent *activity* employed the warm colors (red, orange and yellow) and jagged lines; paintings representing *passivity* were typically large and simple curvilinear shapes, smoothly drawn and using pale rather than intense colors; *chaos* was like activity in representation as far as form was concerned, but there was greater use of dark colors and mass patterns; *orderliness* paintings were almost always geometric in character (straight lines, simple forms) and made use of few colors (an average of three *v.* seven colors in paintings for chaos); to represent *strength*, several modalities were employed – extreme color and/or brightness contrast along with the use of massive forms were common to most, however; *weakness* was typically displayed by uncertain, amorphous lines and/or by faintly blanked out patches having slight contrast and indefinite pattern. These relationships will be recognized as having their counterparts in language metaphor.

To complete the communicative act, we must inquire whether the viewers of these student pastels, in decoding their significances, could recreate the original intentions (activity, strength, orderliness, etc.) of the artists. The answer, as indicated by the results in Table 2 was a qualified 'yes'. A group of seventeen commerce students (University of Georgia) was asked to select one of six adjectives – *active*, *passive*, *chaotic*, *orderly*, *strong* and *weak* – with each of six pastels chosen from the group done by the artists. The paintings to represent *orderliness*, *chaos* and *strength* yielded the expected judgements with a high degree of

Table 2

Selection of Adjectives to Describe Pastels Drawn to Represent Poles of Esthetic Semantic Factors

| Drawings | Adjectives | | | | | |
	orderly	chaotic	active	passive	strong	weak
Extreme orderliness	12	0	1	1	2	1
Extreme chaos	0	10	4	0	3	0
Extreme activity	0	10	3	0	2	2
Extreme passivity	1	0	2	5	0	9
Extreme strength	4	0	1	1	10	1
Extreme weakness	0	2	4	6	1	4

accuracy; the painting drawn to represent *passivity* tended to be judged *weak*, and vice versa; and that drawn to represent *activity* tended to be judged *chaotic*. Recalling the lack of factor structure in the judgements of abstract paintings by non-artists, however, these confusions are not too surprising.

Summary

When either artists or non-artists judge representational paintings against a large number of scales, the dominant factors to appear are recognizable as the same as those derived from judgements of verbal concepts, *evaluation*, *potency*, and *activity*, although the particular scales which represent these factors best in judging esthetic objects are not necessarily the same and the activity factor has relatively more weight. When we consider that highly representational drawings of objects and scenes are facsimiles of perceptual signs, and hence approach functional equivalence to linguistic signs in their capacity to evoke the same mediation processes, this result is to be expected. The essential equivalence of pictorial and verbal signs will be demonstrated again in the next study in this section. When artists and non-artists judge abstract paintings, however, the former display a single, dominant factor (evidence that they have very definite and polarized meanings for these stimuli) whereas the latter display a relatively unstructured system (suggestive evidence that abstracts are essentially meaningless to them). This finding, too, is reasonable. When presented with terms defining the poles of the major esthetic factors (for representational paintings), student artists were able to produce pastel drawings which not only differed in expected ways but also elicited the original polar adjectives with a fair degree of accuracy. These results were obtained on rather small numbers of subjects, however, and need confirmation; further, we would like to extend this type of semantic analysis to other esthetic modes.

References

ODBERT, H. S., KARWOSKI, T. F., and ECKERSON, A. B. (1942), 'Studies in synesthetic thinking: I. Musical and verbal associations of color and mood', *J. gen. Psychol.*, vol. 26, pp. 153–73.

TUCKER W. T. (1955), 'Experiments in esthetic communications' Unpublished doctoral dissertation, University of Illinois.

16 B. Wright and L. Rainwater

The Meanings of Color

B. Wright and L. Rainwater, 'The meanings of color', *Journal of General Psychology*, vol. 67 (1962), pp. 89–99.

Introduction

There are both practical and theoretical reasons for being interested in the connotative effects of color experience. From the practical point of view, we want to know in what way people speak of color so that we can more effectively discuss and study its use in visual communication. Are there consistent connotations along which people discriminate colors? If so, what are they?

From the theoretical point of view, we want to know more about the relationship between perception and connotation – knowledge about this relationship is fundamental to an understanding of the development and structure of thought.

Thoughts and the words which mark them are manifestations of physiological functions, a central one of which is the perceptual system. Connotative or metaphorical meaning is a crucial aspect of thought. We would like to know if there are stable relationships between connotation and perception. Color experience can be fairly well specified perceptually. If there are general connotative dimensions along which colors are described, and if these dimensions are to some extent consistent from person to person and from culture to culture, then this is evidence bearing on the existence and character of such a relationship.

This is a report on a factor analytic study of the connotative meanings of colors. The report is divided into three parts: first, a description of the mechanics of the study; second, a presentation of the six dimensions of connotative meaning found in the factor analysis; third, an analysis of the linear relation between these color connotations and the color perceptions of hue, lightness and saturation.

The Study

Ss were middle- and lower-class men and women living in urban West Germany in 1957. Each S judged a single three-inch square of matt surface color presented in daylight against a neutral background. Judgements were expressed on an Osgood semantic differential (17, pp. 76–85) by circling one of seven positions between pairs of polar adjectives like this:

KALT   ... .   WARM
FROH   ... .   TRAURIG

For the purpose of scoring, the seven rating positions between each adjective pair were weighted linearly one through seven.

Individual interviews were obtained on a door-to-door basis within the structure of an area probability sampling plan for West Germany. Each S rated just one of fifty colors on just one of two different twenty-four adjective pair rating forms. Sample size per color per rating form varied from 20 to 70 with an arithmetic mean of 36. Altogether 955 men and 2705 women participated in these ratings. Age ranged from 16 to 65 with 70 per cent between 25 and 59. The age and sex compositions per individual color were comparable. Since the evidence for sex or age differences in color ratings among the Ss was minor, the data are reported for the group as a whole.

The fifty colors covered the gamut of hue, lightness and saturation. In Munsell color coordinates, hue had a mean of 31 and a standard deviation of 23; lightness had a mean of 5 and a standard deviation of 2·1; and saturation had a mean of 9 and a standard deviation of 3·8.

The three color dimensions were also relatively uncorrelated with one another over the fifty colors. Hue had a correlation of −0·1 and −0·3 with lightness and saturation, and lightness had a correlation of 0·1 with saturation.

Thus the color solid was well filled by the fifty colors and the effect on the data analysis of an artificial dependence among color dimensions in the structure of this sample was small.

In this way a forty-eight row by fifty column matrix of average ratings was accumulated for fifty colors each judged on forty-eight adjective pairs.

The Factor Analysis

The first step in our analysis was to determine whether the variation among average judgements for the fifty colors exceeded significantly the variation within colors and was thus evidence for some kind of color judgement consistency among subjects. To accomplish this we did a fifty-cell one-way analysis of variance on each of the forty-eight adjective pairs. The 99·99th percentile of the variance ratio distribution with forty and several hundred degrees of freedom is about two. The ratio of the variance among colors to the variance within colors for thirty-one of the forty-eight adjective pairs exceeded two. We concluded that the differences among average color ratings were difficult to dismiss as only the product of individual differences.

Having satisfied ourselves that colors evoked judgements to some extent consistent among a wide variety of people, our second step was to analyse the covariation structure of the forty-eight by fifty matrix of average adjective pair ratings to see if some simplification of these judgements could be achieved. This was done by what Cattell calls a 'direct factor analysis' (3, pp. 414–416). A principal component method was used (12, pp. 10–19).

First the row, or adjective-pair means were removed to standardize the observations for average adjective-pair rating level. Then the factor analysis was accomplished by finding the largest proper vectors of the product of this standardized matrix and its transpose. Vectors were normalized by setting the squared length of each vector equal to the corresponding proper value.

The six largest principal components were computed, but the sixth accounted for less than 2·5 per cent of the total variation in the standardized matrix, while the first five claimed altogether 80 per cent. To succeed in gathering 80 per cent of the variation in a 48 by 50 matrix into five uncorrelated components is a substantial simplification. In addition 2·5 per cent is little more than the average variance of a single row. From a substantive point of view this indicates that no real 'cluster' of adjective pairs can have been overlooked. Further analysis was confined to these five largest components.

The loadings on these five components for those eighteen adjective pairs which dominated the covariation structure of the standardized data matrix are given in Table 1. Every adjective pair with at least one loading of 0·30 or more was included. With respect to the one-way analyses of variance mentioned earlier, the ratios of variance among colors to variance within colors for every adjective pair in Table 1 exceeded a value of three.

As can be seen in Table 1, the connotative nature of the five components can be characterized as 'happiness', 'forceful-strength', 'warmth', 'elegance' and 'calming-strength'.

Six clusters of adjective pairs can be identified on the basis of these five components. Each cluster suggests a somewhat different dimension of connotative meaning. The first and dominant cluster with loadings on only the first principal component contains the leading adjectives *happy*, *young*, *fresh*, *clear*, *social* and *graceful*. This dimension will be referred to as 'happiness'.

A second cluster is identified by loadings on both the first and the second principal components. This cluster contains the adjectives *outstanding*, *showy* and *exciting*, and will be referred to as the dimension of 'showiness'.

The third cluster, identified by major loadings on only the second principal component, contains *strong* and *forceful* and will be referred to as the dimension of 'forcefulness'.

Each of the remaining three clusters is located by a succeeding principal component. These dimensions of meaning will be referred to as 'warmth', defined by *warm*, *full* and *healthy;* 'elegance', defined by *splendid* and *elegant;* and finally a second kind of strength dimension, namely 'calmness', defined by the fourth order residual association of the *calming* side of *calming/exciting* with the strong side of *strong/weak*.

In order to clarify as much as possible the face value of each dimension, two prominent adjective pairs were selected from each of the six clusters to embody a dimension of connotative meaning. A dimension score was then formed by averaging color ratings on just these two adjective pairs. The adjective pairs

Table 1

The Loadings of Salient Adjective Pairs on the Five Largest
Principal Components of the Standardized[1] Matrix of Average
Color Judgements over Fifty Colors

	Principal component loadings				
Adjective pairs	I	II	III	IV	V
Froh/traurig	0·66	−0·18	0·20	−0·09	−0·10
Jung/alt	0·63	−0·15	−0·04	−0·15	−0·11
Frisch/abgestanden	0·56	−0·08	0·13	−0·02	0·01
Rein/trüb	0·48	−0·06	0·07	0·10	0·14
Gesellig/einsam	0·44	0·06	0·11	0·00	0·03
Anmutig/plump	0·44	−0·20	0·02	0·11	0·04
Auffällig/unauffällig	0·71	0·39	−0·13	0·10	−0·03
Auffallend/normal	0·66	0·38	−0·21	0·11	−0·08
Erregend/beruhigend	0·52	0·32	−0·15	−0·12	−0·32
Stark/schwach	0·13	0·52	0·15	−0·06	0·32
Energisch/zaghaft	0·16	0·42	0·07	−0·07	0·00
Warm/kalt	0·19	0·12	0·47	−0·12	−0·11
Voll/leer	0·16	0·23	0·33	−0·08	0·11
Gesund/krank	0·24	−0·05	0·32	−0·07	−0·03
Festlich/alltäglich	0·33	0·11	−0·03	0·47	−0·04
Vornehm/einfach	0·25	0·06	0·03	0·40	−0·05
Beruhigend/erregend	−0·52	−0·32	0·15	0·12	0·32
Proportion of total variation[2]	0·462	0·142	0·087	0·059	0·050[3] = 0·800

1. Standardized by removing row, or adjective-pair, means over the fifty colors.

2. Given in the proportion this component's sum of squares forms of the total sum of squares of the standardized observation matrix, computed over all forty-eight adjective pairs.

3. The next largest component accounted for 0·025 of the variation.

selected and the correlation structure within and among the six dimensions over these fifty colors are given in Table 2.

On Table 2 we see that *happy* and *fresh* correlated 0·89 with each other, that *outstanding* and *showy* correlated 0·90, *strong* and *forceful* 0·61, *warm* and *full* 0·70, *splendid* and *elegant* 0·81,

Table 2

Correlations Within and Among the Six Dimensions
of Meaning over Fifty Colors

	Dimension					
Dimension	A	B	C	D	E	F
A. Happiness (froh & frisch)	(0·89)[1]	0·60[2]	0·10	0·43	0·39	−0·38
B. Showiness (auffällig & auffallend)		(0·90)	0·49	0·24	0·56	−0·34
C. Forcefulness (stark & energisch)			(0·61)	0·50	0·16	0·37
D. Warmth (warm & voll)				(0·70)	0·11	0·18
E. Elegance (festlich & vornehm)					(0·81)	−0·1
F. Calmness (beruhigend & stark)						(−0·22)

1. Correlations on the diagonal are those between the two adjective pairs composing each dimension.

2. Correlations off the diagonal are those among dimensions.

but that *strong* and *calming* in the sixth dimension correlated −0·22.

The correlations among the six dimensions are also given. 'Happiness' and 'forcefulness' are nearly uncorrelated. The same is true for 'warmth' and 'elegance'. Otherwise, there are moderate relationships among the dimensions and in particular 'showiness' shares about 70 per cent of its variation between 'happiness' and 'forcefulness' and is thus strongly associated with the combined meaning of these two dimensions. This corresponds closely with the implications of Table 1.

The status of the sixth and last dimension, 'calmness', is somewhat equivocal. The two adjective pairs do not form a cluster in any simple sense. While the fourth-order residual covariation between these two adjective pairs is the major determinant of the fifth largest principal component in the factor analysis, and while their association in meaning has a certain face validity, little communality shows up in their first-order correlation. Their communality depends on first factoring out the other four connotations.

For this reason we take the other dimensions of meaning more seriously at present, and in particular we propose the four least correlated dimensions of 'happiness', 'forcefulness', 'warmth' and 'elegance' as the best bet for a four-dimensional framework within which to study further the connotative effects of color.

The Relation between Color Connotation and Color Perception

The next question is, 'In what way are these fairly consistent color connotations related to the three basic color perceptions of hue, lightness and saturation?' The data on this question are to be found in Table 3. There the partial regression coefficients of each of the six dimensions of color connotation on each of the three dimensions of color perception are given along with their standard errors.

When we come to compare these regression coefficients across different color perceptions, we will want to remember that while the ranges of possible hue, measured in terms of Munsell units, and lightness values are about the same, the range of possible saturation values can be nearly twice as much. If we use the standard deviations of hue, lightness and saturation found in this set of fifty colors as a rough index of this difference in variability, we will boost the regression coefficients on saturation by a factor of at least one and a half when comparing them to those on lightness and hue.

The first things to observe in Table 3 are the multiple correlations given there. It is remarkable how much of the variation among average color connotations can be accounted for by a linear function of the three color perceptions. Although Guilford's work (8, 9, 10) indicates that fundamental relations between color perceptions and color 'pleasantness' may not be linear, the data in Table 3 suggest that a linear model may nevertheless be a useful beginning for understanding the relation between color perception and color connotation.

What, then, are the linear effects of hue, lightness and saturation on these six dimensions of color connotation?

Table 3
The Linear Regression of the Six Dimensions of Meaning on Hue, Lightness and Saturation over Fifty Colors

| Dimension | Partial regression coefficients and standard errors[1] on each color dimension[2] | | | | | | Multiple correlation[3] |
| | Hue | | Lightness | | Saturation | | |
	$b_{H.LS}$	s_b	$b_{L.HS}$	s_b	$b_{S.HL}$	s_b	R_{HLS}
A. Happiness (froh & frisch)	0·014	0·045	0·194	0·049	0·102	0·028	0·67
B. Showiness (auffällig & auffallend)	0·034	0·041	0·118	0·045	0·262	0·026	0·87
C. Forcefulness (stark & energisch)	0·017	0·028	−0·190	0·031	0·142	0·017	0·84
D. Warmth (warm & voll)	−0·088	0·037	−0·115	0·040	0·069	0·023	0·62
E. Elegance (festlich & vornehm)	0·084	0·040	0·061	0·043	0·099	0·025	0·57
F. Calmness (beruhigend & stark)	0·075	0·033	−0·200	0·036	−0·008	0·020	0·71

1. Based on mean square residuals from regression with 46 *df*.
2. Measured in Munsell units with hue expressed in tens.
3. With 3 and 46 *df*.

Beginning with the rows in Table 3 we see that the connotation of 'happiness' is found to depend quite a bit on lightness and saturation, but hardly at all on hue. For example, on the basis of the partial regression coefficient of 'happiness' on color lightness given in Table 3, namely $b_{L.HS} = 0.194$, we might estimate for populations like the one sampled here that an increase in lightness of five Munsell units will be accompanied on the average by a shift of about one rating scale position nearer 'happiness'. Since the saturation of a color in Munsell units can vary at least one and a half times as much as its lightness, we see by the coefficient of 'happiness' on saturation, namely $b_{S.HL} = 0.102$, that saturation also makes a substantial contribution to 'happiness'.

Thus the lighter or the more saturated is a color, the more 'happiness' it connotes.

The connotation of 'showiness' depends on lightness and saturation, but now the emphasis is different. Saturation is the color perception which contributes the most to the connotation of 'showiness'.

Turning to the third connotation in Table 3, we see by the negative regression coefficient that it is color darkness upon which 'forcefulness' most depends. Saturation also plays a part, and so the darker or the more saturated is a color, the more it connotes 'forcefulness'.

'Warmth' is the first connotation in Table 3 to have much of a linear dependence on hue. Since the Munsell color coordinates increase with decreasing wavelength, the negative regression coefficient signifies, as one might expect, that greater redness is the hue change which corresponds with greater 'warmth'.

However, both lightness and saturation also affect the connotation of 'warmth'. Thus in addition to the effect of redness, the darker or the more saturated a color, the more it connotes 'warmth'.

'Elegance', the next connotation, also depends on hue. This time greater blueness is what seems to cause greater 'elegance'. Saturation, however, has even more of an effect. And so it is first of all saturation and second greater blueness which corresponds with a greater connotation of 'elegance'.

The last connotation in Table 3 is the combination of *calming* and *strong*. This connotation, probably because of its strength component, depends mostly on color darkness, but hue also seems to make a contribution. The darker or the more blue is a color, the more it connotes this kind of 'calmness'.

Earlier Research

How do these results compare with previous work on color meaning? Most other studies have been confined to over-all ratings of color preferences. The gist of these studies is that within reasonable bounds greater lightness and greater saturation each correspond with greater color preference (1, 2, 4, 5, 6, 8, 9, 10, 11, 14, 15, 17, 18, 19, 20, 21, 22).

However, these studies vary widely in the way a color preference or 'pleasantness' was operationally defined. In many cases the definitions were quite broad, allowing for such leeway in interpretation on the part of both subject and researcher. One wonders in what sense lightness and saturation are preferred – in the same sense or in senses quite different from each other?

There are also some inconsistencies; for example, Guilford found that the increase of 'pleasantness' with increasing lightness and saturation tended to be concave up (10, p. 457), while Granger found that the increase of 'preference' tended to be concave down (7, pp. 14–15). Indeed, Eysenck suggested that perhaps there were two different types of subjects – those who liked saturated colors and those who liked light colors (6, pp. 388). Thus, in spite of the large number of studies stretching over sixty years and two continents, knowledge concerning the specific effects of color lightness and saturation has remained rather vague.

This study provides some specification of these color effects. In Table 3 we see that greater lightness and greater saturation do correspond with greater 'happiness' and 'showiness', but that there they part company. Greater saturation corresponds with *more* 'forcefulness' and 'warmth', while greater lightness corresponds with *less*. Finally, greater saturation corresponds with more 'elegance', while greater lightness corresponds with less 'calmness'.

What about hue? Several studies report data which suggest that the relationship between hue and color preference may not be linear (1, 7, 8, 9, 10, 14, 21, 22). But only Guilford has dealt with this problem explicitly.

Guilford tried to identify the underlying function by fitting a trigonometric series to the relation between hue and color pleasantness observed in his data (8, 9). His results suggest that color pleasantness may be representable in terms of the combination of a first-order preference for blue over yellow with a second-order preference for primary red, green and blue over in-between hues. This is a particularly provocative preference pattern because of its congruence with physiological theories of color vision.

In so far as the relation between hue and connotation is usefully approximated by a linear model, however, the preference by blue–green over yellow–red in our data is specified by the regression coefficients in Table 3 as due to the connotations of 'elegance', 'calmness', and possibly 'coolness', rather than to those of 'happiness', 'showiness', or 'forcefulness'.

A few previous studies have investigated connotations other than preference or unpleasantness. Several researchers (5, 14, 16, 17, 19, 23) reported that differences in hue corresponded with differences in warmth, activity and excitement — red being warmer, more active, and more exciting than blue. This is in part confirmed by our data.

Greater redness does correspond with greater 'warmth' and less 'calmness' in our data. But on the German adjective pair *activ/passiv*, not included in Table 3 but one of the original forty-eight adjective pairs, the partial regression coefficients on hue and lightness were nearly zero. Only saturation, with a coefficient of 0·094 and a standard error of 0·021, seemed to have some consistent influence on average *activ/passiv* color judgements.

This is of interest since Osgood *et al.* (17, p. 302) reported that differences in the connotation of 'activity' in his data corresponded most of all with differences in hue! Our data suggest, on the other hand, that while excitement may be a linear function of hue, actual activity is a function of saturation.

Both Ross (19) and Osgood *et al.* (17) report data which suggest that greater lightness corresponds with greater passivity and coolness. The data in Table 3 do confirm this. Greater color lightness corresponds with less 'forcefulness' and with less 'warmth'.

Finally Collins (5), Ross (19), and Osgood *et al.* (17) among them related greater saturation to greater warmth, activity and strength. This is confirmed by our data in Table 3, where greater saturation is found to be followed by greater 'warmth', 'forcefulness', and 'showiness'.

Reviewing the over-all picture presented in Table 3, we were impressed by how minor the linear effect of hue was compared to the linear effect of saturation. Hue is the color perception which first appears in primitive language – the one most familiar to all of us, the one most commonly used to explain the emotional effects of color. Saturation, on the other hand, is the color perception last to receive a word designation and generally least familiar. Yet it is saturation which manifests itself most powerfully in this analysis of the relations between connotations and perceptions. This is a finding, we feel, worth thinking about.

Why is it that the least familiar color perception has the strongest linear influence on color connotation? Is this because there is more of an underlying relationship between saturation and connotation than between hue and connotation – a kind of generalized color response? Or is it because the basic hue-connotation relation is more complex, as Guilford suggested for color pleasantness – more complex in a way poorly approximated by a linear model?

With respect to the possibility of a more complex model, the color variables of saturation and lightness have approximately the same form physically and psychologically. This is not true for hue. Physically hue is a manifestation of wavelength, a magnitude; but psychologically hue is perceived as a location on a circle. For example, although blue represents the shortest wavelength and red represents the longest, and there are no clear-cut dominant wavelengths corresponding to the purples, we 'see' continuous steps of color from blue through purple to red, as though there were a continuous variable connecting them. This perceptual phenomena suggests that the relation between hue and connotation might indeed be represented better by a periodic rather than a linear model. We are looking into that possibility further.

What do these relationships between color perception and color connotation mean? Are there underlying physiological processes which are stimulated by color and to which we respond in some regular connotative manner? Or are there early conditioning experiences which are more or less common to all of us? If we can lay bare an orderly relationship between color perception and connotation, then perhaps the character of this relationship will help us to decide.

References

1. G. J. von ALLESCH, 'Die äesthetische Erscheinungsweise der Farben', *Psychol. Forsch.*, vol. 6 (1925), pp. 1–91.
2. E. J. G. BRADFORD, 'A note on the relation and esthetic value of perceptive types in color appreciation', *Amer. J. Psychol.*, vol. 24 (1913), pp. 545–54.
3. R. B. CATTELL, *Factor Analysis*, Harper, 1952.
4. J. COHN, 'Experimentelle Untersuchungen über die Gefühlsbetonung der Farben, Helligkeiten und ihre Combinationen', *Philos Stud.*, vol. 10 (1894), pp. 562–602.
5. N. COLLINS, 'The appropriateness of certain color combinations in advertising,' M.A. Thesis, Columbia University, 1924. Summarized in A. T. Poffenberger, *Psychology in Advertising*, McGraw-Hill, 1932, pp. 450–59.
6. H. J. EYSENCK, 'A critical and experimental study of color preferences', *Amer. J. Psychol.*, vol. 54 (1941), pp. 385–94.
7. G. W. GRANGER, 'An experimental study of color preferences', *J. gen. Psychol.*, vol. 52 (1955), pp. 3–20.
8. J. P. GUILFORD, 'The affective value of color as a function of hue, tint and chroma', *J. exp. Psychol.*, vol. 17 (1934), pp. 342–70.
9. J. P. GUILFORD, 'A study in psychodynamics', *Psychometrika*, vol. 4 (1939), pp. 1–23.
10. J. P. GUILFORD, 'There is system in color preference', *J. opt. Soc. Amer.*, vol. 30 (1940), pp. 455–9.
11. J. JASTROW, 'Popular esthetics of color', *Pop. sci. Mon.*, vol. 50 (1897), pp. 361–8.
12. M. G. KENDALL, 'A course in multivariate analysis', *Griffin's Statistical Monographs and Courses*, no. 2, Griffin, 1957.
13. R. J. LEWINSKI, 'An investigation of individual responses to chromatic illumination', *J. Psychol.*, vol. 6 (1938), pp. 155–60.
14. M. LUCKIESH, *Light and Color in Advertising and Merchandising*, Van Nostrand, 1923.
15. A. MINOR, 'Uber die Gefalligkeit der Sättigungsstufen der Farben', *Zsch. F. Psychol.*, vol. 50 (1909), pp. 433–44.
16. D. C. MURRAY and H. L. DEABLER, 'Colors and mood-tones', *J. appl. Psychol.*, vol. 41 (1957), pp. 279–83.
17. C. OSGOOD, G. SUCI and P. TANNENBAUM, *The Measurement of Meaning*, University of Illinois Press, 1957.

18. S. L. PRESSEY, 'The influence of color upon mental and motor efficiency', *Amer. J. Psychol.*, vol. 32 (1921), pp. 326–56.
19. R. T. ROSS, 'Studies in the psychology of the theater,' *Psychol. Record*, vol. 2 (1938), pp. 127–90.
20. W. E. WALTON and B. M. MORRISON, 'A preliminary study of the affective value of colored lights', *J. appl. Psychol.*, vol. 15 (1931), p. 297.
21. S. J. WARNER, 'The color preferences of psychiatric groups', *Psychol. Monogr.*, vol. 63 (1949), no. 6 (whole no. 301).
22. M. F. WASHBURN, 'Note on the affective value of colors', *Amer. J. Psychol.*, vol. 22 (1911), pp. 114–15.
23. L. B. WEXNER, 'The degree to which colors are associated with mood-tones', *J. appl. Psychol.*, vol. 38 (1954), pp. 432–5.

17 J. Kansaku

The Analytic Study of Affective Values of Color
Combinations. A Study of Color Pairs

J. Kansaku, 'The analytic study of affective values of color combinations.
A study of color pairs', *Japanese Journal of Psychology*, vol. 34 (1963),
pp. 11-12.

Artists and scientists have long been concerned with color 'harmony'. In this study thirty-nine binary combinations of colors
were analysed by the S.D. (Semantic Differential) method in an
effort to determine whether there might not be other affective
values in color combinations.

In this experiment thirty-nine color pairs, each color area being
equal (2 cm × 2 cm), were selected according to degree of color
difference as measured by the color scale of Japan Color Research Institute and mounted on white sheets 6 cm × 10 cm. In
the experimental design of the three attributes of color (hue,
value and chroma), only one attribute was used as a variable and
other two were kept constant. Subjects' reactions to these pairs
were rated on twenty kinds of scales with 9-degree bipolar scale
method which were derived from the free association response in
the previous study. The subjects of this experiment were thirty
(fifteen men and fifteen women). The values for twenty scales on
each pair were calculated and factor analysis done.

The major findings of this study may be summarized as follows:
(1) Four factors of affective value in color pairs were noted in
percentages as indicated: pleasure (43 per cent), brightness (21
per cent), strength (19 per cent), and warmth (8 per cent).

This suggests that pleasure is the dominant factor in paired
colors. Of these four factors, warmth is peculiar to color; that is,
it does not appear in other S.D. studies but one which is concerned
with color of buildings. The first three may correspond to the
factors of evaluation, activity and potency which were discussed
by Osgood and others.
(2) The correlation coefficients between the 'harmonious–
inharmonious' scale and the scales which had high weights of

pleasure were constantly high. But correlation coefficients of the scales highly weighted with other factors were generally low.

(3) It was found that the values on several scales increased or decreased as color differences between two component colors increased. The influence of difference in lightness on the change of affective values was stronger than that in hue or chroma.

As hue difference increased, the values of 'fused, static, dull, vague, sober, weak' feelings decreased and those of 'separated, dynamic, sharp, distinct, gay, strong' feelings increased. When lightness difference increased, 'muddy, light, fused, static, dull, vague, soft, weak' feelings decreased and 'harmonious, smart,

Table 1

Types of factors	Scales
I	pleasant–unpleasant
	tasty–distasteful
	smart–boorish
	chic–rusty
	harmonious–inharmonious
	beautiful–ugly
	refreshing–heavy
	fused–separated
II	bright–dark
	gay–gloomy
	showy–sober
III	strong–weak
	hard–soft
IV	hot–cold
I II	light–heavy
	youthful–mature
I III	sharp–dull
	distinct–vague
I IV	clear–muddy
I II III	dynamic–static

tasty, pleasant, chic, beautiful, clear, sharp, distinct, hard, strong'
feelings increased. And only 'fused, vague' feelings decreased
and 'distinct, hard' feelings increased as chroma difference
increased.

With respect to 'harmonious–inharmonious' values, those of
the present study do not consistently agree with the color harmony theory of Moon and Spencer.

The warmth of color pairs seems to be defined by the mean
value of the warmth of the two components.

(4) Women tended to have the keen harmonious feeling in perceiving color combinations, whereas men did not.

18 R. W. Skager, C. B. Schultz and S. P. Klein

The Multidimensional Scaling of a Set of Artistic
Drawings: Perceived Structure and Scale Correlates

R. W. Skager, C. B. Schultz and S. P. Klein, 'The multidimensional scaling
of a set of artistic drawings: perceived structure and scale correlates',
Multivariate Behavioral Research, vol. 1 (1966), pp. 425–36.

Product-centered research on creativity approaches the criterion problem
of what is to be the referent for creativity through the analysis of tangible
products such as art objects, writing or scientific achievements. The
present research is concerned with the evaluation and study of artistic
drawings contributed by sophomore students at the Rhode Island
School of Design. Multidimensional scaling methods were applied to
similarity judgements obtained from art experts on two separate sets of
twenty-five drawings. Three similarity dimensions accounted for the
interstimulus distances for each set of drawings. Although no statistical
test was available, the dimensions from the two sets appeared to
correspond. Scale values of four drawings common to the two sets
were consistent, and the dimensions appeared to define very similar
stimulus characteristics. It was concluded that multidimensional scaling
procedures provided a means for differentiating among a set of complex, esthetic products. Scale values of drawings on the three dimensions
also correlated differentially with cognitive and achievement measures
available on the students, suggesting that product dimensions identified
via similarity judgements were related to characteristics of individuals
producing the products. Hypotheses were developed as to the psychological meaning of the three product dimensions.

In a recent product-centered study of artistic creativity, Skager,
Schultz and Klein (1966) have shown that even among a group of
expert judges there existed at least two distinct viewpoints about
the esthetic quality of a set of artistic drawings. Furthermore, it
appeared that psychological characteristics of the artists who produced the drawings related differentially to quality of product
depending on which point of view was being considered. For
example, measures of the cultural and economic level of the
subjects' backgrounds appeared to relate to quality of artistic
product as defined by one group of judges but did not relate

to quality as defined by judges holding a different viewpoint.

These results led to the suggestion that the 'product' may provide a more analytical tool for discovering human characteristics related to creativity than we heretofore thought. In other words, since dimensions of preference are likely to be a function of different characteristics of the drawings (Klein and Skager, 1966), an examination of these *product characteristics* may stimulate hypotheses about the *psychological characteristics* of individuals who produce or prefer these drawings. For example, one might hypothesize that chaotic and disorderly drawings are likely to be produced by impulsive individuals.

The determination of dimensions of preference judgements is only one way in which characteristics of products can be identified. In fact, judges holding the same point of view about quality may have based their evaluations on several product characteristics. Multidimensional scaling procedures utilizing similarity rather than preference judgements may identify less complex characteristics by which stimuli are seen as similar or different as well as distinguish product characteristics unrelated to preference. The purposes of the present study are to (1) discover the number and nature of the characteristics by which a set of artistic drawings are perceived as similar, (2) relate the dimensions of similarity to the quality of the drawings as determined by an independent set of preference judgements, and (3) relate psychological characteristisc of the individual who produced the drawings to the dimensions of similarity.

Procedure

Subjects and drawings

Sophomores ($N=191$) from a highly selective school of design were asked to draw a view of the city of Providence from a specified vantage point (see Klein, Skager and Schultz, 1966, for a complete description of this assignment). Because of the excessive number of judgements that would have been required had all the drawings been scaled, a sample of forty-six of the drawings was selected for the present study. However, the selected drawings represented a full distribution of esthetic quality as established in the previous research.

Forty-two of the forty-six selected drawings were divided randomly into two groups (sets A and B). The four remaining drawings were then added to both sets so that each had a total of twenty-five drawings. The selected drawings were photographically reproduced as 9 in × 13 in prints (approximately half of the dimensions of the originals), and each was mounted on a cardboard sheet.

Judges

The judges ($N = 26$) for this study were members of the faculty at nine schools of design located in various parts of the United States.

Preference judgements

The forty-six different drawings were evaluated by each judge on a 7-point scale for personal preference. Ratings of 'creativity' were not obtained for reasons discussed elsewhere (Klein, Skager and Schultz, 1966; Skager *et al.*, 1966).

Similarity judgements

Similarity judgements on each of the 300 possible pairs of the twenty-five drawings in each set were made according to the method of multidimensional successive categories (Torgerson, 1958). Six categories of similarity were used. Twenty-five additional judgements were repeated at the end of the two sets to provide a measure of reliability. Judges were not informed that the repeated judgements had been included.

The judgemental task was in part defined by the following excerpt from the instructions:

You will be rating pairs of drawings for the over-all similarity of the drawings in the pair, taking any characteristics of the drawings into account that you think are relevant, but disregarding completely similarities or differences in materials used and in particular subject matter selected by the artist.

Variables

In addition to the mean of the twenty-six preference ratings on each S's drawing (Variable $H1$), a variety of test scores and items of information were available for the forty-six students whose drawings were evaluated. These variables were:

(2) *Language ability* (L), A.C.E. Psychological Examination (Educational Testing Service, 1954); a measure of general verbal aptitude.

(3) *Quantitative ability* (Q), A.C.E. Psychological Examination (Educational Testing Service, 1954): a measure of general quantitative ability.

(4) *Controlled associations test* (French, Ekstrom and Price, 1963): a measure of the factor of associational fluency.

(5) *Design test:* a test developed and administered by the Admissions Office of the Rhode Island School of Design. The subject is required to fill in parts of a standard figure to form as many different patterns as possible. This test could probably be classified as a measure of the figural fluency factor of the Guilford (1964) system.

(6) *Drawing test:* a score based upon the evaluation of simple line drawings done as a part of the admissions procedure at the Rhode Island School of Design.

(7) *Hidden figures test:* a measure of flexibility of closure. Jackson, Messick and Meyers (1964) have related this test to the personality construct of 'field independence'.

(8) *Figure classification test* (French, Ekstrom and Price, 1963): a measure of induction.

(9) *Rapid associations test I:* a measure of the originality of first associations to a set of stimulus words. Norms for scoring the associations were taken from Bousfield, Cohen, Whitmarsh and Kincaid (1961).

(10) *Rapid associations test II:* the number of associations in the 1 to 10 per cent frequency interval of the Bousfield *et al.* norms.

(11) *Symbol production test* (fluency score) (French, Ekstrom and Price, 1963): this test requires the examinee to produce symbols representing given activities and objects. It is a measure of the semantic adaptive flexibility factor in Guilford's system.

(12) *Symbol production* (originality score): a measure based upon the unusualness of the symbols produced for the first six items of each of the two parts of the *Symbol production test*. This score

351

was calculated only on items completed by all subjects to provide a measure of originality unconfounded with fluency.

(13) *Major in 'applied' arts:* indicates that a student has chosen a major in an area such as industrial design.

(14) *Major in fine arts:* indicates choice of major in an area such as painting or sculpture.

(15) *Major in architecture:* indicates choice of major in one of the architectural fields.

(16) *High school grade point average* (H.S.G.P.A.).

(17) *Grade point average in major field* (major G.P.A.).

(18) *Grade point average in foundation art program* (foundation G.P.A.). Grades in the foundation program are based upon 'fundamentals' courses in design and drawing required for all students at the School of Design.

Analyses and Results

As described above, twenty-five drawing pairs were repeated within each of the two sets of judgements. To provide an indication of the reliability of the similarity judgements, correlations between the first and second judgements were computed across the judges for each repeated pair. The twenty-five correlations ranged from 0·50 to 0·90 ($r=0.70$) for set A, and from 0·22 to 0·89 ($r=0.72$) for set B (average rs were obtained using the z transformation).

Distance estimates were derived from the two sets of similarity judgements by selecting additive constants according to the approach of Messick and Abelson (1956). The resulting distances were scaled by Torgerson's (1958) multidimensional scaling procedure.

Examination of the relative magnitudes of the sums of squares of scale coordinates indicated that at least three dimensions were required to account for the major portion of the variance of interstimulus distances. The values of set A suggested the presence of a minor fourth dimension not evident for the set B drawings. In order to keep the two solutions comparable, three dimensions for each set were rotated by means of Saunders' (1962) equimax criterion. The latter is an analytic rotation procedure that tends

R. W. Skager, C. B. Schultz and S. P. Klein

to distribute variance equally among rotated orthogonal dimensions. Rotated scale values for the similarity dimensions are provided in Table 1.

Table 1

Scale Value Drawings of Set A and Set B[1]

Drawing number	Set A dimensions			Drawing number	Set B dimensions		
	I	II	III		I	II	III
1a	−29	−21	−06	1b	16	24	−07
2a	23	22	−15	2b	−18	−20	−09
3a	03	38	09	3b	−02	04	12
4a	04	13	−16	4b	−20	−19	25
5a	08	−07	−20	5b	−09	02	−33
6a	25	21	−02	6b	13	32	−15
7a	07	03	35	7b	17	09	−06
8a	−26	−04	−16	8b	−46	−06	−05
9a	28	08	04	9b	03	−17	13
10a	00	−23	−01	10b	−24	−35	−01
11a	−44	−04	−03	11b	19	17	−05
12a	−33	−15	−07	12b	22	−01	00
13a	−04	24	22	13b	04	−23	19
14a	−18	03	43	14b	−13	29	04
15a	12	−11	−02	15b	22	02	−13
16a	24	03	−05	16b	−05	−25	13
17a	−12	−25	18	17b	−19	−25	02
18a	20	27	05	18b	−43	08	−08
19a	−15	−17	−20	19b	04	31	04
20a	−26	−29	01	20b	24	04	−00
21a	24	05	−03	21b	19	14	−15
22	05	20	−22	22	11	10	−26
23	08	−04	33	23	11	−02	34
24	24	01	−07	24	20	14	04
25	−09	−27	06	25	−04	−26	12

1. Drawings 22–25 were the same in both sets.

With only four of the drawings common to the two sets it is not possible to provide a statistical estimate of the stability of the similarity dimensions across the two sets of drawings. However, a rough indication of the comparability of the A and B spaces can be obtained by noting the loadings of stimuli 22 through 25 (identical in the two sets of drawings) on corresponding factors. On this basis at least, the dimensions of the two similarity spaces do appear to be similar. The rank order of these four stimuli is the same for each dimension in both sets except for the inversion of 22 and 24 in factor II.

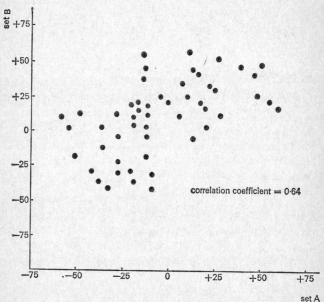

Figure 1. Scatterplot of the corresponding correlation coefficients in sets A and B for the correlation between each dimension and variable

A second source of evidence that corresponding dimensions in the two sets are similar comes from subjective evaluations of the characteristics of the drawings on each dimension in each set. These evaluations were made by comparing the drawings with the highest positive scale values on a given dimension with drawings having the highest negative values on that dimension. The authors' impressionistic reports of the differences have been summarized below. Except for the first factor for sets A and

B almost all descriptive statements seemed to apply to corresponding factors from the two sets. Even for the first dimension, the similarities were considerably more apparent than the differences.

Dimension I

Geometrical or static appearance (high) *v.* impression of dynamic or flowing quality of lines or objects (low).
Simplification (high) *v.* complexity of treatment (low).

Dimension II

Objects de-emphasized or nearly obscured (high) *v.* clear delineation of objects (low).
Organization in part provided by relationship of fields or shapes (high) *v.* organization via relationships among objects (low).
Organization in part provided by use of shading (high) *v.* shading unrelated to organization of drawing (low).
Little use of detail (high) *v.* extensive use of detail (low).
De-emphasis or avoidance of perspective and depth (high) *v.* emphasis on perspective and depth (low).

Dimension III

Impression of precision and control in execution (high) *v.* impression of chaotic, even violent execution (low).
Careful portrayal of objects as they are (high) *v.* simplification or primitization of objects (low).
Unused border at edge of drawing (high) *v.* impression that artist ignored edge of drawing (low).
Neatness (high) *v.* carelessness or disorder (low).

A third source of evidence that corresponding dimensions in the two sets are similar (i.e. in addition to their comparable scale values and stylistic characteristics) comes from the correlations between available information on the student artists and the rotated scale values of their drawings. These correlations are presented in Table 2, and an inspection of this table reveals that the variables which relate to a dimension in set A generally show a similar relationship with the same dimension in set B. For example, the second factors of both sets A and B are positively correlated with the preference ratings, *Design test*, *Rapid associations I* and

Majoring in the fine arts; but negatively related to *Rapid associations II, Symbol production* (Fl) and *Majoring in architecture.* Further evidence that the pattern of correlations between tests and dimensions in the two sets are similar comes from an inspection of the scatterplot (Figure 1) of their corresponding coefficients from Table 2 (e.g. the coordinates for dimension I and 'preference' are 84, 85; the coordinates for dimensions II and 'preference' are 76, 80; etc.).

Table 2

Correlates of Scale Values on Rotated Factors

Variable	Set A scales				Set B scales			
	N	I	II	III	N	I	II	III
Preference	25	85	76	03	25	84	80	35
A.C.E.–L	24	−47	−15	−08	25	09	53	−33
A.C.E.–Q	24	−54	−37	11	25	01	02	24
Cont. Assn	25	00	−14	−10	24	22	13	01
Design Test	24	15	40	−21	24	22	46	−23
Drawing Test	25	24	−21	22	25	28	18	−08
Fig. Class.	25	−19	−30	−04	24	10	09	24
Hid. Fig.	25	−30	−11	15	24	−03	−16	40
Rapid Assn I	19	10	13	−33	19	57	42	−40
Rapid Assn II	19	−59	−48	−15	19	07	−20	38
Sym. Prod., Fl.	23	−10	−28	22	23	−04	−23	30
Sym. Prod., Or.	22	−34	−20	16	24	−12	02	18
App. Arts Maj.	25	−10	−10	28	25	10	17	10
Fine Arts Maj.	25	57	52	−19	25	21	49	−33
Arch. Maj.	25	−42	−37	−13	25	−28	−37	46
H.S.G.P.A.	25	−29	06	−16	23	−33	12	19
Major G.P.A.	25	47	48	−09	22	24	42	−40
Found. G.P.A.	25	63	24	12	24	15	52	−05

There are major differences, however, between the three dimensions that are consistent across sets. Some examples of these differences are: (1) preference ratings and majoring in fine arts are positively related to scale values on factors I and II, but not on

III; (2) factors II and III show correlations in the opposite direction for *Rapid associations I, Symbol production* (Fl.), and *Majoring in fine arts;* and (3) figural fluency reflected in *Design test* and *Major G.P.A.,* is unrelated to factors II and III, but negatively related to factor I.

These results indicate that scale values of drawing dimensions relate in a consistent way to at least some characteristics of the individual artists and that the dimensions appear to define important, even striking ways in which the drawings differ in structure and organization. In contradistinction to previous studies applying multidimensional scaling procedures to colors or geometrical figures, however, the dimensions identified here are not likely to be 'simple' in the sense that they correspond to unitary attributes of the stimuli. A number of factors argue against this conclusion. For one thing, the drawings at opposite poles of each dimension appear to differ in more than one way, even though some integrative generalizations can certainly be made. Also, correlates of the dimensions are themselves rather complex (e.g. *Major in fine arts,* and *G.P.A.*). Finally, the first two dimensions are highly related to preference, itself likely to be based on complex criteria (Skager, Schultz and Klein, 1966). It is true, of course, that a variable may correlate with a complex variable without itself being complex.

It is also relevant to the issue of complexity that the stimulus dimensions are based upon the composite similarity judgements of twenty-six judges. Tucker and Messick (1963) have pointed out that individual judges may not be accurately represented by such composite dimensions. A given judge may use fewer or more stimulus characteristics in his similarity judgements than does the 'average' judge. It is also true that individuals may make judgements on the basis of stimulus characteristics not considered by the majority of the judges, thus contributing to the complexity of the composite dimensions. In other words, there may be more than one point of view among the judges about which characteristic or characteristics of the stimuli define similarity. Moreover, such points of view may differ in complexity – the number of dimensions required to account for the interstimulus distances.

To investigate this possibility, additional analyses were conducted. For the two sets separately, the twenty-six judges were intercorrelated across the 300 similarity judgements. The resulting matrix was factor analysed to determine the number of points of view required to account for the interjudge relationships. Plots of the roots of the unrotated dimensions indicated clearly that there were at least three different viewpoints about stimulus similarity for each set.

Factor plots were then made of the unrotated points of view dimensions with individual judges represented as points in the space. Four judges, represented by points lying in consistent but widely separated positions for both the set A and set B plots, were selected for further study. It was expected that these judges would differ in the number of dimensions each used in making the similarity judgements. Distance estimates for the two sets of judgements of each of the four judges were scaled by the multidimensional procedures already described.[1]

The results of these analyses indicated that the number of dimensions needed to account for the distances did differ for these judges. A single dimension sufficed for one judge, while two, three, and an indeterminate number of dimensions were required for the other three judges, respectively. In general, further study of the data for individual judges did not add appreciably to the analyses of composite judgements in the sense that it did not appear that 'new' similarity dimensions had been discovered that had been obscured in the composite scaling (i.e. the individual judges appeared to be using one or more of the composite dimensions).

Discussion

It is clear from the data reported above that multidimensional scaling procedures offer an effective means for identifying salient dimensions on which complex artistic products can be differentiated from one another. Further, scale values of the drawings on the dimensions thus discovered appear to be differentially related to judged quality as well as to characteristics of the artists who produced the drawings. Such characteristics include cogni-

1. The method can be applied to the distance judgements of a single judge in the same way that it is applied to the composite judgements of several judges.

tive abilities in addition to measures of past performance and choice of major in the arts.

It has also been suggested that inspection of drawings with relatively 'pure' patterns of scale values might aid in generating hypotheses about psychological variables associated with particular product dimensions. While the development of such hypotheses is admittedly highly subjective, such subjectivity is not harmful as long as the hypotheses thus generated are open to verification.

The statements in the previous section summarizing contrasts between drawings at the extremes of the corresponding first dimensions have a common theme. Drawings low on the dimensions are richly complex in organization and detail. The 'dynamic or flowing' quality of the drawings contributes importantly to this complexity. In contrast, drawings with positive loadings give an over-all impression of spareness and simplicity. There is very little in the drawings. What is there is static and unelaborated, with objects carefully separated from one another. This dimension, then, might be labeled *complexity v. simplicity*. In an earlier study of artistic judgements, Beittel (1963) also reported a dimension contrasting complex and simple drawings.

It is, of course, tempting to hypothesize that scale values on this dimension may be related to the cognitive style of complexity–simplicity. Barron and Welsh (1952) reported that artists have strong preferences for complex and asymmetrical design. In the present study the high correlation observed between scale values on the corresponding first dimensions and choice of major in fine arts is consistent with such an interpretation.

This and the following hypotheses can be investigated in future research. For example, measures of complexity–simplicity and related variables such as those reported by Barron (1953) might be administered to another group of artists. Art products, obtained from these same artists, would be rated for complexity, possibly using sample drawings from the present study to help define the concept. Consistent and significant relationships between ratings of the product and the test variables would establish a correspondence between psychological measures of complexity–simplicity and an aspect of performance in art. If complexity of product were also related to judged quality – as in the present study – there would be a reasonable basis for concluding that this particular cognitive style is relevant to one type of creative performance.

The second dimension appears to define differences in the way organization of subject matter is achieved. Thus, drawings with high negative loadings on this dimension show an emphasis on organizing or structuring through the relationships among 'real' objects as compared to an organization based on the relationships of fields or spaces, with objects obscured or seemingly unimportant. There is no ready label for this dimension. However, the positive relationships between scores on the *Design test* and scale values on the second dimension might be explained on the basis of the following reasoning. As a measure of figural fluency the *Design test* presumably taps the ability to produce new combinations of visual elements. This, at a more abstract level, describes drawings with high positive loadings on the second dimension, since an emphasis on relationships between fields or shapes superimposed upon or even obscuring specific objects amounts to a kind of reorganization of what the artist sees. This dimension, then, may be related to cognitive rather than noncognitive variables.

An inspection of the third dimension also suggests a hypothesis about the nature of the artist. In this case, drawings with high loadings appear to be deliberate and controlled, while those with low loadings might be classified as impulsive. Although this dimension does not relate to a drawing's quality (as measured by the preference ratings), it may be that a drawing's loading is related to the personality characteristic of 'control *v.* impulsiveness' in the artist who produced it.

While these interpretations are potentially fruitful, they are based on an assumption. That is, we have implicitly assumed that the subjects in this research, under no special requirements as to how things were to be drawn, followed their own proclivities, and that these proclivities have a basis in the psychology of the individual. Under different conditions the same product dimensions might not be observed. The talented artist is quite capable of modifying at will the way in which he organizes and portrays his subject (Klein, Skager and Erlebacher, 1966).

Taking a 'product-centered' approach to the study of creativity implies that the referent for creativity is based primarily on the study of what people produce rather than on scores on 'creativity' tests or ratings of people on the basis of general impressions about their behavior. While the study of products has a satisfying directness and perhaps promises a greater degree of objectivity, it also poses problems. Some readers may question whether or not the study of products is necessarily relevant to creativity. For example, it might be pointed out that it is impossible to establish that each product is really original for the artist who produced it. In reply, we would suggest that the objection may be an inappropriate one, and that it is the task itself that determines the relevance of the products to the study of creativity. We have simply asked a group of student artists to engage in an activity generally recognized as 'creative', and we have chosen to identify quality of product with degree of creativity. The question of how 'creative' the product is thus inevitably evolves into the operations of the analysis and study of product characteristics.

References

BARRON, F. (1953), 'Complexity–simplicity as a personality dimension', *J. abnorm. soc. Psychol.*, vol. 48, pp. 163–72.

BARRON, F., and WELSH, G. S. (1952), 'Artistic perception as a possible factor in personality style: Its measurement by a figure preference test', *J. Psychol.*, vol. 33, pp. 199–203.

BEITTEL, K. R. (1963), 'Factor analysis of three dimensions of the art judgment complex: Criteria, art objects, and judges', *J. exper. Educ.*, vol. 32, pp. 167–73.

BOUSFIELD, W. A., COHEN, B. H., WHITMARSH, G. A., and KINCAID, W. D. (1961), 'The Connecticut free associational norms', *Technical Report, Department of Psychology, University of Connecticut*, no. 35.

Educational Testing Service (1954), *The American Council of Education Psychological Examination*, Princeton, New Jersey.

FRENCH, J. W., EKSTROM, R. B., and PRICE, L. (1963), *Manual for Kit of Reference Tests for Cognitive Factors*, Educational Testing Service.

GUILFORD, J. P. (1964), 'Progress in the discovery of intellectual factors', in C. W. Taylor (ed.), *Widening Horizons in Creativity*, Wiley.

JACKSON, D. N., MESSICK, S., and MEYERS, C. T. (1964), 'The role of memory and color in group and individual embedded-figures measures of field-independence', *Educ. psychol. Meas.*, vol. 24, pp. 177–92.

KLEIN, S. P., and SKAGER, R. W. (1966), 'Spontaneity vs. deliberateness as a dimension of esthetic judgment', Paper presented at the American Psychological Association, September.

KLEIN, S. P., SKAGER, R. W., and ERLEBACHER, W. (1966), 'Measuring artistic flexibility', *Educational Testing Service Research Bulletin*, no. 66-27.

KLEIN, S. P., SKAGER, R. W., and SCHULTZ, C. B. (1966), 'Dimensions for evaluating art products', *Educational Testing Service, Research Bulletin*, no. 66-9.

MESSICK, S., and ABELSON, R. P. (1956), 'The additive constant problem in multidimensional scaling', *Psychometrika*, vol. 21, pp. 1–15.

SAUNDERS, D. R. (1962), 'Trans-varimax: Some properties of the ratiomax and equimax criteria for blind orthogonal rotation', *Amer. Psychologist*, vol. 17, pp. 395–96 (abstract).

SKAGER, R. W., SCHULTZ, C. B., and KLEIN, S. P. (1966), 'Points of view about preference of tools in the analysis of creative products', *Percep. mot. Skills*, vol. 22, pp. 83–94.

TORGERSON, W. S. (1958), *Theory and Methods of Scaling*, Wiley.

TUCKER, L. R., and MESSICK, S. (1963), 'An individual differences model for multidimensional scaling', *Psychometrika*, vol. 28, pp. 333–67.

Part Eight The Measurement of Preference

There is no reason why tests of aesthetic preference should not be developed to the same degree of technical refinement as tests of intellectual ability. At the outset, however, the problem of the criteria by which a particular judgement is to be marked 'correct' or 'incorrect' presents itself in a fashion different from the criterion problem in other forms of ability testing. Anne Anastasi (Reading 19) discusses this difficulty and reviews some of the available tests. The problems of testing do not end here. As we have pointed out elsewhere in the readings, the question of which aspect of a design is influencing a particular person's judgement can be indeterminate and may not be the aspect 'built-in' to the test by the test designer. Futhermore, correlations between preference and the assumed effective aspects of the design based on average results may be obscuring the true nature of individual response. Both these problems are explored by Moyles, Tuddenham and Block in Reading 20. The possibility that design preference is ultimately dependent upon some neurological aspect of brain functioning has frequently been voiced. Data are scant on this suggestion. However, Lansdell in Reading 21 presents evidence using a standardized test (discussed by Anastasi) of the effect of neurosurgery on test performance, though interpretation of such a finding is extremely difficult.

19 A. Anastasi

Artistic Aptitudes

Excerpt from A. Anastasi, *Psychological Testing* (2nd edn), Macmillan, 1961, pp. 401-9.

Tests of *artistic appreciation* have generally followed a common pattern. In each item, the subject is requested to express his preference regarding two or more variants of the same object. One variant is either an original by an eminent artist or a version preferred by the majority of a group of art experts. The other versions represent deliberate distortions designed to violate some accepted principle of art. Any controversial items, on which a clear consensus of experts cannot be obtained, are normally eliminated from such a test.

In the development of art appreciation tests, both original item selection and subsequent validation procedures depend heavily upon the opinions of contemporary art experts within our culture. It is well to bear this fact in mind when interpreting scores. Essentially, such tests indicate the degree to which the individual's aesthetic 'taste' agrees with that of contemporary art experts. The representativeness of the particular group of experts employed in developing the test is obviously an important consideration. In so far as aesthetic standards or 'taste' may change with time, the periodic rechecking of scoring key and item validities is likewise desirable.

The McAdory Art Test (13, 18) represents one of the earliest attempts to measure artistic appreciation. First published in 1929, this test is now of historical interest only, because many of its items are outdated. The test employed contemporary materials taken from art and trade magazines, as well as art objects chosen from museums and art books. The items cover such varied categories as furniture and household utensils, textiles and clothing, automobiles, and painting and other graphic arts. Each item consists of four variations, to be ranked in order of preference by the

365

subject. The alternative versions differ in shape and line arrangement, massing of dark and light, or color.

The Meier Art Judgement Test (14), a revision of the earlier Meier–Seashore Test (16), is undoubtedly the most widely used test of artistic appreciation. This test, whose first edition also appeared in 1929, was revised in 1940. The revision consisted essentially in the elimination of the twenty-five items having the lowest correlations with total score and, within the remaining 100 items, the allotment of double credit to the twenty-five having the highest correlations with total score.

The Meier Art Judgement Test differs in a number of ways from the McAdory. The materials from which the Meier test was constructed consist of relatively timeless art works, which will not

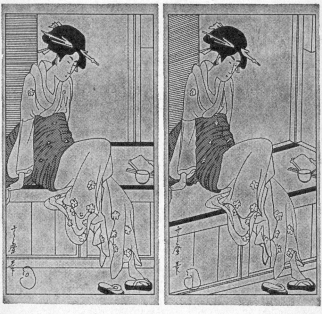

Figure 1. Item similar to those employed in the Meier Art Judgement Test. This item does not appear in the current revised form. The difference between the two versions is in the angle at which the window seat crosses the picture.
(Courtesy Norman C. Meier)

readily go out of date. Most are paintings or drawings by acknowledged masters, while a few represent vases or designs suitable
for pottery. All reproductions are in black and white. Each
item contains only two versions, an original and a variation in
which the symmetry, balance, unity, or rhythm has been altered.
This test thus concentrates upon the judgement of *aesthetic
organization*, which Meier considers to be the key factor in artistic
talent. In order to rule out the contribution of perceptual accuracy
the subject is told in what detail the two versions of each picture
differ. An illustrative item is reproduced in Figure 1.

For more than two decades, Meier and his associates at the
University of Iowa conducted research on the nature of artistic
talent. Although most of their subjects were children, data on
adult groups, including professional artists, were also obtained.
This research led Meier to the conclusion that artistic aptitude
comprises six interlinked traits, namely, manual skill, volitional
perseveration, aesthetic intelligence, perceptual facility, creative
imagination and aesthetic judgement. The Meier Art Judgement
Test is designed to measure only the last of these six traits. The
original plans called for the preparation of creative imagination
and aesthetic perception tests, but little progress was made on the
development of these tests. It might be added that the six traits
listed were not identified by factor analysis, but are based upon
the author's interpretation of a mass of relevant observations.
Corroboration by means of factor analysis would be desirable.
More objective evidence on the relation between aesthetic judgement and the quality of artistic production should likewise be
provided.

Percentile norms are given for three groups: 1445 junior high
school students, 892 senior high school students, and 982 adults,
including college and art school students. All norms were derived
largely from students in art courses, whether in high school,
college or special art schools. Data were gathered in twenty-five
schools scattered throughout the United States. Split-half reliability coefficients between 0·70 and 0·84 are reported for relatively homogeneous samples.

Most of the available evidence regarding validity of the Meier
Art Judgement Test can be summarized under the headings of item
selection and contrasted group performance, although a few

correlations with independent criteria of artistic accomplishment have also been reported. First, it should be noted that the original items were chosen from reputable art works and that the distortions were such as to violate accepted art principles. A large number of items thus assembled were then submitted to twenty-five art experts, and only those items showing clear-cut agreement among the experts were retained. Finally, items were selected on which from 60 to 90 per cent of a group of 1081 miscellaneous subjects chose the original as the preferred version. In the revised edition, it will be recalled, items were further selected on the basis of internal consistency.

Total scores on the Meier Art Judgement Test exhibit a sharp differentiation in terms of age, grade and art training. Thus art faculty score higher than non-art faculty, art students higher than comparable non-art students. The extent to which these group differences result from selection or from previous art training cannot be determined from available data. Although no validity coefficients are given in the manual, a few are reported in other published sources. Correlations ranging from 0·40 to 0·69 have been found between scores on this test and art grades or ratings of creative artistic ability (2, 9, 17).

As in most artistic aptitude tests, the Meier Art Judgement Test has regularly shown negligible correlation with traditional intelligence tests, such as the Stanford–Binet or group verbal tests. This does not mean, however, that abstract intelligence or scholastic aptitude is unrelated to ultimate success at an art career. In fact, there is some evidence to indicate that, for higher levels of artistic accomplishment, superior scholastic aptitude is a decided asset. In one of the investigations conducted at Iowa, for example, the mean I.Q. of successful artists was found to be 119 (20). Similarly, a group of artistically gifted children studied at the University of Iowa had I.Q.s ranging from 111 to 166 (15).

While the McAdory Test employed many contemporary, dated items, and the Meier Test was constructed from relatively timeless art products, the more recently developed Graves Design Judgement Test (4, 5) consists exclusively of abstract designs. Nonrepresentational figures were chosen in order to evoke a purely aesthetic response, unencumbered by associations with specific objects. In the development of this test, about 150 items were prepared, each consisting of two or three comparable designs. In each item, the design was organized in accordance with certain aesthetic principles, including 'unity, dominance, variety, balance, continuity, symmetry, proportion and rhythm'. The other design or designs violated one or more of these principles. The preliminary form of the test was administered to art teachers, art students and non-art students, with instructions to indicate the preferred design in each set. Items were retained on the basis of:

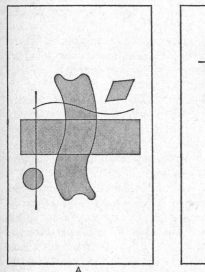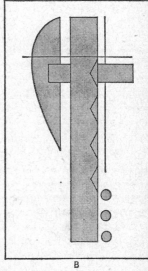

A   B

subject indicates which design he prefers

Figure 2. Item from the Graves Design Judgement Test. (Reproduced by permission of The Psychological Corporation, copyright 1946 ; all rights reserved)

(a) agreement among art teachers regarding the preferred design; (b) more frequent selection of the 'better' design by art students than by non-art students; and (c) internal consistency, i.e. 'better' design chosen more often by those obtaining high scores than by those obtaining low scores on the entire test.

The final test consists of ninety items, eight containing three designs each, the rest containing only two. The designs are executed in black, white and gray. Some are line drawings; others are composed of squares, circles, triangles, and similar two-dimensional figures; still others look like reproductions of three-dimensional abstract sculptures. A sample item is reproduced in Figure 2. Percentile norms are given for several art and non-art student groups at the high school and college level, all tested in New York State. Split-half reliability coefficients in fairly homogeneous groups ranged from 0·81 to 0·93, with a median of 0·86. Validity data are meagre, being based chiefly on significant differences in mean scores between contrasted criterion groups.

Most tests of *creative artistic ability* are actually work samples. As such, they are undoubtedly influenced to a large extent by formal art training and could be regarded as achievement tests. A number of such tests, however, have been designed specially for use in predicting performance in subsequent training and may therefore be included in the present category. Among the best known are the Lewerenz Tests in Fundamental Abilities of Visual Art (12), the Knauber Art Ability Test (10, 11), and the Horn Art Aptitude Inventory (8). The Lewerenz was designed for grades 3 to 12, the Knauber for grades 7 to 16, and the Horn for grades 12 to 16 and adults. The first two include a variety of subtests, covering art appreciation and information, as well as drawing skills and originality. Both are early tests that have not been revised. Insufficient data are reported to permit an adequate evaluation of their effectiveness. In general, however, they appear to be crude when judged in terms of present test construction standards.

The Horn Art Aptitude Inventory was more recently developed and has undergone a certain amount of revision. Concentrating on the measurement of creative artistic abilities, this test has a fairly high ceiling and shows adequate discrimination among applicants for admission to art schools. The test includes the following three parts:

1. *Scribble Exercise:* The subject is directed to make outline drawings of twenty simple objects, such as book or fork, within time limits of two to six seconds for each drawing. This test is designed partly to give the subject confidence and partly to determine quality of line, appreciation of proportion, and skill in composition or arrangement of object on the page.

2. *Doodle Exercise:* The subject is required to draw simple abstract

compositions with given figures, such as six triangles, a rectangle divided by two lines and the like. This test bears a certain resemblance to the Graves Design Judgement Test, although the subject now produces his own designs instead of judging given designs.

3. *Imagery:* This test provides twelve rectangles, in each of which a few lines have been printed to act as 'springboards' for artistic compositions. The subject sketches a picture in each rectangle, building upon the given lines. In Figure 3 will be found one of the given rectangles, together with two different drawings made from the same initial lines.

(a)

(b)

(c)

Figure 3. Sample item from the 'imagery' test of Horn Art Aptitude Inventory. (a) shows the stimulus lines; the other two drawings are made with the stimulus lines. In (b) the card has been turned to a horizontal position (from 8, p. 351). (Reproduced by permission of American Psychological Association)

371

The Horn Art Aptitude Inventory is scored by means of the product scale technique. Samples of excellent, average and poor work are furnished as a basis for rating the subject's drawings. As an additional scoring guide, the manual lists certain factors to be considered, such as order, clarity of thought and presentation, quality of line, use of shading, fertility of imagination and scope of interests. Although the scoring still leaves much to subjective judgement, correlations of 0·79 to 0·86 are reported between the results obtained by different scorers.

Some indication of validity is provided by two preliminary studies conducted with the Horn test. Within a group of fifty-two art school graduates, a correlation of 0·53 was found between test scores and mean instructors' ratings of performance in a three-year art course. The second study was conducted with thirty-six high school seniors enrolled in a special art course. In this group, the test scores obtained at the beginning of the year correlated 0·66 with mean instructors' ratings at the end of the course. A negligible correlation between performance on the Horn test and intelligence test scores was found in the previously mentioned group of fifty-two art school graduates.

As a measure of the more complex and creative aspects of artistic aptitude at a relatively high level, this test appears to have promise. It has, however, been criticized on the grounds that the scoring puts a premium on conformity to tradition in technique and composition, while great artists often deviate from the norm in these respects. Such a criticism could probably be directed against all current art aptitude tests. Whether a test can be devised to measure the degree of originality characteristic of truly great art remains to be seen. In the meantime, many aspects of artistic aptitude can be measured. The skills involved may represent necessary though not sufficient conditions for artistic production.

A more specific limitation of the Horn Art Aptitude Inventory is that it calls for a certain minimum of artistic training or experience. It could obviously be used as either an achievement or aptitude test. As a further illustration of the tenuousness of such distinctions, it might be noted that this test has even been employed by one investigator as a projective technique in the diagnosis of personality characteristics (6).

What can be concluded regarding the present status of art aptitude tests as a whole? First, much more information is needed regarding the validity of all of these tests in terms of clearly defined training and vocational criteria. There is special need for correlations between test scores obtained prior to specific art courses and measures of subsequent achievement. Some available evidence suggests that terminal grades in art courses correlate higher with worksample tests, such as the Lewerenz and the Knauber, than with art appreciation tests, such as the McAdory and the Meier (1). These correlations, however, may simply reflect the influence of earlier art training in other courses.

Another fruitful approach to the further development of art tests is through the factorial analysis of artistic aptitudes. Most, if not all, existing art aptitude tests are based upon certain assumptions regarding the essential factors in artistic aptitude. An objective verification of these assumptions would be desirable.

It would also be of interest to investigate further the effect of cultural differences upon performance on the various art tests. Some scattered data suggest that these tests are restricted in their applicability to specific cultures. Certainly what is known about cultural differences in artistic expression and artistic standards would support such a view. An investigation of approximately 300 Navajo Indian children with the McAdory test found the Indians to fall far below the norms of New York City whites, despite the high degree of artistic development that characterizes the Navajo Indian culture (19). In view of the nature of the McAdory Test this finding is hardly surprising. The application of the Meier Art Judgement Test to artists, art students, college students and other adult groups in Brazil likewise indicated the need for certain revisions if the test were to be used in that culture (3).

References

1. H. D. BARRETT, 'An examination of certain standardized art tests to determine their relation to classroom achievement and to intelligence', *J. educ. Res.*, vol. 42 (1949), pp. 398–400.
2. H. A. CARROLL, 'What do the Meier–Seashore and McAdory Art Tests measure?', *J. educ. Res.*, vol. 26 (1933), pp. 661–5.
3. LEONILDA D'ANNIBALE BRAGA, 'Estudo preliminar da adaptação do teste de Meier ao meio brasileiro' (Preliminary study

of the adaptation of the Meier test to the Brazilian environment), *Arch. brasil. Psicotéc.*, vol. 3 (1951), pp. 7–23.

4. M. GRAVES, *The Art of Color and Design*, 2nd edn, McGraw-Hill, 1951.

5. M. GRAVES, *Graves Design Judgement Test*, Psychological Corporation, 1948.

6. ELIZABETH F. HELLERSBERG, 'The Horn–Hellersberg test and adjustment to reality', *Amer. J. Orthopsychiat.*, vol. 15 (1945), pp. 690–710.

7. C. C. HORN, *Horn Art Aptitude Inventory*, Stoelting, Chicago, 1951–3.

8. C. C. HORN and L. F. SMITH, 'The Horn Art Aptitude Inventory', *J. appl. Psychol.*, vol. 29 (1945), pp. 350–55.

9. MADELINE KINTER, *The Measurement of Artistic Abilities*, Psychological Corporation, 1933.

10. ALMA J. KNAUBER, *Knauber Art Ability Test*, Cincinnati, 1932–5. (Distributed by C. H. Stoelting Co.)

11. ALMA J. KNAUBER, 'Construction and standardization of the Knauber Art Tests', *Education*, vol. 56 (1935), pp. 165–70.

12. A. S. LEWERENZ, *Tests in Fundamental Abilities of Visual Art*, California Test Bureau, Monterey, California, 1927.

13. MARGARET MCADORY, *The McAdory Art Test*, Teachers College Bureau of Publications, 1929–33.

14. N. C. MEIER, *The Meier Art Tests: I. Art Judgement*, Bureau for Educational Research Services, University of Iowa, 1940–42.

15. N. C. MEIER, *Art in Human Affairs*, McGraw-Hill, 1942.

16. N. C. MEIER and C. E. SEASHORE, *The Meier–Seashore Art Judgement Test*, Bureau for Educational Research Services, University of Iowa, 1929.

17. R. S. MORROW, 'An analysis of the relations among tests of musical, artistic and mechanical abilities', *J. Psychol.*, vol. 5 (1938), pp. 253–63.

18. MARGARET MCADORY SICELOFF, *et al.*, *Validation and Standardization of the McAdory Art Test*, Teachers College Bureau of Publications, 1933.

19. M. STEGGERDA, 'The McAdory Art Test applied to Navajo Indian children', *J. comp. Psychol.*, vol. 22 (1936), pp. 283–5.

20. C. TIEBOUT and N. C. MEIER, 'Artistic ability and general intelligence', *Psychol. Monogr.*, vol. 48 (1936), pp. 95–125.

20 E. W. Moyles, R. D. Tuddenham and J. Block

Simplicity/Complexity or Symmetry/Asymmetry?
A Re-analysis of the Barron–Welsh Art Scales

E. W. Moyles, R. D. Tuddenham and J. Block, 'Simplicity/complexity or symmetry/asymmetry? A re-analysis of the Barron–Welsh art scales', *Perceptual and Motor Skills*, vol. 20 (1965), pp. 685–90.

The Barron–Welsh Art Scale has been interpreted as a measure of simplicity/complexity within people. Re-analysis of the test by scaling the individual figures revealed that the stimulus dimension of simplicity/complexity (S/C) was highly confounded with the stimulus dimension of symmetry/asymmetry (S/A). It proved possible to separate these two stimulus dimensions and evaluate their significance independently. S/C and S/A appeared to be of equivalent and usually small importance in determining figure preferences. These results suggest the need for caution in attributing preferences to the single S/C attribute of the stimulus figures, or by extension, to the psychological simplicity or complexity of test-takers.

For the psychologist, the delineation of his variables is a basic task. Unfortunately, there is a fundamental disjunction between the verbal level of theoretical interpretation and the experimental level of observation and measurement. Strict operationism attempted to bind these levels together by defining each construct in terms of the specific procedure eliciting it; but for many researchers, the binding was too tight, purging the theoretical dimension of much of its connotative meaning.

In recent years, the trend has been, instead, toward 'construct validation', i.e. assembling experimental evidence which is at least congruent with the theoretical superstructure. The greater latitude thus allowed the investigator is often paid for by looseness in the specification of the construct.[1] For example, it is not uncommon to find one interpretive label assigned to a measure

1. Campbell and Fiske (1959) have proposed useful criteria for construct validation, but they have seldom been applied.

when, given the stimulus attributes of the measure, other interpretations apply equally well. Such alternatives may not be considered, or an identity of meaning among them may be assumed without demonstration. Hence, it becomes desirable to clarify proposed theoretical interpretations of a measure by determining the empirical relationships among its principal stimulus attributes and evaluating separately their significance. It is to this task, with reference to the Barron–Welsh Art Scale (Barron, 1952), that the present paper is addressed.

In 1949, Welsh reported that a factor analysis of his Figure Preference Test (W.F.P.T.)[2] yielded two orthogonal dimensions: the first, acceptance *v.* rejection (general liking *v.* disliking of the figures); and a second, whose poles as determined by inspection of the figures seemed to be simplicity–symmetry *v.* complexity–asymmetry. Barron and Welsh later constructed a 62-item subscale (Barron–Welsh Art Scale) of the W.F.P.T. by contrasting responses of artists and non-artists (Barron, 1953). This was subsequently revised to equalize the number of 'like' and 'dislike' responses keyed. (See Manual of the W.F.P.T. in Welsh, 1959.)

In his 1953 report, Barron pointed out the same bipolar clustering.

The artists *liked* figures which were highly complex, asymmetrical, freehand rather than ruled, and rather restless and moving in their general effect ... the figures which were *liked* by people in general however, were relatively simple, often bilaterally symmetrical, and regularly predictable, following some cardinal principle, which could be educed at a glance. These figures were described by artists as 'static', 'dull', 'uninteresting' (Barron, 1953, p. 164).

In this paper, Barron singled out the stimulus dimension of simplicity/complexity (S/C) as a basic determiner of preferences on the Art Scale. He then proceeded to suggest, by means of various extra-test correlations, that preferences determined by the S/C property of the stimulus designs could be viewed more generally as manifestations of a pervasively important personality

2. Welsh's report is contained in an unpublished dissertation. However, this finding is summarized by Barron (1952, p. 385). The Welsh Figure Preference Test (W.F.P.T.) consists of 400 drawings in black and white. *S* is asked to categorize each figure according to whether he likes it or dislikes it.

dimension of simplicity/complexity, i.e. the person who prefers simple figures *is* simple; the person who prefers complex figures *is* complex.[3]

The Barron–Welsh Art Scale will hereafter be referred to as a measure of the variable *Complexity*, since it is that feature of the scale which is of interest here, and since the scale is so scored that preferences like those of artists (hence, preference for the complex) earn *S* a high score, while preferences like those of people in general (i.e. preference for the simple) earn a low score. The designations *Complex person and Simple person* will be employed to indicate a modal high scorer and a modal low scorer, respectively, on this particular test (Barron, 1953, p. 165).

Thus, Barron extended what was originally a property of the stimulus designs to a dimension in people and went on to hypothesize its generality in interpersonal relations, religion, social conformity and originality.

The nature and interpretation of the correlates of scores on the Art Scale involve issues and data beyond the scope of this paper. In the present study, we have been concerned with the legitimacy of the projection of the S/C stimulus variable as the central and sufficient construct in terms of which to understand preference behavior in response to the Art Scale figures. We seek to answer three specific questions: (1) What is the relationship in the W.F.P.T. and in its subscales, the Barron–Welsh Art Scale and the Revised Art Scale, between simplicity/complexity (S/C) and symmetry/asymmetry (S/A)? (2) Is it possible to derive *independent* scales of S/C and S/A? (3) Given such independent indices, how important is each as a determiner of preference?

A secondary problem concerns sex differences. Since Barron imputed to the species in general a dimension apparently derived altogether from male *S*s he presumably felt that sex differences were unimportant. We have sought to provide empirical data on this question.

3. One may speculate that Barron focused upon S/C rather than S/A (symmetry/asymmetry) inasmuch as S/A applied to *persons* is more an anatomical than a psychological variable. However, his usage could easily lead to the indiscriminate use of the Barron–Welsh Art Scale for the invidious categorization of 'simple' *v.* 'complex' people.

Procedure

In order to evaluate the relationship between S/C and S/A, it was first necessary to scale all 400 items of the W.F.P.T. separately on each dimension. To obtain these scale values, eleven men and sixteen women of an upper division class in psychology at the University of California Q-sorted the items separately for the two variables. The following explanations were supplied:

Simplicity/Complexity: We are interested in finding out which of these figures you think are the simplest, and which the most complex. You might think of simple as being obvious, uncomplicated, direct, and immediately apparent; complex ones as being complicated, not immediately apparent, and difficult to comprehend.

Symmetry/Asymmetry: We are interested in finding out which of these figures you think are symmetrical and which asymmetrical. You might think of symmetric figures as being in a state of balance, of being static; asymmetric ones as being in an unbalanced or dynamic state.

The items were presented 100 at a time and sorted by successive trichotomizations into nine categories with twelve designs in the middle-most pile, and eleven in the others. To control for order effects our standardization sample was split into two groups: one group sorted the items on the S/C dimension first, the other sorted first on the S/A dimension. Within groups, the order of sorting the four blocks of 100 items was randomized. Design placements were then summed across Ss to obtain the mean placement of each item on S/C and also on S/A.

Next, the two sets of scale values were correlated separately for the complete 400 items of the W.F.P.T., then for the subset constituting the Barron–Welsh Art Scale, and finally for the Revised Art Scale.[4]

In order to obtain indices of S/C and of S/A that would be independent of one another, a subset of items was required that met the following criteria: first, the total range on both dimensions had to be represented; second, the correlation of the scale values of the items on the two dimensions had to be essentially zero.

A set of twenty-four items was found that met these criteria. The items (numbered as they appear in the W.F.P.T.) with their

4. See Welsh (1959) for the items contained in the subsets.

associated scale values on the two dimensions appear in Table 1. The twenty-four items constitute a subset in which the product-moment correlation between S/C and S/A is 0·017.

The twenty-four items were mounted on 3 in × 5 in cards and given to fifteen male and thirty-six female upper division psychology students. Ss were instructed to place the items in two equal piles – those they tended to like and those they tended to dislike. Next, they were asked to convert the preliminary dichotomization into a set of ranks. For each S separately, the preference ranking of the twenty-four items was correlated with the S/C scale values and with the S/A scale values of the items. Thus, for

Table 1

Scale Values for Simplicity/Complexity (S/C) and Symmetry/Asymmetry (S/A) of Twenty-four Selected Items of the Welsh Figure Preference Test[1]

Item no.	S/C	S/A	Item no.	S/C	S/A
6	7·56	3·59	176	2·15	6·78
31	2·70	6·04	181	4·11	7·59
42	5·04	1·93	212	1·78	4·96
43	6·93	7·15	213	7·93	5·19
74	3·30	2·37	234	8·15	6·15
77	1·63	5·48	311	6·30	2·00
82	4·19	1·85	317	5·33	7·85
91	3·52	7·04	322	8·56	4·63
105	8·22	5·11	324	7·52	2·44
111	5·26	8·33	370	6·56	7·41
115	2·11	3·63	396	7·70	6·89
153	2·59	2·93	398	6·52	2·33

1. To select these items, a bivariate plot of S/C scale value v. S/A value was prepared, with all items entered by item number. A subset of twenty-four was then chosen in such a way as to yield a flattened circular correlation surface. For the items listed above, the correlation between S/C and S/A is 0·02.

Note: Low scale values indicate the simplicity and symmetry ends of the scales.

each S, it was possible to evaluate both the absolute and the relative importance of the stimulus dimensions, S/C and S/A, in determining his figure preferences. The mean rankings of the twenty-four items calculated for sexes separately and for sexes combined, were also correlated with their scale values on S/C and S/A.

Results and Discussion

S/C and S/A, as scaled by our sample of judges, are strongly correlated. The values are 0·74 for the entire 400 items of the W.F.P.T., 0·82 for the Barron–Welsh Art Scale, and 0·89 for the Revised Art Scale. Thus, it seems that Welsh's original formulation of the 'fused' stimulus dimension simplicity–symmetry *v.* complexity–asymmetry was accurate. The later omission of reference to the S/A property slights the ubiquitousness of this dimension. However, we were able to derive a set of items in which S/C and S/A were uncorrelated. We take this as evidence that the two dimensions can be distinguished.

Individual *S*s' rank correlations of liking with S/C scale value ranged from 0·51 to −0·49 (men) and 0·54 to −0·79 (women). Corresponding correlations between liking and S/A ranged from 0·58 to −0·30 (men) and 0·55 to −0·39 (women). The algebraic means of these correlations are near zero (0·00 for men and −0·15 for women on S/C and 0·20 and 0·15, respectively, on S/A). However, it is the degree to which the *dimension* is a determinant of preference which is here at issue; hence the means of such correlations with liking should be calculated from the absolute values of the *r*s. These mean *r*s (based on *z*-transformation) are 0·25 and 0·30 for men and for women on liking *v.* S/C, and 0·28 and 0·25 respectively, on liking *v.* S/A.[5]

Clearly, there is not much difference between S/C and S/A as

5. Adjusting these figures for attenuation owing to unreliability would not appreciably increase the importance of S/C or S/A in determining figure preferences. The reliabilities of the S/C and S/A scalings are near unity, since the item values are means based on twenty-seven independent judges. We have no reliabilities for figure preferences, and Welsh reports reliability only for the Revised Art Scale, namely, a retest reliability of 0·90 and of 0·94 in two groups of college students. If a reliability of 0·7 for figure preference on our items is taken as a reasonable guess, then the potency of the S/C or S/A dimensions in determining liking of the Welsh figures climbs only to 0·30 to 0·35.

determinants of liking, and neither is very important for Ss as a group, although for occasional individuals the correlations are substantial. If instead of mean values, attention is shifted to the *number* of individuals whose preferences correlated more with S/C values than with S/A, the results are again inconclusive: nine of fifteen men ($P=0.304$) and nineteen of thirty-six women ($P=0.434$).[6]

While this paper is addressed to a consideration of S/C and S/A as *dimensions*, some interest inheres in which *poles* are most associated with preference. This can be deduced from the algebraic signs of the individual correlations between S/C and S/A on the one hand and preference on the other. For men, liking was associated with complexity in eight cases ($P=0.500$), with simplicity in seven. For women, liking was associated with complexity in twenty-five cases ($P=0.212$), with simplicity in eleven. Turning to the other variable, eleven men preferred symmetry ($P=0.059$), and four asymmetry. Among women, twenty-five preferred symmetry ($P=0.212$) and eleven asymmetry. Only the results for symmetry approach conventional significance levels (one-tailed). However, we have no *a priori* reason to expect one pole to be preferred over its opposite. If the P values are doubled for the two-tailed test, only the data for women reach the 5 per cent level.

To return to the principal issue, it seems likely that for most Ss, the determinants of preference are item-specific interactions between the unique properties of each design and Ss' idiosyncratic esthetics. Generalized attitudes toward S/C and S/A account for only a minor share of the variance. It is noteworthy that, although complexity tends to be strongly linked with asymmetry in W.F.P.T. and in the Art Scale, the modal preferences both of men and of women were for complex but symmetrical designs on the special subset where S/C and S/A are independent. However, it must be remembered that the Ss were not artists. The relationship between S/C and S/A in such a sample remains to be discovered.

6. The indicated P value gives the probability, for the N concerned, of a ratio as large as or larger than the one obtained. (See *Tables of Cumulative Binomial Probabilities*, Ordnance Corps Pamphlet ORDP 20-1, Ordnance Corps, Washington, 1952.)

These results do not bear on the legitimacy of extending the stimulus variable to the intrapsychic domain. However, if neither S/C nor S/A is a very important determinant of liking for designs, then caution is indicated when one infers the psychological simplicity or complexity of Ss from their scores on the Art Scale.

References
BARRON, F. (1952), 'Personality style and perceptual choice', *J. Pers.*, vol. 20, pp. 385–401.
BARRON, F. (1953), 'Complexity–simplicity as a personality dimension', *J. abnorm. soc. Psychol.*, vol. 48, pp. 163–72.
CAMPBELL, D. T., and FISKE, D. W. (1959), 'Convergent and discriminant validation by the multitrait-multimethod matrix', *Psychol. Bull.*, vol. 56, pp. 81–105.
WELSH, G. S. (1959), *Preliminary Manual, Welsh Figure Preference Test*, Consulting Psychologists Press.

21 H. Lansdell

A Sex Difference in Effect of Temporal-lobe Neurosurgery on Design Preference

H. Lansdell, 'A sex difference in effect of temporal-lobe neurosurgery on design preference', *Nature*, vol. 194 (1962), pp. 852–4.

The human brain has a pronounced asymmetry of function: one hemisphere, generally the left, is clearly 'dominant' for speech (Penfield and Roberts, 1959; Lansdell, 1962), and the other is possibly more important for perception (Milner, 1958; Ettlinger, 1966). The present investigation, part of a project on the psychological changes following temporal-lobe surgery, was concerned with a test of artistic aptitude and the impairment that should occur after removal of cerebral tissue from the non-dominant side. The neurosurgery produced asymmetrical effects of this kind; but, unexpectedly, they were found only in men; the lateralized effects in women were reversed. Twenty-two patients with temporal-lobe epilepsy were tested on the Graves Design Judgement Test before and again 13–31 (mean 17) days after undergoing unilateral temporal-lobe surgery for the relief of their epilepsy (Baldwin and Bailey, 1958). Forty-two additional cases were tested for the first time 1–8 (mean 4·2) years after such surgery. The age at surgery for the sixty-four cases was 11–57 (mean 31) years. In one man and two women the dominant hemisphere for speech was on the right side according to the carotid 'Amytal' test (Wada and Rasmussen, 1960); their operations were on the left. One of these women was in the group tested only after surgery. The Graves test was designed to measure 'certain components of aptitude for the appreciation or production of art structure' (Graves, 1948). The test consists of ninety items in a booklet; for each item, the subject is required to choose the preferred design from two, occasionally three, printed on a page. The designs are abstract with little or no 'meaningful' content; the inartistic ones contravene principles of aesthetic order and are often symmetrical designs or nearly so. The only colour used, and not in all items, is a greyish green. Preferences are marked on a standard answer sheet. The test is not timed.

The effect of the surgery on the patients' preferences appeared to be negligible until the sex of the patients was taken into account (Table 1). The group of men with resections in the non-dominant hemisphere showed a drop in mean aptitude score after the operations, whereas the women with non-dominant operations showed a rise. Conversely, with operations in the dominant hemisphere, the men showed a rise in score while the women

Table 1

Pre- and Post-Operative Mean Scores on the Graves Test

Sex and temporal-lobe operated	No. of cases	Pre-operative mean	Post-operative mean
Men, non-dominant	8	35·4	28·0
Women, non-dominant	5	41·8	47·2
Men, dominant	7	41·0	46·9
Women, dominant	2	31·5	26·5

A chance score would be 44; the published means for the test range from 41·0 for 106 non-art students to 77·3 for 54 students in their third year of art school (Graves, 1948).

showed a drop. An analysis of variance showed that this interaction of sex, side and change with operations was significant ($P<0.01$). Since the rank order of the four means after the operations was the same as before, it might appear that the operations accentuated differences which were directly present. However, separate analyses of the pre- and post-operative scores indicated a significant interaction of sex and side only after operation ($P<0.01$).

Three patients had changes in score which were opposite to the general pattern described, and two patients showed no change. For three of these five cases the atypical nature of the operations seems to be pertinent to their inconsistent behaviour. The ablation on the non-dominant side in a man who showed no change in score was done in two stages nine months apart; his score might have dropped had he been tested after the first stage. The operations on the dominant side in two men who showed a drop in score were also unique; one was performed six days after a simultaneous exploration of both temporal areas, the other was interrupted by a laryngospasm and the brain bulging for a few minutes through the cranial opening. Possibly these operations entailed some disruption of functions on the non-dominant side.

The amount of tissue removed in the twenty-two cases was often less than that usually reported for this type of operation, measuring about 3–5$\frac{1}{2}$ cm from the tip of the lobe on the right and about 2$\frac{1}{2}$–4$\frac{1}{2}$ cm on the left, and sometimes gyri or the tip of the lobe were spared. The relation between estimates of the amount removed and the amount of change in scores tended to be inverse although not statistically significant.

The low scores following some of the operations indicate a marked preference for designs which are symmetrical or otherwise too simply structured. These patients could be displaying the concreteness and simplicity in perception often reported in patients with gross brain damage. The better scores after other operations might be a result of the removal of disruptive epileptogenic tissue from the other side. An interpretation of the better scores as a result of practice seems unlikely because no general tendency for improvement was found in nine other cases that had exploratory operations with no removal of tissue.

The changes on the Graves test do not appear to be 'intellectual' in so far as they were not found to be related to changes in the scores on the Wechsler–Bellevue intelligence tests. There was an expected significant drop (Milner, 1958) in the mean of the total weighted scores for the six 'verbal' sub-tests after the operation in the dominant hemisphere ($P < 0.02$, one-tail test).

Although the post-operative changes on the Graves test are clear, they appear to be transitory. No significant relation to the surgery was discernible either for sex or side of operation in the group of forty-two patients tested a year or more after their operations. The mean score for the fifteen women (42·7) was slightly, but not significantly, higher than the mean for the twenty-seven men (38·2). Furthermore, eleven of the original group of twenty-two patients have been tested a third time, with a mean lapse of 17 months since their operations. Ten showed a change opposite to that shown on the first post-operative test; three patients who got better scores on their first post-operative test

385

dropped on the third testing, and the other seven dropped, then rose. A woman whose score was unchanged after a non-dominant operation scored lower on the last test. Finally, combining the data from these eleven cases on their third testing with the data from the other forty-two cases also yielded no significant differences. That the test still did measure something in the latter group of fifty-three cases is indicated by a low but significant, correlation with intelligence ($r = 0.47$).

The results obtained with the women, unlike those with the men, do not conform to the hypothesis that an impairment in some aspect of human visual perception occurs after removals from the temporal lobe of the non-dominant hemisphere. A similar failure of results for women to agree with those for men has been found in an examination of the effect of dominant temporal-lobe operations on an objective test of proverbs: the women were unaffected and the men dropped in score after operation (Lansdell, 1961). The varying proportion of women to men in previous investigations may have been partly responsible for the varied success in demonstrating lateralized effect of temporal-lobe surgery (Meyer 1960; Shalman, 1961).

The effects of the operations suggest that some physiological mechanisms underlying artistic judgement and verbal ability may overlap in the female brain but are in opposite hemispheres in the male. Some data in the psychometric literature could be interpreted in the same way: girls show positive correlations between their level of artistic interest and their competence on tests of verbal reasoning and language usage, whereas boys do not (Bennett, Seashore and Wesman, 1952).

Although the Graves test is considered to be an aptitude test, it is not like the usual speed test which measures efficiency of perception; it is not timed and the subject is not asked to choose 'correct' answers. The Graves test is probably measuring a factor called 'liking for simplicity versus complexity' which has been demonstrated in several experiments on form preferences (Guilford, 1959). Temporary changes in an 'interest' factor as a result of neurosurgery might have been expected. But it is surprising to find that the function of each temporal lobe in regard to this trait appears to be opposite in each sex.

I thank Dr Maitland Baldwin, clinical director of this Institute, for encouraging psychological research on his patients, and Dr E. J. Laskowski for supplying the results of the carotid 'Amytal' tests.

References
BALDWIN, M., and BAILEY, P. (1958), *Temporal Lobe Epilepsy*, Thomas, p. 355.
BENNETT, G. K.. SEASHORE, H. G., and WESMAN, A. G. (1952), *Manual for the Differential Aptitude Tests*, 2nd edn, Psychological Corporation, p. 75.
ETTLINGER, G. (1966), *J. ment. Sci.*, vol. 106, p. 1337.
GRAVES, M. (1948), *Design Judgement Test: Manual*, Psychological Corporation.
GUILFORD, J. P. (1959), *Personality*, McGraw-Hill, p. 451.
LANSDELL, H. (1961), *Amer. Psychologist.*, vol. 16, p. 448.
LANSDELL, H. (1962), *Science*, vol. 135, p. 922.
MEYER, V. (1960) in H. J. Eysenck (ed.), *Handbook of Abnormal Psychology*, Pitman Medical, ch. 14.
MILNER, B. (1958), *Res. Pub. Assoc. nerv. ment. Dis.*, vol. 36, p. 244.
PENFIELD, W., and ROBERTS, L. (1959), *Speech and Brain Mechanisms*, Princeton University Press.
SHALMAN, D. C. (1961), *J. Neur. Neurosurg. Psychiat.*, vol. 34, p. 220.
WADA, J., and RASMUSSEN, T. (1960), *J. Neurosurg.*, vol. 17, p. 266.

Further Reading

Introductory material

Of the following discussions of the area of psychology and art, Frances (1967) and Valentine (1962) are specifically on experimental investigation, while Beardsley (1966) and Sparshott (1963) contain useful discussions of the relations between psychology, art and aesthetics.

M. C. BEARDSLEY (1966), *Aesthetics from Classical Greece to the Present: A Short History*, Collier-Macmillan Ltd.

R. FRANCES (1967), 'L'esthétique expérimentale: rapport de l'esthétique avec la psychologie', *Bulletin de Psychologie*, vol. 20, pp. 575–85.

N. KIELL (1965), *Psychiatry and Psychology in the Visual Arts and Aesthetics: A Bibliography*, University of Wisconsin Press.

H. OSBORNE (1964), 'The elucidation of aesthetic experience', *J. Aesthet. art Crit*. vol. 23, pp. 145–51.

C. C. PRATT (1961), 'Aesthetics', *Ann. Rev. Psychol.*, vol. 16, pp. 71–92.

F. E. SPARSHOTT (1963), *The Structure of Aesthetics*, Routledge & Kegan Paul.

C. W. VALENTINE (1962), *The Experimental Psychology of Beauty*, Methuen

M. A. WALLACH (1959), 'Art, science and representation: towards an experimental psychology of aesthetics', *J. Aesthet. art Crit.*, vol. 18, pp. 159–73.

Psychoanalysis

The literature of psychoanalysis and the visual arts is extensive and much of it is concerned with discussion of individual works of art. Here we restrict our selection to accounts and examples of some of the main approaches. Regarding the present readings, it should be noted that the whole of Waelder (1965) is of great interest, as is Ehrenzweig's (1967) book. Kris (1952) examines psychoanalysis from the point of view of ego-psychology.

I. L. CHILD, M. COOPERMAN and H. M. WOLOWITZ (1969), 'Esthetic preference and other correlates of active versus passive food preference', *J. Pers. soc. Psychol.*, vol. 11, pp. 75–85.

A. EHRENZWEIG (1967), *The Hidden Order in Art: A Study in the Psychology of Artistic Imagination*, Weidenfeld & Nicolson.

E. H. GOMBRICH (1966), 'Freud's aesthetics', *Encounter*, vol. 26 (1), pp. 30–40.

E. KRIS (1952), *Psychoanalytic Explorations in Art*, International Universities Press.

L. MARCUSE (1958), 'Freud's aesthetics', *J. Aesthet. art Crit.*, vol. 17, pp. 1–21.

Further Reading

M. PHILIPSON (1963), *Outline of Jungian Aesthetics*, Northwestern University Press.

A. STOKES (1965), *The Invitation in Art*, Tavistock Publications.

R. WAELDER (1965), *Psychoanalytic Avenues to Art*, Psychoanalytical Epitomes No. 6, Hogarth and the Institute of Psychoanalysis.

Gestalt psychology

Within the readings, the application of Gestalt psychology was restricted to Arnheim's discussion of expression. His own application is far more extensive. Although not related specifically to Gestalt psychology, further discussion of the problem of expression appears in connexion with physiognomic perception in Gombrich (1960) and Werner (1956). Eysenck (1952, chapter 8) criticizes the Gestalt approach dealing with the interaction of colour.

R. ARNHEIM (1956), *Art and Visual Perception: A Psychology of the Creative Eye*, Faber & Faber.

R. ARNHEIM (1967), *Towards a Psychology of Art: Collected Essays*, Faber & Faber.

H. J. EYSENCK (1952), *The Scientific Study of Personality*, Routledge.

E. H. GOMBRICH (1960), 'On physiognomic perception', *Daedalus*, vol. 89, pp. 228–41.

K. KOFFKA (1940), 'Problems in the psychology of art', in *Art: A Bryn Mawr Symposium*, Bryn Mawr College.

H. WERNER (1956), 'On physiognomic perception', in Kepes, G. (ed.), *The New Landscape in Art and Science*, P. Theobald & Co., chapter 7, pt 2, pp. 280–83.

Information theory

Further consideration of the relation between information theory and art can be found in Moles (1966). More general accounts are included in Arnheim (1959), Attneave (1959) and Pierce (1962). A fascinating study of multivariate information measurement applied to interior decoration is described by Staniland (1966, pp. 175–7).

R. ARNHEIM (1959), 'Information theory: an introductory note', *J. Aesthet. art Crit.*, vol. 17, pp. 501–3.

F. ATTNEAVE (1959), 'Stochastic composition processes', *J. Aesthet. art Crit.*, vol. 17, pp. 503–10.

R. EISENMANN and H. K. GELLENS (1968), 'Preferences for complexity – simplicity and symmetry–asymmetry', *Percep. mot. Skills*, vol. 26, pp. 888–90.

A. MOLES (1966), *Information Theory and Esthetic Perception* (trans. J. E. Cohen), University of Illinois Press.

J. R. PIERCE (1962), *Symbols, Signals and Noise*, Hutchinson.

E. E. RUMP (1968), 'Relative preferences as a function of the number of elements in abstract designs', *Aust. J. Psychol.*, vol. 20, pp. 39–48.

A. C. STANILAND (1966), *Patterns of Redundancy: A Psychological Study*, Cambridge University Press.

Individual differences

In these readings we confined our attention to individual differences as exemplified by Child's extensive study and Skager *et al.*'s application of multidimensional scaling techniques to the problem. Other studies by Child investigating aspects of individual differences are listed below, plus a selection of investigations by other authors.

I. L. CHILD (1962), 'Personal preferences as an expression of esthetic sensitivity', *J. Pers.*, vol. 30, pp. 496–512.

I. L. CHILD (1964), 'Observations of the meaning of some measures of esthetic sensitivity', *J. Psychol.*, vol. 57, pp. 49–64.

I. L. CHILD and S. IWAO (1968), 'Personality and esthetic sensitivity: extension of findings to younger age and to different culture', *J. Pers. soc. Psychol.*, vol. 8, pp. 308–12.

R. EISENMANN (1965), 'Aesthetic preference of schizophrenics', *Percep. mot. Skills*, vol. 20, pp. 601–4.

R. FRANKLIN (1963), 'Sex, familiarity and dogmatism as factors in painting preferences', *Percep. mot. Skills*, vol. 17, p. 12.

O. JOHNSON and R. H. KNAPP (1963), 'Sex differences in esthetic preferences', *J. soc. Psychol.*, vol. 61, pp. 279–301.

R. H. KNAPP and S. GREEN (1959), 'Personality correlates of preference for abstract paintings', *Am. Psychologist*, vol. 14, p. 392 (abstract).

R. H. KNAPP L. R. MCELROY, and J. VAUGHN (1962), 'On the blithe melancholic aestheticism', *J. gen. Psychol.*, vol. 67, pp. 3–10.

E. M. SCOTT (1957), 'Personality and movie preference', *Psychol. Rep.*, vol. 3, pp. 17–18.

I. R. STUART and W. G. ELIASBERG (1962), 'Personality structures which reject the human form in art: an exploratory study of cross-cultural perceptions of the nude', *J. soc. Psychol.*, vol. 57, pp. 383–98.

Scaling techniques and art

There is likely to be a considerable growth in the application of multidimensional scaling techniques to problems of art perception and judgement. The use of the semantic differential is included in this and the subsequent section.

G. GUNNAR, G. LINDÉN and L. LUNDSTRÖM (1966), 'An experimental psychological technique for the construction of a characterizing system of art painting and an attempt at physiological validation', Report 33, June, Department of Psychology, University of Uppsala.

E. LOVELESS (1968), 'Dimensions of preference for modern art', *Proc. 76th Ann.Conv. A.P.A.*, vol. 3, pp. 445–6.

B. M. SPRINGETT (1960), 'The semantic differential and meanings in non-objective art', *Percep. mot. Skills*, vol. 10, pp. 231–40.

Colour

The review by Ball (1965) can be supplemented by the bibliographies in Hogg (1969a and b). Child, Hansen and Hornbeck (1968) is one of the best studies of children's colour preferences, while Granger (1955) is concerned with Gestalt psychology and colour.

V. K. BALL (1965), 'The aesthetics of color: a review of fifty years of experimentation', *J. Aesthet. art Crit.*, vol. 23, pp. 441–52.

I. L. CHILD, J. A. HANSEN and R. W. HORNBECK (1968), 'Age and sex differences in children's color preferences', *Child Dev.*, vol. 39, pp. 237–47.

G. W. GRANGER (1955), 'The prediction of preference for color combinations', *J. gen. Psychol.*, vol. 52, pp. 213–22.

J. HOGG (1969a), 'A principal components analysis of semantic differential judgements of single colors and color pairs', *J. gen. Psychol.*, vol. 80, pp. 129–40.

J. HOGG (1969b), 'The prediction of semantic differential ratings of color combinations', *J. gen. Psychol.*, vol. 80, pp. 141–52.

Cross-cultural studies

For reasons given in the Introduction, this area has been excluded from the readings. In addition to the following, other relevant studies appear under the section on individual differences above.

G. JAHODA (1956), 'Sex differences in preference for shapes: a cross-cultural replication', *Brit. J. Psychol.*, vol. 47, pp. 126–32.

I. SUMIKO and I. L. CHILD (1966), 'Comparison of esthetic judgements by American experts and by Japanese potters', *J. soc. Psychol.*, vol. 68, pp. 27–33.

Technical aspects

G. EKMAN and T. KUENNAPAS (1962), 'Scales of aesthetic value', *Percep. mot. Skills*, vol. 14, pp. 19–26.

J. E. KENNEDY (1961), 'The paired-comparison method and central tendency effect in esthetic judgements', *J. app. Psychol.*, vol. 45, pp. 128–9.

E. M. WEST and A. W. BENDIG (1956), 'Esthetic fatigue in ranking', *Am. J. Psychol.*, vol. 69, pp. 285–7.

Art and illusion

Gombrich's book, *Art and Illusion*, has been mentioned several times in these readings. One major discussion of his position that should be noted is Wollheim (1963).

H. OSBORNE (1969), 'On artistic illusion', *Brit. J. Aesthet.*, vol. 9, pp. 109–27.

R. WOLLHEIM (1963), 'Art and illusion', *Brit. J. Aesthet.*, vol. 3, pp. 15–37.

The following papers do not fit directly into the above sections. Hungerland discusses the possible perceptual influences on aesthetic responses and Israeli develops an idiosyncratic but possibly fruitful approach to the psychology of art.

H. HUNGERLAND (1954), 'An analysis of some determinants in the perception of works of art', *J. Aesthet. art Crit.*, vol. 12, pp. 450–56.

H. HUNGERLAND (1957), 'The aesthetic response reconsidered', *J. Aesthet. art Crit.*, vol. 16, pp. 32–43.

N. ISRAELI (1959a), 'Set theory models for research concerning creative thinking and imagination', *J. gen. Psychol.*, vol. 60, pp. 63–96.

N. ISRAELI (1959b), 'Set theory models for research concerning criticism and application', *J. gen. Psychol.*, vol. 60, pp. 97–120.

N. ISRAELI (1962), 'Creative art: a self-observation study', *J. gen. Psychol.*, vol. 66, pp. 33–45.

Acknowledgements

We are grateful to the following for permission to reproduce the material in this selection of Readings:

Reading 1   The American Society for Aesthetics and Thomas Munro
Reading 3   International Universities Press
Reading 4   *British Journal of Aesthetics*
Reading 5   Institut d'Esthétique et des Sciences de l'Art and D. E. Berlyne
Reading 6   *American Psychologist* and E. H. Gombrich
Reading 7   Duke University Press and Irvin L. Child
Reading 8   *Arts Magazine* and E. H. Gombrich
Reading 9   *Acta Psychologica*, R. T. Green and M. C. Courtis
Reading 10   The American Society for Aesthetics and Rudolf Arnheim
Reading 11   American Psychological Association, University of California Press and Faber & Faber
Reading 12   *Canadian Journal of Psychology* and Donald Dorfman
Reading 13   *Psychological Record* and A. M. Noll
Reading 14   *Psychological Reports* and R. A. M. Gregson
Reading 15   University of Illinois Press
Reading 16   The Journal Press, Benjamin D. Wright and Lee Rainwater
Reading 17   The Japanese Psychological Association and Junko Kansaku
Reading 18   Multivariate Behavioral Research and R. W. Skager
Reading 19   Macmillan & Co.
Reading 20   *Psychological Reports*, E. W. Moyles, R. D. Tuddenham and J. Block
Reading 21   Macmillan & Co., Ltd.

Every effort has been made to trace all copyright holders concerned. The publishers would be glad to hear from any copyright owners who have been overlooked.

Author Index

Author Index

Author Index

Subject Index

Subject Index